Emotions and Life

Emotions and Life

Perspectives From Psychology, Biology, and Evolution

Robert Plutchik

American Psychological Association
Washington, DC

First Printing November 2002
Second Printing November 2003

Published by
American Psychological Association
750 First Street, NE
Washington, DC 20002
www.apa.org

To order
APA Order Department
P.O. Box 92984
Washington, DC 20090-2984
Tel: (800) 374-2721, Direct: (202) 336-5510
Fax: (202) 336-5502, TDD/TTY: (202) 336-6123
On-line: www.apa.org/books/
E-mail: order@apa.org

In the U.K., Europe, Africa, and the Middle East, copies may be ordered from
American Psychological Association
3 Henrietta Street
Covent Garden, London
WC2E 8LU England

Typeset in Stone Serif by TechBooks, York, PA

Printer: United Book Press, Inc., Baltimore, MD
Cover Designer: NiDesign, Baltimore, MD
Technical/Production Editors: Jennifer Powers and Jennifer L. Macomber

The opinions and statements published are the responsibility of the authors, and such opinions and statements do not necessarily represent the policies of the American Psychological Association.

Library of Congress Cataloging-in-Publication Data

Plutchik, Robert.
  Emotions and life: perspectives from psychology, biology, and evolution/by Robert Plutchik.—Rev. and updated ed.
    p. cm.
    Rev. ed. of: Psychology and biology of emotion, 1994.
    Includes bibliographical references and index.
    1. Emotions. 2. Emotions—Physiological aspects. I. Plutchik, Robert. Psychology and biology of emotion. II. Title.
    BF531 .P595   2002
    152.4—dc21

                                                          2002015842

British Library Cataloguing-in-Publication Data
A CIP record is available from the British Library.

Printed in the United States of America

With love, to my family,
who have taught me much of what I know about emotions.

Anita, Roy, Lisa, Steve, Lauren, Michelle, Lori, Paul,
Mark, Laurie, Michael, and Derek

The desire to arrive finally at logically connected
concepts is the emotional basis of productive thought.
—*Albert Einstein*

Feeling alone guides the mind.
—*Claude Bernard*

Science starts with fascination and wonder.
—*Frans de Waals*

Contents

Figures and Illustrations

Preface

Most people think of emotions as special kinds of feelings—feelings that we describe by such words as *happy* or *sad*, *angry* or *jealous*, or *in love*. Everyone also knows that emotions are powerful forces influencing our behavior; people laugh, cry, become depressed, or blow up buildings under the influence of emotions. Their emotions may lead them toward alcoholism, drug addiction, suicide, or violence, as well as compassion, kindness, and altruism. Some people are able to hide their emotions, while others are like an open book. Although no one teaches us the meaning of emotional expressions on the face, most of us believe we can read emotions from people's faces. Psychiatrists assure us that almost every one of the current diagnoses of mental disorders involves one or more emotions that have gone awry.

As part of common attitudes about emotions, reinforced by countless articles in popular magazines, it is believed that people's early experiences in their families create the foundation for desirable or undesirable emotional behaviors in later life and that, unless children receive the proper kind of nurturing, they will grow up emotionally disturbed. If such unfortunate events occur, it is widely believed that psychotherapy is an adequate treatment for emotional disturbance.

Family abuse in the form of spousal and child abuse now appears to be surprisingly common, and various groups and agencies have prepared violence checklists to assess risk and have tried to distribute them widely. Despite these checklists, there are strong disagreements between those who believe that sparing the rod will spoil the child and those who emphasize the use of positive rewards only.

Despite the obvious importance of emotions in daily life, the topic of emotions has not received the attention it deserves in academic writings. Most colleges and universities still do not have a course devoted entirely to the subject of emotion. Of course, emotions are discussed to some degree in courses on motivation, abnormal and clinical psychology, child and adolescent development, social psychology, and personality. Yet it seems reasonable to expect that a topic as important as emotions deserves a course of its own.

To be fair, it must be mentioned that there have been some important changes over the past two decades. For a period of about 30 years, from the 1930s until the 1960s, there were few articles or books on emotions. This was partly because behavioristic thinking had achieved considerable dominance in academic circles during this period, and such thinking assumed that subjective reports of feelings (or emotions) were not reliable enough for scientific purposes.

Science does not develop in a linear way with each idea or observation based on a previous one. It more obviously proceeds in fits and starts. In the 1920s there was serious interest in emotions, but the advent of Behaviorism reduced that interest for a time.

In the early 1960s several books and articles on emotions were published that helped give a new impetus to this field of study. Coincidentally, behaviorism was dethroned by the advent of cognitive psychology, and as it developed, cognitive neuropsychology, both of which have had major impacts on the field of psychology.

As these developments were occurring in psychology, a great intellectual mixing of subdomains was also occurring. This was reflected in the new kinds of journals that were being published that dealt with the interaction of two or more subdisciplines. Some examples of these journals dealing with overlapping fields are *Psychophysiology, Cognition and Emotion, Motivation and Emotion, Psychoneuroendocrinology, Brain and Cognition*, and *Emotion.*

As these changes have been taking place, another important element has been added. The most important idea in biology is the concept of evolution. Charles Darwin wrote a book in 1872 that presented an evolutionary approach to emotions. This work was largely ignored until the 1930s, when the development of ethology and its later offshoots reawakened interest in Darwin's ideas about emotion. As a result, in the past two decades, more and more writers have begun to try to apply evolutionary thinking to the study of emotions. As we begin the third millennium, it appears that emotions have finally found a respected place in science.

Clinicians have long been concerned with emotions and what happens when they go awry, but academic psychologists have not always been sympathetic to their views. One result has been the appearance of two parallel tracks that have had limited influence on one another. This, too, may be changing.

In the light of this brief overview, where does the present book fit? This book is based on the assumption that emotions are of fundamental importance to all living creatures and that emotions are best understood in an evolutionary framework. It attempts to integrate a great deal of information about emotions that has been accumulated over the past few decades. It examines in detail the ambiguities of the emotion language and ways that this can be dealt with. It examines the current cognitive approaches to emotion, as well as motivational, evolutionary, and psychodynamic ones, under the assumption that they all have some interesting ideas to contribute to an understanding of emotions. The book describes a number of old and new measurement techniques that have been developed for measuring emotions. It delves into the developmental psychology of emotions with a particular emphasis on attachment theory. It examines the perennial conflicts over the emotional meanings of facial expressions and then explores the recent literature on brain involvement in emotions. The final two chapters deal explicitly with a number of discrete emotions and what we have learned about them in both an academic and clinical context. These emotions are love, sadness, depression, fear, anxiety, anger, and aggression.

In sum, these chapters shed new light on the nature and function of emotion. It is my hope that readers will gain understanding of the fundamental importance of emotions to all living creatures, and their crucial role in ensuring our survival as a species.

Acknowledgments

Every book is a reflection of countless influences. I have been enlightened by many colleagues, and their influences are sometimes noted explicitly in the book, while the origins of others are subtly merged in my consciousness. All have become fused into a coherent tapestry like the colors of a landscape or the notes of a symphony.

Several people have read the entire manuscript and have given me the benefit of their knowledge and expertise. I am especially indebted to Drs. Phillip R. Shaver of the University of California at Davis, Christine R. Harris of the Center for Brain and Cognition at the University of California at San Diego, and Gordon Bauer at New College in Sarasota, Florida. They made detailed and extremely helpful comments about various aspects of the manuscript. I greatly benefited from their suggestions, but the final responsibility for the content of this book is my own.

Finally, I would like to express my deepest appreciation to my wife, Dr. Anita Plutchik, whose collaboration and insights over the years have often helped me avoid ambiguities of expression and thought.

1 The Landscapes of Emotion

> Life is a train of moods like a string of beads.
> *Ralph Waldo Emerson*

PREVIEW

During the past 100 years, dozens of definitions of the word *emotion* have been proposed by psychologists and other scientists. Although the definitions vary widely, some key ideas tend to be repeated. These include the notions that emotions are usually triggered by one's interpretations of events, that they involve strong reactions of many bodily systems, that emotional expressions are based on genetic mechanisms, that they communicate information from one person to another, and that they help the individual adapt to changing environmental situations. Such adaptations contribute in some way to the chances of survival and to the regulation of social interactions among people.

Despite the widespread recognition of these ideas, the systematic study of emotions has been difficult. Some of the reasons for the difficulties in studying emotions are presented in this chapter. These include the diverse descriptions that people give of the same emotion terms, as well as the belief that emotions occur in blind and deaf children as well as lower animals, requiring inferences from various sources of evidence. In addition, the Behavioristic and Psychoanalytic movements in psychology have raised questions about the validity of self-reports as measures of presumed inner states called emotions. Questions have also been raised about the extent to which it is appropriate or ethical to subject people to laboratory stresses designed to produce emotional states. Finally, it is necessary to emphasize that our ideas about emotions are based on a number of diverse historical traditions that have conceptualized and studied emotions in quite different ways.

MOST PEOPLE believe they know what emotions are. They think of emotions as special kinds of feelings that they label with such words as *happy*, *sad*, *angry*, and *surprised*. They recognize that emotions are part of daily life and are constantly being expressed in direct or subtle ways in their relations to friends, parents, lovers, coworkers, and children. The daily newspapers, television screens, and computer screens are filled with references to emotion in politics, war, sports, medicine, and police work. Clinical psychologists and psychiatrists deal with clients who experience emotional disorders. When a computer search for references to the word *emotion* was made, over 965,000 items were identified. When MEDLINE, a library database, was explored for the word, over 69,477 articles were listed. It is clear that emotions are part of the landscapes of our lives.

One recent Sunday newspaper had the following headlines on some of their articles:

- "Father and son share triumph, make history."
- "Compassion is the work of the nation, not just the government."
- "Actor Dennis Arena loves acting game."
- "Church offers hope to homeless outcasts."
- "L. F., 44, was in a coma after he was kicked, stomped and punched outside the Cheetah Lounge . . . . The fight was over L. F.'s son tugging on a lasso B.G., 29, had in his back pocket."
- "Violence declines in the jails and prisons where domestic violence programs are taught."
- "College team starts fast in pounding opponents."

In this small sample of articles, such emotions as *triumph, compassion, love, hope, anger, revenge,* and *assertiveness* are mentioned or implied.

When I asked students in my classes to describe an emotional experience that they had, some interesting stories were told. Here is an example:

> Coming out of the movies with an unimportant date, I saw walking ahead of me a woman I had fallen in love with, but with whom I hadn't been able to maintain the relationship. I was riveted, watching her walk away at a pace I could never keep up with. I felt happiness at seeing her again, longing for her, sadness that we weren't together, and admiration for her. I wondered if she'd seen me in the movie, and felt disappointed and rejected when I thought she must have, and hopeful when I thought maybe she didn't. I was frustrated that I was with my companion and so couldn't run up to talk with her (though I wondered what I could say), and felt wistful as I watched her walk away.
>
> My date noticed this, of course—to my embarrassment—and asked who she was. She seemed a little sympathetic, a little curious, a little jealous, and a little embarrassed that she'd asked and I'd actually told her.
>
> Overall the experience was both pleasant and not. Pleasant for the memories of the old flame, and in the feeling of happiness when I first saw her. But also unpleasant for the same memories. Pleasant for the longing of my love for her, but painful for the same reason.

Here is a second example:

> I am recalling back a few years ago, when my mother had me make three huge gardens in her backyard. I was so mad that she was standing over me supervising me telling me what to do rather than helping me do the labor part of it. I was very angry the entire time I was working. To add that she felt she was actually helping me angered me even more. The topper was when a huge dump truck came pulling up into our front yard and proceeded to dump two tons of dirt into our driveway. I was totally furious yet for some reason I started laughing and every time I thought about all the work I was expected to do, I would just start laughing. Angry as all hell, yet I was laughing. My friends would ride by on their bicycles pointing and laughing yet as mad as I really was, I still laughed with them. I even recall crying a couple of times throughout the day as my hands and body dirtied and blistered from the work that I was so far from finishing. The crying part was embarrassing. Sure, yes I was angry and sad yet I still found myself laughing. When I was not laughing, I was cussing and screaming and when I was not cussing and screaming, I was crying. I worked all day with all sorts of different

emotions bouncing in and out of my mind. I remember a few separate times throughout the day throwing down the shovel and yelling "I quit!" Yet even fear came into play, another strong emotion. I felt fearful as to what pain I was going to suffer when my father came home from work. How mad was he going to be when he saw that pile of dirt in his parking place? Not failing to mention if he found out I had not complied with the orders that my mother had given to me that early spring morning. I cried a little more, then I got very angry and I buckled down, wiped the sweat from my forehead, wrapped my bloody hands, and started working as hard and as fast as I could, just trying to get the job finished.

Of course, as with all the jobs my mother had me start I finished this job with the strong help of anger and fear. If it were not for these two emotions, I can almost assure that I would still be standing there in her backyard with a shovel and an eroded pile of dirt. After it was all said and done, I felt even more emotions. I felt happy it looked so nice, proud that I had done such a nice job, and above everything else I felt relieved. Relieved that I had finally finished and could now go shower up and relax. No worries of my father coming home to reprimand me.

What is especially interesting about these two descriptions is the multiplicity of emotions that were experienced in each incident. Happiness and sadness, disappointment and rejection, embarrassment and wistfulness in the first incident. Anger and sadness, embarrassment and fear, pride and relief in the second. These examples highlight the complexity of people's normal experiences of emotion. Clinicians believe that psychotherapy is concerned primarily with the repair of emotional disorders, that is, emotions that are somehow dysfunctional in an individual's life. Clinicians believe that emotions are related to interpersonal conflicts, that they can be both adaptive or maladaptive, that they relate to personality, and that they are deeper and more complex than is revealed by verbal reports alone.

The ubiquity of emotions in people's lives suggests that the subject should be an important part of scientific research, textbooks, and teaching. Surprisingly, this is not so. Few universities in the United States or in other countries offer courses devoted exclusively to emotions. There was even a period during the 1950s when some psychologists proposed that the concept of emotion was so difficult to define that psychology would be better off without it. For a while, some writers eliminated the word *emotion* from their general textbooks and tried to ignore the topic. It is no surprise, however, that the concept (but not the word) appeared in disguise under such headings as stress, frustration, aggression, conflict, and psychopathology.

On a related theme, Sternberg and Grigorenko (2001) pointed out that the current organization of psychology by fields such as learning, social, and developmental creates oppositions between individuals who may be studying a phenomenon from different vantage points. They wrote, "Psychological phenomena such as imagination, intelligence, wisdom, and even emotion may tend to be ignored in a department if they are not seen as part of the 'core' of a field" (p. 18).

This situation has been gradually changing, and in recent years there has been a marked increase in the number of publications that deal with emotions. Some of the confusions concerning the concept have yet to be resolved.

WHY IS THE STUDY OF EMOTION DIFFICULT?

There are many reasons for the difficulties involved in the study of emotions. Some relate to ambiguities in the language of emotion, some to inconsistencies in definitions of the concept, some to the problem of how and to what extent emotions apply to animals, and some to the impact of different historical traditions. Let us consider some of these points in a preliminary way. They are more fully discussed in other chapters.

The Language of Emotion

If we are asked to describe our emotional states, we can use words like *happy, sad, irritable,* or *jealous*. This assumes that the listener understands these terms because of similar experiences and through empathy. What does one do, however, if the listener does not know what a word such as *depression* means?

A number of years ago, college students were asked to write brief reports about emotional experiences they had (Davitz, 1970). From these reports, a list of 556 words and phrases were obtained of feelings or impulses people had when experiencing emotions.

To illustrate the complexity of these ideas, consider the terms used to describe depression.

> "I feel empty, drained, hollow, understimulated, undercharged, heavy, loggy, sluggish; I feel let down, tired, sleepy; it's an effort to do anything, I have no desire, no motivations, no interest."
>
> "I feel sorry for myself; there is simply no place to go; I lose all confidence in myself and doubt myself; I feel vulnerable and totally helpless; I feel insignificant."
>
> "I want to withdraw, disappear, draw back, be alone, away from others; crawl into myself; everything seems useless, absurd, meaningless; I feel as if I'm out of touch, can't reach others; my body wants to contract."
>
> "I have no appetite; there is a lump in my throat; I can't smile or laugh; it's as if I'm suffocating." (Davitz, 1970, p. 253)

These descriptions of depression present a picture of a complex internal state having many components. There are physical symptoms ("tired" or "sleepy"), attitudes about self ("feel vulnerable"), impulses to action ("want to withdraw"), and physiological changes ("no appetite"). Any one class of descriptions is clearly only a partial image of the total state called *depression*.

In contrast to depression, consider the metaphors used to describe happiness.

> "I have an inner warm glow; I feel like smiling; the world seems basically good and beautiful; the future seems right; I feel safe and secure; I am excited in a calm way; I have a sense of being very open, receptive; I feel bouncy, wide awake; I feel strong inside, a feeling that I can do anything; I feel like singing, like laughing; I want others to feel the same as I do." (Davitz, 1970, p. 254)

These metaphors also refer to inner states, impulses to action, self-attitudes, and physiological changes and indicate the variety of metaphors used to describe a simple emotion like happiness.

Physiological metaphors are particularly common in everyday language when expressing what William James called the "coarser" emotions like anger, fear, and disgust. Consider the following:

> "I was in a cold sweat."
> "He was hot around the collar."
> "My blood ran cold."
> "I had goose pimples."
> "He was a volcano erupting."

It is easy to recognize what emotions are being expressed.

The *Oxford English Dictionary* (*OED*) is the most extensive summary in existence of the origins and meanings of English words. It is instructive to examine the origins of emotion words. Consider, for example, words related to *anger* and its near synonyms such as *annoyance, fury,* and *rage.*

The word *anger* comes from a Norse word that means troubled or afflicted. It can mean physical affection or pain, and it can also be a feeling of *hot displeasure* provoked against an agent.

Annoyance comes from a French word related to the modern word *ennui.* The *OED* provides four definitions of the term: (a) a mental state akin to pain; (b) to be distasteful to, bore, or trouble someone; (c) to affect a person in a way that causes a slight irritation; and (d) to molest, injure, hurt, or harm someone.

The word *fury* comes from a Latin word which means to be mad. It is described in the *OED* as (a) a disorder of the mind approaching madness; (b) fierceness in conflict; and (c) inspired frenzy.

The word *rage* comes from the Latin word which means rabies, or a disease that may occur as the result of the bite of an animal. Nine differing definitions are given; for example, that it is a fit of mania, a violent act, a furious passion, a violent appetite or desire for something, poetic inspiration, and manly enthusiasm or indignation.

These illustrations suggest that the language of emotions is complex and derived from different historical sources, and is used inconsistently even at the present time. It is therefore no surprise that even scholars have difficulty deciding on a single, unequivocal meaning of an emotion term in any language.

To make matters more complex, sometimes emotion terms are used in nonemotional contexts, as when someone says, "I'm *afraid* you didn't do very well on your examination" or "I am *anxious* to get started on my vacation." It is also possible to have emotions about our own emotions. For example, someone might say "I hate being so nervous" or "I am ashamed of feeling so envious of my sister."

Some metaphors imply conflict between emotions. The expressions "to kill with kindness" or "to smother someone with love" suggests this ambivalence.

Sometimes the word *feel* is used in several different contexts.

> "I feel happy" (emotional context).
> "I feel I have given you the right answer" (belief context).
> "I feel a pain in my shoulder" (sensation context).
> "I feel tired" (biological context).

In common parlance, only the first expression would be considered to be part of the language of emotions. It is evident that one can have feelings that are not emotions.

DICHOTOMIES

Reason and Passion

There are additional ways in which the language of emotions is unclear. Many writers have stated that there are various dichotomies that characterize emotions. One dichotomy is between reason and emotion, with emotion often being described as *passion.* The assumption is often made that emotions are irrational and that an individual is not responsible for his or her behavior while under the influence of intense emotion. French philosopher Blaise Pascal wrote that "the heart has its reasons which reason does not understand." The Romans said that "anger is a brief bout of madness" (de Sousa, 1987, p. 4). Some courts of law recognize a "crime of passion" defense, and some recognize that a crime committed during an intense emotional experience is mitigated by this "brief insanity." A woman who violently retaliates against her husband during a period of spousal abuse may be said to be "blinded by passion." If a man finds his wife in bed with another man, he may kill them out of jealousy, a statement that is occasionally considered an acceptable defense in a court of law.

Disorganization and Organization

Another dichotomy that is sometimes discussed in the literature is whether emotions are disorganizing or organizing. Examples are given of people who become tongue-tied with stage fright, or who lose control of themselves during periods of intense anger, or who forget the name of close friends or what they were about to say when embarrassed. In contrast, there are many cases of organized planning for revenge, of organized planning for aggression, and of organized planning for courtship in the interest of love. The possibility exists that emotions can be both. If an event occurs (such as the appearance of an attractive member of the opposite sex) that seems important to an individual, a complete change of direction or action may occur with the result that one ongoing activity is stopped and another begun. This may appear as the disruption of one focus of attention, but it becomes an organized effort to create another focus of attention.

Active and Passive

Emotions are also sometimes described in terms of the dichotomy of *active* versus *passive*. (A more accurate description would be *deliberate* vs. *passive*.) People are said to "fall in love," implying that this just happens and is not a deliberate act. In the movie, *The Godfather*, Michael, during his stay in Sicily, meets a young woman and instantly falls in love with her. His friends say that "the thunderbolt hit him." The person is said to be a passive recipient of the emotion.

A similar passive occurrence of an emotion might be experienced if you saw a child being beaten or witnessed a death at the scene of an accident. In such situations, the observer generally does not believe he or she has deliberate control over the appearance of his or her own emotions. In fact, it is seldom, if ever, possible for an individual to decide to have an emotion and simply create it. Sometimes, however, it is possible to think about a situation (e.g., an injustice, a beautiful setting or person, or an exciting football game) and thus create an emotion. It appears that emotions are generally triggered by particular events or thoughts or appear "out of the blue."

Adaptive and Maladaptive

Still another dichotomy often considered in relation to emotions is whether they are adaptive or maladaptive. On the one hand, there exists an image of a person showing a strong emotion such as rage with disheveled hair, distorted face, wild gesticulations, and foam at the mouth. Such a picture hardly seems useful to the individual, and if there exists the possibility of a stroke or heart attack, the pattern of behavior seems maladaptive. Similarly, if a person becomes so frightened that he or she is "frozen to the spot" and is unable to move in the face of an attacker bent on assault, then this also seems to be maladaptive.

On the other hand, many writers have pointed out the useful nature of emotional reactions. For example, angry behavior can often intimidate a rival and allow the angry person to gain what he or she wishes. Anger can also energize an individual to work harder to obtain a desired goal. Fear typically induces an individual to avoid something or someone perceived as dangerous or threatening. In fact, a similar case can be made for most emotions as being useful to the individual.

Conscious and Unconscious

Some writers have stated that the essence of an emotion is that it is a conscious subjective experience that can be communicated to others (e.g., Masson & McCarthy, 1995; D. Watson, 2000). This idea is the basis for the self-report tests of emotion and mood that exist. However, many investigators have noted that there is a great deal about emotion that is not fully accessible to consciousness. People often report feeling " blue" without knowing why. They report feeling irritable or annoyed without being able to provide any reasons for the feelings. Both moods and emotions can occur without a recognizable stimulus.

People are sometimes mistaken about their emotions. They may report feeling nothing at all while people around them may see signs of depression, rage, or jealousy. Because the language of emotions is ambiguous, an individual may label his or her emotions in a different way than an observer might, or he or she may not understand what is meant by certain emotion terms. For example, in an inpatient study with psychiatric patients, the patients were asked to rate their feelings of anxiety. Many did not know exactly what was meant by the word anxiety, and even staff members had low interjudge reliability when rating the anxiety levels of patients (Platman, Plutchik, & Weinstein, 1971).

Psychoanalytic literature is filled with case histories of patients who were unaware of strong emotions they had but which were revealed through dreams or through extended psychotherapy. Recent research on moods also revealed that people were not good at recognizing what events trigger their own moods (D. Watson, 2000). Social science laboratory research on unconscious processes in social judgment has shown that judgments we make about other groups are often based on knowledge we have of which we are unaware. Specifically, it appears that stereotypes and prejudiced attitudes that may be unconscious operate to influence a person's intentions and self-reflections. People who scored higher on conscious levels of prejudice toward social groups have also been found to have high levels of unconscious prejudice. It appears that emotions need to be conceptualized in such a way as to incorporate the idea of unconscious emotions as well as conscious ones.

Positive and Negative

Emotions are commonly described as being either negative or positive. Emotions such as fear, anger, disgust, and sadness are usually thought to be negative, whereas emotions of joy, interest, and love are described as positive. It should be evident that these terms are metaphors borrowed from mathematics and physics. Although positive and negative numbers and positive and negative electrical charges are neither good nor bad, in ordinary language use, positive emotions are thought to be good or desirable whereas negative emotions are usually described as bad or undesirable.

A number of writers have questioned the use of positive and negative metaphors. One reason is that it is not always evident which emotions fall into each category. For example, in the Middle Ages, the seven deadly sins were considered to be greed, lust, envy, gluttony, anger, pride, and laziness. Today, most people would consider pride to be a positive emotion, and both envy (Ben-Ze'ev, 2000) and anger have also been considered to be positive emotions (Plutchik, 1994).

A psychoanalyst (Jones, 1995) stated that contempt, a form of disgust, is a positive emotion as judged by the fact that it does not feel bad, that it bolsters self-esteem, and that it helps maintain a stable social hierarchy. Jones also claimed that shame plays a key role in helping to maintain status hierarchies and thus plays a positive role in life.

Finally, a number of authors have pointed out that all emotions play an adaptive role in human life and from that point of view are essentially positive. Fear motivates withdrawal behavior in the face of perceived danger, anger motivates the obtaining of survival-related resources, and sadness tends to engender supportive behavior from friends, relatives, and one's community at times of loss. Other functions have been identified for most emotions (Plutchik, 2000). It is possible that the positive and negative metaphors are not the most accurate ways to describe emotions. This issue is discussed more fully later in the book.

The dichotomies that have been briefly described as being related to emotions— reason and passion, disorganization and organization, active and passive, adaptive and maladaptive, conscious and unconscious, positive and negative—reveal how complex the idea of emotions is even in ordinary social discourse. Different scientists have focused their attention on one or another of these dichotomies, which has resulted in confusion in the field and occasional lengthy debates. But there are other important issues that raise difficult problems in the effort to define "emotion" in as broad a context as possible. Let us consider some of them.

EMOTIONS IN NONVERBAL INDIVIDUALS

Many studies of emotion have been carried out with the help of college students who are generally intelligent and verbal. But most people believe that young children and even infants have emotions, too. We accept this idea even though they cannot report their inner feelings with familiar words. Similarly, anyone who has observed severely ill psychiatric patients will admit that they seem to show emotions even though their words may be confusing. Individuals with mental retardation also show emotions even though their verbal statements of feelings are often limited or absent.

An example of emotions in children with mental disabilities may be seen in the research by Eibl-Eibesfeldt (1973), a German ethologist who has spent a great many years studying emotional behavior in natural settings. He took extensive motion pictures of six children who had been born with severe disabilities because their mothers had taken the drug Thalidomide during pregnancy. The result was that five of the six children had slight to extensive brain damage, and all were born deaf and blind. All showed retarded development to varying degrees, and all showed some stereotyped behaviors such as teeth grinding, head or body swaying, and kicking.

Despite the fact that these children could neither see nor hear the world around them and were also greatly impaired in cognitive capacity, they showed many normal emotional reactions. Eibl-Eibesfeldt (1973) noted that all of the children showed smiling behavior during play and that tickling and patting the child elicited the same behavior.

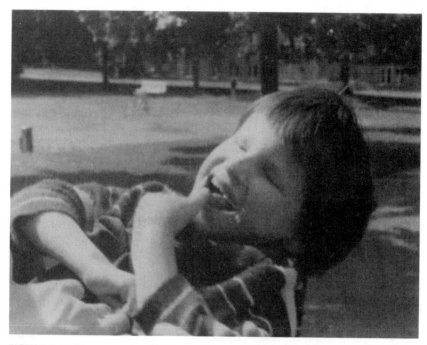

FIGURE 1.1. Photograph of Sabine laughing. Sabine was born blind and deaf because her mother had taken the drug Thalidomide during pregnancy. From "The Expressive Behavior of the Deaf-and-Blind-Born," by I. Eibl-Eibesfeldt. In M. von Cranach and I. Vine (Eds.), *Social Communication and Movement*, 1973, p. 177. Copyright 1973 by Academic Press. Reprinted with permission.

In addition to smiling, the children all showed laughter, generally during rough social play such as wrestling as well as during tickling. The children cried when hurt or when left in an unfamiliar environment. In such cases, the corners of the mouth usually turned down and opened, the eyelids pressed together, and tears were shed. Sometimes the eyebrows were raised, furrowing the brow, at the same time that frown lines appeared between the eyes. Occasionally, angry crying was observed when someone persistently offered a child a disliked object. The children also spontaneously embraced, caressed, and kissed other people on some occasions. At times they showed smiling, laughing, crying in distress, crying in anger, frowning, pouting, surprise, and other expressions that clearly denote emotions. A photograph of one of these children is shown in Figure 1.1. These findings supported the idea that emotions are genetically-based unlearned behavioral adaptations that have value for the individual.

EMOTIONS IN NONHUMAN ANIMALS

There is another reason for doubting the idea that verbal reports of feelings are the only way to recognize emotions, and that is that emotions are believed to occur in animals. From prehistoric times, observations of the behavior and expressions of animals have been used to judge the existence of emotions in these creatures. The belief in animal emotions is the basis for the many studies that have been carried out on animals to determine the factors that produce and modify such emotions as fear and anger.

As a brief illustration of this point, in a report in *Time* magazine, a description was given of a study in which a genetic change had been induced in a group of mice. A gene essential to the synthesis of a neurotransmitter in the brain had been blocked. The result was a group of male mice that were six times as likely to engage in attack and killing behavior on other males as wild-type mice. In addition, these aggressive mice had a much higher frequency of sexual contacts than the control mice. This study dramatically supported the many other studies that confirmed a connection between emotions and genes (Nelson, 1995).

Emotions in Dogs

Most people, particularly those who have had experience with pets, will agree that their animals show emotions. Dogs have been reported to show "depression" when their owners have died or gone away. They also show signs of jealousy. When dogs are scolded their tails droop, their activity slows, and they slink away.

In the United States, there are currently about 52 million dogs, and it is estimated that 20% of Americans share their lives with dogs. Fossil evidence indicates that dogs were domesticated at least 14,000 years ago and were bred from wolves and possibly coyotes and jackals. All these animals can interbreed.

Dogs were bred for puppylike characteristics such as submissiveness and dependency, and the various breeds were developed by selective breeding to emphasize special qualities: large size, small size, herding, pack hunting, individual hunting, fighting, tracking, and guarding. Consistent with these different functions, certain temperamental characteristics resulted from the breeding process.

In the 17th century, French philosopher René Descartes wrote that dogs were simply biological machines without self-awareness or emotional feelings. This dogma led to cruel treatment of dogs over a long period of time.

Participants in the antivivisectionist movement that developed in the 19th century and those involved with animal-rights groups today certainly believe that dogs and other animals can feel pain and by implication pleasure. They point out that the sensory systems of the higher animals at least are very similar to our own, and in some cases surpass human senses in acuity or range of sensitivity. They also note the similarities in the structure of the nervous system of all mammals and the similarities of neurotransmitters such as serotonin and glutamine. Scientists who do research on animals usually find that the results obtained apply to humans as well.

Some dogs can discriminate over 100 spoken human words and can recognize and respond appropriately to gestures. H. Gardner (1983) suggested that there exist at least seven types of human intelligence: linguistic intelligence, logical-mathematical intelligence, spatial intelligence, musical intelligence, kinesthetic intelligence, interpersonal intelligence, and intrapersonal intelligence. According to Coren (1994), a psychologist who has done considerable training of dogs, they are capable of spatial intelligence (making a mental map of the environment), kinesthetic intelligence (coordination of the body for complex skills), intrapersonal intelligence (recognition of limits to one's skills such as an inability to jump over a barrier that is too high), and interpersonal intelligence (ability to get along with others and to assume leadership or followership roles in a group). In brief, to be an animal that can function successfully in a complex social and environmental world requires both intelligence and some degree of mental life.

Not only do dogs respond appropriately to information conveyed by humans, but they are also able to communicate information to humans about three main topics: their emotional states, their social relations particularly with regard to dominance, and their wants (Coren, 1994). With regard to emotions, low-pitched sounds usually indicate threats and the possibility of aggression, whereas high-pitched sounds of short duration usually reveal pain. High-pitched sounds repeated at a slower rate seemed to indicate playfulness. Other examples are continuous rapid barking, mid-range pitch, which appears to be a warning of potential danger; and a single sharp, short bark, lower mid-range pitch, which seems to mean "stop that" and is often given by a mother dog when disciplining her puppies. Soft, low-pitched growling seems to send a message of "Beware," and soft whimpering signals fear or hurt.

A dog's body posture may also communicate information. When the tail is up and slightly curved over the back, the message communicated is of a dominant animal. When the tail is tucked between the legs, this appears to signal low dominance status. When the dog's ears are pulled back flat against the head, it signals preparation for a possible attack.

There are a number of mouth signals that have been identified by trainers. One example is the yawn, which does not indicate fatigue but is believed to be a signal of stress and tension.

Figures 1.2, 1.3, and 1.4 show some expressions of dogs that communicate emotional states according to Coren (1994). In every case, the presence of an emotion in the animal is an inference or interpretation based on several different kinds of information. These descriptions are based on long experience of dog trainers and need to be confirmed in other research settings.

Consider another animal, one that is genetically more similar to humans than are dogs. According to genetic studies, over 98% of the chimpanzee's genome is the same as that of humans. It is reasonable to expect that there would be many similarities in mental as well as biological functioning.

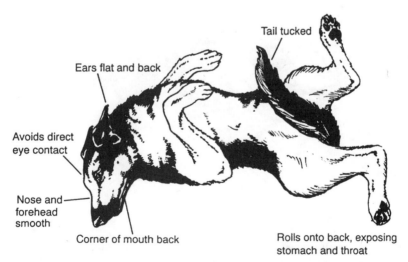

FIGURE 1.2. A dog communicating complete surrender, fear, and submission. From *The Intelligence of Dogs: Canine Consciousness and Capabilities*, by S. Coren, 1994, p. 112. Copyright 1994 by The Free Press. Reprinted with permission.

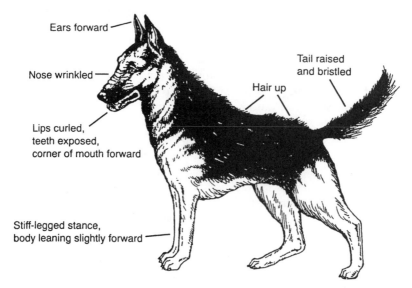

Ears forward

Nose wrinkled

Tail raised
and bristled

Hair up

Lips curled,
teeth exposed,
corner of mouth forward

Stiff-legged stance,
body leaning slightly forward

FIGURE 1.3. A dog communicating dominance and threat. From *The Intelligence of Dogs: Canine Consciousness and Capabilities*, by S. Coren, 1994, p. 111. Copyright 1994 by The Free Press. Reprinted with permission.

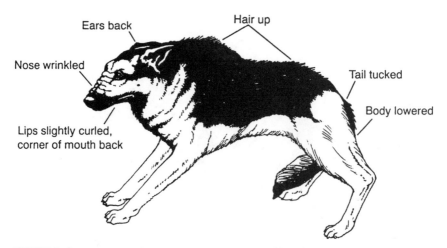

Ears back

Hair up

Nose wrinkled

Tail tucked

Body lowered

Lips slightly curled,
corner of mouth back

FIGURE 1.4. A frightened dog that might attack if pressed. From *The Intelligence of Dogs: Canine Consciousness and Capabilities*, by S. Coren, 1994, p. 111. Copyright 1994 by The Free Press. Reprinted with permission.

Emotions in Chimpanzees

Ethologist Jane Goodall, who has spent over 30 years studying chimpanzee behavior under relatively natural conditions in Africa, has often described emotional behavior in the chimpanzees (Goodall, 1990). She wrote,

> When I began my study at Gombe in 1960, it was not permissible—at least not in ethological circles—to talk about an animal's mind. Only humans had minds. Nor was it proper to talk about animal personality....It was not permissible to present a mere "anecdote" as evidence for anything. (p. 14)

Despite this inauspicious beginning, the work of Goodall has had a major impact on both ethology and psychology. This is also true for other people who have provided theories of mental functioning based on systematic observations, clinical experience, and anecdotal evidence. Examples of such figures are Sigmund Freud, founder of psychoanalysis; Jean Piaget, major contributor to cognitive psychology; and John Bowlby, creator of attachment theory.

Goodall has pointed out that investigators who work with chimpanzees have no reservations about saying that chimps experience such emotions as joy, sorrow, anger, boredom, and jealousy. Such judgments are made because of the similarities of so much of the chimpanzees' behavior to our own. We use empathy to read emotions into similar patterns of behavior. Goodall also points out that the problem of judging emotions in chimps is not fundamentally different from the problem of judging emotions in other humans. Verbal statements are not necessarily true or accurate, and we cannot know for certain what other people experience.

Goodall (1990) described a situation that led to "depression" in Flint, an 8-year-old chimpanzee. Flint's mother, Flo, died when he was 8½ years old, and he began to show signs of depression. He became increasingly lethargic, refused most food, and became sick. Goodall wrote,

> [T]he last time I saw him alive, he was hollow-eyed, gaunt and utterly depressed, huddled in the vegetation close to where Flo had died....The last short journey he made, pausing to rest every few feet, was to the very place where Flo's body had lain. There he stayed for several hours, staring into the water. He struggled on a little further, then curled up and never moved again. (p. 196)

Another illustration that Goodall provides is the case of Merlin, a chimpanzee who lost his mother when he was about 3 years old. Although an elder sibling showed caretaking behavior toward him, Merlin began to show behavior often seen in socially deprived laboratory chimpanzees. These included rocking back and forth, hanging upside down and motionless for minutes at a time, and pulling out his own hairs. His behavior vacillated between submission and aggression. He became increasingly emaciated and died about a year after his mother's death. A picture of Merlin shortly before he died is shown in Figure 1.5.

The work of Goodall and that of many other field ethologists such as Fossey (1983) with gorillas, de Waal (1982) with chimpanzees, Strum (1988) with baboons, and others has increasingly sensitized us to the social complexity of animal behavior. Most people today do not see animals as sensationless robots who feel nothing; they believe that pain and suffering as well as pleasure are part of the life of most animals. It is a simple step from this belief to the belief in emotions in animals.

FIGURE 1.5. A 3-year-old chimpanzee, Merlin, 1 year after his mother's death. He became increasingly listless, stopped playing with other chimpanzees, and developed a number of stereotyped patterns of behavior such as rocking back and forth. From "The Behavior of Chimpanzees in Their Natural Habitat," by J. Van Lawick-Goodall, 1973, *American Journal of Psychiatry, 130,* p. 10. Copyright 1973 by American Psychiatric Association. Reprinted with permission.

Attitudes Toward Animals

There is another argument that is sometimes made to justify the idea of emotions in animals. Almost any kind of animal can become a pet. This includes not only lovable dogs, cats, and birds but also snakes, alligators, bears, lions, lizards, and mice. Humans value companionship and bond to any kind of animal that provides it. Pet owners value animals as distinct personalities with whom they can have affectionate relationships not too different from the kinds of affectionate relationships they have with other people. This would hardly be possible if the pets did not react to human contact in affectionate, trusting, and playful ways—in other words, in emotional ways.

Another aspect of this issue may be seen in some of the attitudes toward animals found in medieval Europe. Witches and sorcerers were believed to engage in sexual rituals with the devil, who was disguised as a large animal. Such offenses, called *bestiality,* were regarded as a horrendous sin, and individuals convicted of this crime were publicly tried and executed along with their animal lovers.

The belief in the human qualities of animals was extended to punishment for crimes committed by animals. In 1457, for example, a pig was arrested in France for murdering and partly devouring an infant. The pig was tried and hanged. Animals were often tortured before execution.

In hunter–gatherer societies of the modern period, the people do not regard the animals they hunt as inferior to themselves but think of them as capable of thoughts and emotions similar to those of humans. In many cultures, the hunters' religious beliefs, known as *totemism*, assume that the tribe traces its origin back to some animal ancestors.

One final example concerns wolves. As forests were cut down, the natural prey of wolves gradually disappeared, and they began to kill domestic livestock for food. These events created a series of myths about wolves that describe them as conscious beings who were evil "vermin" who should be held personally responsible for their actions. The result was an unrelenting attempt in most countries to eradicate the wolf. When caught, wolves were tortured, poisoned, and mutilated.

These various examples support the idea that emotions are part of the lives of animals as well as of humans, a point that is explored in more detail in later chapters. I have presented these ideas to illustrate some of the factors that make the study of emotions difficult. There are several other issues that contribute to the problem that I describe below.

PROBLEMS OF VERBAL REPORTS

Most of us have learned to be cautious about accepting at face value other people's comments about their feelings. One important reason for the distrust we may feel is that we suspect that others censor their verbalizations. This conclusion stems directly from the fact that we are aware of the fact that we often censor our own thoughts and feelings. We learn to "grin and bear it" in embarrassing situations. We learn to smile even when we are angry, and we learn to keep a poker face when necessary. These controls we place on the expression of our feelings have the purpose of avoiding embarrassment or criticism from others and help us get the things we want from other people; for example, goodwill, respect, acceptance, and acknowledgment. Because we recognize the fact that we censor our own expressions of our feelings, we assume that other people do it as well. This contributes to the difficulty in studying emotions.

The Effect of Behaviorism

Another reason for the distrust of verbal reports is the powerful effect that Behaviorism has had on the thinking of psychologists. The early behaviorists such as John Watson and B. F. Skinner were dissatisfied with the introspective tradition in psychology. They believed that the only truly reliable, objective information obtainable about living creatures was information about their behavior, and preferably, as simple behavior as possible. This attitude reduced psychology to the study of behavior and not mind and led to a preoccupation with conditioned responses, simple habits, automatic reactions to stimuli called tropisms, and bar-presses. Emotions were considered to be inner states that could not be reliably observed and were therefore outside of the realm of scientific psychology.

The Effect of Psychoanalysis

Interestingly enough, another quite different tradition led to almost the same conclusion. This was the psychoanalytic tradition. Psychoanalysts have made us aware of the fact that subjective reports of emotions cannot always be accepted at face value. Not only are some emotions totally repressed, and thus unavailable to introspection, but others are frequently modified or distorted. Brenner (1975), a psychoanalyst, presented a case history to illustrate these points.

A patient recalled that once, when he returned home at the end of a college term, he had a daydream in which he imagined his mother and younger sister had been killed. He had this idea without "feeling anything" about it. The patient was not conscious of any of the thoughts that would be expected to accompany the daydream; of a wish to kill, of joy in revenge, or of horror, sadness, or remorse (guilt) at having, in fantasy, done the deed.

Brenner noted that the circumstances "reminded the patient of the time" when his sister was born—a time when his mother had gone to the hospital for delivery and when the patient had felt very alone. What had happened after mother's return had been even worse. She had turned from the patient and focused her affection on her new baby, a girl. From that time on, the patient felt unwanted and unloved. But rage was dangerous, since being a "bad" boy, he learned, would lead all the more to being abandoned by mother, who used to punish him by putting him in a dark closet when he had an angry outburst or, later on, by refusing to talk to him.

When the patient came home to an empty house, he reacted with memories of that earlier time when his sister was born and when he was overcome by jealousy, longing, and rage. He did imagine that his mother and sister had been killed. At the same time, however, he denied that it was his own wish to kill them. (p. 11)

This case history, written within a psychoanalytic framework, illustrates the presence of emotions of which the patient is unaware, and which can be identified only through a long and complex process of analysis. From the psychoanalytic point of view, the presence of emotions is inferred on the basis of various kinds of indirect evidence.

The Problem of Ethical Research

This is another problem that limits the extent to which we may study emotions. That problem concerns the ethics of laboratory research. In other branches of psychology concerned with learning and memory, for example, it is possible to create highly controlled situations in which the stimulus conditions are known and measured and where responses can be equally precisely measured. In the study of emotions, ethical considerations greatly limit the extent to which emotions such as grief, rage, and fear can be created in the laboratory. Almost all academic and research institutions now have review committees that must decide whether research conducted there adequately protects the rights of the subjects and whether the potential benefits are commensurate with the potential risks. Studies that were once acceptable, such as giving strong electric shocks to subjects or deceiving them into believing they have low intelligence or an abnormal personality trait, would probably not be acceptable today in many research settings. As a result, researchers in the field of emotions are frequently forced to study existing clinical conditions such as bereavement, depression, suicidality, and violence. Important as such studies are, they seldom allow causal statements to be made, nor do they permit detailed knowledge of the sources of the observed behavior. Many emotion studies are carried out as field studies such as the kind Goodall has done. The fact that control of variables through laboratory studies of emotions are not often possible does not mean that the data of research by other methods are necessarily less reliable or meaningful.

Are Verbal Reports the Best Measure of Emotions?

The issues that have been raised so far in this chapter suggest that verbal reports of feeling states are sometimes not wholly adequate ways to describe emotions. The following are some of the reasons for this conclusion:

1. Verbal reports of emotion may be deliberate attempts to deceive another person.
2. Verbal reports of emotions may be distortions or partial truths for conscious or unconscious reasons.
3. Reports of emotions depend on an individual's particular knowledge and experience with emotions, as well as his or her facility with words.
4. Reports of inner emotional states usually are retrospective and depend on memory. Remembered events are notoriously subject to distortions.
5. Requests for a report of one's immediate emotional state creates the problem that the process of observing may change the thing observed.
6. Emotions are generally believed to occur in infants and young children as well as adults. Young children have not yet acquired the ability to use language to express their emotions. Therefore, the belief is based on other classes of evidence.
7. Emotions are generally believed to occur in individuals who are mentally defective and mentally deranged. In many such cases, patients are unable to provide any direct verbal reports on their emotional states.
8. The inherent ambiguity of language creates the problem of the "true" meaning of emotion terms. The importance of context in determining meaning implies that the same verbal report of an emotion will have a different referent in another setting.
9. Repression may create false negatives; that is, an observer may erroneously assume that no emotion exists because none has been reported.
10. Emotions are rarely, if ever, experienced in a pure state. More typically, any given situation creates mixed emotions which are difficult to describe in any simple or unequivocal way.

For these various reasons, it seems appropriate to conclude that a verbal report of an inner emotional state is only a rough approximation to whatever that state is. An emotion should not be considered as synonymous with a presumed inner feeling state. Instead it appears that the word *emotion* refers to a complex set of events whose characteristics can only be inferred on the basis of a congruence of various classes of evidence. One of these classes of evidence consists of verbal reports of inner states, but such evidence has no greater logical priority than do the other classes of evidence. This approach is exactly analogous to that taken in other parts of psychology or the physical sciences. Such terms as *memory, perceptions, traits, atoms, genes,* and *DNA molecules* are theoretical constructs whose properties are inferred on the basis of various kinds of evidence.

A FIRST APPROXIMATION TO A DEFINITION OF EMOTIONS

Examination of published papers and books shows that many definitions of the word *emotion* have been proposed over the past 100 years. Although no list can be complete, it is possible to provide a sense of the way psychologists and others have thought about the topic by examining a few of the more influential definitions (see Exhibit 1.1).

■■■■■ **EXHIBIT 1.1. SOME DEFINITIONS OF EMOTION**

My theory...is that the bodily changes follow directly the perception of the exciting fact, and that our feeling of the same changes as they occur is the emotion...

William James, 1884

Ideas are cathexes—ultimately of memory traces—while affects and emotions correspond with processes of discharge, the final expression of which is perceived as feeling.

Sigmund Freud, 1915

An emotion is an hereditary "pattern reaction" involving profound changes of the bodily mechanism as a whole, but particularly of the visceral and glandular systems.

John B. Watson, 1924

The peculiar quality of the emotion is added to simple sensation when the thalamic processes are roused.

Walter B. Cannon, 1929

Emotion is an acute disturbance of the individual as a whole, psychological in origin involving behavior, conscious experience, and visceral functioning.

Paul T. Young, 1943

Emotion can be both organizing (making adaptation to the environment more effective) and disorganizing, both energizing and debilitating, both sought after and avoided.

Donald O. Hebb, 1958

Emotion is the felt tendency toward anything intuitively appraised as good (beneficial) or away from anything intuitively appraised as bad (harmful). This attraction or aversion is accompanied by a pattern of physiological changes, organized toward approach or withdrawal. The patterns differ for different emotions.

Magda Arnold, 1960

An emotion may be defined as a patterned bodily reaction of either destruction, reproduction, incorporation, orientation, protection, reintegration, rejection or exploration or some combination of these, which is brought about by a stimulus.

Robert Plutchik, 1962

Emotional feelings guide our behavior with respect to the two basic life principle of self-preservation and the preservation of the species.

Paul MacLean, 1963

Emotions are phases of an individual's intuitive appraisals either of his own organismic states and urges to act or of the succession of environmental situations in which he finds himself....At the same time, because they are usually accompanied by distinctive facial expressions, bodily postures, and incipient movements, they usually provide valuable information to his companions.

John Bowlby, 1969

Emotion is a complex process that has neurophysiological, motor–expressive, and phenomenological aspects.

Carroll Izard, 1972

An affect is a sensation of pleasure, unpleasure, or both, plus the ideas, both conscious and unconscious, associated with that sensation.

Charles Brenner, 1974

Emotions are tendencies to establish, maintain, or disrupt a relationship with the environment....Emotion might be defined as action readiness change in response to emergencies or interruptions.

Nico Frijda, 1986

Emotions are valenced reactions to events, agents or objects, with their particular nature being determined by the way in which the eliciting situation is construed.

Andrew Ortony, C. L. Clore, and A. Coffins, 1988

Emotion (is) a complex disturbance that includes three main components: subjective affect, physiological changes related to species-specific forms of mobilization for adapted action, and action impulses having both instrumental and expressive qualities.

Richard S. Lazarus, 1991

Emotions are processes that establish, maintain, change, or terminate the relation between the person and the environment on matters of significance to the person.

J. Campos, D. L. Mumme, R. Kermoian, and R. G. Campos, 1994

Affects all are the experiential representation of a nonsymbolic information-processing system that can serve as the central control mechanism for all aspects of human behavior.

Joseph M. Jones, 1995

Emotions are crude predispositions to react to life events, shaped by an evolutionary heritage, but not always adaptive in the modern context.

Denys A. de Catanzaro, 1999

An emotion is a superordinate program whose function is to direct the activities and interactions of the subprograms governing perception; attention; inferences; learning; memory; goal choice; motivational priorities; and physiological reactions, etc.

Leda Cosmides and John Tooby, 2000

An emotion is a phylogenetically evolved, adaptive mechanism that facilitates an organism's attempt to cope with important events affecting its well-being.

Tom Johnston and Klaus Scherer, 2000

Emotions direct and color our attention by selecting what attracts and holds our attention. They regulate priorities and communicate intentions. Emotions are concerned with issues of survival and social status.

Aaron Ben-Ze'ev, 2000

In 1884, James, one of the most influential figures in the history of psychology, defined emotion in the following way: "My theory is that the bodily changes follow directly the perception of the exciting fact, and that our feeling of the same changes as they occur is the emotion" (p. 204). This definition was basically concerned with the question of sequence—that is, which comes first, the feeling of an emotion or the bodily changes associated with it? James believed that for the "coarser" emotions such as fear and anger, the bodily changes (i.e., the increased beating of the heart, the increased blood pressure, the increased sugar in the blood) came first, and the feeling of emotion was based largely on a person's recognition of these changes. This definition or some version of it is still found in many textbooks, and it has influenced the thinking of many generations of psychologists.

John Watson was the founder of Behaviorism as a psychological movement. He defined emotion as follows in one of his publications in 1924: "An emotion is an hereditary *pattern-reaction* involving profound changes of the bodily mechanisms as a whole, but particularly of the visceral and glandular systems" (p. 22). In this definition, Watson introduced the idea that an emotion involved changes in the whole body, that these changes showed different patterns for different emotions, and that all these reactions were based on innate systems.

As an extension of this idea, and in contrast with the views of James, neurophysiologist Walter Cannon in 1929 declared, "The peculiar quality of the emotion is added to simple sensation when the thalamic processes are roused" (p. 369). In writing this, Cannon was summarizing his many studies with cats that seemed to reveal that a certain part of the brain, particularly the hypothalamus, was the integrating center for emotional feelings as well as behavior. This idea was important in that it stimulated many psychologists to become interested in brain functions and led to studies that have taught us a great deal about the roles that different parts of the brain play in determining emotional feelings and displays.

In 1962, I presented a psychoevolutionary theory of emotions that was based on the assumption that there are eight basic emotion dimensions and that all the emotions described in our languages are either one of these eight or a compound or blend of them. The basic emotions were conceptualized as being related to one another by means of a circle or circumplex, somewhat like the relations among colors. The basic dimensions were defined within an adaptive, evolutionary framework as general bipolar dimensions of *destruction* (anger, rage) and *protection* (fear, panic), *incorporation* (acceptance, trust) and *rejection* (disgust, revulsion), *reproduction* (joy, elation) and *reintegration* (sadness, grief), and *exploration* (interest, expectation) and *orientation* (surprise, astonishment). I assumed that emotions exist in all animals and that the different forms of expressions of emotions in different animal groups reflected the operation of evolutionary forces acting on the same fundamental survival mechanisms.

In 1963, Paul MacLean, a neurophysiologist, who had studied the behavior of squirrel monkeys for many years, came to the conclusion that "Emotional feelings guide our behavior with respect to the two basic life principles of self-preservation and the preservation of the species" (MacLean, 1963, p. 17). This view implied that emotions have biological functions and that these functions are related to the survival of the individual as well as survival of the group of which the individual is a part.

A British psychiatrist, John Bowlby, the father of attachment theory (described in a later chapter) in 1969 proposed still another definition of emotion. He wrote,

> Emotions are phases of an individual's intuitive appraisals either of his own organismic states and urges to act or of the succession of environmental situations in which he finds himself. . . . At the same time, because they are usually accompanied by distinctive facial expressions, bodily postures and incipient movements, they usually provide valuable information to his companions. (p. 104)

This definition of emotion emphasized several ideas. It implied that emotions are related to appraisals or interpretations of events going on within an individual's own body as well as events that are occurring around the individual. It indicated that the signs of emotion can be found in facial expressions, postures, and urges to act. And finally, the definition implied that the expressive behavior of an emotion communicates information from one individual to another. These ideas are consistent with Darwin's descriptions of emotional expressions where he stated that emotions communicate intentions.

Another definition of emotion was proposed by psychologist Richard Lazarus in 1991, who suggested that emotion "includes overall an appraisal, outcome action tendencies, a psychological response pattern, and a subjective experience . . . . all this is translated into coping processes that enter the chain after appraisal" (Lazarus, 1991, p. 210). This definition suggests that appraisals are key aspects of emotion, that emotions are patterned reactions rather than disorganized events, and that emotions are closely related to coping processes that attempt to solve problems in an individual's life.

Dutch psychologist Nico Frijda defined emotion as follows in 1986, "Emotions are tendencies to establish, maintain, or disrupt a relationship with the environment . . . . Emotion might be defined as action readiness change in response to emergencies or interruptions" (p. 71). One important idea included in this definition is that emotions are ways that individuals interact with the people and events around them. If the interactions are unpleasant, emotions are attempts to decrease or interrupt the relationship. The other important idea expressed by this definition is that the triggers of emotions are emergencies in the life of the individual and that emotions are responses to these emergencies.

Still another definition of emotion that reflects the so-called cognitive orientation of some psychologists was provided by Andrew Ortony and his colleagues in 1988. He suggested that "Emotions are valenced reactions to events, agents or objects, with their particular nature being determined by the way in which the eliciting situation is construed" (Ortony, Clore, & Collins, 1988, p. 25). The term *valence* is used in the sense of positive or negative, and therefore the definition implies that an emotion involves a pleasant or unpleasant feeling. In addition, the special nature of each emotion is determined by the way that each event is interpreted. This definition thus focuses on the issue of interpretation of events. The same idea has been mentioned by other theorists in terms of the idea of appraisal, evaluation, or cognitive assessment as the basis for emotion.

Joseph Jones is a psychoanalyst who defined *emotion* in 1995 as "the experiential representation of a nonsymbolic information-processing system that can serve as the central control mechanism for all aspects of human behavior" (p. 201). The interesting idea suggested by this definition is that the brain mechanisms that control the expressions of emotions are complex information-processing systems, but it leaves open the question of what triggers emotion in the first place. The definition by Cosmides and Tooby (2000) is similar to that proposed by Jones.

The last two definitions, listed in Exhibit 1.1 and appearing in publications in 2000, emphasize the role of evolution and adaptation in the interests of survival as a basis for emotions. Both definitions imply that emotions are primarily involved in coping with life stresses and with adaptation to the exigencies of life.

Finally, let us examine what *Webster's Third New International Dictionary* says about emotion. The word *emotion* comes from a Latin word that means "to move" or "to stir up." It now has several meanings. It can mean excitement, or agitation, or feelings of pain or pleasure. It is also described as

> a physiological departure from homeostasis that is subjectively experienced as a strong feeling (as of love, hate, desire or fear) and manifests itself in neuromuscular, respiratory, cardiovascular, hormonal or other bodily changes preparatory to overt acts which may or may not be performed. (p. 742)

This definition emphasizes the point that an emotion is a change from a normal or baseline level of activity. It does not say what brings this about, but it does indicate that the changes are extensive and involve most of the systems of the body. The other interesting point made by this definition is that an emotion could, but need not, be expressed in the form of overt action. It could, by implication, simply be a state of mind or a state of preparation for action.

The definitions that have been given here are a sample from a larger group of definitions, but they are useful in that they cover many (although not all) of the ideas about emotion that psychologists and others have proposed over the years. It is evident that there is some agreement and some disagreement. On the basis of these definitions, it may be said that emotions are triggered by our interpretations of events, that they involve reactions of most if not all of our bodily systems, that they can be disruptive of ongoing activity, and yet somehow be adaptive. Emotions communicate information from one person to another, and they may express different feeling states. They may have something to do with survival of the individual and the species, and they may be based on hereditary or genetic processes that influence the way the brain works. In some way, emotions may even have something to do with influencing or regulating the relations between people. All in all, these statements describe a large set of complex ideas.

Some of these ideas have already been summarized by two psychologists seeking to create a consensus on how emotions should be defined. They identified 92 definitions found in various textbooks, dictionaries, and other sources (Kleinginna & Kleinginna, 1981). Their review indicated that certain ideas or themes were frequently repeated, a fact which led them to propose the following integrated definition:

> Emotion is a complex set of interactions among subjective and objective factors, mediated by neural/hormonal systems, which can (a) give rise to affective experiences such as feelings of arousal, pleasure/displeasure; (b) generate cognitive processes such as emotionally relevant perceptual effects, appraisals, labeling processes; (c) activate widespread physiological adjustments to the arousing conditions; and (d) lead to behavior that is often, but not always, expressive, goal-directed, and adaptive. (p. 371)

This definition is useful because it includes many of the diverse ideas found in the literature about emotions. However, it should be considered only as a first approximation. Later chapters will provide additional ideas to help elaborate and refine this definition.

By now, it should be evident that the definitions of emotions are not isolated and arbitrary but that they tend to imply some broader issues or questions. In other words, a definition is, in a sense, a kind of minitheory. It is a way in which the proponent of the definition has decided to describe an area of study. Each definition has, or should have, implications concerning what one should study or measure.

The existence of multiple definitions of the word *emotion* is paralleled by the existence of many different "theories" of emotion. In a review of theories in 1980, I described 24 approaches to an understanding of emotions (Plutchik, 1980). In a similar overview, Strongman (1987) described 30 approaches. Most of these theories tend to be somewhat narrow in focus and are usually concerned with one or two major issues; for example, what parts of the brain are involved in emotional reactions, or how the autonomic nervous system changes during emotions, or what kind of stimulus events trigger what kinds of emotion. Each of these questions is important, but a theory that is broad and general should deal with all of them.

SUMMARY

We have seen that there are a number of reasons why the study of emotions is difficult. Among them is the fact that the language of emotion is complex and often ambiguous; that people are aware of the fact that they, and probably others, disguise or hide their feelings for various social reasons; that the philosophy of Behaviorism implied that we should distrust introspective reports because of their presumed unreliability; and because laboratory research on emotions created ethical dilemmas. Important as these reasons are, there is another major factor to consider when trying to understand why the study of emotions is difficult. This factor concerns the different historical traditions that have directly or indirectly influenced the way scientists and laymen alike think about emotions. These historical traditions will be described in some detail in the following chapter.

2 Major Historical Traditions in the Study of Emotions

Language is the depository of past discoveries, but it is also a hypnotic, blinding the mind to its own concealed, redundant and often erroneous assumptions.

Lancelot L. Whyte

PREVIEW

Although science generally advances by small steps, there are times when exceptional individuals provide important new ways of thinking about the world. This was true, for example, of Newton and Einstein in physics, of Darwin in biology, and of Freud in psychiatry. In relation to the study of emotion, there are a few historical figures who have had a major influence on the way contemporary scientists think about emotions. These individuals are Charles Darwin, William James, Walter Cannon, and Sigmund Freud. Each of them began traditions that are still conceptually powerful today. Three of these individuals were trained as physicians, and Darwin, who was a biologist, also had some medical training.

Darwin, a British naturalist, proposed the theory of evolution in the middle of the 19th century as a way to explain the diversity of living things. He came to recognize that biological diversity was also associated with behavioral diversity, and one aspect of such diversity was the variation in the forms of emotional expression seen in all animals. Darwin came to believe that emotional expressions have an evolutionary history as well as a survival function in the life of animals. His writing on this subject led to the evolutionary tradition in the study of emotions.

James was an American psychologist writing mainly during the latter half of the 19th century. Among his many writings about both psychology and philosophy was a paper on the nature of emotions. In it James proposed a new way to consider the sequence problem, that is, the issue of how subjective feelings were temporally related to changes in autonomic physiology. His views led to a host of studies on the autonomic nervous system and how its activation influences emotional experience. These ideas led to the psychophysiological tradition.

Cannon was an American physician working during the early part of the 20th century who studied the physiological changes that occurred in animals under stress. He used his findings to challenge the hypotheses of James and then proceeded to try to identify the part of the brain that was most involved with the regulation of emotional expression. He also believed that the most important emotions were concerned with either fight or flight behavior. His work had a major influence in stimulating studies of the role of the brain in emotional experience and behavior and helped stimulate the neurological tradition.

Early in the 20th century, Freud, a Viennese psychiatrist, formulated a new way of thinking about the mind. Based on his studies of hysterical patients, and later extended to other types of patients, he concluded that a large part of mental life is unknown to the individual. Emotions, he believed, were not simple feelings, but complex inner states subject to repression, distortion, and modification for conscious or unconscious reasons. Emotions were not obvious feeling states that each of us has access to, but rather are complex events with many historical elements, whose existence and form must be inferred on the basis of limited evidence. Of great importance was his point that we need to infer emotions in ourselves just as we do with other people. These ideas led to the psychodynamic tradition.

These four traditions led to research pursued by individuals in very different academic settings. The evolutionary tradition stimulated the work, mainly with animals, of zoologists, ethologists, and sociobiologists. The psychophysiological tradition influenced the work of psychologists interested in autonomic physiology. The neurological tradition stimulated research on the brain carried out for the most part by physiological psychologists and by neurologists. The psychodynamic tradition had a major impact on 20th-century psychiatry and clinical psychologists and led to major innovations in treatment approaches.

If we assume that each tradition has something useful to contribute to our thinking about emotions, then an ideal solution to the problem of what is emotion might be a synthesis of the best ideas from each approach.

MOST PEOPLE who have written about emotions during the past century, at least until the 1960s, have considered them from one of four points of view. Each of these views was associated initially with the work of a particular individual, and each has influenced the thinking and research of scientists to the present day. This chapter examines the many ideas of these four pioneers in the study of emotion: Charles Darwin, William James, Walter Cannon, and Sigmund Freud. The following chapter deals with a more recent approach to emotions, the cognitive tradition.

CHARLES DARWIN AND THE EVOLUTIONARY TRADITION

Darwin's great work describing his theory of evolution, *On the Origin of Species,* appeared in 1859. In it he explained how different groups of animals gradually appeared on the earth in response to changing environments. The changes that took place in animals in the size and shape of organs, body parts, and lifestyles were interpreted as attempts to adapt to changes in the conditions of life. Those adaptations that were successful led to survival of the group. Inadequate adaptations left traces of groups only in fossil records.

Darwin tried to show that anatomical structures such as fins, wings, hands, and eyes represented successful adjustments of different species to different types of environments. However, Darwin recognized that the process of evolution applied not only to anatomical structures (see, e.g., Figure 2.1) but to an animal's "mind and expressive behavior" as well. He assumed that intelligence, reasoning ability, memory, and emotions had an evolutionary history and that all these activities could be identified at different phylogenetic levels. Darwin began to collect evidence for this point of view and, in 1872, his classic book *The Expression of the Emotions in Man and Animals* was published (Darwin, 1872/1965). This book has had a major influence on contemporary thinking on the subject of evolution and emotion and is the source of the evolutionary tradition (see Figure 2.2 and biographical sketch).

Darwin was not concerned with subjective feelings in lower animals: He focused his attention entirely on expressive behavior such as postures, gestures, and facial expressions. For data he relied on his own observations and on descriptions given him by zoo keepers, explorers, and missionaries concerning the behavior of animals and the expressive behaviors of individuals in nonliterate human groups. His data also included a number of

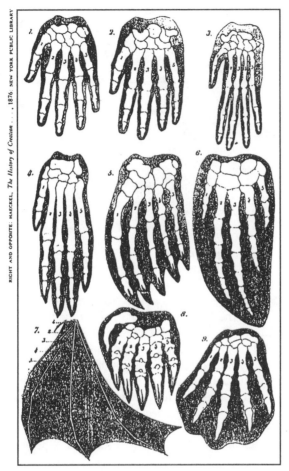

FIGURE 2.1. The feet of different animals. One of Darwin's arguments for evolution was a comparison of features that are similar in all vertebrate mammals. This figure shows the forefeet, or hands, in rows, from left to right: man, gorilla, orangutan, dog, seal, porpoise, bat, mole, and duck-billed platypus, as illustrated in an 1876 book by the German biologist Ernst Haeckel. From *Charles Darwin and the Origin of Species*, by E. Karp, 1968, p. 118. New York: American Heritage Publishing Co.

studies of facial expressions produced artificially by electrical stimulation of facial muscles in humans. In his effort to explain the various expressions observed in humans and lower animals, Darwin suggested three hypotheses or principles. The first principle of *functional value of emotions* was that some expressions or actions are of value in gratifying desires; that is, they have functional value to the individual. The second principle of *antithesis* claimed that because certain states of mind lead to certain useful actions, then opposite states of mind lead to the performance of movements of a directly opposite nature (e.g., an animal's expressions preparatory to attack are often opposite in appearance to those shown in submission). The third principle of *direct action of the nervous system* stated that strong excitation of the nervous system affects various systems of the body (e.g., sweating, trembling of the muscles, color changes in the skin, voiding of the bladder, and fainting).

FIGURE 2.2. Biographical sketch of Charles Darwin.

Charles Darwin
(1809–1882)

In his autobiography, written a few years before he died, Charles Darwin described his good qualities while at school in the following way: "I had strong and diversified tastes, much zeal for whatever interested me, and a keen pleasure in understanding any complex subject or thing" (1892/1958, p. 55). Despite these qualities, Darwin did not consider himself a particularly outstanding student. For 2 years, he studied medicine at Edinburgh, but after he decided he did not want to become a physician, his father sent him to Cambridge to become a clergyman. While at Cambridge, he studied botany and geology and developed a passion for collecting beetles. After graduation, one of his professors recommended that he join the crew of a ship called the *Beagle* as its scientific observer, because it was about to sail around the world on a scientific expedition.

Darwin considered this trip as the most important event of his life in that it sharpened his powers of observation and provided him with a tremendous range of experiences that led eventually to his theory of evolution. As a result of his voyage on the *Beagle*, Darwin developed a theory of the formation of coral reefs, wrote two books on geological topics, another on barnacles, and then his most famous work on the *Origin of Species*. This book was published in 1859, 20 years after he had first conceived of the idea of evolution.

Darwin's book *Descent of Man* was published in 1871 and represented an attempt to apply the concepts of evolution to human beings. Although an entire chapter was devoted to emotions, Darwin recognized that the subject would require a separate treatise. The following year his book *Expression of the Emotions in Man and Animals* was published. This work has been a major source of ideas and a stimulus to research for scientists in many different disciplines who are concerned with the nature of emotions.

Darwin made these contributions despite a long continued illness and a state of near-invalidism that continued for many years. In his autobiography, Darwin concluded by pointing out that whatever success he had was based on four qualities of mind: "The love of science—unbounded patience in long reflecting over any subject—industry in observing and collecting facts—and a fair share of invention as well as of common sense"(p. 58).

Darwin used his various sources of information and these principles to try to account for the particular forms taken by expressions of pain, anxiety, grief, love, hatred, anger, contempt, disgust, guilt, pride, surprise, fear, shame, shyness, and other emotions. The evidence he presented was designed to illustrate the basic continuity of emotional expressions from lower animals to humans. He suggested that the baring of the fangs of the dog or wolf is related to the sneer of the human adult. He noted that flushing of the face in anger has been reported in widely diverse human races, as well as in certain species of monkeys; defecation and urination in association with fear has been observed in rats, cats, dogs, monkeys, and humans.

Some of the flavor of Darwin's descriptions is revealed in his discussion of one of the expressive signs of fear and anger, namely, apparent enlargement of body size. He wrote,

> Hardly any expressive movement is so general as the involuntary erection of the hairs, feathers and other dermal appendages: for it is common throughout three of the great vertebrate classes. These appendages were erected under the excitement of anger or terror: more especially when these emotions are combined, or quickly succeed each other. The action serves to make the animal appear larger and more frightful to its enemies or rivals, and is generally accompanied by various voluntary movements adapted for the same purpose, and by the utterance of savage sounds. (Darwin, 1965/1872, p. 95)

To support these generalizations, Darwin cited observations made of chimps, orangutans, and gorillas in a zoo. He also pointed to the bristling of the mane in lions and the erection of hairs in hyenas, dogs, cats, horses, cattle, pigs, elk, goats, antelope, ant-eaters, rats, and bats. Figure 2.3, from Darwin's book, is a sketch of a cat terrified by a dog and shows the erected hairs of the cat's body and the apparent increase in its body size.

This kind of adaptive behavior has been observed in many different species of animal. Birds ruffle their feathers when threatened by other animals, and Darwin cited similar observations made of chickens, roosters, swans, owls, hawks, parrots, finches, warblers, and quail. Some reptiles have been observed during courtship to expand their throat pouches or frills and erect their dorsal crests. Toads, frogs, and chameleons take in air and swell up in size; and it has been reported that when a frog is seized by a snake, the swelling of the body sometimes allows escape. In humans, a somewhat parallel expansion of apparent body size occurs in anger as reflected by expansion of the chest, thrusting the head forward, standing more erect, and sometimes by erection of body hair.

On the basis of these kinds of evidence, it appears that Darwin's view of expressive behavior is a *functional* one. Emotional expressions serve some functions in the lives of animals. They act as signals and as preparations for action. They communicate information from one animal to another about what is likely to happen. Therefore, they affect the chances of survival.

An illustration of these points is found in the expressive behavior of a cat when confronted by an attacking dog. The cat opens its mouth to show its long incisors, pulls back its ears, erects the hair of its body, arches its back, and hisses. This pattern of emotional expression associated with mixed fear and anger has definite signal value to the attacker. It signals the possibility of an attack in return. It makes the cat look larger and more ferocious and decreases the chances of a direct confrontation. This, in turn, increases survival possibilities for the cat, and eventual reproduction, and anything that increases the chances of survival and reproduction tends to be maintained during the course of evolution.

FIGURE 2.3. Drawing of a cat reacting to a threatening dog. From *The Expression of the Emotions in Man and Animals*, by C. Darwin, 1965, p. 125. Chicago: University of Chicago Press. (Original work published 1872)

Darwin considered another important problem in his book, namely, the question of the innateness of emotional expressions. He believed that many, but not all, emotional expressions are unlearned. He used four kinds of evidence for his conclusions about the innate basis of emotional expressions: (a) Some emotional expressions appear in similar form in many lower animals; (b) some emotional expressions appear in very young children in the same form as in adults, before much opportunity for learning has occurred; (c) some emotional expressions are shown in identical ways by those born blind and those who have normal sight; and (4) some emotional expressions appear in similar forms in widely distinct races and groups of humans.

However, despite his strong belief in the unlearned nature of many emotional expressions, Darwin clearly understood that some expressions are simply gestures that have been learned like the words of a language. This would be true, for example, of joining the hands in reverent prayer, kissing as a mark of affection, or nodding the head as a sign of acceptance. He also pointed out that even though many expressions are unlearned, once they have occurred, they may be voluntarily and consciously used as a means of communication. They also may be voluntarily inhibited except under the most extreme conditions.

What are some implications of Darwin's views? One is simply the idea that behavior patterns are just as reliable characters of species as are the forms of bones, teeth, or any other bodily structures. A second implication is that the near universality of certain emotional expressions confirms to a certain extent the conclusion that man is derived from earlier animal form and supports the belief in the unity of the different races. A third implication is that the study of emotion was expanded from the study of subjective feelings to the study of behavior within a biological, evolutionary context. It became scientifically legitimate to ask the question: In what way does a particular behavior or behavior pattern function in aiding survival? Finally, and of equal importance, Darwin suggested a series of hypotheses and theoretical issues that have guided research in animal behavior to the present time. The modern work of Nobel prize winners Nico Tinbergen and Konrad Lorenz is based directly on Darwin's theory.

WILLIAM JAMES AND THE PSYCHOPHYSIOLOGICAL TRADITION

Twelve years after Darwin had published his book on emotions, American psychologist–philosopher James (1884) published an article in which he presented a new way of looking at emotion, and at the same time founded a second major tradition in the psychology of emotions (see Figure 2.4 and biographical sketch). In his article and in an expanded chapter in his book published in 1890, William James pointed out that the commonsense way to think about the sequence of events when an emotion occurs is that the *perception* of a situation gives rise to a feeling of emotion, which is then followed by various bodily *changes* (e.g., increased heart rate and muscle tension). His theory was that this sequence is incorrect. Instead he proposed that bodily changes directly follow the perception of an event and that the feeling of these bodily changes is the emotion. James (1890) illustrated this idea by saying: "Common sense says we lose our fortune, are sorry and weep:...My hypothesis...is that we feel sorry because we cry, angry because we strike, afraid because we tremble" (p. 1066).

James then proceeded to justify his theory and answer possible criticisms. But first, he began with a qualification. His theory was to apply only to what he called the "coarser emotions" such as grief, fear, rage, and love and not to the "subtler" emotions, which he described as moral, intellectual, and aesthetic feelings (James, 1890).

The first argument in support of his theory is that it is impossible to imagine feeling an emotion if we do not at the same time experience our bodily changes. Emotion disconnected from all bodily feeling is not conceivable, he believed. He then stated that his theory would be challenged if a person could be found who experienced no inner sensations but who otherwise could function normally. James then described one such case, a shoemaker's apprentice who was 15 and who had no bodily sensations, with the exception of one eye and one ear, who had shown shame, grief, surprise, fear, and anger according to a physician who attended him. Despite this apparent contradiction to his theory, James dismissed the case as not studied thoroughly enough.

FIGURE 2.4. Biographical sketch of William James.

William James
(1842–1910)

As a young man, William James wanted to become a painter but eventually decided that he did not have sufficient talent. He entered Harvard University and began training as a physician, but in the middle of his education he left Harvard and went to Germany to study. While there, he became physically ill as well as emotionally depressed, and at one time considered suicide.

After returning to the United States, James completed his medical education but never practiced medicine. He began his career by teaching anatomy and physiology at Harvard. Later he identified himself with psychology and wrote the highly influential textbook *Principles of Psychology* in 1890. In it he presented his views on all aspects of psychology and elaborated on his theory of emotion. He considered emotions to be a kind of *native* or *instinctive* reaction that could be modified by training and habit.

James became increasingly interested in philosophical issues and began to teach philosophy at Harvard. In the last dozen years of his life, he published a number of books dealing with philosophy: *The Will to Believe* (1897), *The Varieties of Religious Experience* (1902), and *Pragmatism* (1907), among others.

Although James's philosophy of pragmatism was often interpreted as emphasizing the practical aspects of life, William James, the man, had a great respect for imagination and its role in human life. Throughout his life, William James had a strong belief in individuality and in the doctrine of live and let live.

Another type of evidence relevant to his theory is found in cases of objectless emotions; that is, when people report feeling anxious, angry, or melancholy without knowing why, James's interpretation of such events is that such people are unusually sensitive to their own bodily changes and that the emotion felt is simply the feeling of their bodily states. He failed to discuss the question of how such bodily states arise in the first place or why they vary in an individual. In a footnote, James did mention that the opposite may occur; that is, a person may report strong emotional feelings and not show any obvious bodily changes. This may happen in dreaming, for example. He provided no explanation of this possibility.

Another possible criticism of his theory is that actors often simulate an emotion without feeling it. James's reply is simply that the visceral and organic parts of an emotion are not present even when the facial expressions or gestures are.

Two basic questions are raised by James's theory. The first concerns the nature of the bodily changes, inner and outer, which are associated with emotions. The second concerns the functional value of the various expressions of emotion. In his brief discussion of these issues, James described Darwin's views approvingly but also added that the functional significance of many bodily changes in emotion such as dryness of the mouth, diarrhea, and nausea are simply not known.

Unfortunately, James never examined other basic questions implied by his theory; for example, how does a perception produce a bodily change in the first place? To follow this line of reasoning further, one may ask: Of all the kinds of perceptions that are possible, why do some lead to emotions and not others?

Given these unanswered questions and conceptual ambiguities, it is reasonable to ask why James's theory has persisted and influenced both writers of textbooks and researchers. (Parenthetically, it should be added that a few years after James proposed his viewpoint about emotion, a Danish physiologist named Carl Lange independently suggested a similar idea; the conceptualization has since become known as the James–Lange theory.)

James was a major figure in 19th-century American psychology. He was educated as a physician, taught in the philosophy department at Harvard, and was a prolific writer of influential books on psychology. Whatever he wrote was taken seriously, and other psychologists almost immediately became concerned with either proving or disproving his ideas.

The James–Lange theory is hardly what we would call a theory today. It was concerned primarily with a kind of chicken-and-egg question: Which came first, the subjective feeling of an emotion or the bodily changes that are associated with it? Its importance obviously did not lie in the narrowness of the issue it posed but rather in emphasizing what was, in fact, a commonsense idea. It reiterated the notion that an emotion is a feeling state, subjective and personal. This was an idea that most psychologists were willing to accept.

The second reason for the importance of his ideas is that they gave a large impetus to investigators to begin examining autonomic changes in relation to emotion. Gradually, a substantial literature developed in these areas, one which is increasingly active and important to this day. It includes studies of autonomic physiology, lie detectors, and physiological measures of arousal. Because James and many who have followed him (e.g., Cacioppo et al., 2000) have been concerned with the relations between introspective states and physiological changes, this approach may be described as the psychophysiological tradition.

WALTER B. CANNON AND THE NEUROLOGICAL TRADITION

A few years after James died, Walter B. Cannon, another Harvard professor working in the Physiology Department of the medical school, began to publish a series of studies concerned with testing and modifying the James–Lange theory (see Figure 2.5 and biographical sketch). These studies led Cannon to reject the basic elements of this theory and to propose an alternative one. In his book *Bodily Changes in Pain, Hunger, Fear and Rage,* first

FIGURE 2.5. Biographical sketch of Walter B. Cannon.

Walter B. Cannon
(1871–1945)

Walter Cannon was raised in a small town in Wisconsin. At the age of 14, he left high school because of a lack of interest in his studies. After working for 2 years in a railroad office, he returned to school, graduated with honors, and won a scholarship to Harvard. Cannon completed both his undergraduate and medical degrees at Harvard and was immediately offered an instructorship in physiology at the medical school, where he remained as a teacher and researcher until he retired in 1942.

Cannon was among the first to use the newly discovered X-rays for research on digestion, but because of a lack of awareness of the dangers of radiation, he received severe burns and eventually developed the radiation-related disease from which he died. By 1911 he began to study endocrine secretions in relation to the autonomic nervous system and was impressed by evidence that emotional states could influence bodily processes. He wrote many papers on this topic, and a general summary of his conclusions appeared in 1929 in his book *Bodily Changes in Pain, Hunger, Fear and Rage*. In this book he presented evidence that he believed refuted William James's theory of emotion. He also included evidence for his own theory that attempted to relate emotional states to brain structures.

In 1932, Cannon's book *The Wisdom of the Body* was published. He pointed out that the stability of the organism is of prime importance for survival and that the many internal and external adjustments and adaptations that organisms make are the basis for stability. He concluded that social institutions are basically in the service of maintaining biological integrity.

published in 1915 and revised in 1929, he presented evidence that raised serious questions about the James–Lange theory. The evidence consisted of five major points.

First, Cannon pointed out that British physiologist Charles Sherrington had cut the spinal cord and vagus nerves of dogs so that no sensory impulse could reach the brain of the animal from the heart, lungs, stomach, bowels, spleen, liver, and other abdominal organs. In addition, Cannon and his associates had removed the entire sympathetic divisions of the autonomic nervous system in several cats so that all vascular reactions controlled by the vasomotor center were abolished: Secretion from the adrenal medulla could no longer be evoked, the action of the stomach and intestines could not be inhibited, the hairs could not be erected, and the liver could not be called upon to liberate sugar into the blood stream (Cannon, 1929). Under these conditions, both Sherrington and Cannon found that their experimental animals showed typical emotional reactions of anger, fear, and pleasure to handling and exposure to other animals. The lack of feedback of visceral changes apparently had no effect on emotional expression, as the James–Lange theory would have predicted.

Cannon's second criticism was based on the fact that stressful stimuli of any type tend to produce similar physiological reactions. For example, fear, rage, fever, exposure to cold, and asphyxia all tend to produce an increase in heart rate, blood sugar, adrenalin excretion, pupil size, and erection of body hair and a decrease in size of arterioles, activity of digestive glands, and amount of gastrointestinal peristalsis. These visceral responses seem to be too uniform to provide a basis for distinguishing between strong emotions, or between emotions and other nonemotional stresses.

Cannon's third criticism simply pointed out that the viscera are relatively insensitive structures and may be cut, torn, crushed, or burned in operations on unanesthetized humans without producing discomfort. In addition, people are normally unaware of the contractions and relaxations of the stomach, intestines, diaphragm, spleen, or liver. Therefore, it appears unlikely that such visceral events could contribute to an individual's recognition of his or her own emotional states.

The fourth criticism that Cannon offered concerns the slow reaction time of visceral organs to stimulation. A number of investigators had reported that the speed of reaction of smooth muscle and glands was anywhere from one quarter of a second to several minutes. Other studies have apparently shown that emotional reactions to pictures, or odors, typically occur within three quarters of a second. It therefore seemed unlikely that visceral events could provide information to the brain quickly enough to help an individual decide what emotional state he or she was experiencing.

Finally, Cannon pointed out that attempts to artificially induce visceral changes typical of strong emotions did not produce emotional feelings. For example, injections of adrenalin into normal or abnormal people produced such extensive bodily changes as palpitations, tightness in the chest and throat, trembling, chills, dryness of the mouth, and feelings of weakness, yet did not induce feelings of fear or any other emotion. These people were therefore able to report their bodily changes without interpreting them as indicating an emotional experience. On the basis of all this evidence, Cannon concluded that visceral feedback is faint and at best plays a minor role in the feelings of emotion.

If Cannon had simply presented these cogent criticisms of the James–Large theory, it would have been a useful contribution. He did much more, however. Cannon went on to present an alternative theory of what bodily changes were related to emotion and also provided an alternative interpretation of the role of visceral changes. Let us consider these ideas.

Surgeons have long known that patients sometimes show strong emotional reactions—sobbing, laughter, or aggression—while under early stages of ether anesthesia. A similar phenomenon is sometimes seen by dentists when their patients are given nitrous oxide (or "laughing gas"). These observations suggest that the temporary abolition of cortical control "releases" those lower brain centers that presumably determine emotional reactions. Similarly, in certain types of hemiplegia (i.e., paralysis of half the body), a patient may be unable to move his or her face on the paralyzed side. However, if the patient hears a joke or learns of the death of a family member, the very muscles that could not be voluntarily controlled may suddenly act to give the face the normal expression of pleasure or sadness. Patients with total facial paralysis have likewise reported their ability to experience emotional feelings, despite the lack of feedback from facial muscles.

Cannon and his associates carried out a series of experiments with cats in which different parts of the brain were removed. They found that the cortex could be removed without affecting the animals' capacity to show emotional behavior. However, when the cerebral hemispheres were removed leaving the other brain structures intact, an interesting effect was observed.

> As soon as recovery from anesthesia was complete a remarkable group of activities appeared, such as are usually seen in an infuriated animal—a sort of sham rage. These quasi-emotional phenomena included lashing of the tail, arching of the trunk, thrusting and jerking of the restrained limbs, display of the claws and clawing motions, snarling and attempts to bite. These were all actions due to skeletal muscles. Besides these, and more typical and permanent, were effects on the viscera, produced by impulses discharged over the sympathetic nerve fibers. They included erection of the tail hairs, sweating of the toe pads, dilation of the pupil, micturition, a high blood pressure, a very rapid heartbeat, an abundant outpouring of adrenalin, and an increase of blood sugar up to five times the normal concentration. This play of a "pseudoaffective" state or sham rage might continue for two or three hours. (Cannon, 1929, p. 246)

Further studies showed that the neural structure associated with the display of rage is located in a part of the brain called the *optic thalamus,* which was later called the *hypothalamus.* In his words, "the peculiar quality of the emotion is added to simple sensation when the thalamic processes are roused" (Cannon, 1929, p. 369). Instead of assuming that there is a linear sequence of events relating perception to feeling as proposed by James, Cannon proposed that the thalamic discharge simultaneously produces both an emotional experience and a series of bodily changes. This hypothesis is sometimes called the Cannon–Bard theory because of the empirical studies of Bard dealing with these issues. Diagrammatically, the two views might be shown schematically as in Figure 2.6, where they are contrasted with the commonsense one.

Several points are worth noting about the diagrams. First, all views include the idea that a perception is necessary to start an emotional process. Second, none of the theories make any attempt to explain how a perception can directly produce an emotional feeling, a motor reaction, or hypothalamic arousal. Third, all of the theories are concerned fundamentally with conscious, reportable, subjective emotional experience. Even when the subjects of experiments are cats and dogs, the assumption is that their emotional behavior directly reflects emotional feelings. Cannon, for example, never seemed to question this relationship. However, whereas James found the sources of emotional feelings in the viscera, Cannon found them in the thalamus. Both men accepted at face value the subjective reports of patients or subjects as valid expressions of emotional feelings.

Cannon had extensive biological training and was well acquainted with the work of Darwin. He was accustomed to asking functional questions about biological events. He therefore asked the question, What is the function of the extensive internal changes that occur during emotional excitement?

Cannon answered this question by concluding that visceral changes did not tell us anything about emotions; rather, they were homeostatic adjustments that helped the body prepare for action. When events occur that create emergencies, if the individual is to survive, he or she must take action. The most appropriate action in most cases is to run away (flight) or to stay and attack (fight). The feelings of fear and anger simply accompany these organic preparations for action.

Some writers have called this conception an emergency theory of emotion. However, it is important to emphasize that this theory represents a view of emotions that is

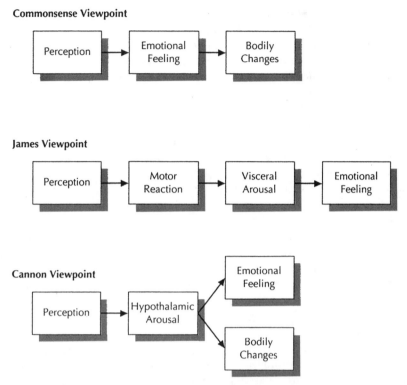

FIGURE 2.6. The sequence problem. Three different ways to think about the problem of what sequence of events occurs in connection with the appearance of an emotion.

logically independent of the thalamic theory. In other words, regardless of the neural structures that may be involved in emotional expression or feeling, the function of emotion may be to handle emergencies connected with problems of survival. A very large number of researchers are currently concerned with studies of brain functions and emotions.

SIGMUND FREUD AND THE PSYCHODYNAMIC TRADITION

In 1895, Freud and his colleague Breuer published a book, *Studies on Hysteria,* that described the development of his new theory of the origin of this illness. At the same time, he laid the foundation for a theory of emotion.

Patients who had hysteria would show puzzling symptoms, related either to sensory losses or to motor paralysis. A patient might suddenly report that a leg or an arm was paralyzed, or that he or she had lost all sensation in a hand. Quite often, the initial appearance of the symptoms was associated with some traumatic event such as an accident, a death in the family, or a war experience. In World War I, many of the soldiers who were diagnosed as having "shell shock" were actually suffering with hysterical symptoms. Some of these patients apparently became blind or deaf, and yet there was no evidence that they were malingering or that they had an actual nerve disease. The terms mentioned above are no longer used but the concept of posttraumatic stress disorder, currently in vogue, describes a related but not identical syndrome.

Of great interest was the fact that the use of hypnotic suggestion could temporarily create or eliminate every one of the symptoms of hysteria in normal people. A number of physicians had already demonstrated this phenomenon. Sometimes they were able to use hypnosis to eliminate the symptoms in patients with hysteria.

Freud's book, *Studies on Hysteria,* which he wrote with another physician, Josef Breuer, is a description of several patients with hysteria who had been treated by use of hypnosis (Freud & Breuer, 1895/1936). One chapter described the now famous case of a young female patient named "Anna," who developed a number of hysterical symptoms during a period when she was helping to care for her dying father. These symptoms included paralysis of one arm, partial paralysis of neck muscles influencing the swallowing reflex, and occasional periods of "absences" or "fits."

Dr. Breuer treated Anna successfully during a 2-year period. Through the use of hypnosis, all of the symptoms were gradually eliminated. Freud and Breuer came to the conclusion that their patients were experiencing memories that had been actively forgotten or repressed. The kinds of memories affected were those that had a strong emotion attached to them, even though the patient might not be aware of the emotion. The hysterical symptom, Freud suggested, acts as a kind of disguised representation of the repressed emotion. At first, Freud believed that the patient could eliminate the symptoms only by an intense expression of the repressed emotion, a process he called *abreaction,* or *catharsis.* The need for such catharses was often suggested to the patient during hypnosis (see Figure 2.7 and biographical sketch).

However, Freud finally changed his mind about the need for catharsis as well as the need for hypnosis after he found that there were some patients he could not hypnotize. He began to think that his "cures" based on hypnosis were unreliable, but he continued to believe in his theory of the origin of the symptoms. In fact, as his experience with patients increased, he came to the conclusion that repression of emotionally charged memories was the basis for all neurotic symptoms and not only those associated with hysteria.

When Freud gave up hypnosis as a technique of therapy, he substituted free association of ideas as the method for patients to use to help identify their repressed memories and emotions. The aim of therapy was no longer to "abreact" an emotion that had been repressed but to uncover repressions and replace them by acts of judgment, which might result either in the acceptance or in the rejection of what had formerly been repudiated. Freud then stopped calling his method of investigation and treatment *catharsis* and substituted the term *psychoanalysis.* Gradually over a period of many years, Freud and his associates built up an elaborate and complex theory of the origin and development of neuroses and aberrant mental states. Explicit or implicit in psychoanalytic writing is a theory of "instincts" or drives, affects, stages of emotional development, fixations, or aberrations of development, conflict, mind, and personality. The details are extensive and beyond the scope of this brief introduction. However, we can consider in somewhat more detail some of Freud's ideas on emotions, or, as psychoanalysts prefer to call them, *affects.* Freud's ideas about affects are based on his theory of drives.

Fairly early in the development of his thinking, Freud assumed that there were two classes of instincts: sexual instincts and ego instincts. (Although most translations of Freud's writings use the word *instinct,* the German term Freud used could just as well have been translated by the more acceptable current term *drive.* In all further discussion, the word *drive* is therefore used instead of the word *instinct.*) These drives were to be thought of as internal stimuli that affected the behavior of each individual by regulating direction and type of action. Each drive was assumed to have a source, an aim, and an object. The source of each drive was to be found in some biological or biochemical internal process;

FIGURE 2.7. Biographical sketch of Sigmund Freud.

**Sigmund Freud
(1856–1939)**

Sigmund Freud lived most of his life in Vienna, Austria. While he was in medical school at the University of Vienna, his special interests were physiology and comparative anatomy. Upon graduation in 1881, he hoped to devote his life to research in neurology, but lack of financial means led him into clinical practice. He studied hypnosis with Jean Martin Charcot, an eminent French neurologist, and then returned to Vienna to enter a medical collaboration with Joseph Breuer.

Together, Breuer and Freud evolved a method for treating hysterical patients based on the use of hypnosis. They called their method *catharsis*, and it required the patient to strongly express emotions connected with traumatic experiences that had apparently been forgotten. Their book *Studies on Hysteria* describing their theories was published in 1895.

At about this time, Breuer withdrew from the collaboration, and Freud went on to develop a complex theory about the mind, about child development, and about psychological treatment, which he called *psychoanalysis*. Key elements of this theory included the concepts of repression and resistance, infantile sexuality, stages of development, and dream interpretations for the understanding of the unconscious.

Among Freud's earlier works are *The Interpretation of Dreams* (1900), *The Psychopathology of Everyday Life* (1904), *Three Contributions to the Theory of Sex* (1905), *A General Introduction to Psychoanalysis* (1910), and *The Ego and the Id* (1923). Gradually, Freud became increasingly interested in broad social or cultural implications of his theories, and he wrote such works as *Totem and Taboo* (1913), *The Future of An Illusion* (1928), *Civilization and Its Discontents* (1930), and *Moses and Monotheism* (1939). Freud developed cancer of the mouth in 1924, but despite much pain and repeated operations, he continued to write until he died.

Freud's ideas were often bitterly attacked, but in spite of the opposition, they gradually became widely known. In addition to becoming an accepted part of psychology and psychiatry, his ideas have influenced anthropology, education, art, and literature.

the aim was discharge and pleasure; and the object of each drive could vary greatly and was dependent on experience and learning. An important characteristic of drives was their variability; they could be displaced, localized, or transformed.

Freud's concept of drives was not a theory of emotion, but it did provide psychoanalytic interpretations of two major affects: anxiety and depression. Let us consider Freud's views of anxiety as an example of his thinking about affects.

The concept of anxiety took a number of different forms in Freud's writings, and they were not all consistent. One view of anxiety that Freud proposed was that it represented a reaction due to an inability to cope with an overwhelming stress. Such a condition first occurs in every individual's life at the time of birth when the sudden massive stimulation of the environment creates a "birth trauma." This trauma produced an *archaic discharge syndrome*, which Freud referred to as primary object anxiety, and which became the prototype for the occurrence of secondary anxiety reactions later in a person's life.

A second hypothesis about anxiety was presented by Freud in 1915. He proposed that affects were primarily a form of energy that required some kind of direct or indirect expression. If repression or inhibition of affect existed, then the energy of the emotion had to be expressed in the form of neurotic overflow mechanisms such as phobias, obsessions, or compulsive rituals. From this point of view, anxiety was seen as the consequence of repression of emotion. Freud also assumed that the emotions involved were always related to conflicts over the sexual drive.

However, in 1926, in his book *Inhibitions, Symptoms and Anxiety*, Freud (1926/1959) formulated a new conception of the nature of anxiety. Instead of anxiety being the result of a conversion of the energy of the affect, it was now interpreted to be the result of an evaluation by the ego (the conscious part of the mind) of dangerous aspects of the external or internal environment. Examples of dangerous types of events that psychoanalysis has been primarily concerned with include birth, hunger, absence of mother, loss of love, castration, conscience, and death. In terms of Freud's later formulation, anxiety was not the result of repression but the reason for repression. Evaluations by the ego determine whether internal impulses or external events are to be considered dangerous. This decision, in turn, determines the subsequent emotional response. This implies that affects include both a cognitive process and a response to this process.

This psychodynamic interpretation of emotion, as exemplified by anxiety, had several implications. It raised the question of whether an emotion could be unconscious, that is, whether an individual could have an emotion and not be aware of it. Although Freud wrote about unconscious guilt and unconscious anxiety, he was dissatisfied with this idea, because he considered an emotion to be a response process. He concluded that the *evaluation* of an event can be unconscious even though the *response* process is not. For example, a free-floating anxiety is evident, but the source of it (the evaluation) is not recognized.

A second implication concerns the question of how to recognize emotion in others. If it is true that emotions may be repressed, how can the analyst identify something that even the patient cannot identify?

Freud made the assumption that various displacements and transformations may occur in the expression of an emotion, but indirect signs of its presence are always noticeable. For example, if someone continually frowns, grinds his teeth, and has dreams in which people are being murdered, we might conclude that this person was angry even if he said he was not. Freud relied heavily on dreams, free associations, slips of the tongue, postures, facial expressions, and voice quality to arrive at judgments about a person's repressed emotions. In other words, in the Freudian psychodynamic tradition, an emotion is a complex state of the individual that is inferred on the basis of various classes of behavior.

Although subjective feelings may provide a clue to a person's emotions, they are only one type of evidence among many others. An emotion is not synonymous with a verbal report of an introspective state.

A third implication of the psychodynamic tradition is that emotions are seldom if ever found in a "pure" state. Any emotion has a complex history that almost invariably produces conflicts, for example, between love and hate, or between envy and awe. The very idea of *psychoanalysis* implies an attempt to determine what the elements of the complex states are.

The psychoanalytic theory of emotion, as represented by these views, contains some interesting ideas. It eliminates the sequence problem (i.e., which came first, the feeling or the bodily change?) by claiming that they both result from an unconscious evaluation. It emphasizes the idea that some aspects of an emotion are unconscious and, therefore, cannot be examined by introspection alone. These emotional processes must be inferred in humans, just as we infer emotions in lower animals. Finally, it suggests that conflicts are involved in all emotions.

Despite these views, Freud never developed a general theory of emotion. Most of his attention was directed toward anxiety, aggression, and depression and their various mixtures. The theory tends to be vague in spots and not entirely consistent, and it relies heavily on metaphorical thinking. Despite these limitations, psychoanalytic theory has stimulated research and has been a major theoretical source in the development of the field of psychosomatic medicine.

ATTEMPTS AT INTEGRATION OF THEORIES

Although the four historical traditions that have been described in this chapter developed along somewhat independent paths, this does not mean that the key figures associated with them were not influenced by each other's ideas. Darwin's writings were well known to William James, and they led James to write about the functions of various psychological states or mechanisms such as learning and memory. His writing in turn stimulated the founding of a *functional school* around the turn of the century.

Cannon was also quite well acquainted with Darwin's writings, and Darwin is cited several times in Cannon's book. He approvingly noted Darwin's view that emotions have developed in the struggle for existence and that the physiological changes that occur during emotions have utility in promoting survival in the face of emergencies.

Freud too was well acquainted with Darwin's writings and referred to him more than 20 times in his writing. He was even said to consider the study of evolution to be essential for the training of psychoanalysts. So important was Darwin's influence on Freud that a book has traced the details (Ritvo, 1990).

Freud's concern with the meaning of symptoms was related to Darwin's idea that all forms of emotional expression had *adaptive* significance in the struggle for survival. Many ideas of Darwin related to the search for historical roots of current behavior. Freud used a similar idea when he suggested a relationship of infant experiences to later adult behavior. Darwin saw evolution as a *gradual* process with no discontinuities, and Freud accepted the same idea in the development of the mind. (The concept of psychosexual stages were only convenient divisions of a continuum.)

Darwin's idea of natural selection seems to imply a continual battle between individuals and species in the struggle to stay alive and to propagate. Freud adapted this concept in terms of the idea of mental as well as interpersonal *conflict*. Freud accepted

FIGURE 2.8. The only visit of Sigmund Freud to the United States, which took place in 1909, was the occasion of a celebrated gathering of psychologists at Clark University. In the front row are E. B. Titchner (second from left); William James (third); G. Stanley Hall (sixth), Freud (seventh), and Carl Jung (eight). Copyright Clark University Archives. Reprinted with permission.

the idea that certain complexes such as the conflict between father and son were innate. Finally, just as Darwin saw the expression of aggression as being in the service of sexual propagation, Freud also considered that sex and aggression were the *basic drives* that motivated humans in their journey through life. Thus, it appears that Freud was influenced by Darwin in some of his ideas about the role of adaptive behavior, about the historical sources of adult behavior, about the gradual process of unfolding development, about the role of conflict, about the role of innate processes in influencing interpersonal behavior, and in the idea of basic emotions.

The various observations that have been made about mutual influences of these four historic figures suggest the possibility that the differences between the modern proponents of their ideas can, in time, be reconciled. It is worth noting that during Freud's only visit to the United States in 1909 when he lectured at Clark University, he met William James, E. B. Titchener, G. Stanley Hall, and other psychologists. An archival photograph (see Figure 2.8) shows the group at Clark.

A RECENT DEVELOPMENT

The fact that these four historical figures have had a major impact on contemporary thinking about emotions does not mean that many other people have not contributed important ideas. For example, another tradition that has gradually developed during the past 30 years or so has stemmed from the work of social psychologists, sociologists, and linguistics and computer experts who have been concerned about the cognitive aspects of emotions. This has become such an important area of research and theory that the next chapter is devoted to it.

SUMMARY

This chapter has described four historical traditions that have influenced the thinking of most contemporary psychologists concerned with the study of emotion. Table 2.1 summarizes the basic ideas within each tradition.

The evolutionary tradition has emphasized the adaptive significance of emotional expressions as signals that tend to increase the chances of individual survival but has had little to say about subjective feelings. The psychophysiological tradition has stimulated the extensive contemporary research and thinking on the relations among autonomic changes, facial expressions, and subjective feelings. The question posed in current terms is this: Are our feelings a "readout" of autonomic changes or changes in facial expressions, or are our feelings independent of such changes? This issue is considered more extensively in the chapter on facial expressions.

The neurological tradition has stimulated the search for the brain structures and systems that organize all the information we use in feeling or expressing our emotions. Numerous researches in recent years have revealed the complex and subtle interactions of information flow from critical sensory receiving areas to hypothalamic and other structures. Many of these developments are described in the chapter on brain mechanisms and emotions.

The psychodynamic tradition has influenced many clinicians to recognize the complexity of emotional states and the ubiquitous presence of mixed states of emotions or blends. They have become aware of the difficulty of relying on only one source of information about emotions, that is, introspective reports of feelings, and have emphasized

TABLE 2.1. Four Historical Traditions related to Emotions

Tradition	Person	Publication	Ideas
Evolutionary	Charles Darwin (1809–1882)	*The Expression of the Emotions in Man and Animals* (1872/1965)	Emotional expressions are communications of intentions in emergency situations and tend to increase the chances of survival.
Psychophysiological	William James (1842–1910)	*What is an Emotion* (1884)	Emotions are subjective feelings based on the awareness of internal autonomic changes associated with actions.
Neurological	Walter B. Cannon (1871–1945)	*Bodily Changes in Pain, Hunger, Fear, and Rage* (1929)	Emotions are subjective feelings resulting from hypothalamic arousal and are usually associated with acts of fight or flight.
Psychoanalytic	Sigmund Freud (1856–1939)	*Studies on Hysteria* (1895/1936)	Emotions are complex states involving conflicts, early experiences, personality traits, and defenses. They can only be inferred on the basis of various kinds of indirect evidence.

the need to integrate multiple sources of information to make meaningful inferences about the presence of emotions. Psychoanalysts have also emphasized the connection between memory and emotions, a subject of increasing interest to contemporary psychologists. They have also recognized the many ways that emotions in humans can be hidden, disguised, manipulated, and distorted.

As time goes on, increasing degrees of overlap occur in the thinking of proponents of these different disciplines about the subject of emotions, and ideas are freely borrowed from one another. Despite the different concerns and emphases that characterize these various approaches, it is reasonable to assume that each theory contains some truth. Any adequate integration of emotion theories should have something to say about the adaptive implications of emotions, about autonomic and brain mechanisms in relation to feeling states, about dynamic sources and complexities of emotional states, and about the role of cognitions.

3 Emotions and Cognitions

Thought is deeper than all speech; feeling deeper than all thought.

Christopher Cranch

PREVIEW

With the advent of the "cognitive revolution" in the 1960s, psychologists became increasingly interested in studying the mind as well as behavior and to make inferences about how the mind works. Extensive research continues on attention, perception, knowledge acquisition, memory, categorizations, and problem solving using concepts borrowed from computer science, linguistics, neuropsychology, and evolutionary psychology.

Conscious thought and reason, often referred to as cognitions, are generally believed to be part of the process of adapting to the environment and have an evolutionarily based structure. Cognitions are also believed to precede emotions and, in fact, determine which emotions follow. This is possible even though many cognitions are inaccessible to the individual; some emotional reactions are very rapid and are based on minimal information.

From an evolutionary point of view, cognitive functions developed with the expansion of the sensory systems and the brain. Several hypotheses are presented to try to account for the rapid development of the brain in humans and for the development of language. It is likely that the main function of a large brain and a highly developed cognitive system is to ensure survival by increasing the ability of individuals to predict the future. In turn, prediction is in the service of emotions and biological needs.

HISTORICAL BEGINNINGS

Behaviorism ✳

The advent of the school of psychology called *behaviorism* is usually dated from the early part of the 20th century, beginning with the research and writings of the psychologist John B. Watson. Like other movements, it began as a protest against an already existing school of thought, introspectionism, and was an attempt to become more "scientific" and reliable.

Watson was interested in explaining Freudian ideas in terms of the concepts of habit and classical conditioning. One of the results of this interest is the frequently cited study of little Albert, a 9-month-old child, who was conditioned to show fear reactions (e.g., crying, startle, trembling) to a rat, a rabbit, a dog, and a fur coat through use of a loud sound as an unconditioned stimulus (J. B. Watson & Rayner, 1920/2000). The history of the ambivalent relations between Watson and psychoanalysis is detailed by Rilling (2000).

In the 1930s B. F. Skinner provided behaviorism with a more consistent philosophical basis. Behaviorism was to be thought of as a guarantee against metaphysical and "mentalistic" explanations of human behavior. Reinforcements were considered to be the controllers of actions, and the environment was to play a major, almost exclusive, role in starting activities; there was to be no inner person or inner mind. The causes of behavior are in the environment. Feelings were not to be considered as causes of behavior; they are simply responses to various states of the body (Skinner, 1985, 1989). There was also little or no place for emotions in behavioristic thinking.

This philosophy dominated the teaching and the research practices of American psychologists from the 1930s until the 1960s, at which time a *cognitive revolution* occurred. This change in thinking was not the result of the contributions of any one person but reflects the interaction of scientists from a number of different disciplines, which included psychology, computer science, philosophy, linguistics, and communication engineering.

One of the key ideas of the cognitive revolution was the concept of feedback as conceptualized by *cybernetics*, the science of control and communication in animals and in machines. The early contributors to cognitive psychology were such individuals as Norbert Weiner, a mathematician; Herbert Simon, an economist and computer scientist; Noam Chomsky, a linguist; and George Miller, a psychologist. (See Plotkin, 1998, for a detailed discussion of this period.) By 1967 the first textbook on cognitive psychology was published by Ulric Neisser. The approach, sometimes referred to as *cognitivism,* became concerned with research and theory related to attention, perception, memory, computer simulation, the nature of language, and brain function (Posner & Di Girolamo, 2000). Cognitive scientists brought mind back into psychology and made it respectable to define *psychology* as the study of the mind rather than the study of behavior.

Gradually, the study of emotions was added to the concerns of cognitive scientists. A particular interest was how cognitions are related to emotions. Here, too, a number of different theorists contributed ideas on this issue.

The Cognitive Tradition

One of the important contributors to the cognitive tradition was a psychologist named Fritz Heider, who wrote an influential book on the *Psychology of Interpersonal Relations* in 1958 (see Figure 3.1 and biographical sketch). Although Heider did not try to present a general theory of emotions, he emphasized the relation between emotions and cognitions. He pointed out that if you can influence someone's beliefs, you can thereby influence his or her emotions. He wrote descriptions of the beliefs that people have that influence such emotions as pity, vengeance, gratitude, envy, and jealousy. He pointed out that different cognitive processes, such as our causal attributions, our sense of what "ought" to be, and our aspirations and goals, all influence our emotions. For example, he said that the violation of our ideas about what ought to be tends to lead to feelings of anger. Your gratitude is aroused if someone intentionally tries to benefit you out of benevolent motives. Envy involves a social comparison between what you have and what someone has who is a member of your own group.

Through such analyses, and many anecdotes drawn from the "naive psychology" of everyday life, Heider tried to relate everyday situations and beliefs to emotional feelings and to show connections between cognitive states and emotions. However, he also

FIGURE 3.1. Biographical sketch of Fritz Heider.

Fritz Heider
(1896–1988)

Fritz Heider was born and educated in Austria. For many years, he considered writing and painting as possible careers, but finally, at the age of 30, he decided to become a psychologist. Some time after World War I, he immigrated to the United States and began teaching at Smith College in Massachusetts. There he spent a number of years of discouragement and frustration because his daily responsibilities prevented the long periods of uninterrupted thought he felt were needed to do his theoretical analyses.

Feeling hemmed in, he began to experience attacks of anxiety. In his attempts to cope with his emotions, he tried to analyze the sources of his feelings of unhappiness and anger. Gradually, he found that he could control his feelings by means of his thoughts. He also came to the belief that the study of commonsense psychology has two values for understanding interpersonal relations. First, commonsense psychology guides our behavior toward other people. We use it to interpret their actions and to predict what they will do under various circumstances. Second, commonsense psychology may contain truths that need to be discovered. For example, the way people think about such concepts as *cause, expect, belong,* and *ought* influences how they deal with one another. Although Heider believed that such cognitions have a major effect on our emotions, he also recognized that emotions may influence cognitions.

In 1958, at age 62, Heider published his book *The Psychology of Interpersonal Relations*. In it, he attempted to analyze the conventional language people use to describe their motivations, their beliefs, and their feelings. This book has had a major impact on the thinking of contemporary social psychologists.

recognized that sometimes the presence of an emotion may alter our cognitions. If you feel anger toward someone, for example, you may exaggerate the faults of this person, blame him for his shortcomings, and plan to get revenge. Thus, cognition and emotion may be related to one another through a kind of circular feedback system (Benesh & Weiner, 1982).

The research literature includes many studies in which the authors have attempted to demonstrate the effect of emotions and mood states on cognitive functions such as perception, attention, recall, and recognition (Rusting, 1998). Heider's concepts have stimulated many social psychologists to pursue the path of trying to identify the cognitive states associated with different specific emotions. Over the years, many social psychologists have been influenced by Heider's ideas.

Other Contributors

Another important contributor to the literature on the relations between cognitions and emotions was Magda Arnold (1960). After an extensive review of the history of concepts concerning the nature of feeling, she concluded that all emotions presuppose evaluations of stimulus situations as good or bad: "The emotion becomes a felt tendency toward anything appraised as good, and away from anything appraised as bad" (p. 182). Such appraisal is often "intuitive," according to Arnold, and depends on "affective memory." In higher animals, she suggested, the appraisal of situations as good or bad is mediated by the brain (Arnold, 1970). The key idea in her view is that cognitions precede emotions.

In 1962, I published a book titled *The Emotions: Facts, Theories and a New Model* in which appeared a discussion of the relations between cognitions and emotions. I pointed out that evaluations initially determine whether stimuli are good or bad, potentially pleasurable or painful for the individual. Depending on which judgment is made, individuals will tend to approach or avoid the source of stimulation.

If something is evaluated as good or beneficial, there are a number of types of reactions that are possible. One class of response to a "good" object is to explore it, another is to ingest it, a third is to orient to it, and a fourth is to mate with it (if appropriate). Each of these reactions represents a distinct type of positive evaluation, and the appropriate responses associated with each type of evaluation I suggested represent distinct classes of basic or primary emotions.

Similarly, if something is evaluated as bad, there are several classes of reaction possible. One is to retreat from it, another is to stop all action and freeze, a third is to cry

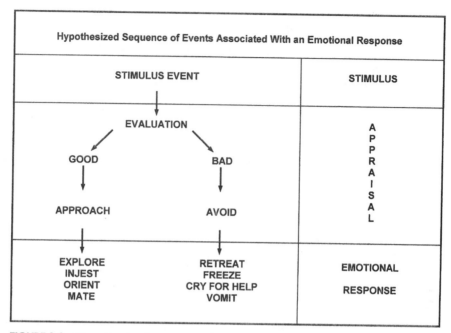

FIGURE 3.2. Hypothesized sequence of events associated with an emotional response.

for help (or emit distress signals), and a fourth is to vomit it out (if it has already been ingested). Again, each of these reactions represents a distinct type of negative evaluation, and the appropriate responses associated with each type of evaluation are considered to represent distinct classes of primary emotions. These ideas are schematically illustrated in Figure 3.2.

Another illustration of the emphasis on cognitive aspects of emotion may be seen in the writings of Richard Lazarus. In 1966, he pointed out that all organisms evaluate their environments and that emotions are a function of such cognitive activity. His view contained two basic assumptions: (a) that "each emotional reaction, regardless of its content, is a function of a particular kind of cognition or appraisal" and (b) that "the emotional response itself consists of an organized syndrome" (Lazarus, Averill, & Opton, 1970, p. 218). Lazarus has continued to elaborate these ideas in his writings, and they are described later.

Another approach that emphasized the cognitive contribution to emotions may be seen in a study by Schachter and Singer, published in 1962. Their basic assumption was that emotional reactions are determined by an individual's interpretation of a situation. However, these authors believed that a state of physiological arousal is a necessary precursor to an emotional feeling and that the specific pattern of arousal is irrelevant to the distinctions people make between different feeling states. The details of this study have been criticized, but these views once had a strong influence on the thinking of many psychologists.

Some Clinical Views About the Role of Cognitions

As the academic psychologists were developing their ideas about the relations between cognitions and emotions, a number of clinicians were independently presenting similar viewpoints. In 1962, Albert Ellis published his book *Reason and Emotion in Psychotherapy* in which he stated that the interpretations people make of their life events are the creators of their emotions. If a man interprets a comment from his wife as a criticism, he may become depressed. If he considers the criticism unfair or unjust, he may become angry. If he believes the criticism was meant as a joke, he may become amused. In essence, the cognitive evaluation of the stimulus determines the emotion. An important part of Ellis's therapy was based on the idea that the therapist could help the client reinterpret the events that created unpleasant emotions.

Ellis also proposed that many undesirable emotions are based on irrational ideas that predispose an individual toward certain interpretations of life events. Here are some examples of irrational interpretations according to Ellis (cited in Plutchik, 1976):

1. I often worry about having an accident.
2. Little inconveniences often make me angry.
3. I am usually afraid to ask questions in a large group because I might look foolish.
4. There are so many injustices in the world that it depresses me.
5. There is a great deal about me that I would be ashamed for others to know.

These ideas have had an important influence on the thinking of many clinicians. For example, Aaron Beck, a psychiatrist, stated that "the affective response is determined by the way an individual conceptualizes a situation" (Beck, 1983, p. 287). Another clinician stated this idea in the following way: "The human organism responds primarily to cognitive representations of its environment rather than to those environments per se" (Mahoney, 1977, p. 7).

The Sequence Debate

As a result of a 1980 paper by Zajonc titled *Feeling and Thinking: Preferences Need No Inferences,* a debate arose over the question of whether emotions (preferences in this case) could occur without a cognitive evaluation. This hypothesis was suggested because subjects expressed preferences for nonsense figures or Chinese ideographs to which they had been repeatedly exposed without an awareness of the repetitions. Zajonc (1980) wrote, "It is possible that we can like something or be afraid of it before we know precisely what it is and perhaps even without knowing what it is" (p. 154).

In the debate that followed, Lazarus (1981) pointed out that "a stimulus does not have to be known in detail for instant recognition of its relevance or potential relevance for one's well-being—in effect, for a person or animal to appraise it as positive, harmful, threatening, or challenging" (p. 222). In a later paper, Lazarus (1991) pointed out that most cognitive psychologists accept the idea that there may be unconscious processing of ideas and evaluations. People cannot directly access the inner cognitive processes related to attention, perception, memory, and impulses to action, but they can be aware of their products. In a more recent review, Bargh and Ferguson (2000) cited research studies that demonstrate the effects of nonconscious perception on behavior, behavioral mimicry (automatic and unintended behavior), the effects of subliminal stimuli on emotions, the development of autonomous, purposive behavior (typing or piano playing), automatic activation of motives (e.g., artistic impulses), and automatic activation of goals (resuming interrupted tasks). These and other studies have revealed that many aspects of cognitions are processes of which an individual is unaware. If one accepts this idea, then it is always possible to state that "cognitions" precede emotions.

Cognitive Research: Some Illustrations

A large body of research has resulted from the cognitive revolution and has revealed many important insights into the nature of the mind. This may be illustrated by some examples. The research of Elizabeth Spelke (2000) has been concerned with core knowledge systems as the building blocks of complex cognitive skills.

Core knowledge systems are mental mechanisms that represent evolutionarily important events, including recognizing objects and their motions, connecting persons to their actions, and understanding simple numerical relationships. Research has demonstrated that core systems are limited to particular events and problems and function independently of other cognitive systems, such as memory and perception. They are found in infants and animals and are believed to be the basis for the development of new cognitive skills in adults. Building blocks are relatively simple innate abilities that, as a result of experience, can combine to form complex mathematical and interpretative skills.

When parallel studies were carried out with animals, it was found that monkeys are able to make consistent choices that indicate that they discriminate between different numbers of objects, just as human infants do. This has also been demonstrated in rats and pigeons. It appears that many animals are able to form abstract ideas about the comparative and appropriate number of objects in groups in much the same ways that humans are able to do. However, exact addition appears to require the use of language systems. Spelke (2000) concluded that "human children and adults may gain new abilities not by creating those abilities out of whole cloth, but by bringing together building-block representational systems that have existed in us since infancy" (p. 1241).

Based on the assumption that emotions are produced by the interpretations people make of certain situations, several attempts have been made to identify the nature of the eliciting situations. For example, Dore and Kirouac (1985) attempted to determine the precise events that are considered by humans to be elicitors of six specific emotions: fear, disgust, happiness, surprise, anger, and sadness. These authors designed a 70-item questionnaire that described situations that were believed, according to several different theories, to elicit specific emotions. Exhibit 3.1 lists the situations that defined each of the assumed basic emotions.

The college student subjects of the experiment were asked to indicate what emotion a person would most likely experience if each of the situations described had occurred. The results indicated considerable agreement among the subjects on the emotion term selected to describe the effects of a particular situation. Agreement, for the 52 students, ranged from a high of 93.3% for happiness to a low of 81.9% for surprise.

Dore and Kirouac (1985) interpreted these findings as implying that humans are very sensitive to the emotional meaning of social situations. No sex differences were found in the ability to judge emotions commonly associated with situations. It was noted, however, that there were several situations that were associated with judgments of more then one emotion. Of interest is the fact that the second most likely emotion judged to be present was surprise. This might possibly indicate that unexpected events of any sort may be associated with the elicitation of emotions.

An alternative approach to studying the relations between appraisals (cognitions) and emotions had been proposed by Roseman, Spindel, and Jose (1990). They assumed that particular patterns of interpretation of events determine which emotions will be felt

EXHIBIT 3.1. THEMES USED AS ELICITING SITUATIONS FOR SIX BASIC EMOTIONS

HAPPINESS

1. Goal-oriented activities or final achievement of a goal
2. To succeed in a new hobby or activity; to have success with a new friend; to see or hear new and pleasant things
3. Recognition of the familiar; to repeat a pleasant activity, to meet someone or to see something that is known
4. Social approval, especially (but not exclusively) from a friend, a relative, an esteemed or important person
5. Benefit in general: money, status, reward, etc.

SADNESS

1. Loss in general
   a. death of a loved one (person or animal)
   b. separation from a loved one (temporary or permanent, real or fictitious)
   c. health problems (chronic disability, disease, pain)
2. To see someone crying or to perceive sadness

FEAR

1. Life in danger: anticipated or learned fear; danger from an event, a person, or an idea
2. Threatening verbal or physical attack: punishment, insult, anger in a stronger opponent
3. Loss of support
4. Strangeness

DISGUST

1. As elicited by sensations
   a. bad or repulsive taste
   b. bad odor
   c. viscous or oily object
   d. sight of something or someone repulsive, dirty, or organically deteriorated
2. Inappropriate behavior violating moral standards, habits, or norms

SURPRISE

1. Unexpected event
2. Unusual sensations (sight, taste)

ANGER

1. Barriers, obstacles, frustrations (psychological or physical, threats from some-one, social constraints, and dangerous attack)
2. Insults (psychological or verbal threats)
3. To be forced to do something
4. To observe or to suffer from an unjust treatment
5. Unrelieved tension which persists and prevents need satisfaction

Note. From "Identifying the Eliciting Situations of Six Fundamental Emotions," by F. Y. Dore and G. Kirouac, 1985, *Journal of Psychology, 119,* p. 436. Reprinted with permission.

in a given situation. The theory proposed that five types of appraisals of events determine which emotion will occur. The five types are as follows:

1. *Situational state:* Are events consistent or inconsistent with an individual's motives?
2. *Probability:* Are events certain or uncertain?
3. *Agency:* Are events caused by other people, by oneself, or are they beyond control?
4. *Motivational state:* Are events consistent or inconsistent with motives to obtain rewards or avoid punishment?
5. *Power:* Does the individual perceive him or herself as weak or strong?

Using this scheme, Roseman et al. hypothesized, for example, that *joy* would be associated with consistent reward-oriented situations, whereas *hope* is associated with uncertain, reward-oriented situations. According to the theory, appraisals of these types determine how to sort situations into groupings for which particular emotional responses are appropriate.

COGNITION AND EVOLUTION

One of the effects of the cognitive revolution has been to bring increased attention to the question of how evolution has created the basic building blocks of the mind, including, as mentioned earlier, the sensory, perceptual, and memory systems, the intelligence systems, and the emotional systems. In an early comment on this point, Attneave (1974) suggested that the usefulness of knowledge and intelligence is to know how to change things for the better and avoid making things worse in the service of increasing the chances of survival. Dember (1974) put the matter this way: "The brain and cerebral cortex have developed as adaptive mechanisms...the brain is the servant of the stomach and the sex organs: cognitive processes are instruments, means to an end" (p. 167).

More recent work has echoed the same theme. Kentridge and Appleton (1990) suggested that emotions are both reactions to important environmental events and preparations for events that are likely to occur. Emotions relate to triggering events for the purpose of reducing the possibility of an undesirable event or increasing the chances of a desirable event. Cognitive capacities are essentially used to predict future events.

Gray (1990) argued that there is an intimate relation between cognitive processes and emotions. This is because living organisms were selected . . . for their capacity to survive and reproduce. This capacity is closely connected with the ability to learn about, remember, and process information concerning . . . stimuli associated with the availability of food, water, shelter, and the opportunity to copulate, on the one hand, and with predators, threatening conspecifics, and other life-threatening dangers on the other. (p. 273)

Similarly, Panksepp (1990) agreed that "cognitive processes evolved (probably along many divergent branches of higher brain evolution) to subserve the homeostatic/ emotional needs of the organism" (p. 293). Panksepp believed that all mammals share similar emotional and motivational systems and that the neurological bases of these systems probably evolved very early in their phylogenetic history.

On the basis of these ideas and many like them in the literature, it seems probable that the evolution of cognitive functions should reveal some important things about the evolution of the emotions. The remainder of this chapter examines this implication. Cognition is considered as more or less synonymous with thinking and includes the many building blocks that make up such functions as perceiving, conceptualizing, and remembering. Cognitive functions have also been described in terms of knowledge acquisition, knowledge development, memory, categorization, and problem solving (Anderson, 1996). The basic question to be considered concerns the relationship between such cognitive or intellectual functions and emotions. This question is considered from a point of view that recognizes (a) that cognitive activities and their material basis, the brain, have a long evolutionary history; (b) that cognitive capacities have evolved along with the evolution of the brain; and (c) that cognitions are intimately related to emotions.

Evolution of the Brain

The first vertebrates appeared in the oceans about 500 million years ago. These creatures were no longer anchored to rocks. They could move around in their search for food, and their survival required both information about distant events and efficient coordination of movements. With the evolution of reptiles about 300 million years ago, the visual sense became highly developed through the development of a complex retina that acted as a small brain for coding spatial relations among external objects.

Because reptiles are cold-blooded, their activity was almost totally limited to the warm daylight hours, and their primary distance sense modality was vision. About 200 million years ago, small mammals appeared as nocturnal animals living on the floors of the forests that were widespread on the earth. These mammals (most living species of which are still nocturnal) developed audition as a distance sense modality to replace vision. They lived in a world that had no polar ice caps, that had oceans 10° warmer than they are now, and that had a tropical or semitropical climate.

By 60 million years ago, the large reptiles had become extinct, and many mammals had not only become larger in size but had also become diurnal land animals. The mammals, especially the primates, reevolved a more elaborate visual distance sense whose neural representation was not in the retina but in the brain. The increase in size of the brain during the course of evolution was limited to birds and mammals and was not an important feature of the evolution of reptiles and fish. The basic reason for the increase in brain size in birds and mammals was that they had entered new environmental niches in which there was an adaptive advantage for larger brains. In other words, neural control systems evolved to cope with the animals' changing environments.

In an important book on the evolution of the brain, Jerison (1973) demonstrated that gross brain size is an index of the total information-processing capacity of the brain and that it is a reasonably good index of the total number of neurons as well as of the degree of proliferation of structures on the nerves called dendrites. He pointed out that the use of the auditory or visual sense to evaluate distant stimuli requires that successive stimuli from the object be recorded, labeled, and compared to construct a perceived object. Such temporal comparisons also imply the existence of a memory. What is true for vision and audition is also true for olfaction. To construct a map of the environment by olfactory cues, an organism would have to encode information received successively over relatively long time intervals. Just as the development of the visual and auditory senses was associated with an increase in the size of posterior and lateral parts of the brain, so too was the expansion of the forebrain of mammals related to the development of the olfactory system.

The evolution of primates from the small mammals called insectivores was apparently due to the availability of a heavily forested zone. According to Jerison (1973),

> In invading that zone, the early primates became more visual than their insectivore cousins and also developed anatomical and physiological adaptations suitable for the active life of mammals that can scamper among branches, feed on the hard nuts of trees, and navigate the unusual environment of forests, leaves, and branches. (p. 365)

The natural camouflage of dense forest led to the reevolution of color sensitivity in primates because color has a selective advantage for identifying objects in this kind of environment. Many factors led to the coevolution of language and the brain. Details of this development are given in Deacon (1997). Some of the ideas he presented are described below.

The Change in Brain Size

Brain size did not change very much among the primates for about 50 million years, but about 15 million years ago certain primates left the forests and became established on the open plains, or savannas, of Africa. There is some evidence that a more arid climate developed in Africa around that time and that there was a reduction in the total forest area. Large and small plains-living mammals evolved and were widely established by the beginning of a series of ice ages, beginning about 2 million years ago.

The fossil record indicates that the major enlargement of the brain of humanlike primate forms took place over a period of less than 1 million years. The stage of *Homo sapiens* is evident in the fossil record beginning about 250,000 years ago; the records indicate a brain volume of approximately 1,200 milliliters. In contrast, the brain of the gorilla is about 500 milliliters. The brain volume of present-day human adults is about 1,400 milliliters.

Many explanations have been proposed for the large increase in the brain size of humans over a relatively short period of time; only unusual selection pressures could have produced such a rapid change. The following hypotheses or interpretations have been suggested as possible bases for this rapid evolution. (It is important to remember that many factors can operate simultaneously.)

1. Primates on an open plain are relatively defenseless against carnivores. Social grouping evolved as a means of cooperative defense. A particular social structure evolved including a dominance hierarchy and a family structure. This phenomenon created some stability of social relations and contributed to the development of language. Language required a complex coding system as well as a good memory; both required a large brain.

2. The relative scarcity of food on the plains led early man to become a carnivore and hence a predator with a large hunting range. However, a hunter without sharp teeth or other natural weapons required tools, cooperative hunting, and stratagems in order to be successful. He also required adequate distance senses and a good memory to deal with both predators and prey. Here, too, language developed as a signaling system for protection as well as a means for increasing the effectiveness of the hunt. Evidence exists that strong predatory pressure on a group exerts a selective influence to increase brain size. The anthropoid apes on the plains of Africa had to deal with the advanced carnivores that already flourished there. The relatively rapid evolution of the human brain may have been one result of this selection pressure.

3. The cold weather associated with glaciation led to the need for an artificial climate, as expressed in the use of fire and clothing. The crowding within the group created a need for social communication; the need for protein eventually led to domestication of certain animals. All these adaptive pressures increased the importance of language, memory, and social controls, with a probable influence on brain size.

4. The male hunt led to a division of labor between men and women and created the genetic basis for food-sharing between husband and wife, parent and child. Longer periods of sexual receptivity in the females might have been selected in evolution because the males were away hunting for a considerable portion of the time. Wife and husband began to recognize each other as economic and sexual partners, further enhancing the use of distinctive names and other aspects of language.

5. In all primate groups except humans, most breeding is endogamous; that is, it occurs primarily between members of a given group, although there is an occasional crossing of group membership. In contrast, the rapid evolution of man seems to have been correlated with the appearance of exogamy (outbreeding), with a resulting large increase in genetic variability. The nearly universal existence of an incest taboo among humans might be seen as a way of increasing genetic mixing. Large genetic variability creates the basis for successful adaptation to changing ecological conditions. Those hominids with large brains made better adaptations to a changing world than those with smaller brains.

The various conditions and reactions described above suggest that many factors may have contributed to the evolution of a large brain in humans. Most important appears to be the need, in order to survive, for good sensory systems for distance perception, a good memory, and a good means of communication. As evolution changed the human brain, humans were able to define stimuli as "objects" with names rather than as "releasers." The excellent memory enabled humans to make internal "maps" of their territories, and to communicate with one another about these "maps" by means of symbols.

The Function of Cognition in Evolution

In a broad sense, we may say that the main function of a large brain and a highly developed cognitive system is to ensure survival. We may, however, describe the cognitive process in a more precise way. From the point of view of evolution, *cognition developed in order to predict the future.*

Cognition is a form of map making. Cognition provides a model of the environment and codes information in a neural code. Early humans, living in a large hunting range filled with prey and predators, needed a great deal of information about their territory so that they could navigate it and locate objects within it. In this environment, there was an evolution of both visual and auditory modalities and a large increase in memory capacity. The combination of sensory input and expanded memory led to the capacity to name objects, create concepts, and relate them.

The development of abstract concepts denoting classes of events meant escape from the present. This increased ability to classify the environment made it possible for humans to develop foresight of future needs. The more precisely the environment could be assessed or mapped, the greater the capacity to make predictions about the likely course of external events and thus to initiate appropriate patterns of adaptive behavior.

Language developed not simply as an extension of the call system, which is widespread in birds and mammals, but rather as a specialized species-specific representation of the evolving cognitive system. Sound signals have rather specific functions in animals. They act as food signals, threat signals, courtship signals, dominance or submission signals, territory markers, or mother–child contact or loss signals. Calls are generally mutually exclusive and occur only in the presence of fairly well-defined appropriate stimuli. Call signals are inborn and represent species characteristics. A large brain is not needed to react appropriately to calls as sensory input.

In contrast, language permits novel combinations of sounds and is not necessarily triggered by particular stimuli. Language symbols can be used to describe events that are not present or that are nonexistent. Although the capacity for speech is based on a genetic endowment characteristic of advanced human primates, the particular symbols used in speech must be learned anew by each individual.

WHY PREDICT THE ENVIRONMENT

In the process of their interaction with the environment, organisms face certain common problems that are identifiable at all phylogenetic levels. To survive, any organism must distinguish between prey and predator, between a potential mate and a potential enemy. It must explore its environment and "map" it to take in information about the beneficial and harmful aspects of its immediate world. The mechanisms by which these functions are expressed will vary throughout the animal domain, but the basic prototype functions will remain the same. In the most basic sense, any organism must predict on the basis of limited information whether there is food, a mate, or danger in its environment. Depending on the prediction made, the organism makes a decision to run, to attack, to play, or to mate. From this point of view, the complex processes of sensory input, evaluation, symbolization, comparison with memory stores, and the like—those processes we call cognitive—are in the service of emotions and biological needs. Predicting the characteristics of environments enables organisms to prepare for those environments.

It is possible to consider the evolution of signaling systems in animal species in this context. Signals are predictions of things to come and indicate the need to prepare an emotional response. Warning signals predict danger and imply the need to flee. Threat signals predict an attack and imply the need for aggressive behavior. Hunger signals imply the need for ingestion of food through contact with a source of nourishment. Courting signals predict the presence of a potential mate and imply the possibility of reproductive behavior. Cognitions may be considered to be certain types of signal or symbol-using functions that have evolved in lower animals and in humans for the purpose of predicting biologically significant events. The predictions are in the service of needs and emotions.

In a paper comparing humans with computing machines, Neisser (1963), one of the early contributors to the cognitive revolution, also discussed the idea of cognitions as being in the service of needs and emotions. He noted that both humans and machines can be goal directed (e.g., a homing missile is goal directed); both can learn from experience (e.g., chess-playing computers learn from experience); and both can occasionally produce novel or "creative" outputs (e.g., some programs have found original proofs for mathematical theorems). The following are some of the major differences between humans and machines: (a) Computers never get bored, people do; (b) computers have single motivations, people have many; (c) computer memories can be instantaneously erased, people have little control over what they will learn or forget; and (d) computers neither dream nor play.

Neisser (1963) pointed out two additional characteristics of humans that are not found in computers. The first is that the particular history of an individual's cognitive development "leaves its mark on a person in the form of a hierarchical organization of purposes as well as strategies" (p. 195). The second is that human thinking is intimately associated with emotions. In the course of early individual development, information from the environment is evaluated in terms of its need-satisfying and need-frustrating properties. In this regard, Neisser (1963) stated:

> The fluctuations of the child's internal states do not have any very obvious relation to the logic of his environment, so that months and years are needed before his thinking and his actions are well attuned to the world around him....One of the most common...modes of learning, that of reward and punishment, operates through an open involvement of strong and historically complicated emotions. (p. 197)

The point has been made by Breland and Breland (1966) and others that most organisms come into the world genetically equipped with a cognitive system that is precoded for certain events. For a given type of environment, these organisms (such as insects and some birds) "know," without the need for a learning period, which events are dangerous or safe, what signals indicate a mate or nonmate, and what foods are edible. In mammals and primates, there are relatively fewer innate responses to particular stimuli; instead, there is a genetically based "curiosity" that impels the animal to explore its environment and gradually to develop an internal "map" of it by conditioning, trial and error, and imitation. What is available is a cognitive system—sensory mechanisms, conceptual building blocks, memory stores, coordinating circuits, and so on—whose parameters have to be established by learning experiences of various kinds. In exactly the same way, the capacity for speech and conceptual thought is innate; only the symbols themselves must be learned.

SUMMARY

The long childhood of most primates allows the child time to learn the major signals needed for survival in a hostile environment. What is particularly significant is that each new cognitive experience that is biologically important is connected with an emotional reaction, such as fear, pleasure, disgust, or depression.

The original function of the evolution of cognition is to enable the organism to map its environment and to predict the future in regard to significant emotional or motivational events. However, once such a complex mechanism has evolved, it can be used for other things, just as a hammer may be used for driving nails or for hitting a chisel to make a sculpture. Once developed, the cognitive mechanism can deal with nonemotional events and symbols as well as emotional ones. It can also deal with the symbols of past events as well as future ones, and the symbols, once in the store of memory, can be used for fantasy productions, art, literature, and play.

From an evolutionary point of view, both emotions and cognitions are part of our primitive heritage. The very first living organisms had to emote—that is, fight or flee, eat or expel, reproduce or orient. These actions are still part of the human behavioral repertoire, changed in form, modified in appearance, reactive to different stimuli, but functionally the same. Cognitions have always been a necessary part of an emotional response, but in sessile organisms fixed to a rock in the ocean, there was little novelty, minimal learning, and almost no perception of distant events. The evolutionary history of cognition is the history of perception through contact to perception of distant events. With this change has come an increase in the size of sensory organs as well as of the central nervous system. The capacity to be conditioned, to learn, and to imitate greatly increased, along with a more extensive central integrating mechanism.

Unusual evolutionary pressures influenced primate evolution and then, in recent geological time, further large environmental changes, acting on preadapted hominids, led to the rapid increase in the brain size of contemporary humans. With a large brain, good distance receptors, and a remarkable memory capacity, the ability to predict the future increased greatly. Although some evolutionary changes have taken place in recent millennia, cultural evolution has far outstripped the pace of organic evolution (Blackmore, 1999). The brain, which evolved as an adaptation to a changing environment, has now helped to create the very environment to which it must continue to adapt.

4 The Language of Emotions

Verbal responses are another, albeit highly sophisticated, type of behavior; they are not a direct window to the emotions.

Neal E. Miller

PREVIEW

Most people believe they know what an emotion is. Despite this belief, they do not always agree on which words in the English language are emotion words and which are not. Psychologists have published many studies that have tried to establish a kind of dictionary of emotion terms by asking college students which words are descriptive of emotional states. The results have been surprisingly inconsistent.

This chapter reviews some of the studies that have used this approach and describes what the studies found. Also included in this chapter is a review of the many historical and contemporary attempts that have been made to describe certain emotions as primary, basic, or fundamental. It appears that such attempts have a long history and that most contemporary psychologists believe that there is a relatively small number of basic emotions. How much agreement there is on this issue is also discussed.

This chapter also examines the question of how the words of the language of emotion are related to one another. It will be evident that emotion words vary in terms of their degree of similarity to one another and that one can recognize families of emotion terms. Different ways of conceptualizing this idea are described.

One way of describing the similarity relations among emotions terms is by means of a circular or circumplex model. Empirical data are given to show how the model applies to English, French, Italian, Spanish, Japanese, as well as preliterate cultures. Information is presented on the cross-cultural study of emotions and its implications for our understanding of the language of emotion.

IN CHAPTER 1, various definitions of the word *emotion* are given, and it became evident that psychologists often disagree over the precise meaning of this term. The tentative general definition that was proposed on the basis of an extensive review of the literature emphasized the ideas that cognitive appraisals were usually involved in emotion, that feelings of arousal and pleasure or displeasure often occur, that physiological changes are not uncommon, and that the emotional behavior is usually goal directed and adaptive. These ideas are examined in detail in subsequent chapters. It is reasonable to consider a definition of a concept as a kind of minitheory and should come at the end of a period of inquiry rather than at the beginning.

TERMS RELATED TO EMOTION

The literature on emotion uses a number of words that are closely related to the concept of emotion; these words are *affect, mood,* and *temperament.* In what ways are they related?

Emotion and Affect

Although the terms *emotion* and *affect* are widely used, an aura of ambiguity surrounds their meanings. Generally, academic psychologists are much more likely to use the term *emotion* in their writings, whereas clinicians are more inclined to use the term *affect,* although sometimes both are used interchangeably. All introductory psychology textbooks have a chapter on emotion but not on affect. In clinical writings, the word *affect* is used; *emotion* is used to denote an emotional disorder or emotional problems.

Is there any way to establish meaningful distinctions between these terms? Over the years some efforts have been made mainly by clinicians to distinguish the terms. In a textbook of psychotherapy, Langs (1990), a psychiatrist, defined affects as "manifest and surface communications" (p. 295). He discussed emotions only in the context of emotional disturbances, which he defined as "all forms of psychologically and emotionally founded disorders. The emotional disturbances range from characterological pathology to psychosis and neurosis. They also include psychosomatic and other psychologically founded physical disorders" (p. 726). Langs suggested that emotional disturbances include disturbances in such affects as anxiety, depression, boredom, and anger, implying that affects are the subjective feelings associated with dysfunction. In contrast, psychologists Greenberg and Paivio (1997) stated

> Affect refers to an unconscious biological response to stimulation. It involves autonomic, physiological, motivational, and neural processes involved in the evolutionary adaptive behavioral response system. Affects do not involve reflective evaluation. They just happen, whereas both emotions and feelings are conscious products of these unconscious affective processes. (p. 7)

Given these confusing and overlapping definitions, it is no wonder that a computer expert who tried to develop a computer program that simulates human emotions defined emotions and affects as interchangeable terms (Picard, 1997).

Two other clinicians have discussed this issue. Vaillant (1997) suggested that the word *emotion* refers to inner bodily experiences, which include drives, affects, and pain. Affect, therefore, would be a subtype of emotion, but one which is difficult to distinguish from emotions.

In his "clinical synthesis" in *Affect in Psychoanalysis,* Spezzano (1993), a psychoanalyst, used the word *affect* almost exclusively and seldom referred to emotion. However, he did provide a number of statements about what affects are. He described affects as internal states that create a demand for action. People, however, are not the final authorities on their own affective states because verbal reports of affects are often inconsistent with behavior.

This brief review of recent writings related to affect and emotion suggests that there is considerable ambiguity in the description of these terms. More often than not, there appears to be extensive overlap in the uses of these terms, and no clear distinctions can be made at this time; they are therefore used interchangeably in this chapter.

Emotion and Mood

In a book describing an extensive program of research on moods, D. Watson (2000) defined *moods* as "transient episodes of feeling or affect. As such, moods are highly similar to the subjective experiential component of emotions" (p. 4). In contrast, Oatley and Jenkins (1996) stated: "The term *mood* refers to an emotional state that usually lasts for hours, days, or weeks, sometimes as a low intensity background...moods are often objectless, free-floating" (p. 125). Yet another way of defining mood is given by Ben-Ze'ev (2000), who said, "Mood has a broad meaning, referring to the entire feeling continuum....Sometimes *mood* is used...as a kind of inclination. Thus we speak of someone being in the mood to make love or to take a walk" (p. 86).

A recent review of the literature on mood describes moods as diffuse and long-lasting states (Gendolla, 2000). Gendolla stated that moods may exist without an obvious stimulus or object that brings them about, and that they are often experienced without an awareness of their cause. In contrast, he believed that emotions are reactions to specific significant events.

Clinicians use the term *mood* in a narrower sense. They refer to *mood disorders* as those that involve some form of depression or its opposite, mania. The *Diagnostic and Statistical Manual of Mental Disorders* (4th ed., *DSM–IV*; American Psychiatric Association, 1994) described at least six mood disorders: major depressive disorder, dysthymic disorder, Bipolar I disorder, Bipolar II disorder, cyclothymic disorder, and substance-induced mood disorder. It thus appears that the concept of mood has as much disagreement and ambiguity as the concept of emotion. These various observations suggest that there is considerable overlap in the literature between the concepts represented by the words *emotion, affect,* and *mood.*

Emotion and Temperament

The concept of temperament is part of an ancient tradition. The Greeks distinguished four temperaments: the phlegmatic, the melancholic, the sanguine, and the choleric. American Indians described four temperaments: the eagle, the bear, the squirrel, and the buffalo (Howard, 1994). In recent years, research psychologists have defined *temperament* "as those aspects of behavior and emotions that are constitutional, that are stable over time and across situations, that have a neurophysiological underpinning, and that have some degree of heritability" (Oatley & Jenkins, 1996, p. 209).

Vaughn and Bost (1999) described temperament as genetically-based traits that can be recognized early in life and have some stability over the life span. They pointed out that such things as maturation rate, intellectual ability, and socially based traits such as shame are not part of temperament. In essence, temperament refers to personality traits (such as sociability and aggressiveness) that are distinguishable in infancy and childhood and that tend to persist over long periods of time.

When a situation arises in which it is not possible to arrive at a simple, clear, and universally acceptable definition of a concept (such as emotion), it is sometimes helpful to examine the language of the field; in other words, to determine how emotion words are used both in daily life and scientific discourse.

HOW CAN WE IDENTIFY THE LANGUAGE OF EMOTION?

One way to attempt to answer the question of how to identify the language of emotion is to ask people to list the words of their language that describe emotions. For example, to find out how consistent people are in identifying emotions, Shields (1984) gave a group of college students a list of 60 words that described subjective states (feelings) and asked them to distinguish the emotion words from the nonemotion words. The list included words like *ashamed, bored, happy, sleepy, hungry,* and *sad.*

The results showed that there was considerable agreement on certain words and relatively little on others. For example, over 80% of the judges considered the following words to be emotions: *angry, happy, sad, loving, jealous, joyful, depressed, embarrassed, frightened, terrified,* and *humiliated.* Over 80% of the judges considered the following words as not referring to emotions: *cold, hungry, thirsty, sleepy, tired, healthy, alert, nauseated, fidgety,* and *strong.* At the same time, there were many words that were considered to be emotions by about half of the judges and not to be emotions by the other half. Examples of these ambiguous words are *startled, curious, confused, astonished, revolted, surprised,* and *scornful.* Shields (1984) concluded that there is no good agreement for many words that refer to feeling states as to whether or not they represent emotions. When the judges were asked to describe their reasons for identifying a state as emotion or nonemotion, they had difficulty in doing so. It appears that *emotion* is an ambiguous category for many college students.

A somewhat different procedure was used by Storm and Storm (1987) to see if they could develop a list of emotion words. They gave a group of college students a list of 72 words that they believed were probably emotions. The judges were asked to sort the words into nonoverlapping groups according to similarity of meaning. The researchers then used a statistical technique called *multidimensional scaling* to identity clusters of terms. The results suggested 18 clusters, with each cluster containing two to five terms. Examples of the clusters are (a) anger, rage; (b) disgust, loathing, revulsion, contempt, hatred; (c) sadness, grief, melancholy, remorse; (d) panic, terror, fear; and (e) elation, jubilation, joy, ecstasy.

To expand this study, Storm and Storm (1987) then asked several hundred children and adults to list every emotion word they could think of. They were also asked to label the feelings of characters in clips from commercial television shows. This resulted in a list of over 500 terms to be further studied. In this phase of the research, four college professors then placed the various words into clusters representing similar meanings. This resulted in 61 separate groups.

Words in these groups could then be reassigned into 20 broader categories. Agreement among the judges ranged from 64% to 84%. When only seven large groups of words were determined, the agreement among the judges ranged from 79% to 95%. The highest agreement was obtained using 193 terms that Storm and Storm (1987) considered to be "clearly emotional."

An examination of the various lists of terms obtained by Storm and Storm (1987), which totaled over 500, revealed that the words often did not correspond to the various definitions of emotion that have been given by various writers. For example, some of the words referred to value judgments such as *good* or *bad* and *evil* or *fine.* Some were simply metaphors. These included such terms as *rotten, empty, sick, stuck-up, butterflies, small, stupid,* and *topsy-turvy.* Some of the terms referred to physical characteristics of a person or thing, such as *ugly, beautiful,* or *heavy.* Some referred to a bodily state of some kind, such as *pain, sick, excited, sleepy, listless, dizzy, queer,* and *strong.* A whole group of terms referred to different states of arousal, from *tired* to *fired up*. After a careful review of the various restrictions, the total count of emotion words was about 350.

Storm and Storm (1987) noted that many of the terms in the list were produced only by adults. Young children typically have a small vocabulary of emotion terms, and these tend to consist of the words *happy, sad, mad,* and *scared.* These observations suggest that children develop a few broad categories of emotion concepts and that these concepts are gradually refined, differentiated, and added to as a result of social development and experience. Storm and Storm also noted that that many of the terms in the list refer to words commonly used to describe personality. Thus, words such as *gloomy, resentful,* and *calm* can describe personality traits as well as emotional feelings. This is an important observation that is discussed in more detail in chapter 13.

Another investigation concerned with identifying emotion words was reported by Clore, Ortony, and Foss (1987). In this study, small groups of about 20 students each rated lists of words taken from the writings of other psychologists. A total of 585 words were rated, some in adjective form, some in verb form, and some in noun form. The students used a 4-point scale to indicate their degree of certainty that each word was or was not an emotion word.

The ratings for degree of certainty were subjected to statistical analyses, and considerable disagreement was found concerning which terms were and which terms were not emotion words. For example, it appeared that intense states such as *astonished, bewildered, flabbergasted,* and *amazed* were all considered emotional states in the general *surprise* family, even though Clore et al. preferred to think of them as *cognitive conditions.* Other examples of words that the students rated as emotion words, contrary to Clore et al.'s expectations, were the terms *determined, disillusioned,* and *lively.* One of the reasons for the inconsistencies in the students' judgments is that the simple presentation of a word does not identify a linguistic context. Thus, for example, the word *good* on the list can be interpreted as feeling good or pleasant or being a good person. If someone interpreted the word as in the first case, it would probably be rated as an emotion word, whereas if it was interpreted as a moral judgment, it might not. Here again, the same term might be used to describe an emotional state or a personality trait.

Another example of the confusion revealed by the data is the fact that the word *courage* (or *courageous*) was considered an emotion word, whereas its opposite *cowardly* was not. Similarly, *optimistic* was considered an emotion word, whereas its opposite *pessimistic* was not. It thus appears that simply asking people to identity emotion words from long lists does not result in much agreement, nor is it a satisfactory solution to the problem of defining the language of emotion.

A study carried out by Averill (1975) provided another possible reason for the discrepant ratings among the participants. Averill was interested in developing a relatively complete list of emotion words in the English language and in describing some of their linguistic properties. To do this, he and four graduate students read through the list of 18,000 psychological terms compiled by Allport and Osbert in 1936. Any term that was considered to be an emotion word by at least two of the five judges was kept in the list. This resulted in a preliminary list of 717 words. These words were then given in random order to a group of college students who were asked to rate on a 7-point scale whether they believed that the average person would consider each term as referring to an emotion. They were also asked to rate whether each word was familiar to them or not.

The results showed that more than half of the words in the list were not familiar to many of the college students. The relatively unfamiliar terms included such words as *bedeviled, beguiled, bewailing, cantankerous, contrite, crestfallen, disconsolate, doleful, droll, enamored, galled, harried, macabre, panged, quaky, scoffing, smitten, testy,* and *volatile.* Only 351 words were rated as familiar by all the students, and it is likely that the final sample of familiar words would be much less if each student was asked to define each term. It is thus likely that the inherent ambiguity of the words of our language, the general lack of a context when words are presented in isolation, and the lack of familiarity with certain words may help account for the highly varied judgments that raters give concerning the question of which words are emotion words and which are not.

What may be concluded about the question being considered, namely, "How can we identify the language of emotion?" The methods that have been described which ask children, college students, or professors to select emotion words from long lists of terms do not seem to provide any clear-cut answers. It appears that there is inconsistency among the judges in deciding which words are emotion words and which are not. These findings are probably due to several reasons:

1. The words are often presented in different grammatical forms, such as adjectives (angry), nouns (joy), and verbs (saddened), thus creating some confusion because the judges have to change expectations or sets.

2. Many words on the lists are obsolete, obscure, or uncommon, and many judges admit to being unfamiliar with these words.

3. The words are presented out of context, thus adding to the ambiguity of the terms.

4. The different experiences of the judges with language in general and emotion words in particular add to the variability in the ratings.

One tentative implication from the data that has been cited is that the ordinary language of emotions, at least in English, probably contains around 300 to 400 words or fewer. It is also worth noting that most studies of emotion use a far smaller sample of this possible set of terms.

Multiplicity of Meanings of Words

The variety of meanings found for emotion words is not surprising and is also found in other linguistic areas that involved descriptions of inner states (e.g., *drug effects, drunkenness, pain, pleasure,* and *sexuality*). For a parallel example of the multiplicity of words and phrases that describe emotional states, consider the vocabulary of drunkenness. Drunkenness is a universal experience in the sense that it can be found in all cultures. Most people have experienced some degree of it in their own lives, and many different words and expressions have been used to describe the experience of drunkenness.

The *Dictionary of American Slang* (Chapman, Kipfer, & Wentworth, 1975) lists 353 terms for being drunk. Examples of synonyms for drunkenness include the following: *crashed, bombed, crocked, gassed, plastered, tanked, looped, floating, glassy-eyed, gone, juiced, lit, loaded, mellow, pickled, potted, smashed, soused, stewed, tight, high,* and *zonked.*

Many of the terms are forceful, or even violent words, whereas others suggest a pleasant state (e.g., *floating, mellow*). Emotion terms are similar to words for drunkenness in their expression of different levels of intensity of feeling, in their partial and limited description of complex inner states, and in the fact that they are triggered by a limited class of stimuli.

Language is a complex structure that has evolved over a period of thousand of years. Within each language, there are many different historical elements. The words of the English language, for example, stem for Latin, Greek, German, and French roots and, to lesser degrees, from various other sources. Over the centuries, a multiplicity of meanings may become attached to a word. In addition, if a word becomes used in a scientific or technical context, it is often given a new or modified meaning.

To illustrate this last point, consider the word *anxiety*. Most people would agree that this is an emotion word, yet the definitions of the term are quite diverse. *Webster's Third New International Dictionary* (1971) stated that the word *anxiety* comes from a Latin root which means to cause pain or to choke. It then provided three different definitions. The first definition is a painful uneasiness of the mind with respect to an impending or anticipated ill. The second definition describes anxiety as a pathological state of restlessness and agitation with a distressing sense of oppression about the heart. The third definition is based on psychoanalytic theory and describes anxiety as an expectancy of evil or of danger without adequate ground, explained as a transformed emotion derived from repressed libido. This last definition is evidently based on theory and not on subjective experience. It is extremely unlikely that a group of college students would ever define anxiety in those terms based solely on their experiences. Therefore, the use of judges to select emotion from nonemotion words is only a limited way to begin to identity the language of emotions. It is likely that emotions will be defined by scientists as part of a body of theory, and the definitions chosen will undoubtedly influence the kind of information that is collected by researchers.

The meanings of words are given not only by explicit definitions but also by identifying related words or synonyms. Thus, to understand a word like *anxiety*, it is useful to list such related words as *fear, worry, foreboding, concern, dread, uneasiness,* and *apprehension*. However, the dictionary adds one other important way to help understand emotions, and that is by listing antonyms as well as synonyms. In this case, words such as *bold, calm,* and *confident* are given as antonyms for *anxiety*. This implies that the concept of opposites (antonyms) or bipolarity is a useful way to describe at least one aspect of emotions.

To further illustrate the complexity of the language of emotions, consider the study by Storm and Storm (1998), who extended their earlier work by selecting one commonly described emotion, love, for further analysis. A list of 28 words was given to participants, and they were asked to indicate whether each word did or did not apply to different types of love relationship. The love relationships were listed as follows: *friendship, sexual love, parental love, brotherly love, sibling love, maternal love, passionate love, romantic love, brotherly love, maternal love, love of pets, physical love, platonic love, sisterly love, marital love, patriotism, erotic love, love of God, homosexual love, love of grandparents, love of humanity, love of work,* and *spiritual love*.

When the data were analyzed across these types of love, six clusters of love-related words were found: *sexuality, respect, attraction, sympathy, nurturant,* and *friendship*. The prototype words for each cluster were the following: *horny, aroused, passionate (sexuality); reverence, awe, admiration, trust (respect); belonging, attracted, enchanted (attraction); compassion, sympathy, pity (sympathy); attached, caring, sentimental (nurturant);* and *fondness, liking (friendship)*. Thus, a single emotion like love, and probably others, can have multiple components or kinds.

Studying Stimulus Situations That Produce Emotions

A study by R. H. Harrison (1986) examined a way of grouping the words of the emotion language on the basis of appraisals made of the situations that tend to elicit emotions. Harrison created 170 imaginary situations and asked participants to describe how they might feel as the central character in each story using any emotion word of their choosing.

> An example of an imaginary situation is: You and your spouse were planning a camping trip for the family during the summer vacation. The family had always been close and done things together as a family. The two of you were all excited about the plans but when you discussed them with your kids, they were very cool: each talked about what he/she had already planned, which was more important than a family vacation. (R. H. Harrison, 1986, p. 257)

The participant was asked, "How would most people feel?" and "How would you yourself feel?"

After idiosyncratic terms used only once or twice were eliminated, 198 emotion words were left for factor analysis and multidimensional scaling. The question asked was, Which emotion terms tend to occur together as alternative responses to the same imaginary situations? This is, in essence, a way of measuring the similarity between each emotion and every other emotion.

One analysis resulted in 32 clusters of emotion words, but this method separated *terrified*, *apprehensive*, and *afraid* into different clusters, even though these words seem to be simply different degrees of the same emotional dimension. A further analysis then produced 10 factors that were labeled with the following terms: *surprise, love, happiness, anticipation, fear, shame, sorrow, achievement, jealousy,* and *anger*. R. H. Harrison (1986) noted that this list is fairly similar to that proposed by Izard (1971) and by Plutchik (1962).

The method described above of clustering emotion words into broad categories represents only one type of approach to reducing the language of emotion to a smaller, more manageable number, at least for research purposes. This might be called a *reductionistic* approach, one that analyzes a complex set into more basic or fundamental units, somewhat as is done in chemistry. The many complex substances of our world can be interpreted as compounds or mixtures of a relatively small number of basic units. It is possible, however, to reverse this conceptual process and begin with certain fundamental units, in this case, basic or primary emotions, and conceptualize all other emotions as compounds or syntheses of the few primary ones. Combining the methods of analysis and synthesis might enable the construction of a kind of periodic table of the emotions. These kinds of attempts are described after a brief discussion of the evolution of languages.

A Note on the Evolution of Languages

Archaeologists and linguists have long been interested in the origins of language. It is believed that human vocal–auditory language is probably only about 50,000 years old. The kind of evidence used for this conclusion relates to the sudden increase in tool use and technological diversification that occurred about this time. In addition, the structure of the mandibles of the human jaw had to reach a certain form before subtle articulations became possible (Harvard, Steklis, & Lancaster, 1977).

It is estimated that about 40,000 years passed before a written mode of language expression developed about 8,000 years ago. Such written language passed through a recognized series of stages, beginning with pictographs, or actual sketches of objects, to increasingly abstract forms.

With a limited number of signs available, a great many different ideas had to be expressed with the same sign. For example, the (hieroglyphic) sign for *foot* meant *foot*, but it meant also *to go, to stand,* and so on. However, although the sign was always the same, the picture of a foot when it was to be read *to go* was read with the special sound which meant *to go,* and when it was intended to indicate the idea of *standing,* it was read in an entirely different way. Thus, every one of the pictures came to be associated with three or four ideas and therefore with three or four sounds (Chiera, 1938).

What was true of the origins of language is still true to some degree today. Words are not precise symbols that have a single, unequivocal meaning. They are inherently ambiguous and depend on context to help establish meanings. Because of this inherent ambiguity, words help to create meanings by influencing the conceptual content of often poorly defined and diffuse inner feeling states. Thus, the statements one makes about one's own inner emotional states are partially dependent on the kinds of words available to the individual and the kind of linguistic community he or she is in. The point being made is simply that verbal reports of inner, private, emotional states are influenced by many factors and, therefore, the nature of the inner states will always remain an inference that requires confirmation by independent sources of evidence.

HOW MANY BASIC EMOTIONS ARE THERE?

From a historical point of view, there is an alternative, and much older, way of trying to understand emotions than by examining lists of emotion words. This alternative approach makes the assumption that there is a small number of emotions that are considered primary or fundamental or basic and that all other emotions are secondary, derived mixtures or blends of the primary ones. From this perspective, one needs to identify the basic emotions and then explain which mixed emotions or blends are derived from them. Over the centuries many philosophers and psychologists have proposed lists of basic emotions. This section reviews some of these proposals.

Between the 3rd and 11th centuries, Hindu philosophers stated that there are eight basic or natural emotions. These have been translated as (a) *sexual passion, love,* or *delight;* (b) *amusement, laughter,* or *humor;* (c) *sorrow;* (d) *anger;* (e) *fear* or *terror;* (f) *perseverance;* (g) *disgust;* and (h) *amazement* (Schweder & Hoidt, 2002).

The French philosopher René Descartes (1596–1650) assumed that there were only six primary emotions or, as he called them, *passions,* and that all others were composed of mixtures of these six or derived from them. He suggested that *love, hatred, desire, joy, sadness,* and *admiration* were primary emotions but gave no justification for his choice.

A more extensive attempt to develop a system of the emotions was presented by the Dutch philosopher Baruch Spinoza (1632–1677), who assumed only three primary affects: *joy, sorrow,* and *desire;* all others were assumed to spring from these.

Spinoza attempted to analyze a number of common emotions using this procedure but gave no justification for his choice of primaries, nor is it evident how he decided on the components of a particular complex emotion. Later, the British philosopher Thomas Hobbes (1588–1679) suggested that there were seven simple passions: *appetite, desire, love, aversion, hate, joy,* and *grief.* Several English philosophers of the 19th century continued making distinctions of a similar kind.

Darwin's book on the expression of emotions does not explicitly say which emotions are primary and which are mixed (Darwin, 1872/1965). However, his chapters deal with seven clusters of emotions that he believed can be identified both in animals and humans. These chapters are titled *Low Spirits, Anxiety, Grief, Dejection, Despair; Joy, High Spirits, Love, Tender Feelings, Devotion; Reflection, Meditation, Ill-Temper, Sulkiness, Determination; Hatred and Anger; Disdain, Contempt, Disgust, Guilt, Pride, Helplessness, Patience, Affirmation and Negation; Surprise, Astonishment, Fear, Horror;* and *Self Attention, Shame, Shyness, Modesty, Blushing.* These clusters presumably reflect the more basic emotions, or at least the ones Darwin considered most important to study.

Early in the 20th century, the concept of primary and secondary emotions was given an extensive analysis by William McDougall, a British psychologist. His views are described in his textbook of social psychology, published in 1921. He pointed out that all animals including humans have propensities and that when these are activated an affective quality, which we call emotion, is associated with each. For example, the propensity to flee from danger is associated with the emotion of fear, the propensity to be aggressive is associated with the emotion of anger, and so on. In all, McDougall assumed seven basic emotions: *fear, disgust, wonder, anger, subjection, elation,* and *tender feelings.* The secondary or complex emotions are illustrated by such things as *hate,* which McDougall defined as a mixture of anger and disgust, or *loathing,* which results from the combination of fear and disgust.

McDougall, however, was one of the few writers on this subject who made some attempt to explain the methods used to decide which emotions are primary. He suggested three criteria (McDougall, 1921):

1. A similar emotion and impulse is clearly shown in the behavior of the higher animals.

2. The emotion and impulse occasionally appear in humans with morbidly exaggerated intensity (which presumably indicates its relatively independent functioning in the mind).

3. Most of the complex emotions can be conceived of as mixtures of the primaries.

This attempt by McDougall to describe behavior in terms of primary emotions is by no means the most recent such attempt. In the 1928 Wittenberg Symposium on *Feelings and Emotions,* Jorgensen proposed his own scheme. He suggested six primary emotions: *fear, happiness, sorrow, want, anger,* and *shyness,* with the possibility that *loathing* might also be included as an emotion. He noted the very important point that the naming of these primaries is partly fortuitous because they each may vary in intensity. Thus, *fear* might also be called *dread, terror, anxiety,* or *apprehension,* and *sorrow* might also be called *grief, despair, pain,* or *despondency.* Using this scheme, Jorgensen interpreted *hope* as a mixture of *want, sorrow,* and *happiness,* and *envy* as a mixture of *sorrow* and *want.*

Several other attempts have been made to identify basic emotions. For example, Cattell (1957) had factor analyzed a variety of descriptive items related to the objective expression of emotions and motivations. He reported 10 factors that he defined as basic emotions and proposed that each emotion has a particular goal, as shown in Table 4.1.

Another list of basic emotions had been proposed by Tomkins (1962). He assumed that there are eight basic emotions or affects. The positive affects are (a) *interest,* (b) *surprise,* and (c) *joy.* The negative affects are (d) *anguish,* (e) *fear,* (f) *shame,* (g) *disgust,* and (h) *rage.* These basic emotions are innately patterned responses to certain types of stimuli and may be expressed by means of a wide variety of bodily reactions. Tomkins, however, emphasized the importance of the face as the primary mode for the expression of emotions. He also assumed that there is a genetic, species-related basis for the expression of the basic emotions.

Izard (1971) had worked closely with Tomkins and has provided evidence that these basic emotions can be reliably distinguished from one another on the basis of posed facial expressions. The list in Table 4.2 is Izard's way of describing these eight emotions; he also provided some defining adjectives for each emotion.

TABLE 4.1. Ten Basic Emotions and Their Goals Determined by Factor Analysis Based on the Work of Raymond Cattell

Emotion	Goal
Sex–lust	Mating
Fear	Escape
Loneliness	Gregariousness
Pity, succorance	Protectiveness
Curiosity	Exploration
Pride	Self-assertion
Sensuous, comfort	Narcissism
Despair	Appeal
Sleepiness	Rest seeking
Anger	Pugnacity

Note. From *Personality and Motivation: Structure and Measurement,* by R. B. Cattell, 1957, p. 112. Copyright 1957 by Harcourt Brace Jovanovich. Reprinted with permission.

In the same year that Tomkins published his book, I also published a theory of emotion that was based on the idea that certain emotions are primary and all others are derived from them (Plutchik, 1962). I assumed that primary emotions are identifiable, in some form, at all phylogenetic levels and that they have adaptive significance in the individual's struggle for survival. Eight such primary emotion dimensions were conceptualized, but it was also emphasized that they could be described in several languages—for example, a subjective language, a behavioral language, a functional language, and so on. By using only the subjective language of introspective feelings, the eight basic emotion dimensions could be described by such words as *joy, sadness, acceptance, disgust, fear, anger, expectation,* and *surprise* or other synonymous terms reflecting differences in intensity, terms such as

TABLE 4.2. Eight Basic Emotions and Some Defining Adjectives Based on the Work of Carroll Izard

Emotion	Adjective
Interest	Curious
Joy	Glad
Surprise	Astonishment
Distress	Sadness
Disgust	Contempt
Anger	Rage
Shame	Embarrassment
Fear	Panic

Note. Based on *The Face of Emotion,* by C. E. Izard, 1971. Copyright 1971 by Appleton-Century-Crofts. Adapted with permission.

ecstasy, grief, trust, revulsion, panic, and so on. The basic emotions are thus conceptualized as emotional dimensions rather than as simple states.

These examples are meant to illustrate the old idea that some emotions are more primary or basic than others. Although there have been different conceptions of just which emotions are primary and which secondary, there has been considerable agreement on the belief that there are only a few such primaries.

In the past three decades, the concept of basic emotions has been embraced by a number of investigators. In a review of this literature, Kemper (1987) provided a table listing the primary emotions that have been proposed; Table 4.3 is based on his review.

These theorists all agree that there are a few emotions that qualify as primary emotions. The smallest number is 3, and the largest number is 11, while most proposals list 5 to 9 emotions. Also of interest is the fact that certain emotions such as *fear* and *anger* appear on every list. *Sadness* (or its synonyms *grief, distress,* or *loneliness*) appears on all but two lists. And *joy* (or near equivalents such as *love, pleasure, elation, happiness,* or *satisfaction*) appears on every list. Less commonly cited as primary emotions are *surprise, disgust, curiosity, expectancy, shame,* and *guilt.* It is important to note that the use of single words such as *joy* or *anger* as primary emotions is simply a shorthand way of representing an emotional dimension. A number of words varying in intensity can represent the same dimension (e.g., *rage* vs. *anger*).

Kemper (1987) believed that there are at least four physiologically based primary emotions: *fear, anger, sadness,* and *satisfaction.* He argued that the rationale for considering them as primary is that they can be observed (or inferred) in most animals, that they are universally found in all cultures, that they appear early in the course of human development, and that they are associated with distinct autonomic patterns of physiological changes. These are important points in that they represent an explicit justification for considering certain emotions as primary.

Similarly, Ortony and Turner (1990) listed some of the reasons that theorists give for assuming the existence of primary emotions: (a) Some emotions appear to exist in all cultures; (b) some can be identified in higher animals; (c) some have characteristic facial expressions; and (d) some seem to increase the chances of survival. These points are very similar to those made by Darwin.

RELATION OF BASIC EMOTIONS TO SECONDARY ONES

The problem remains, however, of explaining how secondary emotions are related to the primary ones. In connection with this point, Kemper (1987) suggested that the secondary emotions result from the attachment of new labels to various aspects of social interaction. Examples of secondary emotions are *hate, jealousy,* and *envy,* which are supposedly mixtures of *fear* and *anger; anxiety,* which is stated to be a mixture of *fear* and *depression;* and *vengeance,* which Kemper suggested is a mixture of *anger* and *happiness.* It is not evident how the components of the different emotions were decided.

In contrast, in 1980, I provided an empirical basis for naming mixtures of primary emotions (Plutchik, 1980). I suggested that there are at least two possible approaches to the problem of naming emotion mixtures.

1. Present a group of judges with all possible pairs of primary emotions and ask them to suggest an appropriate name for the resulting mixture.
2. Present a group of judges with a long list of emotion names taken from the English language and ask them to indicate which of the primaries are present.

TABLE 4.3. Primary Emotions Proposed in Recent Theories

Theory	Emotions
	Evolutionary
Plutchik (1962, 1980a)	fear, anger, sadness, joy, acceptance, disgust, anticipation, surprise
Scott (1980)	fear, anger, loneliness, pleasure, love, anxiety, curiosity
Epstein (1984)	fear, anger, sadness, joy, love
	Neural
Tomkins (1962, 1963)	fear, anger, enjoyment, interest, disgust, surprise, shame, contempt, distress
Izard (1972, 1977)	fear, anger, enjoyment, interest, disgust, surprise, shame/shyness, contempt, distress, guilt
Panksepp (1982)	fear, rage, panic, expectancy
	Psychoanalytic
Arieti (1970)	fear, rage, satisfaction, tension, appetite
	Autonomic
Fromme & O'Brien (1982)	fear, anger, grief/resignation, joy, elation, satisfaction, shock
	Facial expressions
Ekman (1973)	fear, anger, sadness, happiness, disgust, surprise
Osgood (1966)	fear, anger, anxiety–sorrow, joy, quiet pleasure, interest/expectancy, amazement, boredom, disgust
	Empirical classification
Shaver & Schwartz (1984)	fear, anger, sadness, happiness, love
Fehr & Russell (1985)	fear, anger, sadness, happiness, love
	Developmental
Sroufe (1979)	fear, anger, pleasure
Trevarthen (1984)	fear, anger, sadness, happiness
Malatesta & Haviland (1982)	fear, anger, sadness, joy, interest, pain
Etude (1980)	fear, anger, sadness, joy, interest, surprise, distress, shame, shyness, disgust, guilt

Note. Panic is associated with *sorrow, loneliness,* and *grief* (Panksepp, 1982, p. 410); Expectancy is understood as *joyful anticipation* (Panksepp, 1982, p. 414). From "How Many Emotions Are There? Wedding the Social and the Autonomic Components," by T. D. Kemper, 1987, *American Journal of Sociology, 93,* p. 269. Copyright by the American Sociological Society. Reprinted with permission.

It was discovered that the first procedure listed above—that is, the introspective synthesis of primary emotions—is a difficult task that produces more variability than the method of analysis. Because of this, I had relied more heavily on the second procedure. In this connection, a group of judges were asked to examine a long list of emotion terms in the English language and to indicate which two or three of the eight primaries are components. In some cases, there was great consistency; in others, less. Table 4.4 indicates some of those mixed emotions on which there was good agreement.

TABLE 4.4. Judges' Attributions of Words Appropriate to the Description of Mixed Emotions

Primary emotion components		Labels for mixed emotions
Joy + Acceptance	=	Love, friendliness
Fear + Surprise	=	Alarm, awe
Sadness + Disgust	=	Remorse
Disgust + Anger	=	Contempt, hatred, hostility
Joy + Fear	=	Guilt
Anger + Joy	=	Pride
Fear + Disgust	=	Shame, prudishness
Anticipation + Fear	=	Anxiety, caution

Note. From *Emotions in the Practice of Psychotherapy*, by R. Plutchik, 2000b, p. xx. Copyright 2000 by the American Psychological Association. Reprinted with permission.

Examination of this table suggests that the judges sometimes found a single word to represent a mixture, and sometimes a group of words. However, it is evident that when a group of terms is listed they all share a common meaning; they tend to be synonyms (e.g., *contempt, hatred,* and *hostility*; or *anxiety* and *caution*).

The problem of establishing names for emotion mixtures is not easily solved. Interestingly enough, it is somewhat like the problem of naming colors. In 1955 the National Bureau of Standards published a *Dictionary of Color Names* and a standard method for designating colors. In the preface, the authors stated,

> Ever since the language of man began to develop, words or expressions have been used first to indicate and then to describe colors. Some of these have persisted throughout the centuries and are those which refer to the simple colors or ranges such as red or yellow. As the language developed, more and more color names were invented to describe the colors used by art and industry and in later years in the rapidly expanding field of sales promotion. Some of these refer to the pigment or dye used, or a geographical location of its source. Later when it became clear that most colors are bought by or for women, many color names indicative of the beauties and wiles of the fair sex were introduced, such as French Nude, Heart's Desire, Intimate Mood, or Vamp....The dictionary will serve not only as a record of the meaning of the 7,500 individual color names listed but it will also enable anyone to translate from one color vocabulary to another. (Kelly & Judd, 1955, p. 5)

The development of an appropriate and standard color language is called *colorimetry,* and its presence enables people working in a number of fields such as color television, paint and dye development, advertising, mineralogy, and physics to speak a common language. Perhaps the same thing can be done for emotions.

Another analogue to this problem of naming emotion mixtures may be seen in the periodic table of the elements used in physics and chemistry. In the periodic table, there is a limited number of basic elements whose combinations result in the millions of compounds seen in nature. The basic elements can be grouped into a few major classes. Within each major class are a number of related families (e.g., the rare gases, the alkali metals, the halogens). It is not always easy to name all compounds or mixtures; even in the periodic table gaps were discovered, although subsequent research was able to identify the substance on the basis of its familial properties. In relation to emotion, it is possible that the English language may not contain emotion words for certain combinations, although other languages might. Certain combinations may not occur at all in human experience, just as chemical compounds can be formed only in certain limited ways. It is thus evident that the naming of emotions and their mixtures is not a simple task. The widespread existence of emotional blends with subtle variations in the degree of each component is probably one of the major reasons for the inconsistencies in the naming and identification of emotions in the general vocabulary.

A DICTIONARY OF EMOTIONS?

Given the problems that have been described above, is it possible to prepare a definitive list of emotion words in the English (or any other) language? As already noted, various attempts have been made in the past to prepare this type of list, although agreement on the contents of the list is limited.

Little agreement exists on how long these lists should be. Kemper (1987) believed that the number of possible emotions is limitless because society distinguishes new social situations, labels them, and socializes individuals to recognize them. Another possible reason for the lack of a defined number of emotion terms is that words take on different meanings over time or in different situations in terms of the connotations people attach to them. For example, is *aggressive* an emotion, a motivation, or a personality trait? Is it good or bad? Does it represent forceful energy and initiative, offensive action, or self-confidence in expression of opinion? Depending on what choices one makes, the term may or may not appear on a list of emotion words. There is also the question of whether different intensities of the same emotion dimension (such as *sadness* and *grief*) should be counted as two emotions or one. Fortunately, research on emotion is not hampered by the lack of a final answer to these questions.

HOW ARE EMOTIONS RELATED TO ONE ANOTHER?

Although a sizable literature exists that is concerned with the identification of basic emotions and with clusters of emotion, there has been relatively less interest in the question of how the basic emotions (or emotion clusters) are related to one another. Assuming that there is a small number of basic emotions, it is reasonable to ask how they may be related.

One approach to dealing with this question is to recognize some important general characteristics of emotions; for example, that emotions vary in intensity and in similarity and that they show polarities. Most people who have studied emotions have recognized that the language of emotions has an implicit intensity dimension. For most words in the emotion lexicon, it is usually possible to find another word that suggests either a more intense or a weaker version of that emotion. For example, more intense versions of anger would be *rage* and *fury*, whereas less intense forms of anger would be described by such terms as *annoyance* and *irritation*. Similarly, we might recognize the intensity differences of the terms *pensiveness*, *sadness*, and *grief*. The implication of these examples is that most (perhaps all) emotions exist at points along implicit intensity dimensions.

A second point is that emotions vary in how similar they are to one another. This is clearly evident in the case of synonyms such as *fear* and *fright* (which may simply reflect close points along the intensity dimension), but it is also true for the major dimensions themselves. The dimension of anger, for example, is more similar to the dimension of disgust (dislike, loathing) than it is to the dimension of joy (cheerfulness, elation). It is, in fact, possible to systematically study the degree of similarity of the various emotion dimensions, or primary emotions, as is shown shortly.

There is a third important characteristic that is part of our experience of emotions, and that is their bipolar nature. In our everyday experience, we tend to think about emotions in terms of opposites; we talk about *happiness* and *sadness, love* and *hate, fear* and *anger*. William James once pointed out that we can use self-control to influence our own emotional tendencies by practicing opposite emotions: We can deal with our own feelings of hate by trying to love our enemies. Thus, we may conclude that the language of emotions implies at least three characteristics of emotions: (a) They vary in intensity, (b) they vary in degree of similarity to one another, and (c) they express opposite or bipolar feelings or actions.

Use of the Semantic Differential in the Study of Emotions

Several attempts have been made to study these characteristics in a systematic way. One of the earliest of these studies was carried out by Block in 1957. He was interested in determining some of the connotative meanings of emotions in contrast to the dictionary or denotative meanings. *Connotative meanings* refer to the ideas and images that people associate with a word but that do not necessarily define it. Thus, for example, most people tend to associate the color red with anger and the color blue with sadness. Similarly, the expression "gave me the chills" tends to be associated with fear, and the expression "made my skin crawl" suggests disgust or horror.

This approach to understanding a word by finding out what connotations it has is called the *semantic differential* and was developed by Osgood and his associates in the mid-1950s (Osgood, Suci, & Tannenbaum, 1957). When Block adapted this method, he asked a group of male college students and a group of female college students to describe a series of 15 emotions using 20 semantic differential scales applied to each emotion. The scales were 7-point bipolar scales defined at each end by such terms as *good–bad, high–low, active–passive, and tense–relaxed*. The mean rating for each emotion was obtained on each scale to produce a kind of verbal profile for each emotion. Correlations were then computed between each pair of profiles to produce a matrix of all possible pairs of correlations. These correlations were then subjected to a factor analysis. It was possible to plot the data on a two-dimensional graph.

Although the emotion terms were not picked in any systematic way, they fell into a circular order. The circle indicates the relative similarity of the emotions as reflected by their connotative meanings. At the same time they reveal certain polarities: for example, *elation* versus *grief, contentment* versus *worry*, and *sympathy* versus *envy*. It is worth noting that the results obtained from the male and female students were almost identical, and similar results were obtained from a group of Norwegian students.

Studies of the Emotion Circle or Circumplex

In an effort to further study this apparent circular ordering of emotion concepts in terms of similarity, I used an alternative method (Plutchik, 1980). The basic procedure was as follows. Three emotion words were chosen as reference words. The words—*accepting, angry,* and *sad*—were selected because they seemed to be quite different and were clearly not synonyms of each other. Any other diverse set of three such terms could just as well have been used. This point has been demonstrated by Conte and Plutchik (1981) in her analysis of the relative similarity of personality traits. The judges were then asked to rate the relative similarity of 146 emotion words to each of the three reference words. These emotion words were consistently selected by judges as being emotions. The ratings were made on 11-point bipolar scale ranging from *opposite* (−5) to *the same* (+5).

The mean similarity ratings were converted to angular locations on a circle by procedures described more fully in Conte and Plutchik (1981). On the basis of this method, angular placements were obtained for every emotion in the list. This information is presented in Table 4.5 and a sample of the terms is presented in Figure 4.1.

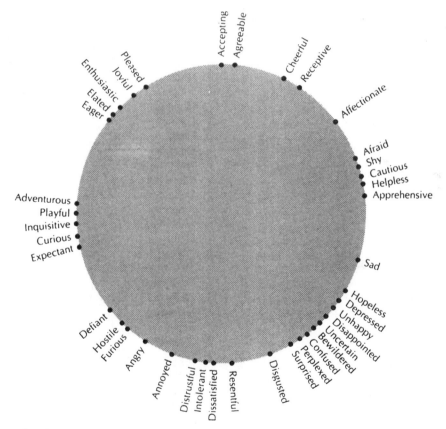

FIGURE 4.1. Angular locations on a circumplex of a sample of emotions based on similarity judgments. From *Emotion: A Psychoevolutionary Synthesis,* by R. Plutchik, 1980, p. 170. Copyright 1980 by Harper & Row. Reprinted with permission.

TABLE 4.5. Angular Placements on a Circumplex for a Population of Emotion Terms

Accepting	0.0	Rejected	136.0	Impatient	230.3
Agreeable	5.0	Bored	136.0	Grouchy	230.0
Serene	12.3	Disappointed	136.7	Defiant	230.7
Cheerful	25.7	Vacillating	137.3	Aggressive	232.0
Receptive	32.3	Discouraged	138.0	Sarcastic	235.3
Calm	37.0	Puzzled	138.3	Rebellious	237.0
Patient	39.7	Uncertain	139.3	Exasperated	239.7
Obliging	43.3	Bewildered	140.3	Disobedient	242.7
Affectionate	52.3	Confused	141.3	Demanding	244.0
Obedient	57.7	Perplexed	142.3	Possessive	247.7
Timid	65.0	Ambivalent	144.7	Greedy	249.0
Scared	66.7	Surprised	146.7	Wandering	249.7
Panicky	67.7	Astonished	148.0	Impulsive	255.0
Afraid	70.3	Amazed	152.0	Anticipatory	257.0
Shy	72.0	Awed	156.7	Boastful	257.3
Submissive	73.0	Envious	160.3	Expectant	257.3
Bashful	74.7	Disgusted	161.3	Daring	260.1
Embarrassed	75.3	Unsympathetic	165.6	Curious	261.0
Terrified	75.7	Unreceptive	170.0	Reckless	261.0
Pensive	76.7	Indignant	175.0	Proud	262.0
Cautious	77.7	Disagreeable	176.4	Inquisitive	267.7
Anxious	78.3	Resentful	176.7	Planful	269.7
Helpless	80.0	Revolted	181.3	Adventurous	270.7
Apprehensive	83.3	Displeased	181.5	Ecstatic	286.0
Self-conscious	83.3	Suspicious	182.7	Social	296.7
Ashamed	83.3	Dissatisfied	183.0	Hopeful	298.0
Humiliated	84.0	Contrary	184.3	Gleeful	307.0
Forlorn	85.0	Jealous	184.7	Elated	311.0
Nervous	86.0	Intolerant	185.0	Eager	311.0
Lonely	88.3	Distrustful	185.0	Enthusiastic	313.7
Apathetic	90.0	Vengeful	186.0	Interested	315.7
Meek	91.0	Bitter	186.0	Delighted	318.6
Guilty	102.3	Unfriendly	188.0	Amused	321.0
Sad	108.5	Stubborn	190.4	Attentive	322.4
Sorrowful	112.7	Uncooperative	191.7	Joyful	323.4
Empty	120.3	Contemptuous	192.0	Happy	323.7
Remorseful	123.3	Loathful	193.0	Self-controlled	326.3
Hopeless	124.7	Critical	193.7	Satisfied	326.7
Depressed	125.3	Annoyed	200.6	Pleased	328.0
Worried	126.0	Irritated	202.3	Generous	328.0
Disinterested	127.3	Angry	212.0	Ready	329.3
Grief-stricken	127.3	Antagonistic	220.0	Sympathetic	331.3
Unhappy	129.0	Furious	221.3	Content	338.3
Gloomy	132.7	Hostile	222.0	Cooperative	340.7
Despairing	133.0	Outraged	225.3	Trusting	345.3
Watchful	133.3	Scornful	227.0	Tolerant	350.7
Hesitant	134.0	Unaffectionate	227.3		
Indecisive	134.0	Quarrelsome	229.7		

Note. From *Emotion: A Psychoevolutionary Synthesis*, by R. Plutchik, 1980, p. 170. Copyright 1980 by Harper & Row. Reprinted with permission.

The first thing to notice about Table 4.5 is that the emotion terms are distributed around the entire circle and there are no gaps. There is nothing about the method for locating the angular placements that would guarantee such a result, and this finding is not, therefore, an artifact of the method.

Additional support for this point is the fact that many terms that are linguistically opposite are found at opposite parts of the circle. For example, the terms *interested* and *disinterested* are almost 180° apart. This is also true for *affectionate* and *unaffectionate* and for *obedient* and *disobedient*. Other examples are *accepting* versus *resentful*, *agreeable* versus *displeased*, and *tolerant* versus *revolted*. Emotions such as *joyful*, *happy*, and *enthusiastic* are opposite the emotions of *gloomy*, *unhappy*, and *grief stricken*.

A second important observation revealed by Table 4.5 and Figure 4.1 is the particular sequence of terms. It is evident that emotions with similar meanings tend to cluster. For example, the terms *lonely, apathetic, meek, guilty, sad, sorrowful, empty, remorseful, hopeless,* and *depressed* are located in consecutive positions covering a range of 88.3° to 125.3°. Similar clusters are found for the fear dimension, the anger dimension, and for other basic dimensions.

A third interesting implication of this empirical emotion circle or circumplex is its possibility for helping to define the sometimes ambiguous language of emotions. For example, the term *worried* is often thought of in the context of fear. However, it was empirically located in the cluster of *depression* words. Similarly, *scornful,* which has a definite element of *rejection* or *disgust* in it, was found to be located in the cluster of *anger* words. This suggests that dictionary definitions may not always correspond to the way people actually use emotion terms. This has also been reported by Heider (1991) in his cross-cultural study of emotion words.

To determine the validity of this emotion circle, I used an independent method to locate the positions of various emotions on the circle. This alternative method involved a factor analysis of semantic differential ratings as described in connection with the study by Block (1957). In this validation, a subset of 40 emotions was selected, and five judges rated the connotative meanings of each term on 20 seven-point semantic differential scales.

The correlations between emotions were factor analyzed, and the data were plotted on a graph. The placements of emotion words were found to form a circular ordering, and the angular position of each of these 40 emotion words could then be obtained. These angular placements were then compared with the angular placements obtained with the first method of direct similarity scaling. The product moment correlation was found to be .90, indicating that the two sets of orderings on the circle were almost identical. This outcome strongly supports the validity of a circular similarity structure for the emotions chosen for the analysis.

Another attempt to establish the validity of this circumplex was reported by G. A. Fisher (1997). Students were asked to rate their moods on 33 emotion words shortly after waking up and shortly before retiring on a 5-point scale ranging from 0 (*does not describe my mood*) to 4 (*definitely describes my mood*). Data were obtained for a 2-week period from each of 141 students.

The data were subjected to statistical analyses that minimize such sources of measurement era as social desirability response bias and were then factor analyzed. Because 17 emotion terms were the same as those used by me in my study, it was possible to make a direct comparison of placements of the words. Figure 4.2 shows the results of this comparison (the comparison was made using a similar circumplex reported by Conte & Plutchik, 1981). The comparison shows remarkably good agreement of approximately .91, which

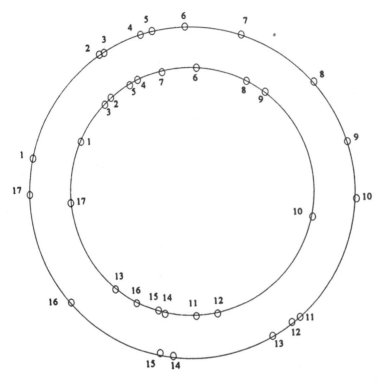

FIGURE 4.2. Plot of the Plutchik circumplex (outer circle) and the independent circumplex obtained by Fisher (inner circle). Loadings have been projected onto the circumference of the circle, and items are numbered as follows: 1 = impulsive, 2 = confident,   3 = enthusiastic,   4 = affectionate,   5 = cheerful,   6 = easygoing, 7 = agreeable, 8 = peaceful, 9 = calm, 10 = reserved, 11 = depressed, 12 = helpless, 13 = nervous, 14 = irritable, 15 = grouchy, 16 = quarrelsome, 17 = aggressive. From "Theoretical and Methodological Elaborations of the Circumplex Model of Personality Traits and Emotions," by G. A. Fisher. In R. Plutchik & H. R. Conte (Eds.), *Circumplex Models of Personality and Emotions,* 1997, p. 261. Copyright 1997 by the American Psychological Association. Reprinted with permission.

lends further support for this circular ordering of many emotion words. Russell (1989) also studied the similarity structure of emotion concepts. In his investigation, judges made similarity estimate of pairs of emotion terms. Results of these comparisons of 28 terms, including words like *sleepy* that are not generally considered to be emotion words, were then subjected to multidimensional scaling and plotted on a two-dimensional surface as shown in Figure 4.3.

The degree of similarity between two words is represented by their closeness in a two-dimensional space. The words fall in a circumplex pattern. In a circumplex, all categories are fuzzy and blend into one another without beginning or end. Terms that are close together (e.g., *calm* and *relaxed*) tend to be synonyms, whereas opposite terms on the circle tend to be antonyms (e.g., *excited* vs. *bored; annoyed* vs. *calm; sad* vs. *delighted*). Variations in the exact placement of terms in different studies is probably due to different samples of emotion terms, different methods of statistical analyses, and different samples of judges.

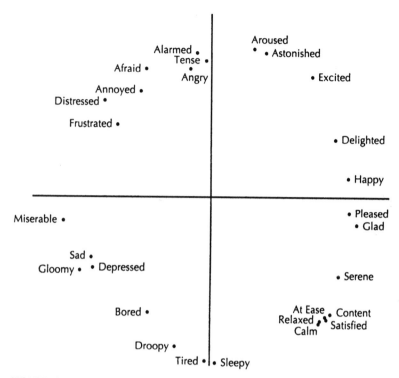

FIGURE 4.3. A circumplex for emotions based on multidimensional scaling. From "Measures of Emotion," by J. A. Russell. In R. Plutchik & H. Kellerman (Eds.), *The Measurement of Emotions*, 1989, Vol. 4, p. 83. Copyright 1989 by Academic Press. Reprinted with permission.

IS THERE A CIRCUMPLEX FOR EMOTION WORDS IN OTHER LANGUAGES?

The question arises as to whether raters who speak different languages will judge emotions in the same way as do English-speaking raters. To deal with this issue, Russell (1983) obtained similarity ratings from native speakers of Chinese, Japanese, Croatian, and Gujarati. Russell used the same 28 emotion terms with a different scaling method and found circumplex orderings in all cases but with some differences in the exact placement of each term. The results for the Japanese sample is presented in Figure 4.4. With a few exceptions, most of the emotion words fall at fairly similar locations on the circumplex figures produced by the different language speakers.

In a study of emotion words among the Cheke Holo people of the Solomon Islands in the Pacific, White (2000) asked five people to list all the words they could think of that referred to feelings. The result was a list of 15 words. Other adult men then sorted the words into groupings according to similarity of meaning. The similarity data were analyzed using multidimensional scaling with results as seen in Figure 4.5.

Although only 15 words were used in this research, the similarity structure closely approximates a circumplex. The English words shown in Figure 4.5 are only approximate terms, but *happy* terms appeared to be opposite *shame* and *sadness* words, *angry* words are opposite *afraid* and *worry* words, and *angry* and *disgusted* are relatively similar to one

JAPANESE

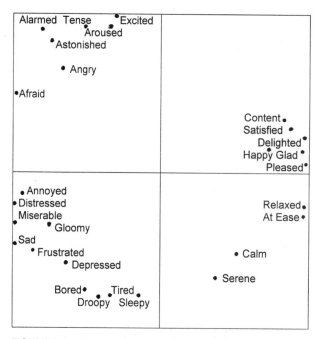

FIGURE 4.4. Circumplex model of emotion concepts based on Japanese. From "Two Pan-Cultural Dimensions of Emotion Words," by J. A. Russell, 1983, *Journal of Personality and Social Psychology, 45,* p. 1285. Copyright 1983 by the American Psychological Association. Reprinted with permission.

another. This patterning is similar to some of the findings regarding the English language already reported.

In another series of investigations based on the work of Dario Galati, an Italian psychologist, and his colleagues, emotion terms from Italian, French, and Spanish dictionaries were selected. The terms had to refer to mental states that were transitory and had recognizable behavioral expressions. This procedure resulted in 84 terms to be used in the Italian study, 108 terms for the study of French, and 86 terms for the study of Spanish emotion words. Thirty judges then made similarity estimates comparing each term with every other term. The results were analyzed by means of multidimensional scaling with results for Italian and French words as shown in Figures 4.6 and 4.7.

The similarity structure for each of these sets of emotion terms approximates a circumplex (Galati & Sini, 1998a, 1998b). Figure 4.8 shows a circumplex for emotion words in the Finnish language based on a factor analysis of 72 terms. The results showing translated English words are generally consistent with those found in other languages. A detailed discussion of many applications of the circumplex concept to emotion, personality, and clinical issues may be found in Plutchik and Conte (1997).

In an extensive research study carried out over a period of many years, anthropologist Karl Heider (1991) collected data on the emotion language of three cultures from Indonesia, Minangkabau, and Java. Indonesian is the national language of Indonesia, whereas Minangkabau and Javanese are regional languages that are spoken by different ethnic groups within the country. The basic aim of the research was to construct

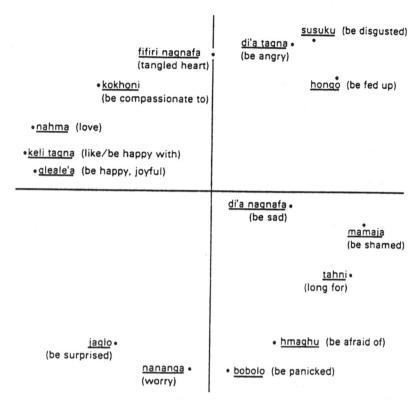

FIGURE 4.5. Two-dimensional scaling of 15 Cheke Holo/A'ara (Solomon Islands) emotion words. From "Representing Emotional Meaning: Category, Metaphor, Schema, Discount," by G. M. White. In M. Lewis & J. M. Haviland-Jones (Eds.), *Handbook of Emotions*, 2000, 2nd ed., p. 35. Copyright 2000 by Guilford Press. Reprinted with permission.

cognitive maps showing the lexical relations among the emotion vocabularies of these three cultures.

On the basis of extensive interviews with informants in these cultures and the use of dictionaries and ethnographic stories of the antecedents and outcomes of emotions, Heider (1991) compiled a list of 229 words that his various informants believed to be emotion words. He then asked 50 respondents in each language to indicate whether each word was "certainly," "sometimes," or "certainly not" an emotion word.

For some words such as *love* (i.e., its equivalent in the languages being studied) and *longing*, there was 100% agreement among the informants that it was an emotion word. Words such as *hate* and *glad* had 85% agreement, whereas words such as *dirty, scorn, cruel,* and *exhausted* had less than 10% agreement. These percentage agreement figures provided the basis for a graphical description of the conceptual closeness of emotion words through the use of a two-dimensional map. Figure 4.9 (top) shows words related to *fear* and that are considered to define the fear cluster.

Words related to fear are the equivalent Javanese words for *terrified, quivering, horrible, sour,* or *sullen.* The lengths of the lines are a rough approximation of the closeness of meaning of the other words to the key word. Figure 4.9 (bottom) shows a cluster map for

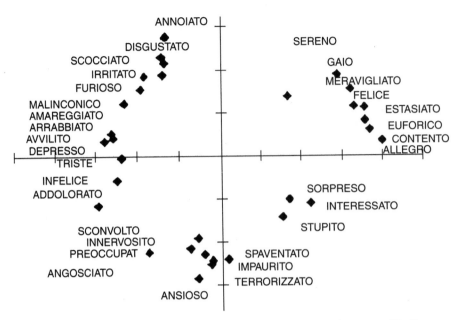

FIGURE 4.6. Multidimensional scaling of 32 terms from the lexicon of Italian emotion terms. From "Les Mots Pour Dire les Emotions: Recherche sur la Structure du Lexique Emotional Italien," [Words for describing the emotions: Research on the structure of the Italian emotional lexicon] by D. Galati and B. Sini, 1998b, *Revue de Semantique et Pragmatique, 4*, p. 151. Copyright 1998 by D. Galati. Reprinted with permission.

the word *jealousy*. Here the related words in Javanese are *depraved, bad, angry, suspicious,* and *prejudiced.*

Heider (1991) constructed 44 clusters from the total emotional vocabulary of these three cultures. Some of these clusters were labeled as *surprise, happy, desire (interest or liking), love, offended, longing, gloomy, fear, jealous, indecision, confused, anger, annoyance, revenge, depressed, shame,* and *arrogant.* Some terms in the list are not what would be considered to be emotions in the West, for example, *consciousness, mocking, lazy, respectful, dirty,* or *poignant.*

Heider (1991) drew the following conclusions from his study

1. It is a mistake to assume that one word in any language is equal to one emotion in that or any other language.
2. Emotions are fuzzy states that cannot be defined by any one set of criteria.
3. The display rules of a given culture determine whether the inner state of the emotion is altered in its public performance through intensification, diminution, neutralization, or masking by another emotion.
4. The words used for emotions are significant data but they are not necessarily the only or the best way to get information about emotions.
5. The influence of cultural norms may result in quite different behavioral reactions to the same basic situation.

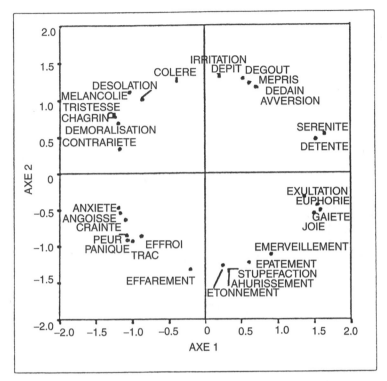

FIGURE 4.7. Multidimensional scaling of 32 terms from the lexicon of French emotion terms. From "Echelonnement Multidimensionnel de Termes du Lexique Francais des Emotions: Une Comparison Entre Trois Procedes d'Analyse" [Multidimensional grouping of terms in the French lexicon of emotions: A comparison of three procedures of analysis] by D. Galati and B. Sini, 1998a, *Les Cahiers Internationaux de Psychologie Sociale, 37,* p. 87. Copyright 1998 by D. Galati. Published by Les Cahiers Internationaux de Psychologie Sociale. Reprinted with permission.

6. What is in English understood as the domain of emotion concepts, and what is understood by specific English emotion words, have general correspondences in other languages and cultures.

7. No word in one language is completely equivalent to a word in another.

8. There are no objective criteria that enables us to map all emotion words with precision.

Other writers who have considered emotions in a cross-cultural context have presented related ideas. For example, Leff (1977) pointed out that Americans with less formal education tend to express emotional distress in somatic terms (1977). This is also true when dealing with people of different cultures. In some African groups (Yoruba, a Nigerian language), it was difficult to find words for *depression* and *anxiety.* The words chosen for use in a research study, when translated back into English, came out as "the heart is weak" (for depression) and "the heart is not at rest" (for anxiety). One problem that is believed to occur because of this linguistic problem is that in rural communities in developing countries there are individuals with severe depression who are untreated.

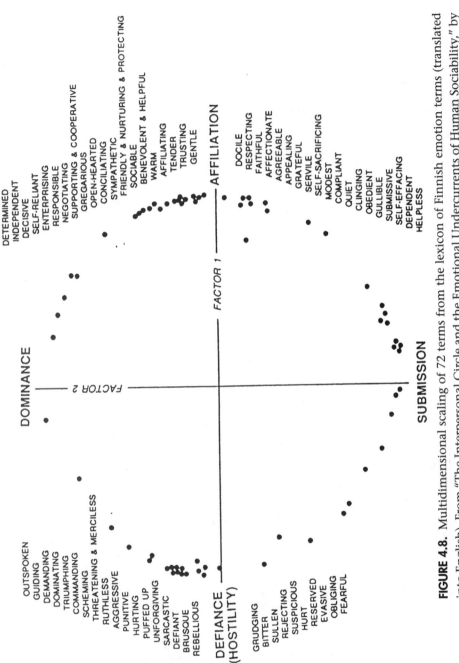

FIGURE 4.8. Multidimensional scaling of 72 terms from the lexicon of Finnish emotion terms (translated into English). From "The Interpersonal Circle and the Emotional Undercurrents of Human Sociability," by R. Myllyniemi. In R. Plutchik & H. R. Conte (Eds.), *Circumplex Models of Personality and Emotions*, 1997, p. 283. Copyright 1997 by the American Psychological Association. Reprinted with permission.

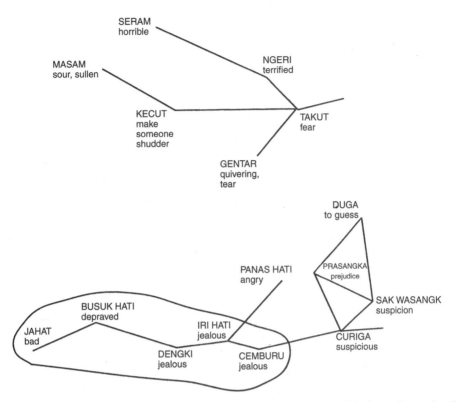

FIGURE 4.9. Cognitive maps in Javanese for the words *fear* and *jealousy*. From *Landscapes of Emotion: Mapping Three Cultures of Emotion in Indonesia,* by K. G. Heider, 1991, pp. 204, 216. Copyright 1991 by Cambridge University Press. Reprinted with permission.

The use of a somatic language to express emotions is not limited to rural communities or to people with limited education. It is quite common for such somatic metaphors to be used in ordinary conversations. Here is an example created by Leff (1977, p. 323):

My heart was in my mouth as I strode up the driveway. Although I hated his guts, my stomach turned over as I approached his house. I knocked on the door and my heart leapt as I heard his footsteps inside. Shivers went down my back as he fumbled with the catch, then as he flung open the door my skin crawled at the sight of him.

"I speak from the heart when I say I can't stomach you", I blurted out. He laughed sneeringly, and I felt my gorge rise.

"You're a pain in the neck", he growled. His retort stuck in my throat.

"I am here because of the woman whose heart you have broken" I asserted, and the thought of Amanda brought a lump to my throat. He turned his back on me so suddenly that I almost jumped out of my skin. My brain reeled as I reached for my...

Careful examination of an emotion word and its antecedent conditions for use may sometimes help us understand an apparently inexplicable emotional state. As example of this is the word *koro*, a condition that affects males in Hong Kong and South East Asia.

It is a condition affecting males in Hong Kong and South East Asia. They develop a fear that their penis is going to invaginate into their abdomen and that if this is allowed to happen they will die. So compelling is this fear that sufferers have been known to persuade relatives to hold on to their penis in relays, or even to secure it with a length of wire to a rock. This fear and the behavior consequent on it appear quite extraordinary to the Western psychiatrist unfamiliar with local beliefs. However, once this phenomenon is viewed in the context of the belief, widespread in that part of the world, that ghosts have no penis, the fear loses its inexplicable quality. It can then be seen as equivalent to hypochondriacal anxiety states in the West, which are characterized by an irrational fear of dying from some disease such as cancer or a heart attack. (Leff, 1977, p. 336)

Cross-cultural research is complex and difficult, and differences will be found in the presence and use of emotion words in different languages. This fact does not necessarily mean that we need a different theory of emotions for each language. What research needs to discover are the historical experiences, environmental events, and cultural norms that influence the specific ways in which the same emotions are expressed.

LATENT SEMANTIC ANALYSIS THEORY

The various observations that have been made in this chapter about the ambiguity and fuzziness of the emotion language may be considered in the light of recent theoretical developments in the theory of meaning, what has been called *latent semantic analysis theory* (Landauer, 1998). This approach does not group words on the basis of features that they have in common. Instead it judges similarity of words in terms of how often words occur near each other in the course of temporal, perceptual experiences. Such experiences are called *contiguity relations*.

This method is somewhat similar to the way that maps of the earth were created. Map makers started with rough estimates of distances from one defined location to another and gradually combined all the observations into a map that preserved the measurements as well as possible. Once these measurements were combined into a map (or space), it enabled the viewers of the map to estimate distances from any point of the map to all other points on the map, including those that had never been measured before. Of course, it was discovered that a map placed on the surface of a globe produced more accurate estimates than one placed on a flat surface.

The latent semantic analysis theory obtains initial estimates of the closeness of two words by finding out how often they occur in the same sentences and paragraphs relative to how often they occur together in different paragraphs. This information provides a correlation index for each pair of words, which is the statistical basis for locating all words in a semantic space. This "map" reflects the meaning of each word relative to all others.

This model suggests that emotion words, like all others, are part of a complex semantic space in which the meaning of any one term is partly dependent on the context, that is, the location of all other nearby terms on the map. Further research using this theory may help us understand more fully the nature of the similarity structure of the emotion language.

SUMMARY

When college students are asked to identify emotion terms from various lists of words, there is good agreement on some words and poor agreement on others. It is likely that the reasons for the discrepancies include the ambiguity of some of the terms, the fact that many college students are not familiar with the terms, and the different experiences of the judges with language in general and emotions in particular. These findings suggest that the identification and meaning of emotion concepts should not depend entirely on naive judgments but should, as in other sciences, depend on their place within a theory.

An alternative approach to identifying the language of emotions, having a long history, is to assume the existence of a small number of basic or primary emotions, somewhat like the primary colors. Almost all theorists who have written on this subject agree that *anger, fear, joy,* and *sadness* should be considered to be basic emotions, and fair agreement exists on such emotions as *disgust (contempt), surprise,* and perhaps *shame.* The assumption of primary emotions implies the existence of secondary ones, or mixed emotions or blends, in order to explain the large number of emotion terms that exist in our language. However, identifying the components of the blends is not an easy task, and more work needs to be done on this problem.

If one accepts the concept of primary emotions, the question arises of their relations to each other. Over the years, a number of studies have been published that indicate that the relative similarity of the primary and other emotions can best be represented by means of a circle or circumplex. The emotion circumplex implies that certain emotions are relatively alike and others are quite dissimilar and that certain emotions are bipolar. The emotions can perhaps be thought of as fuzzy concepts separated by vague rather than sharp boundaries. Despite the lack of sharp boundaries, the prototypes underlying the basic emotions, at least, are well known. It may be concluded that subjective experience is a useful guide to emotions but not an infallible one.

5 Theories of Emotions

Let every student of nature take this as a rule—that whatever his mind seizes and dwells upon with peculiar satisfaction is to be held in suspicion.

Francis Bacon

For every complex problem there is an easy answer, and it is wrong.

H. L. Mencken

PREVIEW

This chapter reviews a number of different theories of emotion that have been proposed in recent years. They reflect the different historical traditions that have been described in chapter 2. These include the theories of Tomkins, Izard, Lazarus, Buck, and Frijda that are concerned mostly with the psychological or communicative aspects of emotion. Clinical theories of affect based largely on psychoanalytical theory are represented by the recent works of Spezzano and Jones. Evolutionarily-based theories are exemplified by the writings of Plutchik, Nesse and Cosmides, and Tooby. Theories of emotion differ partly because they are concerned with different issues; for example, the development of mind, the role of facial expressions, or the functional significance of emotions. In addition, some are concerned with questions that can be studied in the laboratory or through surveys, whereas others reflect clinical experience and clinical applications. Theories also vary in how broad or narrow they are. Some theories appear to be primarily relevant to human adults, whereas others can be seen to apply to children, infants, and animals. Overall there seems to be a trend toward conceptualizing emotions within an evolutionary framework.

IN A BOOK published in 1980, I described 24 theories of emotion that had been proposed in the preceding few decades. In 1987, Strongman briefly described 30 theories of emotion. In most cases, the theories focused on one or two or a few issues, such as how to define the word *emotion,* the role of cognitions in emotion, the nature of the physiological changes that occur in emotion and their relations to verbal reports, functions of emotions, the role of emotions in clinical or psychotherapeutic work, the expressive aspects of emotion (particularly facial expressions), or the role of brain structure and biochemistry in influencing emotion.

Since these theories were published, a great deal of research on these and other aspects of emotion has been carried out and published, and the situation is now changed. There appears to be strong interest in collecting empirical data of all sorts and less concern with presenting broad theories. Theoretical papers now focus on narrow issues such as the development of emotion concepts in children, the generality of facial expressions in different cultures, the relations between mood states and environmental and personality variables, and attachment as a mediating factor in emotional development.

Examination of recent publications reveals that certain ideas that were controversial 20 years ago are now taken for granted by most investigators in the field. This includes the ideas that emotions are about significant events in the life of an individual, that emotions are generally adaptive in an evolutionary sense, that emotions regulate social interactions, and that there are a number of specific emotional circuits in the brain that organize the expression of emotions. Investigators differ on some of the details (e.g., what are the specific functions of individual emotions), but that is as it should be; future research will presumably resolve the differences.

It is also important to emphasize that the contributions to our understanding of emotions come from many sources. Some represent laboratory studies in which the participants' emotions are manipulated by means of deceptions of various kinds (e.g., the Schachter–Singer [1962] study of the effects of epinephrine on judgment of feelings). Many studies are simply descriptions of people's feelings in different situations (e.g., moods at different times of the day). Other studies depend on ratings of or interviews with children and their parents at different ages and settings (e.g., tracing the development of the emotion language). Many investigations are now concerned with identifying parts of the brain that are activated during emotional experiences (using magnetic resonance imaging or positron emission tomography scans). Many investigations have now been carried out by anthropologists who have been especially interested in the diversity of language terms that exist in different cultures and the problems of translation. Sociologists have contributed their insights into emotion, particularly through their concerns with status and power as determinants of affect states. Ethologists continue to study the behavior of animals in natural settings (e.g., field studies of chimpanzees, gorillas, and baboons). Last but not least are the concerns of clinicians, both psychologists and psychiatrists, with problems of emotional disorders and how psychotherapy can recognize and use emotions to effect change. It is thus evident that insights about emotions may be obtained in many ways and with the contributions of different disciplines.

In this chapter, I do not attempt an exhaustive review of different theories but focus on a few general approaches that currently influence the thinking of investigators. The first section deals with some current theories of emotion that have largely emerged from academic settings. The second section deals with clinically based theories of emotion and the third section examines several evolutionary based theories. Other, narrower, theories are discussed in various other chapters; for example, theories of the role of facial expressions, theories of emotional development and attachment, and theories related to brain function in emotion.

PSYCHOPHYSIOLOGICAL AND MOTIVATIONAL THEORIES OF EMOTION

In the 30-year period between 1930 and 1960, the period during which Behaviorism was the dominant philosophy in psychology, there were relatively few books and articles on emotion. However, in 1962 two books were published independently that focused attention directly on emotions and that influenced the thinking of psychologists and others up to the present time. One of these books was written by Sylvan Tomkins, *Affect Imagery Consciousness*. It was followed over the next 30 years by a series of books and articles that elaborated his views (Tomkins, 1963, 1980, 1991, 1992). The other book was written by me and was titled *The Emotions: Facts, Theories and a New Model*. It was followed by three books and many articles that elaborated my views (Plutchik, 1970, 1980, 1994, 1995, 1997, 2000b). Although the contributions of Tomkins and myself were quite independent, there were a number of ideas we had in common. For example, we both assumed that there are at least eight basic emotions (Tomkins sometimes wrote that there were nine). We both made similar distinctions between motivations and emotions. However, whereas Tomkins focused attention more on autonomic physiology, facial expressions, and hypothetical brain processes, I focused attention on evolutionary considerations and on the functional significance of emotions. The following section describes Tomkins's views and is followed by other general views about emotions that have been proposed.

Sylvan S. Tomkins: Affects as Amplifiers

Tomkins (1962, 1970) assumed that there are eight basic emotions or affects. The positive ones are (a) *interest*, (b) *surprise*, and (c) *joy*. The negative ones are (d) *anguish*, (e) *fear*, (f) *shame*, (g) *disgust*, and (h) *rage*. These basic emotions are "innately patterned responses" to certain types of stimuli and are expressed through a wide variety of bodily reactions, particularly through facial responses. For each distinct affect, there are assumed to be specific "programs" stored in subcortical areas of the brain. There is therefore a genetic, species-related basis for the expression of the basic emotions.

Much of the emphasis of the theory is on the distinctions between the affect system and the motivational system. Most psychologists take for granted the idea that motives, such as hunger and sex, strongly drive a person to action. In contrast, Tomkins believed that motives are primarily signals of bodily need and that these signals are then amplified by emotions. As an illustration, he pointed out that oxygen deprivation (anoxia) creates a need for oxygen, but the sense of urgency or panic is created by the affect of fear. In World War II, pilots who neglected to wear oxygen masks at 30,000 feet experienced gradual oxygen deprivation. Although the need was present, the slow process of deprivation did not produce an awareness of the need, and no panic occurred. Without the emotion being present, no action resulted; the pilots took no counter measures and crashed their planes.

The affect system is more general than the drive system. Drives are primarily concerned with getting certain objects into or out of the body and tend to have a rhythmic pattern. Affects can become associated with almost any stimuli (through learning) and can exist for long or short periods of time. Affects are stronger than drives, according to Tomkins, because to get a person to act, all we need do is create an emotional state (e.g., *joy*, *anger*, or *shame*), regardless of the person's state of drive. A person who is frightened by a car will run, regardless of whether he or she is hungry or thirsty.

Drives motivate the individual to act in relation to very specific events: for example, lack of food leading to eating, lack of air leading to breathing, excess of urine leading to micturition, and lack of attachments leading to attachment efforts. Affects are more varied than drives because of the influence of learning, which strongly affects the specific events or situations that trigger the emotional reactions. If anxiety becomes associated with food intake or with sexual reactions, the affect may inhibit the expression of the drive. If one affect becomes associated with another affect (e.g., *anxiety* with *anger*), then the expression of the combined or fused affect will be difficult to identify or label.

Tomkins emphasized that the basic affects are not a series of single states but are part of affect families. For example, the basic emotion of *distress* or *anguish* is actually part of the affect family that includes *sorrow*, *sadness*, *grief*, *despair*, and *woe*. The basic emotion of *anger* is part of the affect family that includes *irritation, annoyance, assertion,* and *fury.* The basic emotion of *interest* is part of the affect family that includes *curiosity, enthusiasm,* and *attraction.*

Each basic affect, Tomkins believed, has a characteristic expressive pattern, one that is most clearly shown through facial expressions. Tomkins's ideas have stimulated Izard (1990) and others such as Ekman (1992) to look for cross-cultural evidence of the universality of the facial expressions of the basic affects. This question is examined in a later chapter. Although Tomkins dealt with clinical issues only peripherally, Vaillant (1997) described a number of clinical implications of his views.

It is worth noting that Tomkins was not a laboratory scientist and did not carry out much research on emotions in relation to his theory. His work is largely theoretical, but it has influenced the thinking of many research scientists.

Carroll E. Izard: Differential Emotions Theory

One of Tomkins's close collaborators has been Carroll Izard. In recent years, Izard has extended the theory first proposed by Tomkins, particularly in relation to the role of facial expressions in emotions.

Izard argued that too much attention has been directed by theorists to feedback from the autonomic nervous system as a major determinant of emotion. Instead, he proposed that affects are primarily facial responses. Patterns of facial reaction that we call emotional are assumed to have a neurological basis in subcortical "programs" for each emotion. Such programs are genetically based. He pointed out that people do not learn to be afraid, or to cry, or to startle, any more than they learn to feel pain. However, it is true that people learn to fear specific things, or to be angry when humiliated. Similarly, the idea of learned anxiety or learned depression is misleading. People do not learn to feel afraid or depressed: They only learn the cues that trigger reactions of anxiety or depression (Izard, 1972).

Following Tomkins, Izard stated that there are several fundamental emotions from which all others can be combined. Sometimes he listed 8 fundamental emotions, and sometimes 10. His longer list included *interest, joy, surprise, distress, anger, disgust, contempt, shame, guilt,* and *fear.* Although many investigators may have assumed that they have studied one or another of these emotions in isolation, Izard argued that this is unlikely. Discrete fundamental emotions rarely occur in isolation in the life of an individual.

To illustrate his ideas about the mixing or patterning of emotions, Izard examined the concept of anxiety. In 1966 he and Tomkins described *anxiety* as a disruptive affect that should simply be identified as fear. By 1972, Izard concluded that anxiety was a multidimensional concept that included the emotions of fear and two or more of the following emotions: *distress, anger, shame, guilt,* and *interest* (Izard, 1972). In addition, he claimed that *love, hostility,* and *depression* were also complex emotions.

Izard suggested that from an evolutionary point of view, it does not seem likely that an animal had to "think" before it could "feel." In fact, to survive, an animal had to have emotional responses (such as fleeing or attacking) triggered by innate releasers, drives, or perceptions, as well as by cognitions. For example, the mating dance of the male stickleback fish will be triggered by the appearance of a certain color on the underside of the female. Izard argued that there is no cognitive process involved in this emotional reaction. Another illustration is the fact, frequently noted in clinical practice, of free-floating anxiety or objectless fear. Izard interpreted this as emotion without a cognitive signal.

Izard also had some ideas about the development of emotions in infants (Buechler & Izard, 1983). What he called basic or discrete emotions developed very early in infancy, and each one has a specific function; in general, they signal the infant's urgent needs for a caretaker. These emotional states are signaled by facial expressions, which Izard believed are tightly linked to emotional experience.

From Izard's point of view, emotions are only one part of the organization of personality. The other subsystems of personality include the homeostatic, the perceptual, the cognitive, and the motor systems. Although each system has some degree of independence, they are all complexly related.

To justify the idea of fundamental emotions, Izard (1991) listed a number of criteria. Fundamental emotions have (a) a specific neural basis, (b) a specific facial expression, (c) a distinct feeling, (d) an origin in evolutionary–biologic processes, and (e) a motivating property that serves adaptive functions.

Izard has reported experiments dealing with factors related to the matching of facial expressions and verbal labels, cross-cultural variables in emotion descriptions, and physiological indices of muscular patterns in the face, among others. He has developed a simple self-report adjective checklist that has been used with various psychiatric populations, and he has stimulated a number of his colleagues to pursue research in this area.

Richard Lazarus: Emotions, Appraisals, and Coping

Richard Lazarus has been concerned during much of his career (Lazarus & Folkman, 1984) with the relations between stress and coping in adults. This research gradually led him to realize that stress and coping are part of a larger area of study of the emotions. In 1991, he published a book, *Emotion and Adaptation,* that described his beliefs about the relations among all these domains.

He pointed out that the study of emotion must include the study of cognition, motivation, adaptation, and physiological activity. Emotions involve a person's appraisals of the environment, his or her relationships with others, and his or her attempts at coping with these relationships. Lazarus therefore referred to his theory as a "cognitive–motivational–relational system of explanation," with the focus being on the person–environment relationship.

The central idea of the theory is the concept of appraisal, which refers to a decision-making process that evaluates the personal harms and benefits existing in each person–environment interaction. Primary appraisals concern the relevance of the interaction for one's goals, the extent to which the situation is goal congruent (i.e., thwarting or facilitating of personal goals), and the extent of one's own ego involvement (or degree of commitment). Secondary appraisals decide on blame or credit, one's own coping potential, and future expectations. This view sees emotions as discrete categories, each of which can be placed on a dimension from weak to strong. It recognizes that several emotions can occur at the same time, because of the multiple motivations and goals involved in any particular encounter. It also implies that each emotion involves a specific action tendency such as anger with attack, fear with escape, shame with hiding, and so forth.

A key ingredient of his concept of secondary appraisal is the idea of coping, which refers to ways to manage and interpret conflicts and emotions. According to Lazarus, there are two general types of coping processes. The first is called problem-focused coping, which deals with conflicts by direct action designed to change the relationship (e.g., fighting if threatened). The second is called emotion-focused (or cognitive) coping, which deals with conflicts by reinterpreting the situation (e.g., denial in the face of threat). The concept of appraisal implies nothing about rationality, deliberateness, or consciousness. One implication of these ideas is that emotion always involves cognition. As Shakespeare said, "There is nothing either good or bad but thinking makes it so."

A question sometimes raised is whether appraisal is necessary for all emotional reactions or whether emotions can occur without appraisal. Lazarus (1991) discussed this at some length and concluded that "appraisal is a necessary and sufficient cause of the emotions. Appraisals determine emotional states." (Refer also to chapter 3, on the theories of Ellis, Beck, and Roseman that emphasize the concept of appraisal.)

In a later book, Lazarus elaborated his ideas about psychopathology (Lazarus & Lazarus, 1994). He concluded that emotions result from the meanings people attribute to life events and depend fundamentally on what is important to each person. "Life and death issues—who and what we are and will be—are the main sources of human anxiety and our emotional life" (p. 5). For an emotion to occur, an individual must appraise a situation as being personally harmful or beneficial. If there is no appraisal of harm or benefit, no emotion will result.

A key hypothesis in his writings is that each emotion is like a script with a distinctive dramatic plot. For example, in the case of shame, the dramatic plot is not having lived up to one's personal ideals. In the case of jealousy, the plot is that an individual is threatened with a loss of another person's affection. The dramatic plot that generates pride is a condition that increases one's sense of importance.

With regard to therapy, Lazarus emphasized the role of cognition in reinterpreting situations so that the scripts may be changed. He suggested that people pay attention to their daily emotions and the thoughts they engage in before and during these emotions. He emphasized the role of coping behavior in dealing with stresses, frustrations, and subjective discomforts, and he believed that people should try to spend less energy protecting their self-image and justifying their behavior.

Lazarus (1991b) summarized his views in the following ways. He believed that emotions in humans can be interpreted as dramatic stories that begin with a provoking stimulus or situation. The meaning of this situation is interpreted by an individual in terms of his or her background (e.g., intelligence, social skills, coping styles, and ways of thinking). The combination of stimulus and background leads to particular appraisals. Such appraisals generally change as actions and reactions provide feedback to both participants, and the appraisals lead to a flow of emotions in both. As the meaning of the relationship changes, so do the emotions.

Lazarus (1991b) also pointed out what he considered to be a common theoretical–research mistake that is made. This is the tendency to make a sharp distinction between positive and negative emotions. He noted that each emotion including those that are often called *negative* such as *anger* and *anxiety* has its own distinctive dramatic story or narrative, and each reveals different information about a person's attempt to cope with a problem. If all emotions are placed into two broad categories, this invariably ignores important information about the life situation an individual is in.

Lazarus stated that emotions often occur in mixed or interacting form. For example, a person may be happy about some pleasant event that has occurred but simultaneously feel anxious about unpleasant things that may follow (e.g., other people's envy). *Love* is considered a positive emotion, yet if unrequited, may be fused with *disappointment* or *rage*. In general, Lazarus proposed that dichotomous thinking be avoided.

Finally, Lazarus provided a brief description of what he referred to as the *core relational themes* associated with a number of emotions. This is shown in Table 5.1. His view

TABLE 5.1. Richard Lazarus's Core Relational Themes for Each Emotion

Emotion	Theme
Anger	A demeaning offense against me and mine.
Anxiety	Facing uncertain, existential threat.
Fright	An immediate, concrete, and overwhelming physical danger.
Guilt	Having transgressed a moral imperative.
Shame	Failing to live up to an ego ideal.
Sadness	Having experienced an irrevocable loss.
Envy	Wanting what someone else has and feeling deprived of it but justified in having it.
Jealousy	Resenting a third party for loss or threat to another's affection or favor.
Happiness	Making reasonable progress toward the realization of a goal.
Pride	Enhancement of one's ego identity by taking credit for a valued object or achievement, either one's own or that of someone or group with whom one identifies.
Relief	A distressing goal-incongruent condition that has changed for the better or gone away.
Hope	Fearing the worst but yearning for better, and believing that improvement is possible.
Love	Desiring or participating in affection, usually but not necessarily reciprocated.
Gratitude	Appreciation for an altruistic gift that provides personal benefit.
Compassion	Moved by another's suffering and wanting to help.

Note. From "Reason and Our Emotions: A Hard Sell," by R. S. Lazarus, 2000, *The General Psychologist, 35,* p. 20. Copyright 2000 by Society for General Psychology. Reprinted with permission.

is that there is a characteristic interpretation that tends to generate a specific emotion. For example, the core theme of *jealousy* is "resenting a third party for loss or threat to another's affection or favor." *Compassion* is being "moved by another's suffering and wanting to help." In many ways, this approach is reminiscent of Fritz Heider's theory (see chapter 3).

Lazarus has had a long and distinguished career in which he has made many contributions to our understanding of stress, adaptation, and coping. He has now added ideas about their relations to emotions.

Ross Buck: Emotion as Communication and Readout

Buck has tried to understand emotions from the point of view of communication theory. His views are best described in *The Communication of Emotion* (1984) and in a theoretical paper (Buck, 1999). Communication theory implies that emotions are meaningful primarily in the context of a system involving the interaction between a sender and a receiver. When emotions occur, an emotional state is encoded in the central nervous system and expressed or sent by means of facial expressions, sounds, or gestures. The receiver attends to these signals, decodes them, and uses the information received in accord with his or her own motivational or emotional state.

Motivation and emotion were considered by Buck to be two aspects of the same underlying processes. Both are concerned with bodily adaptation and maintenance of homeostasis, both involve some external expression of inner states, and both can be directly accessed by subjective experience. The purpose of the motivational/emotional system is to facilitate social coordination through communication of states and intentions. Contrary to the theory of William James, and consistent with that of Walter Cannon, Buck believed that subjective experience is not based on feedback from the autonomic system but is based largely on a readout of neurochemical activity in certain regions of the brain. This idea is derived from the evolutionary argument that it is adaptive for an animal to have knowledge of some of its own motivational and emotional states.

Social animals need to be able to communicate states of fear, anger, and sexual interest in order to accomplish their goals. If the social system is to run smoothly, the individuals toward whom these communications are directed must be able to correctly understand them most of the time. In the course of evolution, certain displays become "ritualized" as a way of sending information in an easily recognized way. For example, some ethologists believe that the evolution of eyebrows in primates functions to accentuate the eyebrow-raise associated with surprise or interest. It has also been suggested that the complex set of facial muscles have evolved to increase the effectiveness of emotional communication.

Buck proposed that there are three aspects of emotion. The first is the maintenance of homeostasis; the second is the expression of displays; and the third is the subjective experience. He suggested that each aspect of emotion should be interpreted as an ongoing progress report or readout of the state of certain brain systems. These readouts make the individual aware of needs for food, water, or air and of his or her impulses toward fight or flight. Such awareness allows a person to anticipate homeostatic problems before they occur.

This communication theory of emotion assumes that cognitive processes are clearly involved in all emotional interactions. Individuals label or appraise stimuli on the basis of past experience and present circumstances, which in turn affects the quality of the subjective feelings that result. Display rules, defined by a given culture or subgroup, influence the extent to which subjective feelings become expressed in overt behavior.

The basic model Buck proposed can be described as follows. External stimuli interact with the motivational/emotional system and with relevant previous learning. The cognitive system of the brain appraises and labels the emotional state. The appraisal process is also influenced by one's homeostatic states, one's expressive tendencies, and one's subjective experience. Display rules then determine to what extent the emotional/motivational state becomes expressed in terms of self-reports, goal-directed behavior, and bodily expressions. Experimental work based on the theory has been concerned mainly with the communication and recognition of emotional displays.

Buck (1999) suggested that basic emotional functions such as arousal, approach and avoidance, and affiliation can be observed (or inferred) even in single-celled organisms. He assumed that these basic emotional reactions may be associated with neurotransmitters such as peptides.

In an effort to propose a typology of so-called "higher-order" emotions, Buck suggested three categories: social emotions, cognitive emotions, and moral emotions. *Social emotions* relate to attachment feelings interacting with certain interpersonal rewards and punishments. *Cognitive emotions* are assumed to be related to an interaction of curiosity and interest with certain life events. *Moral emotions* involve a combination of both social and cognitive emotions and their interactions with certain display rules.

Nico H. Frijda: Emotion as Action Readiness Change

In a book called *The Emotions* (1986), and in papers published since then (e.g., Frijda, 2000), Nico Frijda, a Dutch psychologist, has presented a theory of emotion. He began with a number of principles.

1. Emotions have a biological basis. This means that emotions involve both bodily activity and impulses and that emotions occur in animals as well as humans.
2. Emotions in humans are influenced to various degrees by cognitive factors that may not operate in animals, such factors as norms, values, and self-awareness.
3. The presence of emotions in both humans and animals is invariably associated with efforts at inhibition and control, or more generally with regulation.
4. Emotions differ in terms of mode of activation, in terms of kind of action tendency, and in terms of autonomic response.
5. Different emotions—that is, different action tendencies—are initiated by different stimulus configurations as these are interpreted by an individual.
6. Emotions are evoked by events that are of significance to the life of an individual.

From Frijda's perspective, emotions are defined as changes in readiness for action, or changes in readiness for modifying or establishing relationships with the environment. Emotions deal with concerns related to the satisfactions of the individual.

Where does emotional experience enter this theory? Frijda proposed that emotional experience consists mainly of an awareness of action readiness: that is, impulses to run, attack, or embrace. In this regard, it is similar to the views of William James. Although learning has a major effect on the connection between stimuli and emotional experience and behavior, in many instances there is an innate stimulus–response connection that is based on neural programs within the brain.

Several other ideas about emotions are offered by Frijda. One is that the change in action readiness that defines an emotional state generally occurs in response to emergencies or interruptions. Another is that flexibility of reaction pattern and ability to inhibit or control behavior are essential features of emotion. These factors are what help distinguish between the emotions of a human being and the more limited emotions of an ant. However, because flexibility and inhibitory control are not all-or-none attributes, we cannot clearly say just where in evolution emotions begin.

Frijda's account of emotions is a functionalist theory. Emotions have a purpose; they act to deal with emergency issues related to life's satisfactions, and they do this by evaluating the relevance of events and by organizing appropriate action. Finally, Frijda pointed out that because emotions evolved to deal with emergencies, they are fast-reacting systems based on a minimum amount of information processing. This means that the emotion system occasionally makes mistakes and generates emotion when none is required or generates an emotion that is inappropriate for a given situation. However, in the long run, considering the size of the risks, there is reasonably successful adaptation.

CLINICAL THEORIES OF EMOTION

As described in chapter 2, one historical trend related to emotions involves psychoanalytic theory and its offshoots. Clinicians, both psychologists and psychiatrists, have a primary interest in emotions because their clients or patients are believed to experience emotional disorders. Most patients appear to experience an excess of certain undesirable emotions (such as *depression*), whereas others experience a deficit in the ability to express certain emotions (such as *love* or *anger*). In their efforts to deal with these and other kinds of problems, clinicians have proposed theories of emotion. This section briefly examines two recent contributions to a psychodynamic theory of affect.

Charles Spezzano: Psychoanalysis as the Communication and Interpretation of Affect

One of the more extensive discussions of affect from a psychodynamic perspective has been presented by psychoanalyst Charles Spezzano in a book titled *Affect in Psychoanalysis* (1993). Spezzano pointed out that despite earlier inconsistencies of theory and lack of attention to the topic, psychoanalysis is primarily a theory of affect. Most clinicians think, talk, and interpret in terms of affects. Affects do not need to be verbally identified by the patient in order for them to be known or recognized by the clinician. Empathic understanding is a common experience in psychotherapy.

Spezzano (1993) suggested that there are several characteristics of affect:

1. Affect states are both informative and adaptive.
2. Affects are forms of information about unconscious inner states.
3. Affects are clues to drives and social relations.
4. Affects are transient.
5. Basic affects include at least rage, anxiety, and sexual excitement that combine in various ways to create more complex states like jealousy.
6. Psychological life begins with affects before the development of ideas and the recognition of objects.
7. Affects interact with each other. For example, anxiety inhibits sexual excitement.
8. Affects are modes of communication and action predisposition. In other words, affects imply action; for example, fear implies escape, shame implies hiding.
9. We all have predispositions to maximize or minimize specific emotions.
10. Neuroses are unconscious strategies for managing one's affective life.

Spezzano believed that affects are closely related to drives or motives. To achieve safety and survival, individuals are born with the capacity to feel anxiety. To procreate, individuals are born with the potential to feel sexual excitement and affection. To withdraw from a hopeless situation, individuals are born with the capacity to withdraw and feel depressed. Affective meanings are implied in all human experience, although their unconscious sources often make them difficult to identify. Children experience the need or drive for nurturance, safety, power, curiosity, control, and autonomy. The emotions are the methods by which such drives are satisfied.

With regard to issues of treatment, Spezzano proposed that the development of symptoms is always an attempt to regulate one's own affects. For example, he believed that narcissism involves a central conflict between a wish for security and a wish to do risky things. Narcissistic people tend to have feelings of certainty and perfection as defensive reactions to unsatisfactory events.

In therapy, clinicians recognize that patients are not the final authorities on their own affective states. As Spezzano (1993) stated,

> They claim that they are feeling nothing while simultaneously saying and doing things that would be hard to imagine being done or said by someone who felt nothing. They can also claim they feel one affect while talking or acting in ways we more commonly expect from people feeling a different affect. (p. 53)

Psychoanalysis also has some interesting things to say about the relations between emotions and personality or character. It is a common clinical experience to encounter patients who feel anxious, angry, or guilty most of the time. Such persisting states of emotion are constantly being generated because they keep the patient ready to deal with threats to his or her needs for psychic safety. The process becomes circular because a person in a state of anxious expectation, for example, will find an endless supply of possible dangers. Such persisting states may be described as moods, or if persistent enough, as personality traits or character.

Joseph M. Jones: Affect as Nonsymbolic Control Mechanisms

In a theoretical book called *Affects as Process,* psychoanalyst Joseph Jones (1995) proposed that "affects are the experiential representation of a nonsymbolic information-processing system that can serve as the central control mechanism for all aspects of human behavior" (p. xiv). He distinguished five types of subjective experiences: (a) kinesthetic impulses that regulate movements of the body; (b) sensations of hunger, thirst, pain, fullness, and so on that reveal states of the body; (c) moods such as feelings of irritability or sadness; (d) basic emotions such as *fear* and *disgust;* and (e) complex emotions or mixtures of the basic emotions such as *hate, depression,* and *anxiety.* In clinical as well as ordinary usage, only the last two categories are usually called emotions.

Jones believed that emotions are ways that the brain monitors the relative intensity or importance of different motives. The function of comparisons of different competing emotions is to enable the individual to decide on an optimum course of action and to carry it out in the interests of survival. For example, a hungry animal faced with a dangerous prey has to decide whether the hunger is greater than the potential threat. On the basis of this decision, systems of the body will be mobilized either for attack or retreat.

Jones also suggested that affects are the language of the motivational systems. Affects provide signals both to the individual and to others of what motivational system is active at a given time. The example he gives concerns the complex process of feeding. Hunger signals lead to a search for food. If something is found, emotional feelings signal the palatability or accessibility of the food item. The food will either be found *acceptable* or *disgusting;* both reactions have an adaptive function. In the same sense, *love* is the affect signal of attachment, whereas *grief* is the affect signal of its loss.

Jones emphasized that emotional experience does not have an easily understood language to describe it. In fact, it appears to have many of the characteristics of music: constant flux, fuzzy boundaries, no verbal language to describe the experience of music, and the need for metaphors. These characteristics help us understand why there is such confusion among experts as well as laypeople about how to define emotions and how to specify differences among them. Many people seem to have difficulty distinguishing, for example, between *shame* and *guilt, sadness* and *depression, fear* and *anxiety,* or *envy* and *jealousy.*

Jones, like Lazarus, pointed out some problems that result from using a simple dichotomy of positive or negative affect. *Contempt* is usually considered a negative emotion. However, contempt does not feel bad in the way that *depression* does. According to Jones (1995), "No patient ever arrived at a psychotherapist's office complaining that he was 'feeling contemptuous'" (p. 146). Contempt does appear to bolster self-esteem and may even play a role in the development of dominance hierarchies. For these various reasons, Jones suggested that contempt may be considered a positive affect; dichotomies miss many situations of this sort.

Jones showed the relevance of his views to a number of clinical issues, particularly with regard to infants and children. He also suggested names for the combinations of certain emotions. *Love,* he proposed, is a mixture of affection plus the idea of goodness; *hatred* is a mixture of anger plus the idea of sadness, and so on. He concluded,

> In many ways, this ability to add or subtract ideas to our core affects is similar to the painter's ability to create literally thousands of colors through the process of tinting (adding white) or toning (adding black or brown) to the primary colors. The composition of some of these complex affects—love, hatred, futility—is relatively easy to figure out; however, others—compassion and serenity—have a much more complicated mix and depend on a high level of affective and intellectual development. Whether explicitly stated or not, one of the goals of any type of uncovering therapy is the expansion, both in breadth and in depth, of the affective palette. (Jones, 1995, p. 206)

CURRENT EVOLUTIONARY THEORIES OF EMOTION

The theory of evolution has been described as one of the most important ideas in biology. It has had a major impact on the thinking not only of biologists but of investigators in the physical and social sciences as well. As Darwin recognized, evolution implied changes over generations in both physical structures and mental (or behavioral) systems.

Evolutionary ideas have gradually entered the thinking of psychologists concerning the nature of emotions. These include the idea that emotions are forms of communication signals that have adaptive or survival value. It also includes the notion that there are certain basic or primary emotions that may interact to produce the great varieties seen in social encounters. The implications of these and other ideas are seen in some recent writings on emotion. My own views are described here and are followed by two other evolutionarily based theories.

Robert Plutchik: A Psychoevolutionary Theory of Emotions

My book appeared the same year as Tomkins's book (1962), and my later writings directed attention to the evolutionary bases of emotion. The work reflects a general Darwinian position and is influenced by the research of ethologists, by clinicians, and by those concerned currently with evolutionary psychology.

The psychoevolutionary theory consists of three interrelated models. These have been called the *structural*, the *sequential*, and the *derivative* models. Each deals with different fundamental questions.

The Structural Model

If we consider the language of emotions, it is evident that there exists an implicit intensity dimension. For most words in the emotion lexicon, it is usually possible to find other words that suggest either a more intense or a weaker version of that emotion. For example, more intense versions of *anger* would be *rage* and *fury,* whereas less intense forms would be *annoyance* and *irritation.* Similarly, we recognize the intensity differences of *pensiveness, sadness,* and *grief.* The implication of these examples is that most (perhaps all) emotions exist at points along implicit intensity dimensions.

A second point worth noting is that emotions vary in how similar they are to one another. This characteristic is clearly evident in the case of synonyms such as *fear* and *fright* (which may simply reflect close points along the intensity dimension), but it is also true for the major dimensions themselves, as discussed in the previous chapter. The dimension of *anger,* for example, is more similar to the dimension of *disgust (dislike, loathing)* than it is to the dimension of *joy (cheerfulness, elation).* It is, in fact, possible to study systematically the degree of similarity of the various emotion dimensions or primary emotions.

A third important characteristic that is part of our experience of emotions is their bipolar nature. In our everyday experience, we tend to think about emotions in terms of opposites; we talk about happiness and sadness, love and hate, fear and anger. Thus, we may conclude that the language of emotions implies at least three characteristics of emotions: (a) They vary in intensity, (b) they vary in degree of similarity to one another, and (c) they express opposite or bipolar feelings or actions.

It is possible to combine these three ideas of intensity, similarity, and polarity of emotions by means of a simple three-dimensional geometric model that looks like a cone. The vertical dimension represents intensity of emotion, any cross-sectional circle represents similarity of emotions, and bipolarity is reflected by opposite points on the circle. This cone-shaped model looks very much like the color solid, and in fact many observers over the years have suggested how similar emotions and colors seem to be in terms of their general properties (e.g., intensity, hue, and complementarity; Plutchik, 1980).

The color wheel was created by Sir Isaac Newton in the early part of the 18th century and later elaborated by Goethe and others (Varley, 1980). The primary pigment colors are red, blue, and yellow. The secondary colors, purple, orange, and green, are obtained by mixing two primary colors. Combining these few colors at different intensities (obtained by having different amounts of white or black) produces millions of colors. Complementary colors are directly opposite each other on the color wheel, and their combinations tend to neutralize the hues of the respective components and to produce a gray tone. William James was interested in the parallels between colors and emotions and stated that the naming of emotions is difficult partly because emotions merge endlessly into each other (as do colors; see also discussion in chap. 4). Neither colors nor emotions are clear-cut categories with sharp boundaries.

To these ideas is added one important concept to complete the structural model. For many generations, philosophers have assumed that there is a small number of primary emotions and that all others are derived from them. In recent years, investigators have proposed from 3 to 11 emotions as primary. All include *fear, anger,* and *sadness,* and most include *joy, love,* and *surprise* (Kemper, 1987).

If we combine the idea of primary emotions with the three characteristics of the language of emotion, we can conceptualize a three-dimensional structure with eight slices representing the (assumed) basic emotions. This is shown in Figure 5.1. The idea that there are eight basic emotions is a theoretical one but should be evaluated partly in terms of the

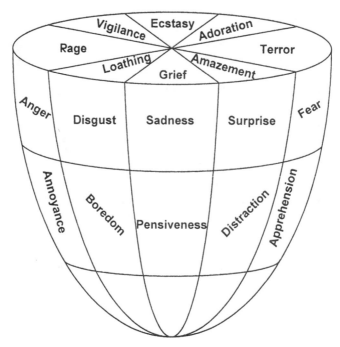

FIGURE 5.1. A multidimensional model of the emotions. The vertical dimension represents intensity. The eight families of basic emotions are arranged in order of degree of similarity. From *Emotions in the Practice of Psychotherapy*, by R. Plutchik, 2000, p. 63. Copyright 2000 by the American Psychological Association. Reprinted with permission.

inferences and insights to which it leads, the research it suggests, and the extent to which empirical data are consistent with it.

If we imagine a cross-section through the emotion solid, we obtain an emotion circle as shown in Figure 5.2 for a midlevel cross-section on the intensity dimension. A number of studies summarized in chapter 4 and Plutchik and Conte (1997) support this circular or circumplex set of interrelations among emotions.

If there are eight basic emotion dimensions (each with a number of synonyms or related terms), how can we account for the total language of emotions? The review of the literature on the language of emotions implies that the total number of emotion words is a few hundred at most, and they tend to fall into families based on similarity. If we follow the pattern used in color theory and research, we can obtain judgments about what results when two or more emotions are combined. When this was done, the results were clear; judges agreed that the mixture of *joy* and *acceptance* produces the mixed emotion of *love*. The blending of *disgust* and *anger* produces the mixed emotional state of *hatred* or *hostility*. Such mixtures have been called primary dyads in the theory. By mixing two or more emotions at different intensity levels, it is possible to create hundreds of terms representing the language of emotions.

Another important idea stemming from the structural model is the fact that many of the terms that judges used in describing mixtures of the emotions are words that are typically used to describe personality traits. In fact, it is evident that most of the terms used

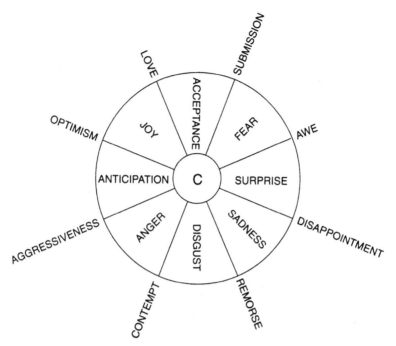

FIGURE 5.2. A circumplex for emotions based on a cross-section of the multidimensional model of emotions. Inside the circle, the eight basic emotions represent a moderate intensity level. The outside terms represent the new emotions (primary dyads) created by combining adjacent pairs of basic emotions. The C at the center stands for the idea of conflict which is produced by mixing opposite or near-opposite emotions. From *Emotions in the Practice of Psychotherapy*, by R. Plutchik, 2000, p. 64. Copyright 2000 by the American Psychological Association. Reprinted with permission.

to describe emotions are also used to describe personality traits. For example, words such as *gloomy, resentful, anxious,* and *calm* can describe personality traits as well as emotional feelings. The distinction between emotional states and interpersonal personality traits is largely arbitrary (Allen & Potkay, 1981). Often the same adjective checklist can be used to measure both states and traits by a simple change in instructions. If the research participants are asked how they feel now, or within the past few days or so, we are asking about emotional states or moods. If, however, they are asked to describe how they usually feel, we are asking about personality traits. Thus, from the point of view of this theory, emotions and personality traits are intimately connected, and in fact, personality traits may be considered to be derived from mixtures of emotions. This idea of derivatives of emotion is elaborated later in this chapter.

The Sequential Model

Ever since the writings of William James on the question of which comes first, the feelings of an emotion or the physiological changes (see the discussion in chapter 2), psychologists have been concerned with the sequence of events in emotion. Despite considerable interest in the question, no definitive answers have been found.

A major reason for this lack of closure is the fact that emotions are not simply linear events; that is, A does not always follow B, D does not always follow C, and so on. In contrast, clinicians have stated that emotions are circular or feedback processes. For example, Weisman (1965) stated that the function of affect is to restore the individual to a state of equilibrium, or in other words, the acts associated with emotions tend to reduce the emotions that produced them. Relatedly, Karasu (1992) pointed out that each person tries to maintain a certain level of affective equilibrium in everyday life with only moderate fluctuations. Unexpected or unusual events (external or internal) change this affect level, and the resulting behaviors are attempts to reestablish the preexisting state. Greenberg and Paivio (1997) argued that emotions provide us with feedback about our own reactions to events and basically function to promote survival. In an emotional reaction, once the goal of aggression or escape, for example, has been achieved, and the individual's relation to the environment has changed, the emotional response declines. These observations imply that emotions involve feedback processes to change the relation between the individual who experiences the emotion and the stimulus or event that started the process in the first place.

From an evolutionary perspective, the functioning elements of any complex system must be kept within certain limits or the system will not survive. This is well known in biology under the concept of *homeostasis*. In the human body, for example, there are a large number of control systems that act to keep various physiological parameters within narrow limits: blood sugar levels, blood pressure, body temperature, white and red blood cells, rate of coagulation of blood, and others.

Bowlby (1969) pointed out that goal corrections (i.e., stabilization of important parameters) take place not only within an individual's body but also in the relations between one individual and another, or between an individual and certain events that may occur in the external environment. This is clearly seen in attachment behavior between mother and child, in which such behavior acts to protect a child from a wide range of dangers.

> When a goal-corrected behavior sequence, such as locomoting toward the caregiver in order to make physical contact, is activated, the child continuously orients his or her behavior and selects alternative behaviors, based in part on the feedback received from the effects of the behavior. When the set goal is achieved, the perceived discrepancy between the set goal and the organism's state is reduced to zero, and the behavioral plan terminates. (Marvin & Britner, 1999, p. 49)

An alternative way of describing these regulatory mechanisms is to note that the homeostatic system is actually composed of the mother and child as a unit. Several behavioral systems act to bring the child into close proximity to the mother, continue to keep the child close, and function to help reunite a separated child with his or her mother (Polan & Hofer, 1999).

Watson (2000), in his studies of moods, also pointed out the circular nature of mood functioning. Moods are often considered to be the effects of various life experiences (e.g., cloudy days, being on a cruise ship, doing poorly on an examination). Once they exist, however, moods can influence one's behavior and thinking.

The psychoevolutionary theory accepts the idea that emotions are part of complex, circular feedback systems. It assumes that stimulus events, either external or internal (as in dreams), act as the primary triggers that start the emotion process going. However, events need to be interpreted in order for them to have an effect on the individual.

A picture of an American flag may elicit feelings of pride and enthusiasm in an American, but it may elicit feelings of hate and vengeance in someone from, say, Iraq. Sometimes the interpretation is obvious and occasionally less so. For example, individuals sometimes take an instant dislike to someone they have just met. The reason may not be obvious either to an observer or to the individual himself or herself. In such a case, we assume that an interpretation or a cognition has occurred that may be unconscious and so we make an inference about the cognition on the basis of the behavior shown. The psychoevolutionary theory assumes that following the cognition or interpretation, a feeling state occurs as well as a physiological state of arousal, if appropriate. Walter Cannon and many others have pointed out that arousal states are generally preparations for action or self-protective changes that may be functionally useful in situations of danger. No one has satisfactorily resolved the question of whether feeling states precede or follow states of physiological arousal; it is just as feasible to argue that they occur together.

Feeling states tend to be followed by impulses to action. Such impulses may be expressed by tensions in the muscles, by facial expressions, by clenching of the fists, or by preparations for running, attacking, or yelling. Clinicians are well aware of the fact that impulses to action are not always followed by action, often for fear of retaliation or fear of embarrassment. However, action often does occur; the individual runs, attacks, criticizes, cries, compliments, kisses, or withdraws.

Such overt behavior is, however, not the end of the emotion process. Such behavior generally has an effect on the stimulus or condition that started the chain of events in the first place. For example, running from a source of threat reduces the threat and tends to reestablish the condition that existed before the threat occurred. Similarly, if a major loss occurs in an individual's life, such as the death of a parent, the crying and grieving that result tends to produce supportive and helpful contacts from other members of one's social group and, at least in a symbolic way, provides a kind of reintegration or reattachment with the lost parent. Overall, this process is a kind of homeostatic process, but one that is carried out by behavioral rather than internal changes. This process is called a *behavioral homeostatic feedback system*. From this point of view, an emotion is not simply the feeling state but the entire chain of events including the feedback loops.

Figure 5.3 depicts this process in general terms. Feedback loops may influence the impulses to action, the feeling states, the cognitions, as well as the initiating stimulus. This process is what leads to the idea that feelings and behaviors can affect cognitions, just as much as cognitions can influence feelings. Also implied by this model is the idea that the term *feelings* is used to represent subjective, reportable states such as joy, sadness, anger, or disgust, whereas the word *emotion* is used in a much broader sense to refer to the entire chain of events that include feelings, but also cognitions, impulses to action, display behaviors, and the various loops that occur; an individual may not be consciously aware of some of these components.

Table 5.2 summarizes the theory's assumptions about some of the key elements involved in the emotion sequence. For each of the eight basic emotions, a general description of the stimulus event that triggers it is described, followed by descriptions of the probable cognitions associated with each of the emotions, the subjective feeling states, the overt behaviors, and the effect of the behavior in reducing the disequilibrium.

At the heart of all these descriptions is the idea that emotions have a purpose in the lives of individuals. This idea stems from the evolutionary perspective, is consistent with psychodynamic thinking, and is becoming more and more accepted in the writings of contemporary clinicians. For example, Hauser (1996) pointed out that the primary care that young organisms require is for food, protection, and transportation and that

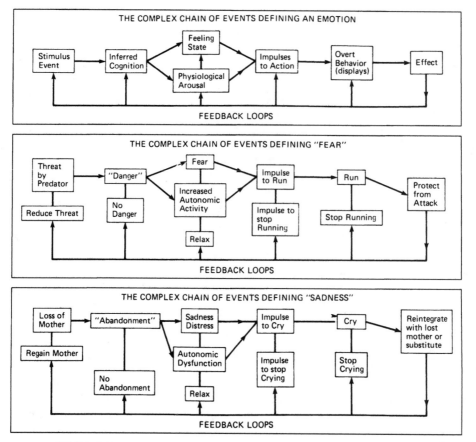

FIGURE 5.3. Illustrations of the complex chain of events defining an emotion.

crying is a major method for getting such care. Spezzano (1993) suggested that people use love or intimidation to keep others invested in their personal agendas. Vaillant (1997) discussed the adaptive functions of a number of emotions. Sorrow, for example, increases one's feelings of closeness to others, and listeners often feel compassion and the desire to be helpful. Interest, or anticipation, is often energizing and increases one's involvement with others. Fear protects the self, initiates withdrawal, and allows general functioning to continue. Shame leads to remorse and a decrease in the probability of repetition of the shameful act. All of these examples imply that emotions are part of an adaptive circular or feedback process.

The Derivatives Model

One of the most important ideas of the psychoevolutionary theory is the concept of *derivatives*. This term is used in three different senses. First, it can mean that certain human behaviors are seen in lower animals; for example, the sneer of the human may be said to be derived from the snarl of the wolf. Second, it can mean that certain behaviors seen in adults are derivatives of certain behaviors seen in infants. An example might be the feeding and babyish behaviors sometimes seen between adult lovers. A third meaning of

TABLE 5.2. Key Elements in the Emotion Sequence

Stimulus event	Cognition	Feeling state	Overt bhavior	Effect
Threat	"Danger"	Fear	Escape	Safety
Obstacle	"Enemy"	Anger	Attack	Destroy obstacle
Gain of valued object	"Possess"	Joy	Retain or repeat	Gain resources
Loss of valued object	"Abandonment"	Sadness	Cry	Reattach to lost object
Member of one's group	"Friend"	Acceptance	Groom	Mutual support
Unpalatable object	"Poison"	Disgust	Vomit	Eject poison
New territory	"Examine"	Expectation	Map	Knowledge of territory
Unexpected event	"What is it?"	Surprise	Stop	Gain time to orient

Note. From *Emotions in the Practice of Psychotherapy*, by R. Plutchik, 2000, p. 69. Copyright 2000 by the American Psychological Association. Reprinted with permission.

the concept is the idea that certain concepts are derived from other, more primitive events or concepts. This is the sense in which the term is used here. It means that a number of conceptual domains are systematically related to one another.

Take, for example, the domain of personality. The topic is usually taught in universities as if it had little to do with emotions. Yet the language of emotions and the language of personality are remarkably similar. An individual can feel depressed or be a depressed person, can feel nervous or be a nervous person, or can feel joyful or be a joyful person.

In addition to the overlap in the language of the domains of emotion and personality, there is also the fact that both domains can be represented by means of a circumplex model. This has been illustrated by Conte and Plutchik (1981), who used two independent methods to establish a circumplex structure for personality traits that is quite similar to the one established for emotions (see also previous chapter).

The psychoevolutionary theory of emotions assumed that emotions, because of their fundamental adaptive role in all organisms, are the precursors of the ways in which emotions become expressed in other related domains such as personality. It is in this sense that personality traits are derivatives of the more fundamental emotional states, just as most colors in nature are derived from mixtures of a few primary ones. When emotions occur in persistent or repeated form in an individual over long periods of time, we tend to consider them as more or less permanent (dispositional) characteristics of the individual. We then tend to use the language of personality traits to describe the person rather than the language of emotional states. The idea of derivatives is shown in Table 5.3.

This table describes a number of conceptual languages that the psychoevolutionary theory hypothesizes are systematically related to one another. For example, proceeding from left to right across the table, the term *fear* is part of the subjective language of emotions, as are terms like *anger, joy,* and *surprise*. From an evolutionary point of view, it may be asked what the function of each emotion is; the second column describes them. The

TABLE 5.3. Emotions and Their Derivatives

Subjective language	Functional language	Trait language	Diagnostic language	Ego defense language	Coping-style language
Fear	Protection	Timid	Dependent; avoidant	Repression	Avoidance
Anger	Destruction	Quarrelsome	Antisocial	Displacement	Substitution
Joy	Attachment	Sociable	Hypomanic	Reaction formation	Reversal
Sadness	Reintegration	Gloomy	Dysthymic	Compensation	Replacement
Acceptance	Incorporation	Trusting	Histrionic	Denial	Minimization
Disgust	Rejection	Hostile	Paranoid	Projection	Fault finding
Expectation	Exploration	Controlling	Obsessive compulsive	Intellectualization	Mapping
Surprise	Orientation	Indecisive	Borderline	Regression	Help seeking

Note. From *Emotions in the Practice of Psychotherapy,* by R. Plutchik, 2000, p. 73. Copyright 2000 by the American Psychological Association. Reprinted with permission.

function of fear is *protection*; of anger, the *destruction of a barrier* to the satisfaction of one's needs; of sadness, symbolic reintegration with a lost object in the form of *nurturance*; and of disgust, the *rejection* of a toxic substance or experience.

Emotions and Personality

When emotional states persist over time or are frequently repeated, we tend to describe the individual as having a particular personality trait. Thus, repeated expressions of fear lead to the designation of someone as *timid*. Repeated expressions of anger or irritability lead to the description of someone as *quarrelsome*, and repeated expressions of rejection of others leads to such trait designations as *hostile* or *cruel*.

When personality traits exist in fairly extreme form, we use a new language to describe the situation—the language of personality disorders. Thus, an extreme form of quarrelsomeness may be diagnosed as antisocial personality disorder, and a person who shows an extreme form of timidity might be diagnosed as a dependent personality type. Similar parallels may be drawn for each of the major clusters of personality, which are in turn derived from the basic emotions. Extensive documentation of these ideas may be found in Plutchik and Conte (1997).

The ego defense language and coping-style language are theorized to be ways of dealing with particular emotions. Ego defenses such as repression and denial are usually considered to be unconscious, whereas coping styles such as minimizing and avoiding are considered to be conscious methods people use to deal with problems that generate emotions.

Examination of the three models—structural, sequential, and derivatives—indicates that many ideas are necessary to provide an understanding of the nature of emotions. In all, the theory has emphasized the importance of evolutionary thinking in this quest. Empirical studies have supported the idea of the circumplex as a model for describing emotions, certain classes of personality traits, personality disorders, and ego defenses. The theory also points the direction for future research.

Randolph M. Nesse: Evolutionary Functions of Specific Emotions

In recent years, with the development of evolutionary thinking as applied to psychology, a number of ideas about the evolutionary meaning of emotions have been suggested. One important contributor to these ideas is Randolph Nesse, a psychiatrist. He pointed out that a theory of emotion should have great utility for clinicians who deal with emotional disorders. His belief was that our understanding of emotions will increase most rapidly if we can develop explicit evolutionary explanations for the functions that emotions serve (Nesse, 1990).

Biological explanations are of several types. *Proximate* explanations deal with how a system works (e.g., How is blood pressure control carried out in the human body?). *Evolutionary* (sometimes called ultimate) explanations focus on how a given mechanism or function was produced by natural selection over countless periods of time to increase biological fitness (i.e., to enable an individual to leave offspring that survive to reproduce). Exhibit 5.1 describes Nesse's concept of an evolutionary explanation for emotions.

▬   **EXHIBIT 5.1. OUTLINE FOR AN EVOLUTIONARY EXPLANATION OF AN EMOTION**

I. Proximate explanation of the physiological and psychological mechanisms that mediate and regulate the emotion
   A. Cues that elicit the emotion
   B. Mechanisms that assess the cues and regulate the emotion
   C. Characteristics of the emotional state
      1. Physiological
      2. Behavioral
      3. Cognitive/subjective
II. Ontogeny (development from birth to old age) of the proximate mechanisms
III. How was the emotional capacity shaped by natural selection; that is, how did its functions increase fitness?
   A. The situation in which the emotion is adaptive in relation to threats and opportunities.
   B. Adaptive significance of the emotion
      1. Physiology
      2. Behavior
      3. Cognitions
      4. Sensory changes
IV. Phylogenetic (evolutionary changes that occur over millions of years) history of the emotion

Note. From "Evolutionary Explanations of Emotions," by R. M. Nesse, 1990, *Human Nature, 1,* p. 266. Copyright 1990 by Aldine de Gruyter. Reprinted with permission.

Proximate explanations should identify the stimuli that elicit emotions, the cues that regulate them, and the physiological, behavioral, and cognitive characteristics that they process. Such explanations should also identify infant and childhood factors that influence the frequency and form of expression of emotions. Evolutionary explanations are an attempt to identify how natural selection has created particular emotions that increase the prospects of survival of an individual and his or her genes. To do this, one needs to precisely identify the kinds of situations in which the emotion is adaptive.

Biological systems are usually defined in terms of functions. For example, the immune system has the function of protecting the body from pathogens. Similarly, each emotion should correspond to a significant situation that has occurred repeatedly in the course of evolution. Different subtypes of fear are aroused by predators, high places, strangers, groups of people, and diseases. People who have a social phobia may not be afraid of heights, but will be frightened by being the center of attention. Table 5.4 expresses Nesse's ideas about the situations that correspond to different types of fears.

Any emotion (such as *panic*) represents not a wild disorganization of the behavior of an individual but a coordinated pattern of behaviors that are useful in the event of a possible attack. "Panic disorder is a disease that results from faulty regulation of panic, but panic itself, like cough, is not a disease, but a defense against a particular kind of danger" (Nesse, 1990, p. 271).

Nesse also suggested that the expressions of *happiness* and *sadness* have been shaped by natural selection. From an evolutionary point of view, *joy* is elicited by situations that increase fitness (i.e., reproductive success). This could mean having sex, having

TABLE 5.4. Subtypes of Fear and Their Corresponding Situations

Subtype of Fear	Corresponding Danger or Situation
Panic	Imminent attack by predator or human
Agoraphobia	Environment in which attack is likely
General anxiety	Environment that is unsafe in general
Conflictual anxiety	Socially unacceptable impulses
Social anxiety	Threats to status or group membership
Small animal phobias	Dangerous small animals
Hypochondriasis	Disease
Separation anxiety	Separation from protective parent
Stranger anxiety	Likelihood of harm from strange humans
Personal inadequacy	Rejection by allies or group
Obsessive cleanliness	Infectious disease
Obsessive hoarding	Lack of food or other resources
Blood/injury	Possibility of death

Note. From "Evolutionary Explanations of Emotions," by R. M. Nesse, 1990. *Human Nature, 1,* p. 271. Copyright 1990 by Aldine de Gruyter. Reprinted with permission.

children and grandchildren, and being loved. In contrast, *sadness* is generally elicited by events that signal decreasing fitness; sickness, loss of status, loss of resources, social rejection, loss of a friend or lover, or death of a family member.

As a psychiatrist, Nesse pointed out that although many emotions are useful responses to a threat or loss, there may be true emotional diseases caused by abnormal regulatory mechanisms. This issue has been particularly raised with regard to depression. The question is whether depression is basically adaptive, but extreme, or whether it has a function that is unrelated to adaptation (Nesse, 2000). Clinicians have suggested a number of different functions for depression, for example, a cry for help; a communication designed to manipulate other people into providing resources; a failed adaptation; a way of resolving social competitions by signaling the absence of threat; a way to obtain sympathetic consideration on the part of important people in one's life; or a way of disengaging from an unreachable goal. Just as anxiety inhibits dangerous actions, depression possibly inhibits futile efforts. Nesse (1998) also pointed out so-called negative emotions are useful or they would not exist. Nesse's work is important not only because he provides a somewhat different perspective for considering emotions but also because he has attempted to show the clinical usefulness of these ideas.

Leda Cosmides and John Tooby: Evolutionary Psychology and Emotions

These authors have devoted a good deal of attention in recent years to showing the relevance to psychology of ideas about evolution. In a recent publication, they have outlined a general approach to emotions from this perspective (Cosmides & Tooby, 2000).

A fairly well-accepted belief among evolutionary psychologists is that the mind consists of a large number of neural programs or modules, each of which is specialized for dealing with specific problems that arose during evolutionary history. These specific programs include such things as face recognition and predator avoidance. From this perspective, emotions are functional subprograms that evolved to solve certain kinds of survival-related problems that reoccurred repeatedly in evolutionarily ancient times. These emotional programs function to organize a variety of different bodily systems such as attention, memory, arousal, and action to solve a survival-related problem. Any one system (such as physiological) cannot be the only or best description of an emotion, nor can subjective experience, which is a relatively late evolutionary development.

Adaptive problems for individuals from the point of view of inclusive fitness (i.e., survival of genes in future generations) are either about reproductive opportunities (such as problems of mate selection) or about reproductive obstacles (such as conflicts between males for access to females). In order for emotion programs to evolve, a number of conditions are necessary:

1. An evolutionarily recurrent situation or condition.
2. An adaptive problem.
3. Cues that signal the presence of the situation.
4. Situation-detecting algorithms (subprograms)
   a. Programs that monitor for relevant cues
   b. Programs that detect situations
5. Programs that assign priorities among competing motives.
6. An internal communication system (to turn on all relevant body functions).
7. Programs for switching physiological mechanisms on and off. (Cosmides & Tooby, 2000)

The view developed by Cosmides and Tooby has a number of implications. For example, they suggested that seemingly "pointless emotions" such as *grief, playfulness, guilt,* and *depression* have no function in the short term but may have over the long run. They suggested that there may be emotions that have not yet been named, such as "predatoriness," which is a complex of feelings and behavior involved in hunting prey. They also proposed that a number of mental states that are not currently considered to be emotions should be so designated. These include feelings of malaise, coma, shock, appreciation of beauty, homesickness, nausea, and others.

Finally, they hypothesized that there are criteria for judging whether a person is in an emotional state regardless of whether the person is aware of it, or whether a given culture has a word for it. This is simply because having an emotion means that a particular set of programs in the brain are being run. They added that even facial expressions are not necessarily part of the definition of an emotion.

SUMMARY

This chapter has reviewed some of the more general theories of emotion, and the various theories described in the chapter are briefly summarized in Exhibit 5.2. It is evident that there is an overlap of ideas in the different theories. Most current views recognize that emotions have an evolutionary history as well as systematic relations to one another. The most recent approaches explicitly try to relate evolutionary considerations to the functioning of emotions. There are still a number of unanswered questions with which theories have yet to deal.

■■■■■ **EXHIBIT 5.2. KEY IDEAS OF SOME CURRENT THEORIES OF EMOTION**

Psychophysiological and Motivational Theories of Emotion

Sylvan Tomkins

He assumes eight basic emotions which influence our drives (motivations). Emotions amplify behavior. Each emotion is believed to have a characteristic expressive pattern based on a neurological program.

Carroll Izard

Emotions have a genetic basis. He assumes there are 10 basic emotions and that others are combinations of these ten. Emotions are part of personality.

Richard Lazarus

Individual appraisals of harm or benefit determine emotional reactions. Coping styles are ways to manage emotions. Emotions are like scripts with distinctive dramatic plots each of which has a core theme.

Ross Buck

Emotions are readouts or interpretations of one's own inner signals from body, face, and brain. Emotions are concerned with adaptation to the environment and the maintenance of homeostasis. The concept of emotions applies to relatively primitive animals as well as humans.

Nico Frijda

Emotions are changes in readiness for action usually brought about by emergencies or interruptions; they organize appropriate action. Individuals are constantly involved in trying to control their emotions.

Clinical Theories of Emotion

Charles Spezzano

Emotions provide information about unconscious inner states such as drives and social impulses. Most emotions are complex states made up of more basic ones. Emotions appear very early in life and act as communication signals. Psychological disorders are believed to be unconscious strategies for managing one's emotional life.

Joseph Jones

Emotions are control mechanisms for regulating behavior. Emotional reactions are adaptive and influence one's chances of survival. Emotions are basically nonverbal reactions that reveal states of the body. They are constantly changing, have fuzzy boundaries and are often best understood through metaphors.

Evolutionary Theories of Emotions

Robert Plutchik

Emotions are complex feedback processes that attempt to restore homeostatic balance when certain significant life events create disequilibria. The theory includes three models: a *structural* model that conceptualizes the relations between emotions in terms of a three-dimensional cone; a *sequential* model that describes the complex, feedback loops involved in all emotions; and a *derivatives* model that shows systematic connections between emotions, personality, personality disorders, ego defenses and coping styles.

Randolph Nesse

Evolutionary explanations of emotions try to identify how natural selection has created particular emotions that increase the chances of individual and genetic survival. All emotions have adaptive functions. So-called negative emotions are useful or they would not exist.

Leda Cosmides and John Tooby

Emotions are functional subprograms in the brain that evolved to solve certain kinds of survival-related problems. They organize other body systems such as memory and action to attempt to deal with such problems. Emotions can exist even if a person is not aware of them, or even if the culture has no words for them.

6 The Measurement of Emotions

> Were any man to keep minutes of his feelings from youth to old age, what a table of vanities they would present—how numerous, how diverse, how strange.
>
> *August W. Hare*

PREVIEW

How we measure emotions depends on how we define them and the theories we have about them. Each different theory of emotion has some implications for assessment of emotions. For example, cognitive theories usually describe the situational and conceptual triggers of emotional reactions. Motivational theories are likely to direct the researcher's attention to autonomic changes that occur within the body and are also likely to use facial expressions as indicators of emotion. Evolutionary-based theories are likely to focus attention on the measurement of expressive behavior of humans and animals. Psychoanalytic theories imply that measures of emotion that best reflect the unconscious, mixed states typical of humans consist of projective and drawing techniques.

However, because of the increasing overlap of theoretical ideas, we see overlap of measurement techniques as well. Thus, we find four general approaches to measuring emotions, most of which tend to be used by proponents of all viewpoints. One method involves the use of self-reports of subjective feelings, a procedure that is useful mainly with human adults. A second method for judging emotions is through ratings made of the behavior of an individual. Such ratings can be used with adults, children, people who are mentally retarded, and lower animals. A third way to evaluate emotions is through a rating of the product of someone's behavior, for example, an individual's handwriting or figure drawings. Finally, emotions may be assessed through the use of recordings of physiological or neural changes. Each of these methods is described in this chapter.

SELF-REPORT MEASURES OF EMOTIONS

One of the most common, and deceptively simple, ways to measure emotional states in human adults is by means of adjective checklists. Such lists consist of a series of adjectives, such as *calm, nervous, fearful,* and *bored,* that individuals identify as reflections of their current feelings. Although this seems like a simple enough idea, there are problems with it. One concerns the question of which words we should use that are descriptive of current feelings. The second concerns the question of how best to group terms to represent scales or dimensions, and the third concerns the question of how long an emotion lasts.

117

Adjective Checklists

One of the earliest adjective checklists was developed by Gough and his associates (1960). They selected 300 words that included such terms as *affectionate, charming, deceitful, absent-minded, prudish, sexy, slow, weak, quiet, relaxed,* and *gloomy*. Other authors have included words like *droopy, tired, sleepy,* and *aroused* (Russell, 1989). The problem with these choices is that people do not always agree on which words are emotion words and which are not. Some students, for example, believe that *hunger* and *thirst,* as inner states, are emotions and that states of *fatigue* or *excitement* are also emotions. Many do not agree with these judgments. Fortunately, there is good agreement that words like *fearful, sad, angry,* and *happy* describe emotions, and such terms or their synonyms are generally found on every checklist.

The second question concerns the issue of how to group emotion words to form scales or dimensions. For example, a common practice is to group emotion words into two broad categories called *positive affect* and *negative affect*. An illustration of this approach may be found in the research by D. Watson, Clark, and Tellegen (1988), who described the development of brief measures of positive and negative affect. They started with 60 emotion words and through use of factor analysis reduced this list to 10 words that strongly reflected positive affect and 10 that expressed negative affect, with relatively little overlap. Examples of positive emotions are *interested, excited, happy, proud, alert,* and *optimistic*. Examples of negative emotions are *distressed, upset, guilty, hostile, nervous,* and *afraid*.

One of the problems with lists of this type is that many of the words are vague; it is not clear just what is implied by them. For example, the word *excited* could be associated with rage. Similarly, the word *upset* could mean that one feels bad, sick, uncomfortable, or depressed. One of the puzzling things about emotion words is that we sometimes find puzzling associations. Watson et al. reported that the two positive-sounding words *delighted* and *healthy* were omitted from their list of positive affects because their factor analysis showed that they seemed to be related to the negative emotions.

Profile of Mood States

An attempt to develop an adjective checklist with different clusters of words was made by Lorr and McNair (1984) and is called the Profile of Mood States, or POMS. This test consists of 65 words representing six emotion dimensions: Anger–Hostility, Depression–Dejection, Vigor–Activity, Fatigue–Inertia, Tension–Confusion, and Friendliness. Examples of the words used on the scales are *friendly, tense, angry,* and *worthless*. Participants make intensity of feeling judgments on a 5-point scale ranging from *not at all* to *extremely*. The POMS has been useful in a number of investigations concerned with the effects of drugs and antidepressants on mood states.

Emotion–Mood Index

Another checklist, the Emotion–Mood Index (Plutchik, 1980), is shown in Table 6.1. It consists of 72 terms placed into nine clusters. The first eight groupings of terms reflect eight basic dimensions of emotion: Trust, Dyscontrol, Timidity, Depression, Distrust, Control, Aggression, and Gregarious. These correspond to the eight basic emotions in the *psychoevolutionary* theory described in chapter 5. The last cluster represents an activation or arousal dimension with terms such as *weak, strong,* and *restless*.

TABLE 6.1. Emotion–Mood Index

Trust	Depression	Aggression
Trusting	Depressed	Aggressive
Friendly	Gloomy	Furious
Obliging	Sad	Bossy
Contented	Empty	Boastful
Cooperative	Cooperative	Annoyed
Tolerant	Helpless	Quarrelsome
Calm	Discouraged	Irritated
Patient	Hopeless	Angry
Dyscontrol	**Distrust**	**Gregarious**
Alert	Disgusted	Sociable
Fascinated	Uninterested	Generous
Surprised	Bored	Cheerful
Confused	Distrustful	Affectionate
Attentive	Bitter	Happy
Wondering	Sarcastic	Satisfied
Puzzled	Resentful	Delighted
Bewildered	Fed up	Fed up
Timidity	**Control**	**Control**
Afraid	Hopeful	Slowed-down
Scared	Inquisitive	Sluggish
Nervous	Curious	Relaxed
Timid	Eager	Weak
Worried	Interested	Active
Anxious	Daring	Strong
Shy	Impulsive	Energetic
Cautious	Nosy	Restless

Note. From *Emotion: A Psychoevolutionary Synthesis*, by R. Plutchik, 1980, p. 206. Copyright 1980 by Harper & Row. Reprinted with permission.

An example illustrates its use. The Emotion–Mood Index was administered weekly to a group of psychiatric inpatients on a research ward. All patients had been carefully screened and were diagnosed as manic–depressive. All had repeated experiences of mania, depression, or both (Platman, Plutchik, Fieve, & Lawlor, 1969).

During the course of the study, 26 patients were judged by the psychiatric staff as being in a manic state, 42 were evaluated as depressed, and 79 were assessed as being in a (temporary) normal state. Comparisons were made between the frequencies of self-reported moods in manic and depressed states for each adjective. It was found that every one of the Trust, Gregarious, and Depression adjectives significantly discriminated between the manic and depressed states. In addition, many adjectives from the other scales also discriminated significantly between these two states.

Separate comparisons were then made between the normal state and the manic or depressed state using the total number of items checked in each scale as the basis for

TABLE 6.2. Dimensions Measured by Various Adjective Checklists

Checklist/No. of Words	Adjectives
Borgatta (1961), 40 adjectives	Lonely (depressed), warmhearted, tired, thoughtful, defiant (aggressive), startled (anxious)
Clyde (1963), 132 adjectives	Friendly, aggressive, clear thinking, sleepy, unhappy, dizzy
Zuckerman & Lubin (1965), 89 adjectives	Depression, hostility, anxiety
Plutchik (1966), 8 adjectives	Happy, agreeable, fearful, angry, interested, disgusted, sad, surprised
McNair, Lorr, & Dropleman (1971), 57 adjectives	Anger–hostility, depression–dejection, vigor–activity, fatigue inertia, friendliness, confusion
Izard (1972), 30 adjectives	Interest, joy, surprise, distress, disgust, anger, shame, fear, contempt, guilt
Plutchik & Kellerman (1974), 66 adjectives	Sociable, trusting, dyscontrolled, timid, depressed, distrustful, controlled, aggressive
Curran & Cattell (1975), 96 adjectives	Anxiety, stress, depression, regression, fatigue, guilt, extraversion, arousal
Lorr & McNair (1984), 72 adjectives	Composed, anxious, agreeable, hostile, elated, depressed, confident, unsure, energetic, tired, clear-headed, confused
Howarth and Young (1986), 60 adjectives	Concentration, anxiety, anger, depression, potency, sleep, control, cooperation, optimism, skepticism
Watson, Clark, & Tellegen (1988), 20 adjectives	Positive (e.g., proud) and negative (e.g., upset)

Note. From "Measuring Emotions and Their Derivatives," by R. Plutchik, 1989. In R. Plutchik and H. Kellerman (Eds.), *The Measurement of Emotions* (Vol. 4, p. 16). Copyright 1989 by Academic Press. Reprinted with permission.

comparisons. It was found that every scale significantly discriminated between the normal and depressed states. Three scales—Depression, Aggression, and Control—discriminated between the normal and manic states. It thus appears that the Emotion–Mood Index is capable of distinguishing among several affective states.

Table 6.2 provides information on the range of emotions covered by the various adjective checklists that have been described in the literature. Ten different instruments are listed. The number of adjectives per test ranges from 8 to 132, whereas the number of dimensions or subscales varies from 3 to 10.

Adjective checklists for the measurement of emotional states have come into wide use in recent years. Their advantages are that they are usually brief, have obvious face validity, (i.e., they appear to measure emotions or moods), and can be easily self-administered. Devices have been constructed that enable mood ratings to be recorded at any time of the day or night. Participants carry a small electronic mood-recording device and are signaled by radio at designated or random intervals to register their mood or emotion. The device records the time and registers a feeling and enables rapid later data analysis (Hoeksma, Sep, Vester, Groot, Sijmons, & de Vries, 2000).The checklists can also be used to provide indices of transient states of emotion as well as long-term emotional dispositions. Their disadvantages include the fact that they are easy to fake. In addition, many of the checklists have no theoretical justification for the particular dimensions or scales that are scored. Despite these problems, such checklists have been widely used.

SOME RECENT STUDIES OF MOOD

Measuring the Effects of "Ecstasy"

A hallucinogenic amphetamine derivative (MDMA, which stands for methylene-dioxymethamphetamine), called *ecstasy* in street talk, became popular in the mid-1980s and, although illicit, has become widely used as a recreational drug. In the past few years, a number of cases, due to the use of the drug, have been reported of convulsions, hyper-thermia, and neurological dysfunction, including memory impairments.

In an effort to study the effects of this drug, Parrott and Lasky (1998) were able to find individuals who regularly visited a large nightclub in London, England. Fifteen of them were regular ecstasy users (had used it on 10 or more occasions); 15 were novice ecstasy users (had used it on 1–9 occasions); and 15 were controls who had never used ecstasy.

Using a hand-held computer, the participants were asked to complete an auditory word recall task, a visual search task, and a mood scale. The mood scales were presented as single lines with a 100-point scale marked from *do not feel at all* (0) to *feel completely* (100). Sixteen descriptions were used for the mood scales: *abnormal, calm, clear-headed, depressed, drowsy, energetic, good tempered, ill, interested, quick-witted, sad, sober, steady, unpleasant, unsociable,* and *well-coordinated.*

On the Saturday night that the participants were tested at the nightclub, no significant differences in mood were found among the three groups. However, 2 days later, the ecstasy users reported feeling significantly more depressed, abnormal, unsociable, unpleasant, and less good tempered than the control participants. Memory was also found to be significantly impaired in ecstasy users.

Mood and Sexuality

A study from the Kinsey Institute for Research on Sex, Gender, and Reproduction was concerned with the effects of fragrance on female sexual arousal and mood during different phases of the menstrual cycle (Graham, Janseen, & Sanders, 2000). Forty women volunteers, ranging in age from 19 to 45 years, were exposed to three fragrance conditions: female fragrance, male fragrance, and a control (no fragrance) condition. Fragrances were defined in this way on the basis of ratings by an independent group of 20 women.

The participants were exposed to these fragrances while watching an erotic film and during a brief period of sexual fantasy. Each participant was tested twice, once during the periovulatory (prior to release of eggs and when the woman can be impregnated) and once during the follicular (or nonfertile) phase of their menstrual cycles.

Sexual arousal was measured by means of a photoplethysmograph, which recorded changes in blood volume within the vaginal tissue. Subjective arousal was measured by having the participants make marks along a line that ranged from 0 (*not at all*) to 10 (*very strongly*). Such ratings were made for genital sensations, vaginal lubrication, the desire for sex, and desire to masturbate. Mood items included *interested, happy, sexy, attractive, confident,* and *disgusted.*

Results were complex. Among the findings were the following:

1. The male fragrance was rated as more intense than the female fragrance.

2. The women rated the male fragrance as sexier, more pleasant, and more appealing than the control fragrance.

3. The erotic film led to stronger feelings of sexual arousal than did the sexual fantasy condition.

4. The women had higher ratings on genital sensations, vaginal lubrication, and desire for sex during the periovulatory phase than during the follicular phase.

5. The mood measures were not significantly related to the different fragrances.

Another recent study using mood measures was concerned with the effects of large doses of testosterone on mood and aggression in normal men (Pope, Kouri, & Hudson, 2000). Clinical reports over the past few years have indicated that male hormones (testosterone and its synthetic analogs) are widely used by young men to improve athletic performance or personal appearance. Occasionally, with high doses, aggression, hypomania, and mania have been reported, and withdrawal from long-term use has been associated with depressive symptoms and suicide.

Participants in Pope et al.'s (2000) study were recruited from colleges and gyms. The 53 participants agreed to receive injections of testosterone or placebo over a 25-week period. Three dose levels of testosterone were used: 150 mg, 300 mg, and 600 mg. Psychological measures included a depression rating scale, an aggression questionnaire, a symptom checklist, and a mania rating scale, as well as diary entries.

Results indicated that testosterone doses up to 300 mg per week had few effects on any of the measures used. However, with doses of 600 mg per week, 12% of the participants became hypomanic, and 4% became manic. It thus appears that high doses of testosterone (i.e., over 300 mg per week) may lead to prominent psychiatric symptoms in a subgroup of users.

Checklists for Measuring States and Traits

One of the confusing problems connected with the study of emotions concerns the distinctions we tend to make between emotions that last a short time and those that last a long time. For example, we may use the word *anger* to describe a transient feeling associated with someone accidentally stepping on your toe. We may also use the same word to describe a person who seems to be irritable much of the time: that is, we think of this person as an angry person. In the first case, the word *angry* refers to a brief state; in the second case, the word *angry* refers to a long-term trait, the kind that we usually think of as a personality trait. Some psychologists suggest that moods are emotional states that may last for hours, days, and weeks, but as stated in an earlier chapter, the distinctions are not precise, and the terms are often used interchangeably.

In general, we assume that emotional states are feelings evoked by immediate changes in a situation (e.g., winning a lottery, threats, losing a job) or by temporary physiological changes (e.g., being very hungry, having a bad headache, being massaged). Traits, in contrast, are usually considered to be stable patterns of behavior that are manifested in a variety of situations. Thus, for example, someone may feel *anxious* in anticipation of an examination. At the other end of the continuum are people for whom *anxiety* is a constant part of their lives, and they are said to have an *anxiety disorder*.

Although the two ends of the continuum are fairly obvious, it has often been pointed out that the distinction between states and traits is largely arbitrary (Allen & Potkay, 1981). Often the same adjective checklist, or other emotion test, can be used to measure both states and traits by a simple change in instructions. If the participants are asked to describe how they feel now, or within the past few days or so, we are asking about emotional states or moods. If, however, participants are asked to describe how they usually feel, we are dealing with long-term traits. This implies that the distinctions between emotions and personality traits are not sharp and that these two domains may represent extremes of the same underlying dimensions. There is thus no simple or single answer to the question of how long emotions last. Whether we call a condition an *emotion* or a *personality trait* is a matter of degree with no clear-cut boundaries separating categories.

SELF-REPORT QUESTIONNAIRE SCALES

In addition to adjective checklists, self-report questionnaire-type scales have been extensively used to assess emotions. Such questionnaires or scales usually ask the respondent to answer questions of the following kind:

- Are you afraid of snakes?
- Do you lack self-confidence?
- Do you feel lonely and blue?
- Are you able to tell other people what is on your mind?
- Do you easily lose your temper?

The answers to such questions presumably reflect emotional states or emotional traits in a person, depending on the nature of the instructions. If the question refers to the present moment or recent past only, the answers probably reflect emotional states, moods, or feelings that may be relatively transient. If the question refers to typical or long-term behaviors or feelings, then the answers reflect emotional traits or dispositions. Questionnaire scales may be illustrated by some of the tests used to measure anxiety.

Taylor Manifest Anxiety Scale

In the early 1950s, Janet Taylor, an experimental psychologist, developed a test to measure manifest anxiety (Taylor, 1953). It was originally constructed by having five clinical psychologists select items from the Minnesota Multiphasic Personality Inventory that the judges agreed had face validity for measuring manifest anxiety. The final version of the scale that was used in many studies had 50 items.

Several studies then compared groups of participants rated high on anxiety with those rated low. By using such extreme groups, it was found that fewer than 20 of the 50 Taylor Manifest Anxiety Scale (MAS) items discriminated between the high- and low-anxiety participants (Hoyt & Magom, 1954). On the basis of these findings, Bendig (1956) then developed a short form of the MAS using only 20 of the items that had approximately the same internal reliability as the long version. Some of the items in the 20-item version are as follows:

- I work under a great deal of tension.
- I frequently find myself worrying about something.
- I certainly feel useless at times.
- I am a high-strung person.
- I sometimes feel that I am about to go to pieces.

The person taking the test is asked to indicate whether each statement is true or false for him or her. It is also evident that the statements imply the existence of per-sisting characteristics and are thus meant to measure trait anxiety. However, the same statements can be used with instructions to respond in terms of recent events (e.g., a 1-week period); the resulting scores would then presumably reflect the existence of a current state of anxiety.

State–Trait Anxiety Inventory

Another scale for measuring anxiety was developed by Spielberger, Gorsuch, and Lushene (1970). The respondent is presented with 20 statements and is asked to indicate on a 4-point scale the extent to which each describes his or her feelings at the present moment. Some of the items are as follows:

- I feel tense.
- I feel upset.
- I feel nervous.
- I am worried.

A second scale measures trait anxiety: The respondents are asked how they generally feel. Examples of items are as follows:

- I wish I could be as happy as others seem to be.
- I lack self-confidence.
- I try to avoid facing a crisis or difficulty.
- I am inclined to take things hard.

The authors of these scales have found that the test–retest reliability of the state anxiety questionnaire is much lower than that of the trait anxiety questionnaire. This is reasonable in that the trait represents a kind of average of many states over time.

Emotions Profile Index

The anxiety scales that have thus far been described are essentially empirical in origin. They stem from daily observations or clinical experience and may have practical value in research. In contrast, the Emotions Profile Index (EPI; Plutchik & Kellerman, 1974), based on a theory of emotion, has been used both as a measure of emotion and as a measure of personality. It provides an index not only of fear and anxiety but also of other emotions and their combinations.

The EPI provides measures of the eight basic emotions first postulated by Plutchik in 1958 and described more fully in subsequent publications (1962, 1970, 1980, 1990). It is based on the idea that all interpersonal personality traits can be conceptualized as resulting from the mixture of two or more primary or basic emotions. This means that those who describe themselves as *shy* or *gloomy* are implicitly telling us something about the primary emotions that go to make up these traits. *Shyness,* for example, implies frequent feelings of *fear,* whereas *gloominess* implies frequent feelings of *sadness.*

The EPI was developed initially by having 10 clinical psychologists rate the primary emotion components of a large number of traits. Twelve trait terms were selected on the grounds of high interjudge consistency on the components and a wide sampling of the trait universe described by factor-analytic studies. These 12 terms were then paired in all possible combinations, yielding 66 pairs. Four of the pairs were found to have identical scoring categories and so were dropped, thus leaving 62 pairs of trait terms for the final form of the test.

The EPI is a forced-choice test. The person taking it is simply asked to indicate which of two paired words is more descriptive of him or her: for example, is he or she more *quarrelsome* or *shy?* The choices are scored in terms of the primary emotions implied by the trait word. Each time the respondent makes a choice between two trait words, he or she adds to the score on one or more of the eight basic emotion dimensions. Thus, rather than measure only anxiety, the test also simultaneously measures anger, sadness, joy, and so on. Because the implications of the choices are not always clear to the respondent, the test has something of a projective quality since the subject does not usually recognize the implicit scoring system. Finally, because of the forced-choice format of the EPI, it tends to reduce response bias associated with a set to choose socially desirable traits. This is true because many of the choices must be made between two equally undesirable or two equally desirable traits. In addition, a bias score is built into the test as a measure of the respondent's tendency to choose socially desirable (or undesirable) traits in those cases in which the items are not matched.

The 12 terms used in the EPI are the following: *adventurous, affectionate, brooding, cautious, gloomy, impulsive, obedient, quarrelsome, resentful, self-conscious, shy,* and *sociable.* A brief definition is provided in the test for each term. The total score for each of the eight primary emotion dimensions is converted into a percentile score based on normative data. The percentile scores are then plotted on a circular diagram, as illustrated in Figure 6.1 for a group of patients with severe depression. The center of the circle represents zero percentile, and the outer circumference of the circle is the 100th percentile. The larger the dark wedge-shaped area, the stronger the emotional disposition that is revealed.

Figure 6.1 shows that the depressed patients are highest on the Depression scale and moderately high on the Timidity (anxiety), Distrust (rejection), Aggression (anger), and Control (expectation) scales. They tend to be low on Dyscontrol (interest in novelty) and Gregariousness (socializing with others). Areas of conflict are revealed by high scores on opposite emotions on the circle. Thus, with this group of patients, a major conflict seems to be between Aggression (anger) and Timidity (anxiety).

Thus far, this chapter has discussed the use of subjective reports of feeling states as measures of emotion. Although several different approaches to such measurement have been developed, the most common is based on the use of adjective checklists of various kinds. Many studies reduce such checklists to a small number of basic dimensions, but at present there is no general agreement. Various investigations have revealed that self-report emotion measures can be reasonably stable and can be valid indices of life stresses or

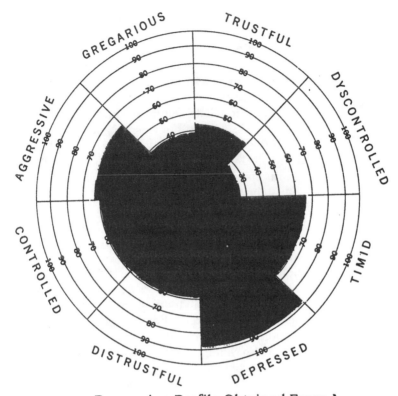

Depression Profile Obtained From A
Group of Manic-Depressive Patients

FIGURE 6.1. Depression profile based on the Emotions Profile Index obtained from a group of manic–depressive patients. From the Psychology and Biology of Emotion by R. Plutchik, p. 117. Copyright 1994 by Robert Plutchik. Reprinted with permission.

other conditions. Such measures thus appear to be useful measures of emotion. However, those that are based on a formal theory of emotion are more likely to reveal important interconnections among variables and to be of general use.

With regard to possible biases in self-report checklists, a recent study has shown that such lists are susceptible to various response biases related to scale type, instructions, and format (Green, Goldman, & Salovey, 1993). When such biases are corrected, mood studies show good evidence of bipolarity of positive and negative terms (e.g., *happy* vs. *sad*) rather than independence. According to Green et al., the best way to correct biases is to use a series of short questions in different formats and to combine the responses. For example,

1. Select the adjectives that describe your feelings (e.g., *nervous, irritated, calm*).

2. Indicate the degree to which you agree or disagree with each statement on a 5-point scale (e.g., *For some reason, I've been feeling sort of nervous*).

3. Indicate the extent to which each statement describes you on a 4-point scale (e.g., *I have felt rather distressed*).

4. Rate on a 7-point scale the extent to which each term describes you (e.g., *scared–not scared*).

A CROSS-CULTURAL QUESTIONNAIRE STUDY
OF EMOTIONS

During the past few years, Scherer and his associates (1986, Wallbott & Scherer, 1989) have been engaged in an extensive cross-cultural study of emotions using questionnaires. These investigators recognized that it is extremely difficult (and unethical) to try to create strong emotions in the laboratory. They therefore decided to rely on the recall of real-life experiences.

The questionnaire they constructed asked for information about the situations that aroused each particular emotion, how the individual felt during the emotion, and how strongly an attempt was made to control the emotion. Initially, four emotions were studied—*joy, sadness, fear,* and *anger*—on the grounds that nearly all theories agree that these emotions are basic or fundamental. Later, the emotions of *disgust, shame,* and *guilt* were added. So far, data have been obtained on 2,235 college students ranging in age from 18 to 35 years, in eight countries: Germany, France, Switzerland, Great Britain, Italy, Israel, Belgium, and Spain.

Among many findings, the questionnaire study threw light on the kinds of physiological nonverbal changes that are likely to occur when people experience different emotions. These results are summarized in Table 6.3.

Subjective experiences of temperature changes in the body appear to be an important discriminator of some emotions. Feeling warm, for example, is exclusively associated with joy, feeling hot is mostly associated with anger, and feeling cold is associated primarily with both fear and sadness. Some bodily changes appear to occur in a wide variety of emotions, a faster heartbeat, for example. The fact that silence is often reported for most of the

TABLE 6.3. Frequent Reactions Associated With Different Emotions Based on 2,235 Respondents in 8 Countries

Emotion	Reaction
Joy	Feeling warm, heartbeat faster, muscles relaxing, laughing, smiling, moving toward, lengthy utterance, speech disturbances.
Anger	Heartbeat faster, muscles tensing, change in breathing, feeling hot, changed facial expression, changes in voice, moving against, lengthy utterance, speech tempo change.
Disgust	Silence, changed facial expression, lengthy utterance, muscles tensing, withdrawing.
Sadness	Crying, sobbing, lump in throat, withdrawing, heartbeat faster, muscles tensing, feeling cold.
Fear	Heartbeat faster, muscles tensing, perspiring, change in breathing, feeling cold, changed facial expression.
Shame	Silence, heartbeat faster, feeling hot, changed facial expression, withdrawing.
Guilt	Silence, heartbeat faster, lump in throat, muscles tensing.

Note. From "Assessing Emotion by Questionnaire," by H. C. Wallbott and K. R. Scherer. In R. Plutchik and H. Kellerman (Eds.), *The Measurement of Emotions*, 1989, Vol. 4, p. 72. Copyright 1989 by Academic Press. Reprinted with permission.

emotions suggests that many individuals exercise self-control over the expression of their emotions. In all, however, it is evident that different patterns of physiological symptoms, nonverbal reactions, and verbal behavior exist for different emotions. It should be emphasized that these patterns are verbal descriptions and are not based on actual observations or measurements of physiology or behavior. Thus, social expectations and stereotypes may have some degree of influence on the reported results.

MEASURING EMOTIONS BY RATING BEHAVIOR

It is obvious that there are certain kinds of populations for whom self-reports of emotional states are not possible. These include severely ill psychiatric patients, patients who are mentally retarded, children and infants, and animals. This section provides a description of some of the types of rating scales that have been developed for use with these populations. Such scales usually require detailed observation of the behavior of an individual by experienced judges. For some scales, the rater is expected to identify the presence of certain classes of behavior assumed to reflect emotions. For other scales, the judge is expected to make an inference about the presence of emotions without necessarily specifying what behavior is being observed. Interjudge reliability is obviously important in all such ratings. The following sections illustrate the types of scales used with these various populations.

Scales for Rating Psychiatric Patients

The psychiatric literature contains many examples of rating scales used to assess emotional states in psychiatric patients. This abundance of rating scales reflects the fact that psychiatrists are usually not inclined to accept a patient's self-descriptions at face value; they assume that repression, denial, and lack of insight often prevent an accurate self-description. Therefore, psychiatrists typically make ratings after an interview with a patient or after ward observation.

The use of rating scales may be illustrated by a study reported by two psychiatrists (Clancy & Noyes, 1976) that was designed to identify the behavioral correlates of anxiety. The records of over 4,000 patients referred for psychiatric consultation over a 5-year period were reviewed. Of this total, 82 patients were given a primary or secondary diagnosis of anxiety neurosis, had complete records, and had no other medical condition. From these records, the frequency of report of various symptoms was determined; the list is presented in Table 6.4. This list includes symptoms found in patients diagnosed as experiencing persistent anxieties. It provides a way of identifying the relative importance, as measured by frequency of occurrence, of many symptoms. It is evident that anxiety states include a large number of physiological symptoms that can only be determined by observation or examination.

Scales for Rating Patients With Mental Retardation

A number of scales have been developed for rating the behavior of patients with mental retardation. Although the focus of these scales is usually on cognitive or functional skills, some include items that relate to emotions. In one of the more widely used scales

TABLE 6.4. Symptoms of Anxiety Obtained From the Records of 71 Patients

Symptom	%	Symptom	%
Chronic nervousness	97	Abdominal pain or discomfort	44
Attacks of nervousness	92	Depressed mood	41
Shortness of breath	70	Crying spells	37
Muscle aching or tension	65	Anorexia	31
Sweating, flushing, or chills	61	Fear of death or dying	24
Chest pain	56	Difficulty swallowing	23
Fatigue or tiredness	56	Blurred vision	21
Insomnia	52	Restlessness	20
Numbness or tingling	52	Weight loss	15
Trembling	52	Poor concentration	14
Headaches	51	Irritability	10
Palpitations	48	Dry mouth	8
Nausea or vomiting	46	Fear of insanity	8
Weakness	45	Urinary frequency	8
Fainting or lightheadedness	45	Nightmares	7
Dizziness	44		

Note. From "Anxiety Neurosis: A Disease for the Medical Model," by J. Clancy and R. Noyes Jr., 1976, *Psychosomatics*, 17, p. 92. Copyright 1976 by The American Psychosomatic Society. Reprinted with permission.

(Nihira, Foster, Shellhaas, & Leland, 1970), there are a number of ratings to be made about the emotional behavior of the patient with mental retardation. Here are two examples:

Item 1: *Select all statements that are true of the person.*
1. Uses threatening gestures
2. Indirectly causes injury to others
3. Spits on others
4. Scratches or pinches others
5. Pulls others' hair, ears, etc.
6. Bites others
7. Kicks, strikes, or steps on others
8. Throws objects at others
9. Uses objects as weapons against others
10. Chokes others
11. Hurts animals

Item 2: *Select all statements that are true of the person.*
1. Is timid and shy in social situations
2. Hides face in group situations
3. Does not mix well with others
4. Always prefers to be alone.

It is evident that the first group of behaviors is designed to measure the emotion of anger or the trait of aggressiveness, whereas the second group attempts to provide an index of timidity. Interjudge reliability is reported to be high.

Scales for Rating Children

The fact that young children cannot be expected to clearly articulate their feelings has led developmental psychologists to rely heavily on behavior rating scales to evaluate emotions in children. Of the well-known standardized scales, one of the earliest introduced into general use was the Fels Child Behavior Scales (Richards & Simons, 1941), developed at the Fels Institute at Antioch College. There are 30 Fels scales suitable for children in the first few grades as well as for preschool children. Judges are asked to make a rating along a line that represents different degrees of a trait. Such emotions or traits as aggressiveness, affectionateness, emotional control, and vigor of activity are rated. Interjudge reliability is reported to be high.

Another example of rating states used to measure emotions in children was reported by Brody, Plutchik, Reilly, and Petersen (1973). In this study an attempt was made to determine the relations between personality traits of third-grade children and the extent to which the children showed problem behavior in the classroom. In addition, relations among personality traits, IQ, and absence records were determined.

A random sample of 60 children was selected from the 600 children in the third grade of a school district. The home room teacher for each of these 60 children was asked to rate each designated child on 12 personality traits using a 9-point scale of intensity. For example, some of the descriptions were as follows:

- Someone who often tries new activities for excitement.
- Someone who starts arguments.
- Someone who feels timid with other people and in new situations.

A second measure, the Problem Inventory, simply listed 10 problems that children have been reported to show in a school setting. These include reading problems, speech problems, withdrawal, temper tantrums, stealing, hyperactivity, fighting, unable to get along with other children, disruptive, and daydreaming. Each designated student was rated by a teacher on a 3-point scale that ranged from *not a problem* to *slight problem* to *serious problem*.

Results showed that the girls were significantly more sociable and affectionate than the boys, and the boys were significantly more quarrelsome than the girls. No other sex differences were found in personality. It was also determined that children who were rated high on the traits cautious, self-conscious, quarrelsome, or impulsive tended to have more problems, and children who were rated high on sociable had fewer. In terms of the frequency of problems, 8% of the children were described as having a serious problem in getting along with other children, 6% were seriously withdrawn, and 3% had severe temper tantrums or severe hyperactivity. One of the conclusions of the study emphasized the point that there are different kinds of emotional difficulties that children have and that each type has its own spectrum of problems associated with it. Such a conclusion would not have been possible without a set of rating scales that covered a wide range of emotional states.

Behavior Ratings of Infants

In what many consider to be a classic study of this type, Birch and his colleagues (1962) studied temperament in infants and the changes that occur over time. For this purpose, they obtained information on 95 infants from age 2 months to age 24 months at 3-month intervals for the 1st year and at 6-month intervals during the 2nd year. Information on each child was based on the mother's reports, plus direct observations of the child in the home, in a playroom, and in nursery school.

From a content analysis of the records of the first 22 children, nine categories were defined as "primary reaction characteristics" and labeled as follows: (a) activity level, (b) rhythmicity (predictability of behavior over time), (c) approach or withdrawal to new stimuli, (d) adaptability to altered situations, (e) intensity of reaction, (f) threshold of responsiveness, (g) quality of mood (pleasant vs. unfriendly), (h) distractibility, and (i) attention span and persistence.

Analysis of the data showed that some children respond quietly and placidly to a new situation, approach it at once, and adapt quickly and smoothly. At the other extreme are those children who withdraw sharply and violently, persist tenaciously in their old behavior, and adapt irregularly and slowly to a new situation. Birch et al. hypothesized that these reaction patterns are the bases for later emotional and personality development or, in other words, the sources of temperamental differences among individuals. A follow-up study by Scarr and Salapatek (1970) examined these ideas in greater detail. They explored the development of a variety of fears in infants during the first 2 years of life and tried to relate these fears to the primary reaction characteristics described by Birch and his colleagues. Ninety-one infants between the ages of 2 and 23 months were exposed to a series of six stimuli that have been reported to produce fear reactions in infants and young children. The stimuli were as follows: strangers, heights, jack-in-the-box, mechanical dog, loud noises, and masks. The child's fear reaction to each stimulus was rated on a 3-point scale: 1 = *no evidence of fear; 2 = sober, cautious, stops ongoing activity; 3 = fretting, crying, fleeing to mother.* The nine temperamental characteristics were rated after a structured 3-hour interview with the child's mother.

The results showed that the fear of heights tended to increase linearly up to the age of about 18 months but that the fears of the mechanical dog, noise, and jack-in-the-box remained fairly constant over the 7–24-month age range. Fears of strangers and masks increased to a maximum at about age 10 months and then remained constant. It was also found that a particular temperament pattern correlated with fear behavior. Infants who had generally depressive moods, low threshold of response, poor adaptability, and low rhythmicity were more likely to show fear across situations. Finally, there appeared to be a fair amount of stability of fear reactions over a 2-month period when the same infant was tested twice. Scarr and Salapatek (1970) concluded that these findings suggest a possible genetic role in the development of fear during infancy.

SCALES FOR RATING EMOTIONS IN ANIMALS

Comparative psychologists and ethologists have been rating the emotional behavior of animals for a long time. In fact, all those who have followed the Darwinian tradition have no difficulty with the idea that animals show emotional behavior and that such behavior can reliably be rated. This section provides some illustrations.

The identification of emotions in animals requires careful observation of the animal's behavior, some knowledge of its history, observations of the consequences of its behavior, and knowledge of how other animals react to the animal under observation. Using this framework, one of the most detailed studies of social behavior and emotions in animals was carried out by Van Hooff (1973) on a chimpanzee colony of 25 animals at a research laboratory in New Mexico. Over 200 hours were spent in direct observation of these animals, and a catalog of observed behaviors was developed, with a record kept of the relative frequency of each behavior. Also noted were interactions between animals and the effects of each action.

From these observations, Van Hooff identified 53 behavior elements that were scored as frequently preceding or succeeding other elements, thus creating a list of behaviors in their typical sequential context. A type of factor analysis was then used to identify clusters of behaviors that tended to occur together. The results of this analysis are summarized in Exhibit 6.1.

▬▬▬   EXHIBIT 6.1. CLUSTER ANALYSIS OF CHIMPANZEE BEHAVIORS

Group I: The Affinitive System
Examples: Touch, cling, hold out hand, smooth approach, silent pout, groom, embrace, pant, mount.

Group II: The Play System
Examples: Relaxed open mouth, grasp, poke, gnaw, gnaw-wrestle, pull limb, gymnastics, hand-wrestle.

Group III: The Aggressive System
Examples: Trample, tug, brusque rush, bite, grunt-bark, sway-walk, hit, stamp, shrill bark.

Group IV: The Submissive System
Examples: Flight, crouch, avoid, bared-teeth scream, bared-teeth yelps, parry, shrink-flinch, hesitant approach.

Group V: The Excitement System
Examples: Squat-bobbing, rapid "ohoh," rising hoot, upsway.

Note. From "The Structural Analysis of the Social Behavior of a Semi-Captive Group of Chimpanzees," by J. A. R. A. M. van Hooff. In M. von Cranach and I. Vine (Eds.), *Social Communication and Movement*, 1973, p. 243. Copyright 1973 by Academic Press. Reprinted with permission.

Most of the behaviors tend to fall into five groups, which Van Hooff called the *affinitive* system, the *play* system, the *aggressive* system, the *submissive* system, and the *excitement* system. These terms clearly relate to emotional states, and it is evident that animal social behaviors do not occur in isolation but always as part of a complex emotional interaction. It is interesting that Jane Goodall (1987), after years of observations of chimpanzees in Africa, arrived at a fairly similar classification of their social and emotional behaviors. Her list includes the following terms: (a) *flight and avoidance,* (b) *frustration,* (c) *aggressive behavior,* (d) *submissive behavior,* (e) *reassurance behavior,* (f) *greeting behavior,* and (g) *communications related to sex, play, and mothering.* It is thus evident that emotions enter into the basic fabric of all social encounters.

The Rating of Emotions in Baboons and Chimpanzees

Another interesting way to assess emotions in animals has been described by Buirski, Kellerman, Plutchik, Weininger, and Buirski (1973). These investigators selected and defined a set of 10 terms descriptive of emotional behavior: *belligerent, fearful, inquisitive, irritable, defiant, depressed, dominant, playful, sociable,* and *submissive.* The emotion components of each of these states was determined by consensus of a group of judges. The terms were then paired in all possible combinations, and the resulting form was used in a study of baboons at the Nairobi National Park in Kenya, Africa.

Three observers watched a small troop of 7 baboons for 35 hours over a 3-week period. Every incident of grooming was noted in terms of who groomed whom and the length of time of the act. At the end of the 35 hours of observation, the baboons in the troop were independently ranked on dominance. Each rater simply picked one word from each pair that best described the behavior of the baboon being observed. Interrater reliability for most of the scales was high.

Among the many interesting findings of this investigation is the fact that there was an almost perfect correlation between the dominance rank and some of the indices of grooming. The most dominant animal, Big Harry, was groomed most. In general, the higher dominance animals had briefer but more frequent grooms by others, and they did less grooming of others. It was also found that the animals rated lowest on the fearfulness dimension of the scale and highest on the aggressiveness dimension were groomed the most by the other baboons.

This same measurement technique was adapted by Buirski, Plutchik, and Kellerman (1978) for use with chimpanzees. Observations were made at the Gombe Stream Research Centre in Tanzania, East Africa, on 23 free-living chimpanzees: 13 males and 10 females. This Centre had been established by Jane Goodall. Ratings were made by seven graduate students living at the camp who were quite familiar with the day-to-day behavior of most of the chimps. Raters were asked to rate those chimps whose behavior they were most familiar with, in terms of the defined scales. They picked one word from each of the 45 pairs that best described the behavior of the chimp under observation. Most of the interjudge reliabilities were greater than .70.

The dominance rank of each male was independently estimated from brief biographies of the animals. The rank position was then correlated with each of the eight emotion dimensions. The set of correlations suggested a profile: Dominant animals tend to be aggressive and distrustful, whereas nondominant animals tend to be timid, impulsive, and trustful. Sex differences were also found. The female chimpanzees were rated as more timid, more depressed, and more trustful than the male chimpanzees, who were judged as more gregarious and more distrustful.

There are a number of implications of this study of chimpanzees. In terms of emotions, chimpanzees have been reported to show depression, curiosity, aggression, jealousy, affection, timidity, and other states (Goodall, 1987), and there is no reason why these emotions cannot be reliably rated by experienced judges.

It is important to emphasize that the use of the emotion and personality language does not mean that we are using a subjective, imprecise terminology. All important terms in psychology are about inferred states, including such common terms as *learning, memory, conditioning, displacement, pair bonds,* and *ritualization.* In chimpanzees, an extensive non-verbal communication system is evident; they bow, kiss, hold hands, touch and pat each other, embrace, tickle one another with their fingers, bite, punch, kick, scratch each other, and pull out one another's hair. Not only do many of these movements look remarkably like many of the expressive postures and gestures of our own species, but the contexts likely to elicit the behaviors may be strikingly similar in chimpanzees and humans. In addition, each call of the chimpanzee is fairly reliably associated with some specific emotion (Van Lawick-Goodall, 1973). The point being made is that terms like *gregarious, timid, depressed,* and *aggressive* are fundamentally no more subjective or less useful than other terms currently used in psychology or ethology.

An Example of Abnormal Behavior in a Chimpanzee

An interesting clinical observation resulted from a study by Buirski and Plutchik (1991). Among the sample of chimps that were observed was one female, named Passion, whose ratings suggested considerable variation from the average of other females. For example, Passion was judged to be considerably more aggressive than the other females, more depressed, and more distrustful. She was also rated as less timid and less controlled. The overall impression of Passion was that of an isolated, aggressive individual who would be considered in human terms to be severely disturbed.

This image of Passion may be considered in the light of her past history and subsequent behavior. Passion's daughter Pom was born in 1965, and from the beginning Passion was observed to display extraordinarily inefficient and indifferent maternal behavior. In all respects Passion was a somewhat unnatural mother. Whereas other chimp mothers are protective of their infants, Passion seemed dissatisfied and neglectful. It appeared that Pom had to fight continually for her own survival. Passion was not a nurturing mother and did not facilitate her daughter's suckling, often ignoring Pom's whimpers completely. If Pom happened to be suckling when Passion wanted to travel, she typically moved off without waiting for her daughter to finish. Passion showed a similarly callous attitude toward Pom when her daughter was learning to ride and later walk. Pom would often be seen frantically trying to catch up with Passion, who had suddenly gotten up and walked away. Later on, rather than being able to separate from her mother to wander off a distance in play or exploration, which would be age-appropriate behavior, Pom needed to sit or play very close to Passion. For months on end, Pom could not play freely with other infants without holding tightly to her mother's hand. Pom seemed to fear being abandoned by Passion.

A year or so after these ratings were made, Passion, in collaboration with her daughter Pom, was observed to steal three tiny chimpanzee infants from their mothers and then to kill and eat them. Passion and Pom worked as a team in attacking the mothers of their victims. Passion, heavier and stronger, grappled with the mother while Pom pulled at the baby. Once they had possession of the babies, no further aggression was directed toward the victims' mothers. Only Passion and Pom were ever observed to show predatory interest in infant chimps. Over a 4-year period, these two were believed to be responsible for the disappearance and deaths of as many as seven other chimpanzee infants. After Passion died, Pom was never seen to engage in these kinds of behaviors again. The observation of Passion and Pom's infanticidal and cannibalistic behavior is unique and bizarre, not only in the chimpanzee literature but in all primate literature.

The point of this description is to illustrate the fact that emotional states or traits can be reliably related in animals as well as humans and that they can be related meaningfully to other classes of behavior.

Measuring Aggression in Rats

As was stated earlier in this chapter, to measure something, one must have some idea of what the concept is that is to be measured. In trying to measure aggressive behavior in animals, one must have some ideas of what aggression is. Ethologists, who observe animals in natural settings, have provided many insights into this issue. For example, Moyer (1983) described seven types of situations that usually elicit aggression in animals: predatory, intermale, fear-induced, territorial, irritable, maternal, and instrumental. An alternative scheme proposed by Brain (1981) listed five types of aggression: self-defensive, parental, predatory-attack, reproduction termination, and social conflict; Eibl-Eibesfeldt (1979), another ethologist, suggested that aggression be defined as all behavior patterns

Offensive Postures in the Rat

(a) The alpha rat displays sideways offensive posture; the submissive animal is boxing.
(b) The full aggressive and full submissive postures.

A

B

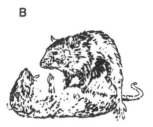

FIGURE 6.2. Offensive postures in the rat. (a) The alpha rat displays sideways offensive posture; the submissive rat is boxing. (b) The full aggressive and full submissive postures. From "Measuring Animal Aggression," by D. Benton. In R. Plutchik and H. Kellerman (Eds.), *The Measurement of Emotions* (1989, Vol. 4, p. 263). Copyright 1989 by Academic Press. Reprinted with permission.

that lead to the spacing out of conspecifics (i.e., members of the same species) or to the domination of one individual over another.

On the basis of these ideas, aggression has been measured in a variety of ways. Examples are the following (based on the review by Benton, 1989):

1. The latency to start fighting.
2. The total time spent fighting.
3. A single rating of aggression on a scale.
4. The percentage of animals that fight.
5. The number of bouts of fighting.

However, Benton pointed out that aggressive encounters are so complex that single measures are bound to be inadequate. Figure 6.2 shows some of the aggressive and submissive postures seen in rats when fighting.

Table 6.5 reveals the variety of specific acts or behaviors seen when two male mice are placed together. Benton (1989) concluded that a single measure will not adequately reflect the multiple factors that inevitably influence the behavior of an animal. Aggression is not a unitary phenomenon and multiple measures are needed to reflect the complexities of such behaviors.

MEASURING EMOTIONS THROUGH THE PRODUCTS OF HUMAN BEHAVIOR

Another approach to measuring emotions depends not on the observation of behavior but rather on studying the effects or products of behavior. For example, if we see a child throwing a stone through a school window and shattering it, we might make an inference that the child was angry about something. But what if we see only the broken window? Can we also make a reasonable guess that it was broken by someone who was angry?

There are many situations that occur in everyday life that are like that. For example, we may read a poem and conclude that the author was depressed, or see a modern painting

TABLE 6.5. Behaviors Observed in a Dyadic Encounter of Male Mice

Posture	Comments
	Offensive
Aggressive groom	Vigorous grooming of immobilized opponent.
Biting attack	Bites opponent.
Chase	Pursues opponent.
Circle	Cycles of approaching and leaving with no intervening activity.
Fight	Intense biting and kicking of opponent.
Lunge	An "intention movement" for biting opponent.
Sideways offensive	Attention to opponent, eyes slitted, and ears flattened; orientation toward opponent with at least one forepaw on the ground.
Tail rattle	Tail vibrated against ground.
Upright offensive	Upright or vertical position, ears flattened, eyes slitted; head horizontal and extended toward opponent.
	Defensive
Crouch	All paws on ground, body hunched; generally immobile with slight scanning movements of the head.
Flag/evade	Avoids opponent.
Flee	Runs from opponent.
Freeze	Immobile in any position except crouch.
Kick	Fends off other mouse with hindpaws or forepaws.
Sideways Defensive	Lateral orientation to opponent, head up, eyes open, and ears extended; at least one forepaw on the ground.
Upright defensive	Forepaws off the ground, head up, eyes open, and ears extended; sometimes regarded as a submissive response.
	Social
Approach	Moves toward opponent.
Attempted mount	Palpitation of opponent's sides with forepaws, pelvic thrusting.
Attend	Directs head toward opponent.
Body sniff	Sniffs opponent's body.
Crawl under	Tunnels under opponent.
Follow	Moves after opponent.
Genital sniff	Sniffs perianal region of opponent.
Groom	Grooms opponent.
Head groom	Grooms head of opponent.
Head sniff	Sniffs head of opponent.
Leave	Ambulates away from opponent.
Nose to nose	Sniffs face of opponent.
Stretched attention	Orientating to opponent at a distance—an extreme version of attending.
Walk round	Locomotion around opponent at close quarters.

TABLE 6.5. (*continued*)

Posture	Comments
	Nonsocial
Abbreviated dig	Forepaws kick sawdust backward.
Back rear	One or both forepaws on opponent's back without nose or whisker contact.
Dig	Forepaws and hindpaws used in alternation.
Explore	Ambulation around cage with sniffing.
Jump	Orienting to opponent at close quarters
Push dig	Forepaws push sawdust forward.
Scan	Scanning movements of head while standing; attention not on opponent.
Scratch	Scratches self, often with hindpaw, like a dog.
Self groom	Auto grooming.

Note. From "Measuring Animal Aggression," by D. Benton. In R. Plutchik and H. Kellerman (Eds.), *The Measurement of Emotions*, 1989, Vol. 4, p. 278. Copyright 1989 by Academic Press. Reprinted with permission.

that suggests strong feelings of anger or anguish in the artist, as was probably the case when Picasso painted the Guernica picture based on the bombing of a Spanish town. Such judgments may be wrong, of course, yet clinical psychologists often make them. They infer something about a client's emotions on the basis of the fantasy behavior of the client. These are the so-called projective tests.

A well-known example is the Rorschach Ink Blot Test, in which an individual is presented with a series of symmetrical inkblots and is asked to describe what he or she sees in each one. Depending on the images seen and the number of responses obtained, clinical psychologists make inferences about the client's anger, anxiety, hatred, and mental status. Similarly, the Thematic Apperception Test, or TAT, requests an individual to make up a series of stories on the basis of cards depicting scenes of various kinds involving people.

Figure 6.3 is an illustration of this idea. The picture is an etching made in the 19th-century and shows a seated man surrounded by many children. A woman stands at the door in the background with her arms around the shoulders of two small children. What kind of story would you create about this scene?

When shown to one student, she said,

> This is a clinic, and the man in the center is the doctor in charge. The doctor is a very kind man, and very permissive. He is trying to make the new child brought by the young man, comfortable. The woman at the door is bringing her two children.

Another student said:

> This is a man that everyone looks up to—like a doctor. The mother in the corner with her two children really needs help. She is frightened.

In these brief descriptions, one student emphasizes the permissive quality of the key figure, whereas the other student describes him as having high social status. The first student

FIGURE 6.3. An illustration of an ambiguous picture about which stories can be created to reveal emotional states.

ignores the emotions of the woman, whereas the second emphasizes the woman's frightened appearance. From such stories, one may gain some limited insight into the emotions of the viewer.

Figure Drawings as Measures of Emotion

One of the more widely used projective measures of emotions is the Figure Drawing Test. In this test, the client is simply asked to draw a male figure and a female figure. Depending on such things as details included on the figures, their location on the page, and the style of the drawing, many inferences are made about the emotions and psychological adjustment of the client.

This can be illustrated by a study that compared figure drawings in normal and abnormal geriatric and nongeriatric groups (Plutchik, Conte, Weiner, & Teresi, 1978). In this investigation, figure drawings were obtained from 72 normal adults, 48 adult psychiatric inpatients, 30 senior citizens living in the community, and 33 elderly inpatients in a mental hospital. The drawings were coded, and then each was rated without knowledge of the group to which it belonged. Ratings were made on 12 emotional indicators that had been previously identified. These indicators included such things as shading on the face or body, gross asymmetry of the limbs, strongly slanted figures, crossed eyes, teeth shown, and big hands. From these drawings, experienced clinicians were to make blind ratings on such emotions as aggression, depression, anxiety, emotional conflict, and impulsivity. The use of several independent judges revealed that these ratings could be made reliably. Examples of the drawings are shown in Figure 6.4.

Figure Drawings

These drawings were drawn by (a) normal adult, (b) psychiatric adult patient, (c) normal elderly, (d) psychiatric elderly patient. The figures are not presented in their original true proportions.

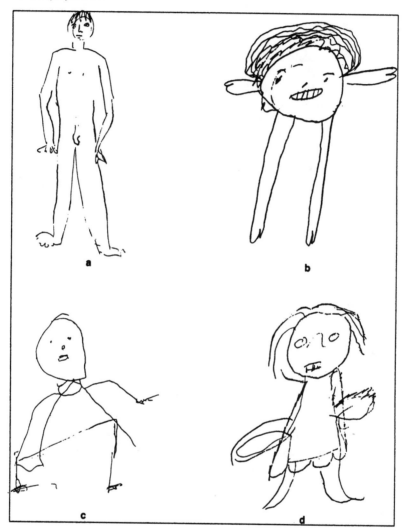

FIGURE 6.4. Figure drawings obtained from (a) normal adult, (b) psychiatric adult patient, (c) normal elderly person, and (d) psychiatric elderly patient. The figures are not presented in their original true proportions. From "Studies of Body Image: IV. Figure Drawings in Normal and Abnormal Geriatric and Nongeriatric Groups," by R. Plutchik, H. R. Conte, M. Weiner, and J. Teresi, 1978, *Journal of Gerontology, 33,* p. 72. Copyright 1978 by the American Geriatrics Society. Reprinted with permission.

The results showed that various measures of dysfunction increased with age. The figures were smaller, and ratings of such problems as emotional conflict and depression increased. It was also found that adult psychiatric patients tended to draw small figures, lacking in sexual differentiation and with signs of emotional conflict and depression. The differences between adult patients and adult nonpatients were similar to the differences between adult nonpatients and elderly people of any status. When the figure drawings obtained from normal elderly individuals were compared with psychiatric patients (elderly or adult), very few differences were found.

These findings indicated that clinicians might easily confuse the figure drawings of a normal elderly person with those of a psychiatric patient. Norms based on figure drawings of children do not apply to the elderly population, and considerable caution should be used by clinicians when using figure drawings as a measure of psychopathology in elderly people. The study cited is important not only in revealing these facts but in showing that emotions may reliably be rated from figure drawings, thus providing another indirect measure of emotions.

An illustration of projective measures of emotion used with children is seen in the study by Warren, Emde, and Sroufe (2000). Five-year-old children were asked to complete 16 stories based on brief initial statements. The following are some examples of the initial statements:

1. In a park, the child kicks a ball away from the family. Suddenly a scary dog appears and barks loudly.
2. It's nighttime and the child is alone. Suddenly the lights go out, and the child thinks he/she hears a monster.
3. The child has been looking forward all day to visiting with a friend, but Mom tells the child that he/she can't go.

The child's narratives were coded for emotional content and related to measures of child behavior (the Child Behavior Checklist) and to a self-report measure of anxiety. It was found that the child's anxious expectations measured at 5 years of age predicted diagnosis-related anxiety symptoms at age 6 years. Warren et al. concluded that children who tell stories indicating difficulty in separating from parents and who are unable to seek help from parents may be at risk for later anxiety.

PHYSIOLOGICAL AND NEURAL MEASURES OF EMOTION

Physiological Measures

Ever since William James claimed that an emotional feeling was basically a perception of internal bodily changes, there has been much interest in the measurement of autonomic changes as measures of emotion. Most of this research, however, has dealt with generalized stress or arousal rather than with particular emotions, and the results have not always been consistent.

One result of this interest in autonomic changes in the body under conditions of stress has been the development of the field of "lie detection." By the mid-1980s, lie detection tests were used very widely, mostly by private corporations, in an effort to detect theft or identify "honest" employees. Government employees who deal with classified information are now required to take lie detector tests during investigations of leaks. However, because of the criticisms leveled against such tests, the U.S. Congress in 1988 passed a law prohibiting most nongovernmental lie detector testing. What then is the nature of the claims and the counterclaims?

A lie detector is simply a polygraph used to measure a number of different physiological changes in a person while he or she is being asked "yes" or "no" questions related to a possible theft or crime. Typically, the measures obtained are breathing pattern, pulse rate, blood pressure, and the electrical resistance of the palm of the hand, which is believed to reflect level of sweating. It is assumed that when a person tells a lie, this will be associated with some degree of stress as compared with parts of the record when no lie is told. If this assumption is true, there should be noticeable changes in the physiological indices when the lie is told. This assumption does not mean that there is an unambiguous connection between any one emotion and the recorded autonomic changes, only that any emotional state related to stress might be reflected by these measures of arousal.

Over the years many studies have been carried out in an effort to determine how accurate the lie detector polygraph is. The results of such studies suggest that a trained administrator will detect deception at better than a chance level, but far from perfectly. The result of these findings is that most state courts do not accept polygraph evidence in criminal cases. Although the study of deception by measuring autonomic changes is still in vogue, it is debatable how much this research has contributed to our understanding of emotions.

Exhibit 6.2 lists the many kinds of physiological measures that have been used in studies of emotion. They represent most of the organ systems of the body, and although many hundreds of studies have been carried out using such measures, great differences exist, not only in relation to the conclusions of such investigations but also with regard to the actual methods of measuring those variables. For example, although the electrical properties of the skin have been examined in literally thousands of studies, there is still disagreement on such basic issues as whether to measure skin resistance or skin potential, what types of electrodes are best, whether to use direct current or alternating current stimulation, whether to use constant voltage or constant current, and whether to use electrode paste and skin-rubbing techniques. Such issues apply to all the measurement procedures to some degree. No one knows to what extent inconsistent reports reflect variations in instrument techniques.

Another problem that has frequently been noted with regard to the use of physiological measures is that there seems to be considerable independence in the modes of reaction of the different organ systems. This results in little or no correlation between different measures of autonomic reactivity. It means that multiple measures of physiological activity must be used in order not to miss physiological reactions when they occur and also to avoid overgeneralizing from single measures. No single measure can serve as an accurate index of general arousal.

Problems connected with identifying physiological correlates of emotion relate not only to the measuring instruments but to other factors as well. First, such research requires an independent measure of emotion, which must be based either on self-report or on behavioral observations (or both). Unfortunately, some studies have assumed that changes in skin resistance or heart rate necessarily mean that an emotion has occurred, without some independent assessment of the emotion. Second, because most research situations in which subjects are evaluated are complex, it is likely that complex, or mixed,

---

EXHIBIT 6.2. PHYSIOLOGICAL MEASURES MOST OFTEN USED IN STUDIES OF EMOTION

1. Electrical phenomena of the skin (skin resistance or conductance and skin potentials).
2. Blood pressure (systolic and diastolic pressures).
3. Electrocardiogram and heart rate.
4. Respiration rate, depth, and pattern.
5. Skin temperature.
6. Pupillary response (expansion and contraction of pupil).
7. Salivary secretion.
8. Skin sweating.
9. Analysis of blood, saliva, and urine (e.g., blood sugar, hormones, metabolites).
10. Metabolic rate (oxygen consumption).
11. Muscle tension (muscle potentials).
12. Tremor (of striated muscles).
13. Eye blink and eye movement.
14. Evoked potentials (measures brain responses to repeated stimulation).
15. Electroencephalograph (electrical activity of the brain).
16. Positron Emission Tomography (PET; measures metabolic activity in the brain).
17. Functional Magnetic Resonance Imaging (FMRI; measures blood flow in specific areas of the brain).
18. Magnetic Resonance Spectroscope Imaging (MRSI; measures the metabolism of specific chemicals in the brain).
19. Magnetoencephalography (MEG; measures changes in weak magnetic fields due to electrical currents in the brain).
20. Near Infrared Imaging (NIR; measures brain blood flow).
21. Event-Related Optical Signal (EROS; measures movement of light through local brain areas).

Note. From *The Psychology and Biology of Emotion,* by R. Plutchik, 1994, p. 137. Copyright 1994 by HarperCollins. Reprinted with permission.

---

emotional states are aroused. The problem then becomes one of relating some pattern of physiological changes to some pattern of mixed emotion, an extremely difficult problem. Third, present technology is capable of recording many covert and subtle responses of which a subject is totally unaware, such as EEG changes or skin resistance changes. In such cases it is especially difficult to relate the physiological index to an emotional state. A fourth problem is that each physiological system has several different functions within the body. For example, the sweating system and the cardiovascular system act not only in relation to emotions but they regulate temperature as well. The result is that different environmental conditions, and different fatigue and hunger conditions, will influence the pattern of physiological changes that occur in response to an emotion-producing stimulus. They will therefore obscure the nature of the physiological response. Finally, it has been demonstrated that different emotional states (e.g., fear and anger, pleasure and pain) have some physiological changes in common.

The result of all these problems is that it is very difficult to establish clear-cut relations between emotional states and physiological responses. There is no way that we can read a skin resistance meter or a cardio-tachometer and say: "This person is experiencing an emotion, and that emotion is fear." The emotional life is richer, more subtle, and more varied than are physiological changes. There is no one-to-one correspondence between self-reports of emotions and physiology that has yet been established. For all these reasons, it is easier to study the relations between emotional behavior and physiology in lower animals.

Brain Functioning Measures

One example of this approach is a study by Morton (1986) that measured regional brain activity in rats or mice during emotional behavior. In this investigation, a form of sugar used by the brain during metabolism (2-deoxyglucose) was injected into a rat's blood with some radioactive tracer in it. During a 30-minute period while the rat was engaged in some form of emotional behavior, the radio labeled glucose was deposited in active brain sites. After the animal was sacrificed, X-ray film was used to detect the brain structures where increased or decreased metabolic activity occurred during the emotional behavior, in contrast to control rats.

Three emotional situations were studied: fighting induced by introducing an intruder male into the colony cage, fear induced by the experimenter approaching the animal in a confined area, and copulatory behavior. Eighty-six brain loci were analyzed for each of 52 rats in the study.

The results showed significant increases in glucose uptake in the fearful rats in the prefrontal cortex and in the corpus callosum and significant decreases in parts of the hippocampus and amygdala. In the attacking rats, there was an increase in lateral hypothalamus glucose uptake and a decrease in septal metabolism. The copulating rats showed large increases in metabolic activity in the globus pallidus of the forebrain and in the cerebellar cortex. Almost all the changes that were found were in limbic or limbic-associated brain structures. These brain structures are described in the chapter on the brain (chapter 11).

The value of this method for studying emotions in animals is that it allows examination of the functioning of the brain uninfluenced by drugs, electrodes, or lesions. This method is also similar to positron emission tomography (or PET scans), which can be used with humans. Through the use of similar methods in humans and animals, it may be possible to reveal emotional continuities across phylogenetic levels.

In recent years, a number of highly sophisticated electronic-computer systems have been developed to study the way the brain functions. Although these developments were designed primarily for medical applications, psychologists have begun collaborations with neurologists and other scientists to apply these new technologies to psychological problems.

Figure 6.5 shows a magnetic resonance image and a simultaneous positron emission image obtained from a single patient with depression. The rate of glucose metabolism in the amygdala can be measured from these scans. The metabolic rate in the right amygdala appears to predict some arousal of emotion in the patients with depression (Abercrombie, Schaefer, Larson, et al., 1998).

Another study examined 100 patients with focal brain lesions. The patients were asked to rate the intensity of six emotions from facial expressions, to match facial expressions with the names of the six basic emotions, and to sort facial expression photographs into emotion categories (Adolphs, Damasio, Travel, Cooper, & Damasio, 2000). A nonpatient control group was also used.

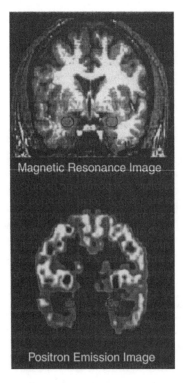

FIGURE 6.5. Magnetic resonance image (top) and a corresponding positron emission image for one patient. The lines forming a box are around the amygdala. From "Metabolic Rate in the Right Amygdala Predicts Negative Affect in Depressed Patients," by H. C. Abercrombie, S. M. Schaefer, C. L. Larson, et al., 1998, *NeuroReport, 9*, p. 3305. Copyright 1998 by Lippincott, Williams and Wilkins. Reprinted with permission.

Scores on these various tasks were related to lesion location and size, as illustrated in Figure 6.6. It was found that lesions in somatosensory cortex, which impaired some somatic sensations, were associated with impaired recognition of emotions from facial expressions. This was true only for lesions in the right hemisphere. Adolphs et al. (2000) concluded that the recognition of facial expressions of emotions involves right-hemisphere regions that respond to visual cues, brain representations of certain somatic states, and links between the two. These findings appear to be consistent with reports that facial expressions produced by voluntary contractions of specific muscles tend to induce feelings consistent with the expression produced (Levenson, Ekman, & Friesin, 1990).

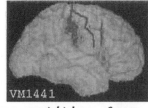 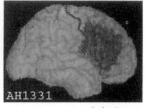

score partition: lower   lower   higher

FIGURE 6.6. Three examples of individual patients' lesions in the right frontoparietal cortex. The central sulcus is shown as a black line. From "A Role for Somatosensory Cortices in the Visual Recognition of Emotion as Revealed by Three-Dimensional Lesion Mapping," by R. Adolphs, H. Damasio, D. Travel, G. Cooper, and A. R. Damasio, 2000, *Journal of Neuroscience, 20*, p. 2686. Copyright 2000 by Society for Neuroscience. Reprinted with permission.

SUMMARY

Because emotions are complex states of the organism that involve feelings, behavior, impulses, physiological changes, and efforts at control, the measurement of emotions is also a complex process. Many approaches to measuring emotions have been developed. These include adjective checklists, structured and unstructured questionnaires, behavioral rating techniques, observations of the products of behavior through the use of projective techniques, and physiological indices. No one method is necessarily better than any other, and all have sources of bias connected with them. Some, such as behavior ratings, are obviously more useful with psychiatric patients, children, and animals. Others, such as projective methods, are useful in getting at emotions that are hidden or repressed and that even the respondent may not be aware of. Physiological measures of autonomic functions require appropriate equipment and may measure general arousal better than specific emotional states. Combinations of measures of different types are being used to an increasing degree.

In addition to the need for multiple measures of emotions, there is a need for a theoretical framework that provides a rationale for the measurement technique to be used. The idea that theory should guide and determine measurement methods is well established in the physical sciences. It should also be the basis for measurement in psychology.

7 Facial Expressions and Emotions

> The face is the mirror of the mind, and eyes without speaking confess the secrets of the heart.
>
> *St. Jerome*

> He that has eyes to see and ears to hear may convince himself that no mortal can keep a secret. If his lips are silent, he chatters with his fingertips, betrayal oozes out of him at every pore.
>
> *Sigmund Freud*

PREVIEW

The study of facial expressions already had a venerable history by the time Charles Darwin began to study the role of facial expressions in animals and humans. Over the years attempts have been made to determine if participants can agree on the emotions expressed in posed pictures of the face, unposed pictures, and pictures of parts of the face. Evidence has begun to accumulate on the cross-cultural meanings of facial expressions. Other evidence to be described on the meaning of facial expressions comes from studies of children who are born blind and deaf. Facial expressions are part of a general nonverbal system that includes gestures, posture, voice quality, and other expressions, all of which communicate information. Several theories have attempted to explain emotional expressions. Peripheral theories assume that feedback from facial expressions influences emotional feelings. Central theories assume that facial expressions reflect inner feeling or brain states. Functional theories assume that facial expressions are communications that attempt to influence a social encounter regardless of inner feelings. The chapter then considers the evolutionary origins of facial displays.

STUDIES OF FACIAL MUSCULATURE

By the time Darwin wrote his book on emotional expression in 1872, a number of other scientists had already studied the expressions of the face. It had been noted, for example, that during screaming, loud laughter, sneezing, and vomiting, the orbicular (eyelid) muscles of the eye contract strongly, thus forming part of the expression associated with these actions. In all such cases, the muscles of the chest and abdomen strongly contract, and at the same time the muscles around the eyes also contract. Darwin suspected that the eyelid contractions had some protective role.

Another early investigator of facial expression was the French physiologist G. Duchenne de Boulogne, who published a book that showed the role of particular muscles in producing facial expressions (Duchenne de Boulogne, 1862/1990). He did this

FIGURE 7.1. When Darwin showed this picture to 23 adults, most said it expressed horror or agony, whereas some said that it looked like anger. From *The Expression of the Emotions in Man and Animals*, by C. Darwin, 1872/1965, p. 306. Copyright 1965 by University of Chicago Press. Reprinted with permission.

by using small electric currents to produce contractions of various muscles of the face and then took pictures of the resulting expression. Figure 7.1 is a copy of a photograph produced by Duchenne using electrical stimulation of facial muscles. When this picture was shown by Darwin to 23 adults, most said that it expressed horror or agony, whereas some said it looked like anger.

Some of the muscles involved in facial expressions are shown in Figure 7.2. In Duchenne's photograph (Figure 7.1), the muscles mostly involved are the corrugators (frown) muscles, the frontal (forehead) muscles, the orbicular (eyelid) muscles, and the platysma (neck) muscles.

Although differences of opinion exist among anatomists on the precise description of all the muscles of the face, there is reasonable agreement on the functional units of facial expression. From this point of view, Ekman and Friesen (1976) tried to identify those facial muscles or groups of muscles that produce visible changes in particular parts of the face, such as the eyebrows or nose, that human observers can reliably distinguish. Table 7.1 presents their list of facial actions and the muscle or muscles that produce those actions. This work is based on the prior efforts of Swedish psychologist Carl Herman Hjortsjo (1970), who carried out detailed studies of the facial muscles associated with different expressions. Figure 7.3, for example, presents a schematic presentation of sad, mournful expressions. According to Hjortsjo, these expressions depend on the cooperative action of the following

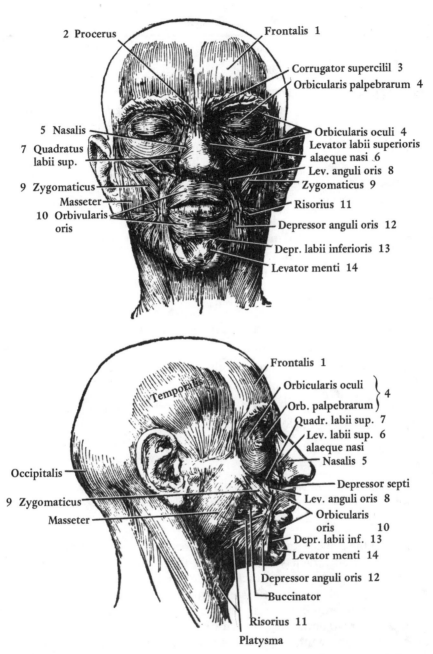

2 Procerus

Frontalis 1

Corrugator supercilil 3
Orbicularis palpebrarum 4

5 Nasalis

7 Quadratus
labii sup.

Orbicularis oculi 4
Levator labii superioris
alaeque nasi 6
Lev. anguli oris 8
Zygomaticus 9

9 Zygomaticus
Masseter
10 Orbivularis
oris

Risorius 11

Depressor anguli oris 12

Depr. labii inferioris 13

Levator menti 14

Frontalis 1

Temporalis

Orbicularis oculi
Orb. palpebrarum } 4
Quadr. labii sup. 7
Lev. labii sup. 6
alaeque nasi
Nasalis 5

Occipitalis

Depressor septi
Lev. anguli oris 8

9 Zygomaticus
Masseter

Orbicularis
oris   10
Depr. labii inf. 13
Levator menti 14

Depressor anguli oris 12

Buccinator

Risorius 11

Platysma

FIGURE 7.2. Muscles involved in facial expressions. From *The Driving Forces of Human Nature*, by T. V. Moore, 1948, p. 110. Copyright 1948 by Heinemann. Reprinted with permission.

TABLE 7.1. Single Action Units in the Facial Code

Facial action code name	Muscular basis
Inner brow raiser	Frontalis, pars medialis
Outer brow raiser	Frontalis, pars lateralis
Brow lowerer	Depressor glabella, depressor supercilli, corrugator
Upper lid raiser	Levator palpaebrae superioris
Cheek raiser	Orbicularis oculi, pars palebralis
Lid tightener	Orbicularis oculi, pars palebralis
Nose wrinkler	Levator labii superioris, aleque nasi
Nasolabial fold deepener	Zygomatic minor
Lip corner puller	Zygomatic major
Cheek puffer	Caninus
Dimpler	Buccinnator
Lip corner depressor	Triangularis
Lower lip depressor	Depressor labii
Chin raiser	Mantalis
Lip puckerer	Incisivii labii superioris, incisive labii inferioris
Lip stretcher	Risorius
Lip funneler	Orbicularis oris
Lip tightener	Orbicularis oris
Lips part	Depressor labii, or relaxation of mentalis or orbicularis oris
Jaw drop	Masetter, temporal and internal pterygoid relaxed
Mouth stretch	Pterygoids, digastric
Lip suck	Orbicularis oris

Note. Action units in The Facial Action Code. From "Measuring Facial Movement," by P. Ekman and W. V. Friesen, 1976, *Environmental Psychology and Nonverbal Behavior, 1,* p. 61. Reprinted with permission.

facial muscles: the glabella depressor, the eyebrow depressor, the sphincter muscle of the eye, the upper lip and the nasal wing levator, the incisive muscles of the upper lip and the lower lip, and the sphincter muscles of the mouth. Generally, every facial expression involves the cooperative action of a large number of individual muscles.

Darwin's interest in facial expressions stimulated a number of psychologists early in the 20th century to begin the systematic study of facial expressions in humans. One of the questions they were interested in was whether college students could correctly judge emotional expressions from posed photographs. They were also interested in the relative importance of different parts of the face in influencing such judgments. What did they learn from these studies?

STUDIES OF PHOTOGRAPHS

Judgment of Posed Facial Expressions

The early studies of this problem involved posed photographs or drawn portraits. These were presented one at a time to college students who were asked to label each

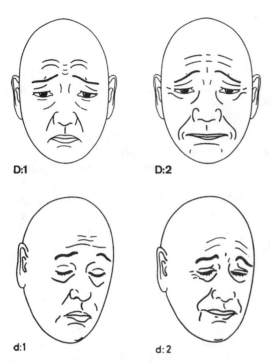

FIGURE 7.3. Schematic presentation of expressions of sadness and grief. The letters represent different orientations of the face. From *Man's Face and Mimic Language*, by C. H. Hjortsjo, 1970, p. 88. Copyright 1970 by Nordens Boktrycheri, Malmo, Sweden. Reprinted with permission.

picture with an emotion word or phrase. Widely used for such studies was a set of posed photographs of an actress who provided her own labels as to what she meant to convey with each expression. Her labels were defined as the correct response for each picture (Feleky, 1914).

The results of this and other similar studies were ambiguous. Some expressions such as *surprise* and *disgust* were judged correctly by most students, whereas other expressions such as *hate*, *religious awe*, and *breathless interest* were not often judged correctly. It gradually became obvious that what was called a correct judgment depended too much on the arbitrary (and even whimsical) opinions of the actress doing the posing (who is, after all, only another judge). This led Woodworth (1938) to examine the overlapping of terms used to describe a given pose, with the result that considerable consistency was found. For example, the *fear* pose was often confused with *surprise* and *suffering* but never with *contempt* or *love*. The *disgust* pose was often confused with *anger* and *contempt* but never with *surprise*. Therefore, if synonyms of the correct word of the posed expression were accepted as correct, it turned out that the judges were in fairly good agreement.

A second way to increase agreement of judgments was by limiting the number of responses each judge could make. The need for this became apparent when the posed picture for *hate* was called *mental pain* by some judges, *disgusted dread* by others, and *self-sufficiency* by still others.

The increase in consistency of judgments resulting from a limited set of response words is illustrated in the study by Tomkins and McCarter (1964). These investigators prepared 69 photos of facial expressions designed, in their opinion, to exemplify either a neutral feeling or one of the following eight emotions: *interest, joy, surprise, distress, fear, shame, disgust,* and *rage.* These are the emotions that Tomkins considered basic or primary. The judges were given the pictures in random order and were asked to identify the emotions expressed using words selected from nine brief lists of terms. For example, the judge could choose a word from the following list: *afraid, frightened, panicky, or terrified,* or from this list: *joyful, happy, smiling, pleased,* or *delighted.*

Results showed considerable agreement between the judges' responses and the intended posed emotions. It was found that *joy* and *shame* were almost always judged correctly, whereas the accuracy of judgments of *surprise* and *interest* was only moderate. Certain overlappings or confusions were also found. *Surprise* and *interest* were often confused. So too were *fear* and *surprise, anger* and *disgust,* and *shame* and *distress.* These confusions suggest an implicit similarity structure of emotion expressions. Schlosberg (1941), using the data reported by Feleky (1914), came to the conclusion that the overlap of judgments about facial expressions of emotion leads to a circular scale rather than a linear one. In a circular scale, adjoining expressions are similar, but the end of the scale is similar to the beginning.

Despite the relatively good agreement among judges found by Tomkins and McCarter (1964), they suggested a number of reasons the judgments were not unanimous. First, they pointed out that the actors who posed for the pictures did not always express the pattern the investigators wished. These actors also had some unique lines or expressions on their own faces that influenced the final pose to some degree. Second, and perhaps more important, is the fact that an emotional response is an event that occurs over time. The smile involves an increasingly widening mouth. The eyeblink in surprise is a progressive narrowing of the eyelids. The sneer of contempt is a progressive lifting of the upper lip. Any still photograph is a very limited sample of this complex, temporal pattern. Third, the naming of affects is often ambiguous because each individual has a different personal history connected with the learning of the emotion language. Finally, there are many facial expressions that are mixtures or blends of two or more primary emotions. If a judge is asked to select only one name for a facial expression, it is bound to be inadequate to some degree.

Unposed or "Natural" Expressions

Probably the best-known study of this sort was carried out by Landis in 1924. He asked college students to allow themselves to be subjected to various conditions, mostly unpleasant, while he took motion pictures of their facial expressions. The students were asked, for example, to look at pictures of people with ugly skin diseases, to accept a strong electric shock, and to cut off the head of a live rat with a knife. To facilitate later analysis of his pictures, Landis marked the major muscle outlines of each participant's face in black charcoal.

When he analyzed his film records, he found little evidence of any clear-cut relations between the students' reported feelings in a situation and patterns of facial expression. He concluded that facial expressions are not typically associated with any verbal reports of emotions (Landis, 1924), and this idea has often been repeated in psychology textbooks as proof that facial expressions and emotions are not linked in any meaningful way.

This study can be criticized on a number of grounds. For one thing, many of these students, standing in front of a camera with black marks on their faces, showed a sheepish grin throughout most of the situations. There is thus a strong likelihood that all emotions generated in this context were mixed emotions, containing such elements as *embarrassment, disgust,* and *surprise,* and therefore no simple connection between one emotion and expression could be established. Second, Davis in 1934 reanalyzed Landis's data and showed that smiling occurred in cases of reported pain in 7% of the observations, whereas smiling occurred in 60% of the emotional responses reported as sexual. A particular muscle group of the face was found to be involved in 3% of reported cases of sexual feelings and in 50% of cases of reported pain. In addition, the facial expressions seen when looking at pornographic pictures were quite recognizably different from those seen when the participants were listening to music. Davis concluded that there were definite tendencies for certain muscles to be involved in one emotion and not in another.

It should be evident that it is difficult to study facial expressions in humans through the use of still photographs of facial expressions. The following are among the many problems:

1. Still photographs are poor samples of the variety of changes that actually occur over time during emotions.

2. Still photographs reveal little or nothing about the situation an individual is in, which is part of the information people usually use to judge the likelihood of an emotion being present.

3. It is difficult to establish a standard to determine what emotion is being expressed.

4. Judges typically use a wide variety of words to describe what they see in a photograph. If every word is taken to mean a different emotion, agreement among judges is poor. If, however, the words are grouped in terms of similarity of meaning, agreement among judges is relatively good.

5. It is evident that the language of emotions contains hundreds of possible words to describe emotions, whereas the number of different facial expressions is relatively limited. Asking judges to label facial expressions with whatever terms come to mind is therefore likely to produce many inconsistencies. If broad categories are used, agreement is greater.

Another factor that influences the degree of agreement of judges is the intensity of the facial expression. Mild expressions are more likely to produce differences in judgment than extreme ones. This may be illustrated by Figure 7.4, which shows drawings of a number of extreme facial expressions. Most of these expressions are easier to identify than more neutral, less intense ones.

THE SEARCH FOR UNIVERSAL FACIAL EXPRESSIONS

Are Facial Expressions Learned or Innate?

Are facial expressions of emotion learned like the words of a language or are they innate? Darwin believed that some facial expressions in humans are innate, just as many expressions in chimpanzees and other primates are innate. The evidence he presented for this point of view included the following: (a) Some facial expressions appear in similar form in lower animals, particularly primates; (b) some facial expressions are seen in infants and young children in the same form as seen in adults; (c) some facial expressions are shown in identical ways by those born blind and in those who are normally sighted; and (d) some facial expressions appear in similar forms in widely distinct races and groups of humans.

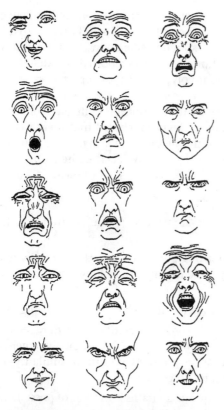

FIGURE 7.4. These drawings illustrate a number of extreme facial expressions that are easier to judge than less intense expressions of emotion. From *Manwatching: A Field Guide to Human Behavior*, by D. Morris, 1977, p. 26. Copyright 1977 by Harry N. Abrams, Inc. Reprinted with permission.

Based on these kinds of observations, Darwin concluded that facial expressions act as signals or as forms of communication between individuals. He believed that facial expressions reveal something about the likelihood of action. There is usually some probability that making an angry face will be followed by angry words, threats, or physical attacks. If one individual can judge the probable behavior of another individual, or accurately estimate his or her intentions, this fact can be very useful. It will allow the second person to adjust his or her behavior and thus possibly affect the outcome of the interaction. Such communications and adaptations may even influence the chances of individual survival. In recent years, many studies have been reported that deal with these issues. Of particular interest has been the question of the universality of facial expressions of emotion.

Judgments of Facial Expressions in a Nonliterate Society

In 1969, Ekman, Sorenson, and Friesen published a cross-cultural study concerned with recognition of facial expressions. Out of 3,000 photographs, these investigators selected 30 that, in their own judgment, showed only pure expressions of single emotions.

These 30 photographs represented six emotions that Tomkins and others have proposed as primary or basic: *happiness, surprise, fear, anger, disgust,* and *sadness*. The photographs were of White males and females, adults and children, actors, and patients with mental illness. The pictures were shown to college students in the United States, Brazil, and Japan and to adult volunteers in New Guinea and in Borneo. The six emotion words were translated into each appropriate language, and the judge was requested to pick a word from each group of six to name the facial expression.

The results showed high agreement by the students in the United States, Brazil, and Japan, with percentage agreement ranging from the 60s to the high 90s. Similar results have been reported by Izard (1971) for seven other literate cultures. Relatively less agreement was found for the two preliterate societies: *Happiness* was judged consistently (92%) in Borneo and in New Guinea, but the percentage agreement for *anger* (using medians) was around 56%, for *sadness* about 55%, for *fear* 46%, for *surprise* 38%, and for *disgust* 31%. All of these results are better than chance judgments, but it is evident that the preliterate groups do not judge the facial expressions in quite the same way as do the literate groups. Ekman and his colleagues concluded that their findings support Darwin's suggestion that some facial expressions of emotion are similar among humans, regardless of culture, because of their evolutionary origins. This conclusion is undoubtedly an overgeneralization in view of the various limitations of the study; for example: use of only 30 pictures; use of only 15 judges in Borneo and 14 in one of the New Guinea groups; use of only six affects; and less agreement among the preliterate groups than the literate ones. In addition, it could be argued that people even in the preliterate societies have seen Western-made motion pictures, thus recognizing some of the emotions displayed in the pictures.

To deal with this last criticism, Ekman and Friesen (1971) provided a detailed report of a study carried out with members of the South Fore linguistic cultural group of Southeastern New Guinea. Until 1960, these people were an isolated "Stone Age" culture with little or no contact with Westerners. The judges used in the study were selected because they had seen no movies, neither spoke nor understood English or Pidgin (simplified speech used for communication between people with different languages), had not lived in any government towns, and had never worked for a White person. These criteria were met by 180 adults and 130 children.

Because of reading and other problems that the judges had, the judgment task was made very simple. The judge was read a simple story and then shown three pictures simultaneously. He or she was to select the picture in which the person's face showed the emotion described in the story. Some other members of the South Fore tribe served as research assistants and recruited participants, read and translated the stories, and were discouraged from prompting.

With this technique, extremely high agreement was found among both adults and children for almost all emotion expressions. For adults, the median agreement for the happiness picture was 92%; for the anger picture, 87%; for the sadness picture, 81%; for the disgust picture, 83%; for the surprise picture, 68%; and for the fear picture, 64%. In this sample, fear and surprise expressions were often not clearly separated.

As a result of these studies, Ekman and Friesen (1971) concluded that certain facial expressions are generally associated with particular emotions. However, they emphasized that cultural factors and learning may influence emotional expression. For example, the people in all cultures have to learn what to be afraid of and how to manage their feelings when they occur.

These studies by Ekman and Friesen (1971) have been criticized by Russell (1994) partly on the grounds of methodology. It is possible that the forced-choice method of providing the judges with a very limited number of choices may unduly bias the results. In his rejoinder, Ekman (1994) answered the criticisms by noting that culturally variable display rules regulate when to show or not show an emotion, and also influence the conflicts that invariably result.

An example of the role of display rules may be seen in a study in which participants' facial expressions were videotaped without their knowledge while they watched both neutral films and stress-inducing films of body mutilation. Such videotapes were obtained on 25 Japanese college students and 25 American students. The Facial Affect Scoring System (shown in Table 7.1) was used to identify the facial muscles and expressions resulting from the stress. It was found that the frequency with which American and Japanese students showed anger, fear, disgust, surprise, sadness, and happiness was quite similar. The correlation was .88. However, when a fellow countryman entered the room, the facial behaviors of the two groups of students was quite different. The Japanese students tended to show polite smiles, whereas the Americans replayed the expressions they originally had. These observations imply that different display rules may operate in different cultures (Ekman, 1993).

COMPUTER SIMULATION STUDIES OF FACIAL EXPRESSION

In recent years, computer-generated facial expressions ("morphs") have contributed new insights into the meaning of facial expressions. Several such studies are described here.

In one photograph, real faces of the six basic emotions most often studied—*happiness, sadness, fear, anger, disgust,* and *surprise*—were compared with computer-generated synthetic images, line drawings in this case (see Figure 7.5). It was found that although all judgments were better than chance, the real faces were judged somewhat more accurately than were the line drawings (Wehrle, Kaiser, Schmidt, & Scherer, 2000). Although the line drawing expressions of *sadness* and *happiness* were recognized as well as the photographs, the expression of *fear* was very poorly recognized, and the expression of *disgust* was consistently confused with *anger*.

When drawings representing high versus low intensity of expression were used, judgments were somewhat more accurate with high-intensity images, although "hot anger" at high intensity was judged as "fear" by 50% of the participants. When low-intensity stimuli were used, the recognition scores were at a chance level.

When the line drawings were presented in a dynamic form, that is, by videotape in a series of animated movements from a neutral expression to the final form of the expression, the recognition scores for the emotions were higher. This was interpreted to mean that dynamic presentation of facial expressions adds important cues to emotion.

Use of Noh Masks

To illustrate how subtle variations in head position and orientation may influence judgments of emotion, a study by Lyons et al. (2000) used Japanese Noh masks held in different orientations; these were compared with a human face in comparable positions. (The human face is seen in Figure 7.6).

When the Noh mask was tilted forward, it was often described as *happy,* whereas a mask with a backward tilt was often judged as *sad.* These results were replicated with the human face. Such findings help account for the variations that have been reported in the judgment of emotional expressions.

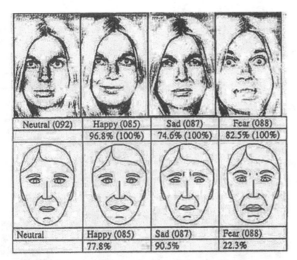

FIGURE 7.5. The upper photographs are taken from the *Pictures of Facial Affect* (Ekman, 1976). Percentages refer to the degree of agreement of the observers (Ekman's percentages are in parentheses). The lower figures are computer synthesized images corresponding to the photographs in the upper part. Percentages are the degrees of agreement on the emotion label. From "Studying the Dynamics of Emotional Expression Using Synthesized Facial Muscle Movements," by T. Wehrle, S. Kaiser, S. Schmidt, and K. R. Scherer, 2000, *Journal of Personality and Social Psychology, 78,* p. 110. Copyright 2000 by the American Psychological Association. Reprinted with permission.

Composite Images

Further support for the idea that more extreme, or intense, expressions of emotion are easier to recognize may be found in the study by Benson, Campbell, Harris, Frank, and Tovee (1999). In this investigation, Benson et al. first produced a computer-generated composite facial image from natural photographs of the expressions of the six basic emotions typically studied. They then exaggerated (caricatured) the composite images on the computer in relation to a neutral expression. This is shown in Figure 7.7.

FIGURE 7.6. The same facial stimulus tilted at varying degrees from the vertical results in the attribution of different emotion labels. From "The Noh Mask Effect: Vertical Viewpoint Dependence of Facial Expression Perception," by M. J. Lyons, R. Campbell, A. Plante, M. Coleman, M. Kamachi, and S. Akamatsu, 2000, *Proceedings of the Royal Society of London B, 267,* p. 2240. Copyright 2000 by the Royal Society of London. Reprinted with permission.

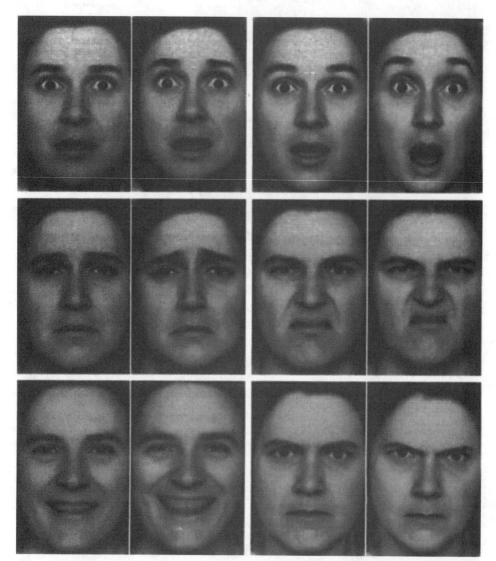

FIGURE 7.7. Images on the left of each pair are prototypes obtained by averaging expressions from six individuals with the computer. Images on the right in each pair are caricature (enhanced) stimuli. Expressions from top-left are: fear, surprise, sadness, disgust, happiness, and anger. From "Enhancing Images of Facial Expressions," by P. J. Benson, R. Campbell, T. Harris, M. G. Frank, and M. J. Tovee, 1999, *Perception & Psychophysics, 61*, p. 262. Copyright 1999 by the Psychonomic Society. Reprinted with permission.

It was found that the caricatured faces were judged as more clearly representing each emotion than were the composite faces. It was also reported that there were confusion errors between *fear* and *surprise* and to a lesser degree between *sadness* and *anger*. The caricatured images also did not speed up the naming of the facial expressions. This may have been due to the possibility that caricature morphing increased the appearance of mixed emotions on the face.

Finally, based on composite faces generated by computers, a new two-process theory of facial perception was proposed (De Bonis, De Boesk, Perez-Diaz, & Nahas, 1999). In this study, computers were used to morph combinations of upper and lower parts of a face, as shown in Figure 7.8.

Prototypical expressions

a. Happy   *b. Fearful*

Chimeric expressions

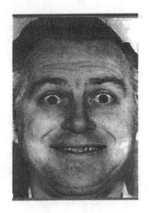

c.   *d.*
Happy(up)-Fearful(low)   *Fearful(up)-happy(low)*

FIGURE 7.8. Faces (a) and (b) are, respectively, prototypical happy and fearful expressions of a single individual from a standard set. Faces (c) and (d) are computer-generated expressions in which the upper and lower parts of the prototypical expressions have been fused to create a chimerical expression. From "A Two-Process Theory of Facial Perception of Emotions," by M. De Bonis, P. De Boesk, F. Perez-Diaz, and M. Nahas, 1999, *Life Sciences, 322,* p. 672. Copyright 1999 by Academie des Sciences/Elsevier, Paris. Reprinted with permission.

Four types of faces were created:

1. HH: Both upper and lower parts of the face had a happy expression.
2. FF: Both upper and lower parts of the face had a fearful expression
3. HF: The upper part of the face had a happy expression, and the lower part had a fearful expression.
4. FH: The upper part of the face had a fearful expression, and the lower part had a happy expression.

The faces were taken from a standard set of pictures of emotional expression published by Ekman and Friesen (1976). The composite faces, called *chimerical faces,* were then shown to a group of medical students who were asked to label every emotion represented in each face using a list of 19 emotion words. The emotion words included *admiration, affection, cheerful, connected, enjoyment, interested, relaxed, warm, angry, confused, contempt, distant, embarrassed, fearful, pained, repulsed, sad,* and *surprised.* Agreement between judges was high (intraclass coefficient was .82).

Statistical analysis revealed that only four features accounted for most of the judgments made. For example, a happy lower face (a smile) largely determined the responses of *admiration, affection, amused, cheerful, enjoyment, relaxed,* and *warm.* A fearful upper face (wide open eyes and raised furrowed brow) largely determined the responses of *confused, embarrassed, sad,* and *surprised.* Some emotion responses were determined by two features; these included *anger* (happy upper face and fearful lower face), *contempt* (happy upper face and fearful lower face), *pained* (fearful upper and lower faces), and *sad* (fearful upper and lower faces).

Of interest was the fact that the morphed faces often produced more than one emotional label. This was measured in terms of the probability of each response. For example, the morphed picture of a face designed to have a fearful upper and a fearful lower expression resulted in the following probability of response: *fearful* ($p = .93$), *embarrassed* ($p = .87$), *confused* ($p = .79$), *repulsed* ($p = .74$), *pained* ($p = .50$), and *sad* ($p = .48$).

Ekman and Friesen (1976) concluded that the perception of emotion from the face reflects a probability estimate of the relevance of certain features. In the study by De Bonis et al. (1999), happy and fearful expressions appear to share component expressions with other emotions. The authors also noted that the artificial expressions, the chimerical faces, were generally perceived by the judges as genuine, but complex, emotions. It is also likely that the results reflect the general fact that all emotions have varying degrees of similarity to one another. This has been shown in studies of the language of emotions in many cultures and has been expressed by a circumplex. The findings of these authors suggest that a circumplex (as described in chapter 4) may also apply to facial expressions.

Facial Expressions and the Circumplex

In an effort to test the hypothesis that a circumplex could be used to describe the relations among facial expressions, Myllyniemi (1997) selected 16 photographs of a professional actor who created emotional expressions based on the descriptions given by Ekman (1976) and Izard (1971). The expressions were based on the emotions of *aggression, fear, nurturance,* and *trust* and their combinations. The labels given to the expressions were based on agreement by two independent judges.

The photographs were then shown to college students who rated them on 18 five-point rating scales on such dimensions as dominance, submission, affiliation, defiance, trust, and nurturance. The mean ratings on all 18 scales were obtained for each photograph, creating a profile of mean ratings per photograph. These profiles were then intercorrelated and analyzed using multidimensional scaling. The result was a circumplex of facial expressions as shown in Figure 7.9. It appears that the judges saw emotional meaning in the faces and that they could be represented in terms of both polarity and similarity. Myllyniemi (1997) concluded that the interpersonal circle (or circumplex) may reflect the types of social behavior needed to build a dominance hierarchy and, in turn, social cohesion.

STUDIES OF ANTHROPOLOGICAL ARTIFACTS

Several studies in recent years have examined the issue of cross-cultural similarities in emotional expressions in an indirect way. For example, Aronoff, Barclay, and Stevenson (1988) were interested in the ways that different cultures show threat through facial expressions as revealed by their art work. To study this problem, Aronoff et al. began by asking American college students to imagine themselves in a primitive society and to then draw a picture of a mask they would wear to frighten their victims into surrender. From these drawings, coders compiled a list of elements that were commonly drawn. These included horns or pointed head, disheveled hair, pointed ears, diagonal eyebrows, vertical lines between eyebrows, eyes oriented diagonally, triangular eyes, pointed chin, pointed beard, and so on.

Pictures of masks were then obtained from ethnographic sources representing "threatening" and "nonthreatening" wooden masks as constructed in 18 different subcultures. These pictures were then coded for the number of threatening signs appearing on each mask. The total number of threatening signs was considered to be an index of the amount of threat present in each mask. The results showed that all but one of the threat characteristics (pointed chin) significantly discriminated between the threatening and nonthreatening masks. Aronoff et al. concluded that the basic underlying feature that most of the signs had in common was the geometrical pattern of diagonal lines and angularity (i.e., the use of diagonal and triangular forms).

As a follow-up of this conclusion, 10 features were selected from the list of threat characteristics and were then presented as abstract patterns to another group of college students who were asked to rate their emotional reactions to the pattern. The ratings involved semantic differential scales measuring *evaluation* (e.g., *bad–good, dangerous–safe, cruel–kind, unfriendly–friendly*), *potency* (e.g., *weak–strong, feminine–masculine, cowardly–brave*), and *activity* (e.g., *passive–active, inert–energetic, calm–excitable*).

Examples of the patterns used are shown in Figure 7.10. The students who evaluated the patterns found the diagonal and angular displays significantly more potent, active, and negative than the comparison figures. Aronoff et al. suggested that certain geometric patterns act cross-culturally as displays that signal threat or danger, although an underlying reason for this generalization was not proposed.

Anthropological analyses have also been used extensively by German ethologist Irenaeus Eibl-Eibesfeldt (see Eibl-Eibesfeldt & Sutterlin, 1990). He has been studying emotional displays in various preliterate cultures around the world and has reported many parallels in the patterns of emotional expression revealed in their art and sculpture. He reported that the facial expressions of threat, fear, and submission are universally found.

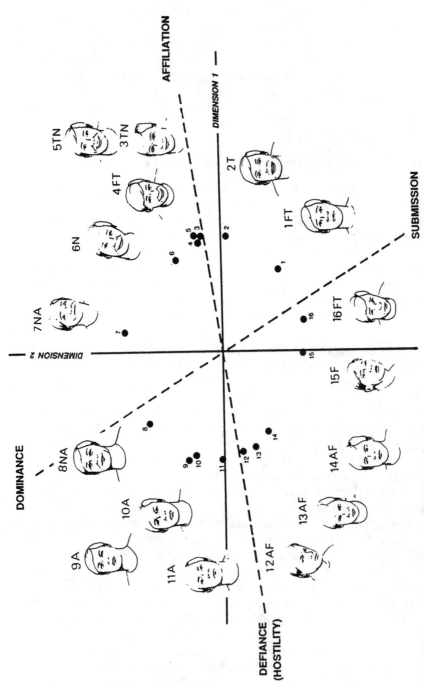

FIGURE 7.9. A multidimensional scaling analysis of the similarity structure of 16 posed photographs. A = aggressive; AF = aggressive-fearful; F = fearful; FT = fearful-trusting; N = nurturing; NA = nurturing-aggressive; T = trusting; TN = trusting-nurturing. From "The Interpersonal Circle and the Emotional Undercurrents of Human Sociability," by R. Myllyniemi. In R. Plutchik and H. R. Conte (Eds.), *Circumplex Models of Personality and Emotions*, 1997, p. 286. Copyright 1997 by the American Psychological Association. Reprinted with permission.

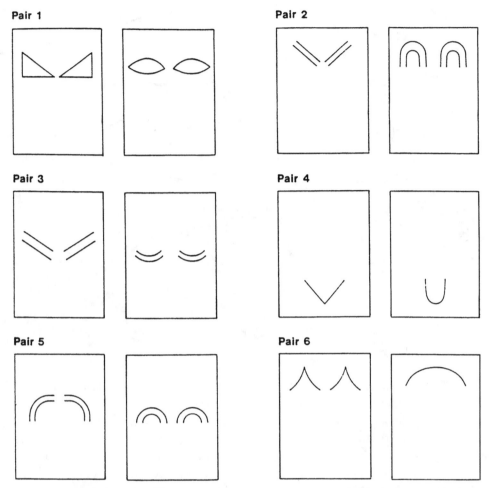

Pair 1

Pair 2

Pair 3

Pair 4

Pair 5

Pair 6

FIGURE 7.10. Geometric forms reflected in masks. For each pair, the more threatening stimulus is presented on the left. From "The Recognition of Threatening Facial Stimuli," by J. Aronoff, A. M. Barclay, and L. A. Stevenson, 1988, *Journal of Personality and Social Psychology, 54,* p. 652. Copyright 1988 by the American Psychological Association. Reprinted with permission.

Staring at an opponent, for example, is a widely used expression to intimidate. Lowering and tilting the head together with pouting and gaze avoidance are submissive signals. Showing clenched teeth by pulling down the corners of the mouth is widely seen as a display of anger both in some primates and in humans.

Because dangers and threats are universal, avoidance, flight, and defensive responses are found in all animals, including humans. The need for protection from strangers and enemies is manifested in many ways. For example, *apotropaeic figurines* (also called *scare devils*) are found all over the world. These sculptures show stare threats, teeth threats, phallic displays, female genital displays, and anal threats in an exaggerated manner. In Gothic churches all over Europe, there are stone sculptures commonly called *grotesques*. Many of them appear as frozen expressions of threat intended to scare away or appease evil spirits or demons. An example of such faces is shown in Figure 7.11, along with a similar sculpture

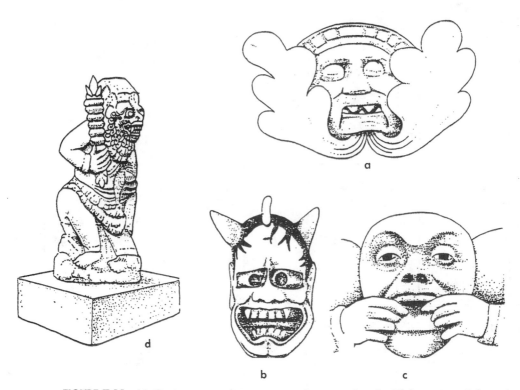

FIGURE 7.11. (a) Grotesque sculpture expressing emotion in 12th-century Johanni Church, Schwabisch Gmund, Germany; the threatening face shows a "biting" expression with a widely open mouth and exposed teeth. (b) A Japanese amulet devil's mask in the form of a typical scare-face, with exaggerated teeth. (c) Corbel figure from the Gothic church of Notre Dame in L'Epine, France; the gesture of pulling the mouth apart with both hands is common in grotesque sculpture and mimics furor. (All drawn from photographs by I. Eibl-Eibesfeldt.) (d) An Eastern example before a temple in Ubud, Bali, Indonesia. (Drawn from a photograph by C. Sutterlin.) From "Fear, Defense and Aggression in Animals and Man: Some Ethological Perspectives," by I. Eibl-Eibesfeldt and C. Sutterlin. In P. F. Brain and S. Parmigiani (Eds.), *Fear and Defense*, 1990, p. 143. Copyright 1990 by Harwood. Reprinted with permission.

standing before a temple in Bali, Indonesia. Sticking out of the tongue is another facial display that is often seen in old churches. Figure 7.12 shows this pattern. Eibl-Eibesfeldt believed it to be a universal expression derived from spitting and disgust. Rozin and Fallon (1987) have also cited evidence that tongue protrusion is seen in disgust in all cultures that have been studied. It is also seen in various primate species (W. J. Smith, Chase, & Lieblich, 1974). The widespread appearance of these facial displays around the world and in higher primates suggests that human beings have some common patterns of expression related to basic protective and defensive experiences. Does this mean that emotional displays are innate or genetically determined? How consistent is such a conclusion with the obvious fact that human beings can control the expression of their emotions to varying degrees? Is it possible to disentangle the complex issue of the connection between innate emotional expressions and the influence of learning?

FIGURE 7.12. An expression of disgust. This figure is found at the entrance to the Placenza Cathedral, Italy. The extended tongue is widespread in avertive figures in all cultures and is derived from ritualized aggressive behavior of spitting and disgust. From "Fear, Defense and Aggression in Animals and Man: Some Ethological Perspectives," by I. Eibl-Eibesfeldt and C. Sutterlin. In P. F. Brain and S. Parmigiani (Eds.), *Fear and Defense*, 1990, p. 144. Copyright 1990 by Harwood. Reprinted with permission.

EMOTIONAL EXPRESSIONS IN CHILDREN BORN BLIND

Darwin was the first to bring to our attention the importance of observing children who were blind from birth as evidence concerning the innateness of facial expressions of emotion. In his 1872 book, Darwin stated that children born blind blush from shame and display emotions in the same way as do children with normal eyesight.

Almost no attempt was made to try and follow up these observations until the third decade of the 20th century. In 1932, Goodenough reported her observations of a 10-year-old girl who had been born blind and deaf and who had had almost no training. This child showed typical signs of surprise on her face when something unexpected occurred; she whimpered and looked sad at the loss of an object; she frowned when she was frustrated; and she laughed and smiled when given pleasant things. She showed resentment by pouting of the lips, and when she was happy, she often danced.

These kinds of observations were replicated by Thompson (1941). Photographs were taken of 26 blind children, ages 7 weeks to 13 years, in "natural" emotional states. Similar photographs were taken of a matched control group of seeing children. It was found that facial activities of laughing, crying, and smiling were comparable at all ages in both groups. During mild punishment, children in both groups showed a pouting expression, as well as the downturned mouth characteristic of sadness. Judges accurately judged the facial expressions of both the blind and seeing children in about 70% of the photographs.

In a second study of this type (Fulcher, 1942), 118 seeing boys and girls, ages 4 to 15 years and of normal intelligence, were asked to look happy, sad, angry, or frightened. Their facial expressions were compared with those of 50 congenitally blind boys and girls of approximately the same age and intelligence who were asked to do the same task. It was found that both the seeing and the blind children showed distinct patterns of facial expression for each of the different emotions. In addition, the patterns shown by the blind and seeing children were quite similar.

Another study of children born blind and deaf was reported by Eibl-Eibesfeldt (1973) and has been described in chapter 1. Despite the fact that these children could neither see nor hear the world around them and were also greatly impaired in cognitive capacity, they showed many normal emotional reactions. In addition to smiling, the children all showed laughter, generally during rough social play such as wrestling or during tickling. The children cried when hurt or when left in an unfamiliar environment. In such cases, the corners of the mouth usually turned down and opened, the eyelids pressed together, and tears were shed. Sometimes the eyebrows were raised, furrowing the brow at the same time that frown lines appeared between the eyes. Occasionally, angry crying was observed when someone persistently offered a child a disliked object. The children also spontaneously embraced, caressed, and kissed other people on some occasions.

Most studies of blind children have been carried out using relatively few participants and had generally used the judgment of the investigators to evaluate the facial expressions that were observed. There are two recent studies that used relatively large numbers of participants and an objective system of facial expression coding. These are briefly described.

In one study (Galati, Scherer, & Ricci-Bitti, 1997), a group of 14 adults who had been blind since birth was compared with a group of 14 adults with normal sight. Each person read a brief description of a situation that might induce one or another of six emotions: *surprise, anger, joy, disgust, sadness,* and *fear.* They were told to imagine the situation and to then pose the facial expression of the emotion likely to have been elicited by the situation. Photographs of their faces were taken during each simulated emotion. The photos were then coded for action units on the faces. A separate group of college students was shown the photographs and was asked to label the emotions that were shown.

The results indicated that there were few differences in facial expressions between the two groups for the different emotion situations. Both groups also did not show expressions that corresponded closely to what previous research using coached actors might lead one to expect. It was found that some emotions were expressed in a more standard way than others (e.g., *joy, sadness,* and *surprise*). Some individuals in both groups posed their faces in the standard ways much better than did others. The college student raters had a little more difficulty recognizing the facial expressions of the blind participants than those of the normally sighted. Galati et al. (1997) concluded that very little is known about the process of producing voluntary expressions of emotions.

The second study examined the facial expressions of emotions in very young, congenitally blind children to determine the extent to which they could be recognized (Galati, Miceli, & Sini, 2000). The participants of this study were 10 blind children ranging in age from 6 months to 4 years and 10 normally sighted children of the same age range. Each child was then separately exposed to seven situations that were chosen to induce different emotions. The seven situations were the following:

1. Interruption of a behavioral plan (*anger* situation)
2. Positive interaction with a caregiver (*joy* situation)
3. Contact with a repulsive stimulus (*disgust* situation)
4. Sudden interruption of a stimulus (*surprise* situation)
5. Stimulation by multiple objects or events (*interest* situation)
6. Separation from the caregiver (*sadness* situation)
7. Loss of balance or support (*fear* situation)

Facial reactions of each child in each situation were filmed, and the facial expressions were coded using the Max coding procedure (Izard, 1979), which codes three regions of the face: the brow area, the eye–cheek area, and the mouth. Coders were unaware of the stimulus situations that generated each expression. The brief videos, each lasting about 5 seconds, were then shown to 280 college students who were asked to rate the emotion expressed (if any) and whether it was intense, pleasant, or unpleasant.

Results showed that the facial expressions produced by the blind and sighted children were quite similar. It was also found that the expressions of fear and sadness were often confused by the judges. Finally, the judges correctly interpreted the facial expressions with a frequency greater than chance.

These two studies have been interpreted to mean that certain facial expressions probably have neural programs that determine their forms. It may mean that some facial expressions of emotions are activated by subcortical motor centers, whereas voluntary facial expressions are determined by cortical centers. The latter are more influenced by learning and visual information than the former.

These studies of deaf-and-blind-born children and the studies of blind children indicate that these children all show emotional expressions that are very similar to the expressions shown by normal children. This occurs without imitation or other kinds of direct information about how one is supposed to behave. These observations strongly support the position that some emotional expressions are not learned but reflect basic neuromuscular, genetically determined programs. Such a view does not require that all facial expressions are innate because some expressions may be learned like the words of a language (e.g., winking at someone to express approval, or wrinkling the nose to express disdain). The belief that certain emotional expressions are innate also does not mean that such expressions cannot be modified, suppressed, or inhibited. It is an empirical research problem to determine which expressions are innate and the extent to which such patterns can be modified by experience. In addition, it should be emphasized that there are many emotional expressions that are not facial expressions but bodily expressions, a point we now consider.

BODILY EXPRESSIONS OF EMOTION

Facial Expressions as an Aspect of Nonverbal Behavior

Everyone knows that parts of the body other than the face also express emotions. Apart from facial expressions, the erection of body hairs, the flushing of the skin, the raising of the shoulders, and restless pacing all can reveal something about emotional states. People often say one thing but imply another by tone of voice or by gesture. It is evident that nonverbal behaviors are intimately related to emotions. The range of nonverbal communicative behaviors is quite large. Examples of nonverbal events that can communicate affect states are facial expressions, eye movements and gaze direction, gestures, posture, voice qualities such as pitch and inflection, speech hesitations, nonlanguage sounds such as laughing or yawning or grunting, use of social space, touching, odors, and sniffing.

Body Odors as Expressions

Body odors also convey emotional messages, although we seldom talk about them. The intensity of our concerns about odors, however, is reflected in the billions of dollars spent every year on soaps, deodorants, perfumes, and mouthwashes. Some odors are obvious and simply reflect poor personal cleanliness. Others are more subtle, or even not recognized, and yet have an influence on our emotions. Such subtle odors are called *pheromones*, and they have been detected and measured in both humans and lower animals. The typical sniffing behavior that takes place between most animals functions to identify sexual and emotional signals. They enable animals to recognize mates, mark territory, and indicate sexual receptivity.

Sweating as Expressions

In humans there are two types of sweat glands: eccrine glands and apocrine glands. The eccrine glands are the true sweat glands and occur over most of the body. They produce a relatively odorless secretion whose evaporation aids the body to lose heat and regulate salt balance. The apocrine glands are found in both men and women and are located in only a few places in the body: on the eyelids, in the armpits, on the nipples and areola, and in the genital and anal areas. They secrete a slightly oilier substance than the eccrine glands as well as pheromones. Although most people cannot detect the pheromones consciously, they are still influenced by them. In one study, a group of married women was given a perfume containing a pheromone derived from secretions of musk deer. A control group of women was given an identically smelling perfume but without the pheromone. All the women applied the perfume before going to bed at night. Questionnaires completed by both husbands and wives, after a trial period, revealed that overall sexual activity markedly increased in about one quarter of the women who had received the perfumes containing the pheromones (Marsh, 1988).

VOCAL EXPRESSIONS OF EMOTION

Compared with studies of facial expression, the vocal mode of affect expression has been relatively neglected. This is probably related to the fact that special electronic methods for measuring vocal characteristics are required, and their results are not always easy to interpret.

Studies of animals have led to some tentative conclusions concerning the relations between vocal sounds and emotions. As summarized by Scherer (1989), in states of relaxation and play, one tends to find repeated short sounds with relatively low frequencies (e.g., purring). Defense calls tend to be short, high-amplitude sounds with a broad frequency spectrum (e.g., shrieking). Submission calls are usually long, high-frequency sounds with repeated frequency shifts.

On the basis of studies of calls made by squirrel monkeys, Jurgens (1979) described warning sounds as short, loud sounds, with a rapid decrease in energy from high to low frequencies. He is in agreement with Morton (1977) that birds and mammals tend to use relatively low-frequency sounds when threatening and high-frequency sounds when frightened, appeasing, or approaching in a friendly manner.

Human speech makes use of vocal sounds, but it represents a complex mixture of both linguistic patterns (i.e., the codes we call words) and nonlinguistic elements, which refer to such things as loudness, pitch, variability, breathiness, and nasality. The problem of separating out these two components of human speech is an extremely difficult one. However, although words of a language are obviously learned, the specific vocal quality is probably largely determined by genetic factors. Speech patterns seem to be as characteristic of a person as are fingerprints, a fact that is well known to the police of all nations.

Research in this area has two major traditions: one is concerned with the process of encoding emotions in speech (i.e., what aspects of speech reflect emotions), and the other is concerned with decoding (i.e., the ability of judges to recognize emotion in speech). Data on encoding reveal some differences between emotions (as least as generated by actors who are engaged in role playing), but the overlap is great. For example, in a summary of this literature, Scherer (1989) reported that the emotion of *joy* is characterized by high pitch, large variability in pitch, loud sound, and fast tempo. *Anger* is described by a high pitch, wide frequency range, large variability, loud sound, and fast tempo. *Fear* is similar to anger. *Grief* has a low pitch, narrow range, soft sounds, and slow tempo. The overlap, especially among *joy, anger,* and *fear,* is evident. This may be due, in part, to a lack of knowledge of what best to measure.

With regard to the ability of humans to decode the emotions in human speech, a review of 30 studies has revealed an average accuracy of about 60% in contrast to chance agreement of 12%. This is about the same degree of agreement found when making judgment from photographs (Scherer, 1989).

GESTURES AS COMMUNICATIONS

In an effort to find out what certain common gestures mean, Morris, Collett, Marsh, and O'Shaughnessy (1979) identified 20 gestures and showed pictures of them to 1,200 people at various locations in England and Europe. The judges were asked to indicate what each gesture meant. Illustrations of the gestures used are shown in Figure 7.13. Some of the gestures involve the face and others involve only the hand. The most common meanings given to each gesture are listed in Table 7.2.

A more detailed explanation may be given for some of the gestures. The *fingers cross* is believed by most to mean protection. It originated as a sign of the cross and as an attempt by the devout to gain protection or ward off evil. We now say "Keep your fingers crossed" to hope for luck. *Thumbing the nose* is almost universally seen as insult or mockery. It apparently originated in medieval Europe as a jester's way of insulting his audience. It implies that someone has a bad smell, and at the same time the face often takes on an expression of disgust. The *forearm jerk* is widely recognized as a sexual insult. It appears to be a phallic gesture implying insertion by a large penis. It is usually used by men against each other, and therefore it suggests anal threat. In primates, dominant males make phallic threats against subordinate males, usually by mounting and by making some pelvic thrusts without anal insertion. The forearm jerk is an enlarged version of the old middle-finger jerk (known by the Romans as the obscene finger). In Malta, the gesture is so obscene that one can be arrested for using it in a public place. The fig is an ancient shape meaning a sexual comment or insult or as a protection. The ancient Greeks carried amulets of female genitals (in the shape of a fig) as a way to avert evil. Such amulets are still popular today. Another meaning of the fig is as a reference to a woman being sexy and available, usually made as a comment from one man to another. It has also been interpreted as a symbol of copulation.

What may be concluded about nonverbal gestures and emotions? It appears that gestures are a kind of visual slang, with some gestures having an ancient origin and others (such as V for victory) having a quite recent origin. They express emotions just as words do, but they are not spontaneous or unlearned. They often have somewhat different interpretations in different places and, when used, tend to emphasize the spoken word. Gestures are more common and acceptable in the lower social classes and in children or younger people. They are more often used by men rather than women. Most people have no idea of the historical sources of the gestures they use. Most important in the present context,

FIGURE 7.13. A study of the meanings of 20 common gestures. The interpretations of each gesture are found in Table 7.2. From *Gestures: Their Origins and Distribution*, by D. Morris, P. Collett, P. Marsh, and M. O'Shaughnessy, 1979, p. 114. Copyright 1979 by Stein & Day. Reprinted with permission.

TABLE 7.2. The Meanings of Gestures

Gesture	Meaning
Fingertips kiss	Praise, salutation
Fingers cross	Protection
Nose thumb	Mockery
Hand purse	Question, good, fear, lots
Cheek screw	Good
Eyelid pull	I am alert, be alert
Forearm jerk	Sexual insult, sexual comment
Flat-hand flick	Go away
The ring	OK, good
Vertical horn	Cuckold
Horizontal horn	Cuckold
The fig	Sexual comment, sexual insult
The head toss	Negative, beckon
Chin flick	Disinterest, negative
Cheek stroke	Thin and ill, attractive
Thumb up	OK
Teeth flick	"I will give you nothing," anger (defiance) revenge
The ear touch	Effeminate, warning
Nose tap	Complicity ("it's a secret" or "keep it a secret"), be alert
Palm back V-sign	Victory, two, sexual insult, sign in WWII

they express strong emotions, usually of anger, disgust, mockery, disinterest, wariness, fear, praise, and acceptance. Most of these things may be said of facial expressions as well.

It is important to emphasize that interpersonal communication of emotions is not limited to facial expressions alone. In one study concerned with how couples express love in a nonverbal way, the investigators recorded the cues shown by romantic partners as they discussed a recent pleasant event. Self-reports of affection for the partner were found to be correlated with smiling and nodding the head. Other cues such as licking the lips and coy glances were found to be correlated with self-reports of desire for sex (Keltner, Kring, & Bonanno, 1999).

THE NEUROPHYSIOLOGY OF FACIAL EXPRESSION

The face is capable of providing information of many kinds about an individual. The size, shape, and color of the features provide information about the beauty, race, and age of an individual. The gradual accumulation of wrinkles and pouches provides more detailed information about age and health. Rapid changes in the face are usually produced by muscles and to some degree by alterations of blood flow and skin temperature. These changes are what are usually considered when studying emotions. To understand them and their functions requires some knowledge of the underlying physiology and neurology of the face. This has been reviewed by Rinn (1984), and the following description is based on his account.

Facial Muscles

Facial muscles are evolutionary offshoots of the respiratory muscles of fish. In humans, some of the nerve connections to the facial muscles are from the autonomic system, and for this reason some anatomists classify the face muscles as viscera. Some of the major face muscles are involved primarily in chewing and eating, whereas others are involved in speech and lip articulation. One of the results of these functions is that the oral region is moved by many small muscles in almost any direction. In contrast, the brows are moved by fewer muscles and can move only up, down, or in a vertical furrow. Unilateral movements of the lips, for example, are easy, but the movements are difficult in the upper face (brow) because of differences in the ways that muscles are connected to nerves (Feyereisen, 1986).

Two major nerve pathways enervate the facial muscles: the fifth (trigeminal) and seventh (facial) nerves. The muscles innervated by the trigeminal nerve control chewing movements. In contrast, the muscles innervated by the facial nerve do not move any skeletal structure. Instead they are specialized for communication.

The transneuronal tracts for each side of the face are independent of each other, which means that a nerve injury may conceivably affect only one side of the face. The pattern of innervation also shows considerable individual variation. In the brain, the motor area that controls lower facial movements is much larger than the part of the motor area controlling upper facial movements.

Effects on Facial Expressions of Neural Injuries

Of great interest is the fact that there are two motor pathways from the brain that influence facial movements. One is through the pyramidal tract, whereas the other is through the phylogenetically older extrapyramidal tract. These differences have important clinical implications. For example, a lesion or injury of the cortical motor area on one side may produce a paralysis for voluntary movement of half of the face (hemi-paralysis). However, the same patient may show a normal bilateral smile to an amusing joke. In contrast, a patient with a lesion of the extrapyramidal motor system as in Parkinson's disease may retain the ability to move the facial muscles to verbal commands but loses all spontaneous emotional movements. Separation of voluntary from involuntary function is also seen in cases of multiple sclerosis and some cases of stroke. Many patients with this condition (pseudo bulbar palsy) often find themselves laughing or crying with slight or no provocation. Once the response starts, these patients are unable to inhibit it.

> These episodes are generally indistinguishable from normal laughing and weeping. The face muscles contract into convincing smiles or crying faces, the face reddens, tears flow. The respiratory and vocal responses are also at least grossly identical to emotional responses. The only obvious difference is that these patients report no emotional experience during these bouts, or may even report the presence of an emotion incompatible with the expression (e.g., anger or pain while laughing) .... It appears that the involuntary expressions stem from an inability to involuntarily inhibit those motor release phenomena through normal cortical influences. (Rinn, 1984, p. 64)

Some kinds of laughter are a manifestation of epilepsy. The laughter is inappropriate to the situation and inconsistent with any reported feelings and may be associated with other epileptic symptoms such as falling or spasms. Patients may not recall the laughing fit and will deny any feeling of amusement (Moody, 1979).

Drug use may also produce laughter that is unrelated to any precipitating situation. Nitrous oxide (laughing gas) was used for its laughter-inducing capacities long before it was used as an anesthetic agent. Marijuana users often show hilarious laughter during their "highs." Manganese miners and workers who assembled dry cell batteries would often develop laughing spells. In all these instances, the laughter was a symptom of acute drug intoxication or poisoning.

From the point of view of evolution, in simple organisms, simple reflex neural circuits handle survival issues related to feeding, mating, fight, and flight. Stimulation of the hypothalamus produces coordinated threat displays in cats and in rhesus monkeys (Plutchik, McFarland, & Robinson, 1966). During the course of evolution, the simple circuits are not eliminated as more complex systems evolve, but the functions of some of the systems do change. For example, dogs and cats without a cortical motor system can still walk, eat, fight, and show sexual activity. A comparable lesion in humans would produce massive paralysis. Some primitive responses that are organized neurally at the level of the brain stem and hypothalamus would remain. These include coughing, sneezing, swallowing, gagging, laughing, and crying. Most of these reactions cannot be performed voluntarily except as an approximation, and most can be only partially inhibited.

Facial Expressions in Infants

It has been pointed out that infants can produce almost all of the discrete facial movements that adults produce, but the capacity to inhibit these expressions does not appear until middle childhood when frontal lobe development is complete. Infants born with no cortex still show facial expressions of crying and disgust, which implies that the integration of these expressions occur at subcortical levels. Cortical control is a relatively late evolutionary development, but as a result of the learning of display rules the cortex influences the degree and form of expression of facial movements. Rinn (1984) concluded that any given behavior is the product of both cortical and subcortical influences. Facial expressions of emotion are complex expressions of the interaction of both the involuntary and voluntary systems of the brain.

THEORIES OF FACIAL EXPRESSIONS OF EMOTIONS

Theories are designed to explain facts. Good theories explain more facts than poor ones, and they stimulate research as well. What are some of the facts that need explaining in relation to facial expressions of emotion? Here is a partial list.

Key Issues

1. Most people are strongly influenced by, and interested in, the face. They keep pictures of other people's faces on their desks, in albums, and on the walls. The faces of great men and women are often photographed and enlarged to gigantic proportions. Our preoccupation with mirrors suggests that we constantly examine our own face as well.

2. Our faces express some emotions clearly but not all emotions. We believe that we can easily read expressions of anger, fear, surprise, sadness, joy, and disgust from

the face, but there are many emotions that are harder or impossible to judge from the face; for example, guilt, envy, curiosity, jealousy, and boredom.

3. In laboratory studies, the ability of judges to correctly read, or decode, emotions from photographs is relatively poor. The rate of correct judgments increases if the judges are given a restricted list of emotion words to use, and if synonyms and near-synonyms are grouped as correct answers.

4. The use of photographs of posed or spontaneous expressions is probably not an ideal way to study emotions in view of the fact that emotional expressions have a beginning, a time course, and an ending. Still photos miss much of the complexity of facial expressions.

5. Infants show many of the same facial expressions as do adults, apparently without the benefit of learning. Children born blind and deaf also show what appear to be typical emotional expressions on the face. This suggests that there are genetically determined brain mechanisms that organize the expression of at least some emotions.

6. Electrical stimulation of certain subcortical neurons or pathways produces typical emotional expressions in animals. This supports the notion of specialized brain centers for organizing emotional expressions.

7. Observations of humans with various kinds of brain or nerve damage reveal that a person can show strong emotional expressions (such as laughing or crying) and not report being either happy or sad. Individuals with other types of nerve lesions (e.g., hemiparalysis) cannot voluntarily show typical emotional expressions, yet amusing or sad events may trigger normal patterns of expression.

8. Young children begin the process of learning how to hide some of their emotional expressions, and many adults are very adept at this (e.g., poker face). Adults are also quite capable of voluntarily creating any expression they wish regardless of how they may feel at the moment. They may smile when they are sad and appear friendly even when angry.

9. Most investigators assume that an emotion is a feeling that an individual can report. This ignores the fact that many people have difficulty finding words for their feelings, that feelings may sometimes be repressed or distorted, or that people may sometimes deceive others about their true feelings. These facts make it difficult to interpret simple correlations between reported feelings and overt expressions, no matter how accurately the expressions may be measured.

10. Emotional expressions seldom, if ever, occur in isolation. Ambivalence and conflict are the rule in human and animal social relationships. Therefore, facial expressions will generally reflect mixtures or blends of emotions and mixtures of cortical and subcortical influences.

11. Considerable evidence exists that a small number of facial expressions—fear, anger, disgust, sadness, and enjoyment—are judged fairly consistently in a wide range of cultures, including those having little or no contact with Western societies.

12. According to Ekman (1993), emotions can occur without any characteristic facial expressions. In addition, some emotions have no distinctive expressions at all.

To provide an appreciation of the complexity of facial expressions in everyday life, consider the newspaper photograph shown in Figure 7.14. This is the famous picture

FIGURE 7.14. A photo of Lee Harvey Oswald, the assassin of President John F. Kennedy, being shot by Jack Ruby. Reprinted with permission of Robert Jackson.

taken when Jack Ruby shot Lee Harvey Oswald in the police station shortly after the assassination of President Kennedy. Oswald's face expresses a mixture of pain, horror, and surprise, whereas the policeman's face seems to register shock, disbelief, and fear. There may be other emotions involved as well. Are these expressions readouts of inner states, functional attempts to influence a social encounter, or contemporary expressions of a phylogenetic history related to responses to crises? How do these observations relate to the various theories that have been proposed about the nature of facial expressions?

Darwin's Principles

As stated earlier in chapter 2, Darwin suggested three hypotheses to help account for expressive behavior. The first (*the functional value of expressions*) stated that some expressions are of value in gratifying desires. If, for example, showing teeth with the mouth open acts to intimidate others or reduce threats, it has survival value and is likely to be maintained. The second principle (*antithesis*) states that if certain feelings lead to useful expressions, then opposite feelings will lead to movements of an opposite appearance. Thus, smiling brings the lips up in a U-shape, whereas sadness brings the lips down in an inverted U. This makes sense, because signals between individuals should be easy to recognize and to discriminate. Signals that are easy to detect, easy to discriminate, and easy to remember should represent important characteristics for development during the course of evolution (Guilford & Dawkins, 1991). Darwin's third principle (*direct action of the nervous system*) stated that strong excitation of the nervous system affects various systems of the body, resulting in such expressions as blushing, pallor, sweating, and trembling.

Darwin's central notion was that facial (and other bodily) expressions were forms of communication designed to influence important life events such as mating, dominance, and access to food. Because Darwin was concerned largely with animals lower than man, he had little to say about subjective feelings.

Peripheral Theories of Facial Expression

Stemming from the theories of William James, a number of contemporary theories have developed the implications of his ideas in relation to facial expressions. These theories are called peripheral theories because they assume that the muscles in the face (i.e., near the periphery of the body) generate sensory feedback that is evaluated to produce emotional feelings. These muscular responses are organized at subcortical centers where specific programs for each distinct emotion are assumed to be stored.

One contributor to these ideas about the role of facial feedback is Izard (1990). He assumed that there are 10 basic emotions and that there are separate, innately programmed neural mechanisms for each of the fundamental emotions. These are present in infants and are revealed through distinctive facial expressions. He believed that the development of facial expressions of the fundamental emotions is largely a function of maturation. The intensity of an individual's emotions, however, can be modified by voluntary control of facial movements. This idea has been supported by some research that suggests that intensifying or inhibiting facial expressions in pain can increase or decrease both the self-report of pain and the physiological reaction to it. Izard assumed that facial actions (through feedback from muscles or skin) play a major role in generating feelings of emotion.

Another theory consistent with this general approach has been proposed by Zajonc, Murphy, and Inglehart (1989). This theory assumed that muscle movements of the face regulate blood flow to the brain and thereby affect the temperature of the brain. Variations in brain temperature are believed to influence feeling states. Limited evidence on this point was found when cool air introduced directly into the nasal cavity was experienced as pleasurable, whereas warm air similarly introduced was experienced as unpleasant. Zajonc, Murphy, and Inglehart (1989) concluded that changes in the vascular system of the face tend to generate emotional feelings. They therefore believed that emotional expression and temperature regulation of the brain are closely related. As developed thus far, the theory has something to say only about pleasant versus unpleasant feeling states but has nothing to say about specific emotions, that is, why anger feels different from fear or grief, for example.

Central Theories of Facial Expressions

Most people assume that facial expressions reflect inner emotional states; that is, we cry or look sad when we are grieving and we smile when we feel pleased. From this point of view, facial expression are a *readout* of inner feeling states.

However, in various studies in which attempts were made to correlate facial ratings of emotion with self-reported emotional states, the correlations were often low. In addition, facial expressions of disgust as measured by Ekman's Facial Action Coding System correlated with a number of different self-reported emotions, including anger, sadness, fear, pain, and disgust (Ekman, Friesen, & Ancoli, 1980).

A problem with this central view of facial expressions is that many people (including participants in these kinds of studies) often show little or no facial expressions, even though they report feeling emotions. This observation has usually been explained by assuming that each person is socialized to use certain *display rules* about what emotions to show and under what conditions. For example, it is often assumed that girls are taught to easily display feelings of sadness as well as joy, whereas boys are taught not to cry or show fear. Support for this idea is seen in the study cited earlier indicating that Japanese and American students show similar expressions (to an unseen observer) while watching a distressing film but show different expressions when asked to talk about the film in public. However, there is little empirical data on the nature of display rules and their effects on people.

Another issue that arises in connection with a central theory of facial expressions is that there are large numbers of emotions, as well as mixtures of emotions, for which no discrete facial pattern is known. How does one express on the face whether one is jealous, remorseful, proud, sarcastic, or curious? Many people also deliberately prevent their face from revealing any emotions if it is to their benefit to do so. And many people will deliberately show an emotional expression they do not feel to accomplish some goal, such as hiding their anger when criticized or looking friendly despite a wish for revenge. These observations suggest that there may be, and often is, a discrepancy between an inner emotional feeling and its outward expression on the face. People sometimes fake facial expressions. This is particularly true in certain occupations where one might be expected to smile without feeling the corresponding emotion (e.g., this is part of a salesperson or flight attendant's job). Such dissimulation is not easy to detect.

An interesting study illustrates both the controlled nature of the facial response and its impact on other people. In this study, participants were asked to deliver electric shocks to another participant (actually a confederate of the experimenter). Some victims were told to smile during the shock experience, whereas others were told to look angry. The results revealed that victims who showed anger received less shock, whereas smiling victims were given increasing levels of shock (Savitsky, Izard, Kotsch, & Christy, 1974). These findings suggest that people can deliberately choose, if they wish, to show certain expressions on their faces to elicit sympathy and support, or to create fear or anger. This implies that facial expressions are forms of communication that we use to satisfy our needs, wishes, and motives.

A Functional Theory of Facial Expressions

Instead of thinking of facial expressions as a reflection of an inner state of emotion or as a generator of emotional feelings, various authors (beginning with Darwin) have suggested that facial expressions are simply forms of communication. From this point of view, facial expressions reflect intentions or attempts to influence or regulate a social encounter, regardless of inner feelings.

It is evident from observations of infants that they cry when they are hungry, tired, or in pain, and they smile when a mother or caretaker arrives. Fridlund (1994) suggested that cries and smiles function to make sure that the mother is attentive and will probably carry out actions useful to the infant's' survival. From an evolutionary viewpoint, selection pressures exist on children to capture the attention of their parents, particularly in settings in which there may be multiple children all competing for parental attention.

From a similar functional viewpoint, the cry face is a signal that one needs or wishes help. The threat face is an indication that one is ready to fight or that one has the ability to fight. This view of facial expression does not imply that emotions do not exist or that the face does not show emotions at times. Rather it assumes that in most situations, people and animals use facial (and other) displays to try to influence others so they may get what they want. Some theorists have called this process *deception*, but it does not imply some kind of evil-doing, nor does it necessarily imply a conscious intent to deceive. Deception, as a form of protection, is found widely throughout the plant and animal kingdom. Camouflage markings are forms of deception, as are eye-spots on the wings of butterflies. These are natural, survival-related adaptations. Presumably, the same is true for human facial displays.

EVOLUTIONARY ORIGINS OF FACIAL DISPLAYS

An ethologist, Shirley Strum (1988), who has long studied baboons in natural environments in Africa, commented on the functional value of facial expressions:

> All animals need to communicate with one another. Solitary creatures who reproduce sexually need only to be able to communicate about mating. Creatures who care for their offspring need to be able to exchange information about themselves and their children. Animals who live in social groups, temporarily or permanently, need to be able to communicate on a much more sophisticated level . . . . As a result signals were borrowed from one context—sexual behavior, for example—and used in another—parenting or social communication—with a shift in meaning to extend the dialogue. (p. 263)

Baboons

As a result of closely observing several groups of baboons for 15 years, Strum (1988) developed considerable insight into their social interactions. The following summary is based on her book, *Almost Human: A Journey Into the World of Baboons*.

When a sexually receptive female presents her bottom for a male to inspect, this is a communication about sexual intentions. However, presenting can also be an invitation from an adult female to an infant to approach, or it can be a greeting asking permission to approach. When two males show a slight variation on the presenting position, and at the same time grunt, narrow their eyes, and smack their lips together, they convey friendly intentions but also some nervousness. Presenting can also be a request for grooming. Embraces can be a type of greeting, usually between an adult and an older infant. When two adults embrace, it usually occurs after an upsetting incident in the troop.

Aggressive displays can vary greatly in intensity. At low intensity, raising the eyebrows reveals white eyelids. As aggression increases, an open-mouth threat (with canines showing) is added to the eyelid signal as well as some erection of body hair. At more intense levels, sounds and ground slapping are added. Submissive displays often occur in response to aggressive threats. In such cases the animal makes short staccato grunts, shows an open-mouth fear-face that looks somewhat like a grin, and crouches low. Play behavior is accompanied by a special facial display called a play-face that signals that the ensuing behavior is not serious.

Of great importance is the fact that most social interactions among the baboons are confused and ambivalent. Males will often first exchange friendly greetings, then threats, and then friendly greetings again. Strum (1988) concluded that these various displays communicate emotions and imply such statements as "I am angry," "I am content," "I am ambivalent," or "I am not aggressive."

Guenons

In another interesting book about primates (Gautier-Hion, Bourliere, Gautier, & Kingdon, 1988), a great deal of information was provided about a group of African guenons, which include the patas monkeys and the hamadras baboons, macaques, colobines, and mangabeys, among others. These monkeys live mainly in forest areas or tall grass and communicate largely by vocalizations. They have three types of calls: alarm calls, cohesion calls, and spacing calls. In addition, their faces and bodies show bright colors, for example, a blue face, white belly fur, and red sexual swelling, all of which provide instant information from one individual to another about sex, rank, and age.

In this species, the underside and inner linings of arms and eyes are pure white, and cheeks and brows are also very pale. Adult males respond to a monkey puppet with stereotyped threat behavior. The threat response goes from a *cutoff* phase in which the animal is hunched over and is apparently avoiding interaction, to an *advertising* phase in which various body parts are exposed while the posture is changed. The third phase is one of *threat* (hard stare and lunge) plus vocalization followed by another cutoff. During the cutoff, the dullest areas of the animal are exposed to view. These examples are given to illustrate the role of facial and other displays in regulating the course of social interaction.

The Origins of Facial Expressions

Ethologists have long been interested in the origins of these various displays. It is usually assumed that displays developed from patterns of behavior that originally possessed no communication value. These patterns include regulation of body temperature, intention movements (i.e., initial movement of attack or retreat, and protective reactions). Protective reactions include eye closure, arrested respiration, repeated tongue protrusions, and lateral shaking of the head.

In a review of the origin of calls and facial expressions in primates, Andrew (1963) came to the conclusion that primate calls and facial expressions probably originated from protective reflexes evoked by unpleasant or startling stimuli. For example, if a noxious fluid is placed in the mouth, the head is usually shaken from side to side, the mouth corners and lips are drawn back, and the tongue is repeatedly protruded. The eyebrows tend to be lowered and the eyes closed. Finally, a throat reflex closes the glottis or mouth of the windpipe to prevent the noxious material from being ingested.

Another expression frequently seen in primates is the grimace. In this display, the corners of the mouth and lips retract to expose the teeth. This expression is frequently observed in animals that are the target of an attack or threat, or in response to a close approach by another animal. In one study of baboons, a subordinate animal gave 97% of the grimaces to a dominant one (Redican, 1982). Ethologists believe that the function of the grimace is appeasement. Supporting this idea is that in most circumstances potential or actual attack terminates as a consequence of the display.

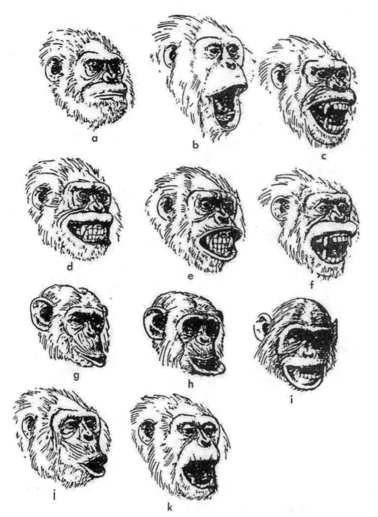

FIGURE 7.15. Some facial expressions of chimpanzees drawn from photographs and descriptions provided by van Hooff (1973) and van Lawick-Goodall (1973): (a) "Glare"; anger, Type 1. (b) "Waa bark"; anger, Type 2. (c) "Scream calls"; fear-anger. (d) "Silent bared-teeth"; "Type 1, horizontal bared-teeth"; submission. (e) "Silent bared-teeth"; "Type 2, vertical bared-teeth"; fear-affection (?). (f) "Silent bared-teeth"; "Type 3, open-mouth bared-teeth"; affection. (g) "Pout face"; desiring-frustration (?). (h) "Whimper face"; frustration-sadness (?); Type 1, or Type 1-2 transition (infant). (i) "Cry face"; frustration-sadness; Type 2 (infant). (j) "Hoot face"; excitement-affection (?). (k) "Play face"; playfulness (the question marks indicate ambiguity about the emotion being expressed). From "Facial Expression of Emotion in Nonhuman Primates," by S. Chevalier-Skolnikoff. In P. Ekman (Ed.), *Darwin and Facial Expression*, 1973, p. 211. Copyright 1973 by Academic Press. Reprinted with permission.

According to Andrew (1963), some ethologists believe that the grimace evolved from high-frequency vocalizations such as screeching or screaming heard in fear-inducing situations. This vocalization evolved into a silent scream. Hence, the assumption is that the emotional state typically associated with the grimace is fear.

Other ethologists have suggested that the grin seen in primates is a facial expression that has evolved from lip retraction as a response to potentially dangerous foods. In a social context, the grin generally indicates fear and submission. Primates of lower status are much more likely to show the grin than those of high status. In humans and the higher primates, the grin has evolved into the smile, which acts as a signal of affiliation and appeasement (de Waal, 1989).

Another aspect of a fear-related display is gaze aversion. Avoiding visual contact is a means of avoiding social interaction. Primatologists consider gaze aversion to express less fearfulness than does the grimace.

In threat, the mouth was originally opened with no lip retraction. Baboons and lemurs raise the upper lip before an attack in an expression that looks like a snarl. Facial snarls are also seen in apes such as the chimpanzee. Ear flattening is observed in threats against equals and often in connection with overt attacks. The effect of ear flattening is to raise the eyebrows, seen in baboons as a rapid threat signal.

Both apes and humans frown in threat. This appears as a lowering of the eyebrows and through the action of the corrugater muscles as a vertical line in the skin between the eyes. The eyes remain wide open. This kind of frown is believed to have originated from the intense scrutiny of a nearby object. Throughout the primates, a steady gaze is one of the features of confident threat.

Andrew (1963) emphasized the close connection between the production of sounds (calls) in different situations and the evolution of facial expressions. Changes in facial expressions come to alter the quality of calls, so that calls carry more specific information. He concluded that the various facial expression components are elicited by a variety of types of environmental situations in different primates, and that therefore no perfect correlation is possible between any particular facial component and any single emotional state. Figure 7.15 shows a variety of chimpanzee facial expressions. They highlight the fact that different species have different ways to communicate the same underlying emotional states.

Facial expressions are essential to the welfare of animals that live in groups. Through facial expressions, vocalizations, and other displays, animals avoid or approach one another, determine the timing of reproductive activities and, in general, regulate social interactions.

SUMMARY

The literature reviewed in this chapter reveals that facial expressions are imperfect communicators of emotional states. Emotions and facial expressions are only partially related, and the connections between the two classes of events are subject to many disrupting influences. Evidence exists to support the idea that certain facial expressions can be seen in many different cultures in fairly similar forms; this implies that there is a genetic basis for some facial expressions of emotion. However, it is also likely that certain facial expressions (such as winking or sticking out the tongue) may be learned like the words of a language. Generally, learning helps determine the stimuli to which facial expressions are made, as well as the mixtures of facial expressions. It is probable that most expressions are based on genetically determined brain programs; the overt appearance of an expression depends on the presence of particular stimuli and their interpretation, which in turn depend on social learning and the current state of the individual. Certain patterns of reaction (or displays) are elicited by significant stimuli in the life of an individual. But in many situations, facial expressions are muted, hidden, or deceptive and are largely controlled by the wishes or needs of the individual, needs for power, acceptance, love, and intimidation. This viewpoint interprets facial expressions as compromises between innate tendencies to react in protective ways to dangerous situations and desires to accomplish one's aims indirectly with the help of camouflage. Facial expressions are only one aspect of general social signals, which include various types of vocalizations as well as other types of nonverbal behavior.

Studies of patients with neurological injuries that produce partial paralysis of facial muscles have shown that integrated laughing and weeping can still occur. The interpretation of such findings is that facial expressions of emotion are complex expressions of the interaction of both the involuntary and voluntary systems of the brain.

Three general types of theories of facial expression are described. *Peripheral* theories assume that the muscles and skin of the face generate sensory feedback that is then evaluated to produce emotional feelings. *Central* theories assume that facial expressions reflect inner emotional states. *Functional* theories assume that facial expressions are forms of communication that attempt to influence a social encounter, regardless of inner feelings. Evidence for each of these viewpoints exists, although the functional theory is more general and has been shown to apply to lower primates as well as to humans. A number of speculations have been offered by ethologists on the evolutionary origins of expressions of emotion.

8 Emotional Development

> I used to think in terms of the evil emotions of fear and anger as opposed to the good emotion of love, but considering that all of these can lay claim to having had survival value over the evolutionary eras, none can properly be considered to be entirely evil.
>
> *Harry Harlow*

PREVIEW

The study of emotion in infants and young children creates many conceptual problems. If emotions are considered to be inner feelings or experiences, it is obviously no more possible to discover such inner feelings in an infant than in a chimpanzee. If an emotion is something other than a feeling, just what is it? If we choose to attribute emotions to infants, on what basis do we make such inferences? How many emotions do infants start with, and how do they develop? Although there are no simple answers to these questions, they should be addressed. Therefore, in this chapter we consider the many behavior patterns infants exhibit, the criteria we use in making judgments about infant emotions, the functions of emotions in infants, the nature of infant attachments, facial expressions in infants and what they mean, and how young children learn emotion concepts.

BEHAVIOR PATTERNS IN INFANTS

It is obvious that inferences about emotions in infants must be based on evidence other than verbal reports. Most discussions of this issue rely on an infant's facial expressions or vocal output such as crying, and relatively little attention has been paid to other responses or behavior. However, from an evolutionary point of view, it is possible that too much attention has been paid to the face. In most lower animals, there are relatively few facial expressions to communicate information, but many other display behaviors reflect emotional states. For example, in lower animals, the displays, which involve various parts of the body, are used in special ways in the following contexts: greeting, recognition, courtship, mating, dominance, submission, warning, alarm, defense, challenge, distress, defeat, victory, feeding, and food begging. These kinds of displays are thought of by ethologists as signals; that is, they function to communicate important information from one animal to another. In most cases, these display reactions appear without prior explicit learning or experience and are apparently genetically programmed. Some of these displays are found in young organisms as well as mature ones.

From an ethological point of view, it would be expected that some of these display behaviors should be found in humans, at least in rudimentary form. For example, the cry of the newborn human infant is remarkably like the cry of the newborn chimpanzee and newborn gorilla (Lieberman, 1975), and the grasp reflex is found in human newborns just as it is found in monkeys. If we are to understand the nature of emotions in infants, therefore, it would be useful to consider the many different expressive behaviors of which infants are capable.

Darwin's Observations

Charles Darwin was probably the first to systematically attempt to investigate emotions in infants. In his autobiography, Darwin (1892/1958) wrote,

> My first child was born on December 27, 1839, and I at once commenced to make notes on the first dawn of the various expressions which he exhibited, for I felt convinced, even at this early period, that the most complex and fine shades of expression must all have had a gradual and natural origin. (p. 50).

In his book, *The Expression of the Emotions in Man and Animals* (1872/1965), Darwin described some of the observations he made on his own infants and those of others. For example, he noticed that infants will utter screams when in hunger, pain, or discomfort and that the facial expression will be the same in all of these situations. When screaming, the eyes are closed, the skin around the eyes are wrinkled, and the forehead is contracted in a frown. The mouth is widely open, with the lips retracted in such a way as to create a squarelike form, with the teeth or gums exposed. Darwin also reported that tears are not associated with crying until the 2nd to 4th month of life and that sobbing is observed only in humans and never in lower primates. He also suggested, without further elaboration, that the crying associated with pain was different from the crying associated with grief. Some of the pictures he took of his children are shown in Figure 8.1.

Watson's Observations

Despite these intriguing beginnings of a comparative psychology of infant development, relatively little attention was paid to the problem until well into the 20th century, when John Watson, the founder of behaviorism, provided a major contribution. Watson was influenced both by Darwin and by Sigmund Freud. In his book *Psychology From the Standpoint of a Behaviorist* (1929), Watson pointed out that humans are innately endowed with various adaptive life-conserving propensities that influence food intake, waste elimination, and procreation. These functions serve humans as they serve lower animals. He went on to write,

> Man at birth and at varying periods thereafter is supplied with a series of protective attack and defense mechanism, which while not nearly so perfect as in animals, nevertheless form a substantial repertoire of acts. They need supplementation by habit before being of direct utility to the individual in his struggle for food, against enemies, etc. These are the protective and defense reactions—the unlearned part activities at first predominate .... The principal role of all unlearned activity, neglecting the vegetative and procreative ... is to initiate the process of learning. (p. 35)

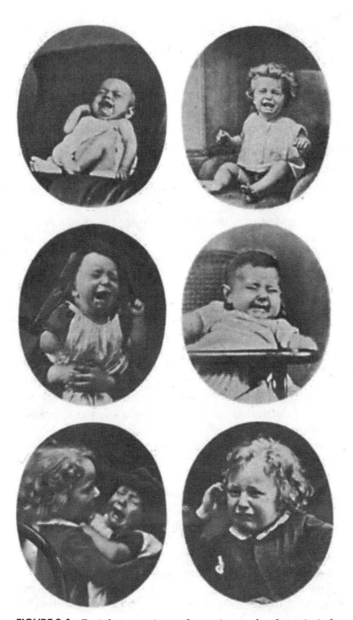

FIGURE 8.1. Facial expressions of weeping and sadness in infants and young children. From *The Expression of the Emotions in Man and Animals*, by C. Darwin, 1872/1965, p. 147. Copyright 1965 by University of Chicago Press. Reprinted with permission.

Watson performed a series of experiments with infants designed to identify the reactions that could be elicited by various stimuli. He tried the following kinds of stimuli:

1. sudden dropping of the infant
2. loud sounds
3. slight shaking when the infant was falling asleep

4. holding the infant's arms at side

5. holding the infant's head to prevent movement

6. tickling

7. shaking

8. gentle rocking

9. patting

10. stroking an erogenous zone

11. odors such as oil of peppermint, asafoetida, butyric acid, and ammonia

12. light pinching of nose or inner surface of knee.

Watson noticed that within hours after birth, the infant showed a variety of spontaneous behaviors as well as reactions to stimuli. These included sucking; sneezing; hiccuping; yawning; crying; erection of the penis; defecation; urination; turning of the head; raising the head; and various hand, arm, and leg movements. Also included are various infant reflexes, such as the *rooting reflex* (turning the mouth toward a tactile stimulus); the *Babinski, or plantar, reflex* (spreading of the toes when the sole of the foot is scratched); the *grasp reflex* (clinging to an object with the hands); and the *Moro reflex* (extension of the limbs and arching of the back elicited by a loud noise).

After observing many infants exposed to the stimuli listed above, Watson came to the conclusion that they showed three major patterns of reaction that could be called $X, Y,$ and Z. He then indicated that there are other common psychological terms that might label these patterns, which he proposed with great hesitation: *fear, rage,* and *love.* Parenthetically, Watson (1919) stated that his use of the word *love* was approximately the same as Freud's use of the word *sex.*

Watson then reported that the fear (X) response was produced by sudden dropping of an infant, by loud sounds, and by shaking the infant as he or she is just falling asleep. The rage (Y) response was produced by hampering the infant's movements. Stroking or manipulation of an erogenous zone of the infant produced the love (Z) response. Relatively little information was given on the exact forms of these responses. Watson also assumed that individual differences were largely a result of differences in the type of environment to which an individual was exposed.

Although Watson's observations were interesting, his stimuli were not standardized, and many psychologists began to systematically examine infants and young children in an effort to confirm or disprove these ideas. Let us examine one such recent study concerned with the development of anger expressions in infancy (Stenberg & Campos, 1990).

Anger in Infants and Young Children

Anger is an important and probably universal experience in human life, but relatively little is known about its earliest manifestations. In one study of anger in infants, Stenberg and Campos (1990) used restraint of the infant's arms as the stimulus condition designed to produce anger, and this was applied to 48 infants, divided into four equal groups ranging in age from 1 to 7 months. The investigators measured facial and vocal expressions, flushing, and crying. Independent raters sampled several 3-second episodes taken before, during, and after the restraint and coded the facial expressions by means of a coding system developed by Izard (1979)—MAX (Maximally Discriminative Facial Movement Coding System). The MAX system had already identified the facial component expressions that are believed to be associated with anger in adults; Stenberg and Campos attempted to determine the extent to which the infants' facial expressions during restraint matched the adults' expressions.

The results indicated that the infants did not show the anger expression spontaneously before the arms were restrained. However, both 4- and 7-month-old infants clearly showed the anger pattern following restraint, whereas the 1-month-old infants never did. Flushing of the face was observed in 92% of the babies following restraint. None of the babies except one shed any tears during restraint. Also of interest is the fact that the anger facial displays in 4-month-old infants appeared to be directed toward the immediate source of the frustration, whereas by 7 months, the expressions seemed to be directed toward the mother who was sitting nearby. It thus appears that the capacity to exhibit the organized expression of anger develops in infants some time between the 1st and 4th months of life.

In a review of anger and its development, Lemerise and Dodge (2000) pointed out the functional significance of anger in children. When restraint of movement occurs, or a barrier is placed between a child and a desired object, anger energizes behavior in an attempt to overcome the barrier. In addition, anger signals often enable a child to obtain desired goals, by having other people respond to the anger in such a way as to reduce it. Although anger does not always work in this way, it is often effective enough to perpetuate its use.

Less is known about the socialization of anger. It is known that there are marked individual differences in the threshold response to anger-eliciting situations. It is also recognized that some children have more difficulty in regulating their emotions. An active area of current research is the concern with socialization techniques that regulate anger and its expression.

In a study dealing with a related issue and somewhat older children, Stein, Trabasso, and Liwag (2000) asked parents to describe recent instances during which their young children (ages 2–4 years) expressed anger, sadness, fear, or happiness. In a later interview, the children were told their parents' recollections and were asked if they remembered the event, recalled their feelings, and recalled what they thought and did during the event.

Stein et al. (2000) then identified what they called prototypic precipitating events as seen by the parents and separately as seen by the children. Table 8.1 summarizes these feelings.

It is evident that the parents' ideas about what kinds of events precipitate emotions in young children are often at variance with the ideas of their children. For example, 22% of the children recalled that punishment by their parents precipitated their anger, whereas none of the parents believed that punishment produced anger in their young child. With regard to sadness, none of the parents thought that punishment of the child produced sadness, whereas 20% of the children reported sadness as a result of punishment. None of the parents believed that nightmares and bad dreams produced fear, whereas 13% of the children recalled their bad dreams as a precipitating event for fear. Such findings are puzzling. Stein et al. (2000) suggested that young children use both conscious and unconscious processes to understand their own emotions.

TABLE 8.1. Prototypic Precipitating Events for Four Different Emotions

Event	Parent recall (%)	Child recall (%)
Angry		
Child is punished	0	22
Child's goals are in conflict with another's	15	0
Child's possessions are taken away/destroyed	14	0
Child is forced to do something	14	0
Child is intruded upon	12	0
Sad		
Child is separated from significant others	32	10
Child is punished	0	20
Child is denied desirable objects	0	10
Child is unable to engage in desirable activities	0	10
Afraid		
Child perceives a threat to self or others	23	40
Child experiences undesirable sensory stimuli	22	0
Child's emotions are elicited by imaginary animate beings	14	20
Child had nightmares/bad dreams	0	13
Happy		
Child engages in/masters desirable activities	22	21
Child gets desirable objects	18	19
Child participates in family activities	14	0
Child plays	0	18

Note. From "A Goal Appraisal Theory of Emotional Understanding: Implications for Development and Learning," by N. L. Stein, T. Trabasso, and M. D. Liwag. In M. Lewis and J. M. Haviland-Jones (Eds.), *Handbook of Emotions* (2nd ed.), 2000, p. 442. Copyright 2000 by Guilford Press. Reprinted with permission.

VARIETIES OF INFANT BEHAVIORS

Brazelton (1976) described the range of behaviors of which newborns are capable. His Neonatal Assessment Scale listed 26 behavioral and 20 reflex activities of the human neonate in interaction with an adult. These include the following:

1. Turning head in direction of human voice
2. Responding to a female vocal pitch over a male voice
3. Humanoid sounds preferred to pure tones
4. Using the eyes to follow a picture
5. Responding to milk smells rather than sugar water.

It is now known that newborn infants have a surprising ability to process sensory information. Infants show the pupillary reflex; visual pursuit behavior; sustained fixation; color sensitivity; tracking objects with coordinated movements of the head and eyes;

visual accommodation; the ability to discriminate visual patterns; differential attention and preferences for some patterns over others; sensitivity to pitch, intensity, and duration of sounds; head and eye movements to locate a source of sound; and a preference for human speech over other types of sound.

Many other researchers have mentioned the behavioral characteristics of infants. For example, infants show automatic walking movements, eyes-closed smiling, and spontaneous erections. They are able to imitate mouth and tongue movements, vocalizations, and hand movements, and they often synchronize hand or arm movements with vocalizations or facial grimaces (Trevarthen, 1977).

Trevarthen (1977) also claimed that when a mother shows a lack of response or an inappropriate response, 8-week-old infants show expressions of confusion, distress, or withdrawal. Spitz (1957) pointed out that infants show rooting behavior (a head-turning response to touching of the cheek called an oral orientation reflex) as well as head nodding. Kinsey, Pomeroy, and Martin (1948) described evidence of orgasm in infants. Andrew (1974) drew our attention to patterns of behavior that are found in the young of lower animals (as well as in the mature animal). He mentioned respiratory reflexes that cause dilation of the nostrils and contribute in some degree to facial expressions. He described thermoregulatory responses such as sweating, panting, and flushing, which act to cool the body, and the total body response of immobility. He also mentioned secretions (odors) and excretions (defecation), which play an important role in social displays.

These studies have revealed the presence of many different behaviors and expressions in infants during the first year of life. Most such patterns have not been studied intensively, and only a few of them have been considered as measures of emotion. However, it is possible to consider infant behaviors somewhat the way ethologists examine animal behaviors. They do this by creating an ethogram, which is briefly described next.

The newborn infant is not simply a blank screen on which experience writes. Within the first hours and weeks after birth, many organized behavior patterns may be identified either as reactions to stimulations or as spontaneous events. For example, there are a number of reflexes that can be elicited in most human infants at birth but usually disappear after 3 or 4 months. As listed earlier, these include the rooting reflex, the plantar reflex, the grasp reflex, and the Moro reflex.

Although many behaviors are observable in infants, few investigators have attempted to catalog them in any systematic way. However, Young and Decarie (1977) compiled what might be called an *ethogram* of human infant behaviors. The term is taken from the terminology of the ethologists who generally study animals in their natural environments; it describes an exhaustive list of behaviors observable in a given species of animal under naturalistic conditions.

Young and Decarie established a list of facial expressions and vocalizations that might be broadly considered as related to emotional expressions. This meant that observers had to judge the behavior as social, affective, or communicative in nature. Such behaviors as sneezing or coughing were not included.

The ethogram was established by first observing 6 infants in different situations (e.g., approach of a stranger with the mother present, departure of mother, physical restraint). These infants and their reactions were videotaped, and a preliminary catalog of behaviors was drawn up. The catalog was applied to 30 other infants and further refined. Then it was finally applied to another group of 40 infants approximately ages 8 to 12 months.

The result was a catalog of 42 facial expressions and 10 vocalizations. On the basis of the situations connected with each expression, an inference was made of the hedonic tone, that is, the pleasant or unpleasant quality presumably associated with the expression.

TABLE 8.2. An Ethogram of Facial and Vocal Behaviors in 8- to 12-Month-Old Infants

Inferred Hedonic Tone		
Positive	*Negative*	*Ambiguous*
Close mouth smile	Tremble	Yawn
Coy smile	Tight-lip face	Wide-eyes stare
O-mouth smile	Square-mouth face	Tongue out
Open-mouth smile	Kidney-mouth face	Blink
Shy smile	Clenched-teeth face	Brow-raise stare
Semismile	Pout	Lip roll
Slight open-mouth smile	Sad face	Sigh
Positive face	Negative face	Somber frown
Brighten	Grimace	Sober stare
Sparkle	Frown	Surprise face
Play face	Fear face	Perplexed face
Babble	Disgust face	Shy face
Coo	Harsh wail	Detached face
Laugh	Soft wail	Frozen face
Squeal	Wail	Attentive face
Positive vocalization		Ambivalent face
		Ambivalent smile
		Undifferentiated face
		Normal face
		Ambivalent vocalization
		Undifferentiated vocalization

Note. From "An Ethology-Based Catalogue of Facial/Vocal Behavior in Infancy," by C. Young and T. Decarie, 1977, *Animal Behavior, 25,* p. 104. Copyright 1977 by Animal Behavior Society. Reprinted with permission.

This resulted in 16 positive expressions, 15 negative ones, and 21 neutral, ambivalent, or undifferentiated ones. These expressions, as labeled by Young and Decarie (1977), are presented in Table 8.2. They are assumed to be "basic" expressions of interpersonal communication that combine in numerous ways to produce all the complex emotional expressions observed in infants and older children. For example, the kidney-mouth or square-mouth faces were often accompanied by wails (or soft wails) and tended to be evoked in situations in which the mother frustrated the child. However, it should be emphasized that a behavior expression does not occur at a single moment in time but occurs in sequences and combinations of units over varying periods of time. In other words, a sequence starts and later stops, and somehow most observers recognize the beginning and end of each sequence.

INFERRING EMOTIONS IN INFANTS

Although the descriptions given above demonstrate that infants are capable of a wide variety of behaviors, it is not at all evident that babies have subjective feelings that are anything like those in adults. At best, one can only make guesses or inferences about inner states in infants. However, if one accepts the definition of emotion proposed by the ethologist Marler (1977), it is reasonable to infer emotional states in young babies. Marler proposed that inferences about emotional states are based on the following: (a) that emotions are generalized, (b) that they affect many patterns of behavior, (c) that autonomic arousal is often involved, (d) that there appears to be a sense of urgency when they appear, (e) that they have a momentum that makes rapid stops difficult, (f) that they seem to involve the involuntary muscles mostly, (g) that they are not easily trained, (h) that they are often associated with approach or avoidance behavior, and (i) that they are usually directed toward other individuals in the environment.

Smiles

It is important to emphasize that one or more of these characteristics may be absent and the judgment of the presence of an emotion may still be made. An example of the role of inference in judging emotions in infants may be given in regard to the smile. Certain smiles are not triggered by social events, are not conditionable, and are related to rapid eye movement (REM) states of drowsiness. A certain stage of sleep is associated with eye movements that can be seen through the closed eyelids. This sleep stage, REM sleep, is found in adults, infants, and many animals. Other smiles are clearly responses to the caretaker, appear to be anticipatory reactions, and appear at times of high alertness. The latter smiles are inferred to be emotional, whereas the former smiles are not.

Surprise

Similar issues have been raised with regard to the emotion of surprise. Camras (2000) noted that a current view of emotional development in infants assumes that a species-specific set of emotions develops over time and is reflected in a set of recognizable infant facial expressions (Izard et al., 1995) that express inner emotional states. However, an interesting body of evidence revealed noncorrespondence between emotions and facial expressions. Several illustrations of this point may be given.

1. Fear expressions on the face have not been found in infants who showed other signs of fear due to a stranger, or when placed on a visual cliff (discussed later).
2. More than one typical facial expression has been described for the same emotion, for example, interest. The Facial Action Coding System contains over 10 expressions that can be called *surprise*.
3. Surprise expressions are often seen when infants open their mouths in anticipation of putting something into their mouths.

Such inconsistencies between facial expressions and probable emotions cannot be explained by reference to display rules, which possibly apply only to older children and adults.

A cross-cultural study of 48 American infants and 23 Chinese infants examined their facial reactions to a situation designed to produce surprise in the child (Camras, 2000). Only 4 infants out of this large group showed a facial expression that could be coded with certainty for the emotion of surprise.

Camras (2000) concluded that emotion-type facial expressions may occur even when no emotion is present (as judged on the basis of other evidence). Conversely, an observer may infer emotions in an infant even when the infant does not show corresponding facial expressions. These observations do not imply that emotional communication between infants and adults is therefore impossible. Converging evidence based on a variety of observations (e.g., knowledge of stimulus situations, verbal behavior, postural changes, facial expressions, and changes in these observations over time) determine the probability of certain emotions being present. Perfect predictability is not necessary for effective communication (even in adults); the observer only needs to be correct more often than not.

INFERRING EMOTION IN MONKEYS

A parallel problem exists with regard to inferring emotions in monkeys. Seyforth, Cheney, and Marler (1980a) noticed that vervet monkeys seemed to show appropriate emotional reactions to alarm calls emitted by other monkeys. For example, so-called leopard alarms were associated with other monkeys running into trees; eagle alarms were associated with monkeys looking up; and snake alarms were associated with monkeys looking down. These alarm signals were tape-recorded and played back to the vervets in the absence of actual predators, with comparable results. In addition, it was found that age, sex, context, and various acoustic properties had little effect on the animal's reactions. Thus, the convergence of various kinds of evidence led to the conclusion that an emotional signal of a specific kind had been emitted.

SOCIAL ATTACHMENT AND FEAR IN INFANTS

Social attachment in infants and children is considered to be an expression of an emotion. The judgment of social attachment in infants is also based on a variety of observations. Freedman (1974) stated that social attachment is inferred on the basis of the following kinds of data: (a) the attempt to maintain physical proximity, (b) the appearance of mutual watching, (c) mutual smiling, (d) mutual cooing, (e) mutual laughter and play, and (f) signs of protection of the young. It thus appears that the inference of attachment is based on an evaluation and interpretation of specific behaviors engaged in by the mother and infant.

The judgment of fear in an infant is usually based on observations of gaze aversion and crying when a stranger approaches. But these reactions may also be evoked by placing the child on a glass table several feet above the floor. This setting is called a *visual cliff*, and although it is not dangerous for the child, it does evoke crying and aversive reactions. (The visual cliff reaction is discussed is more detail later in the chapter.) Inferences about emotions should rely on as many sources of information as possible. Of particular importance is a description of the stimuli that precede the emotional expression, the detailed appearance of the response itself, and the kind of effects the expression appears to have on other organisms in the immediate environment. Figure 8.2 shows the reaction of a 7-week-old infant to the experimenter wearing a plastic mask. Infants stare, frown, and stop smiling. Some begin to cry, as shown in the figure. The inference made is that the mask is aversive.

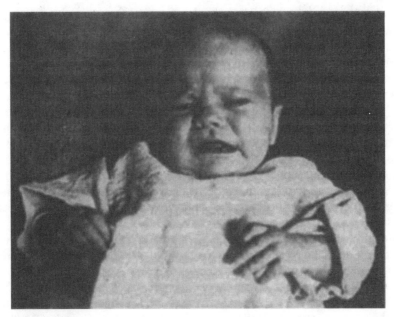

FIGURE 8.2. A 7-week-old infant's reactions to the investigator wearing a plastic mask. From *The Development of Behavioral States and the Expression of Emotions in Early Infancy*, by P. H. Wolff, 1987, p. 57. Copyright 1987 by University of Chicago Press. Reprinted with permission.

VOCALIZATIONS AS EXPRESSIONS OF EMOTIONS

An illustration of this approach to defining emotion may be found in the study of kitten vocalizations by Haskins (1979). Kittens were exposed to cold stimuli, restraint, and isolation at various times during their first 6 weeks of life. The results showed that the kittens cried more during restraint than during either cold exposure or isolation. The entrance of the mother into the litter box also increased the frequency of crying, as did shifts in position of the mother during nursing. Crying decreased when kittens congregated in huddles. The crying of the kittens also influenced the mother to come into the litter box and to make nursing possible. Sound spectrograph analysis revealed that the peak fundamental frequency of the crying was significantly greater during the cold stress than during either isolation or restraint. These results imply that vocalizations carry information about the stimulus conditions to which kittens are exposed and have an effect on the caretaker that is related to the probability of survival of the young. They also imply that we make judgments about probable emotional states by considering the stimuli that seemed to trigger the response as well as the effect the response had on the mother cat.

Another illustration of a similar approach was reported by Scoville and Gottlieb (1980). They recorded the vocalizations of Peking ducklings from several hours before hatching to 48 hours post hatching. Vocalizations were recorded in a variety of situations, for example, in the presence of other ducklings, during exposure to maternal calls, and during social isolation. Sound spectrograph analysis revealed two acoustically distinct types of sound patterns: (a) *contentment calls*, which have short note durations, fast repetition rates, and low pitch and are elicited by the presence of peers or maternal calls, and

(b) *distress calls,* which have longer note durations, slower repetition rates, and higher pitch and are emitted during social isolation. The second category of sounds appear to attract attention of the hen to any duckling that has become separated from the brood. Such attraction serves to maintain group cohesion and to increase the chances of survival of the ducklings.

In a similar type of investigation, Scott (1980) recorded distress vocalizations in puppies and tried to identify variables that would either increase or decrease them. Food, novel objects, and tranquilizers had no effect, although an antidepressant (Imipramine) reduced distress vocalizations in certain breeds of dogs. Morphine also reduced these vocalizations, as did exposure to a warm (29° centigrade) incubator. The most effective reducer of these vocalizations was social interaction with other puppies or adult dogs. These and other observations led to the conclusion that these vocalizations are, in fact, emotional signals of distress and that they function to increase the probability of social contact with other animals.

There is one further point to be made in regard to the issue of inferring emotions from indirect evidence. One of the important reasons that emotional states are sometimes difficult to define in a simple, clear-cut way is that emotions are often mixed states and reflect the interaction of opposite tendencies. Hinde (1966) gave many examples from the animal literature of the concept that overt displays often reflect combined impulses of approach and avoidance, attack and flight, or sex and aggression. Van Hooff (1973) identified five display systems in the chimpanzee that he called play, aggression, submission, affinity, and excitement systems. He concluded that all facial expressions seen in the chimpanzee are a result of the conflict of two or more of these motivational systems. Harlow and Suomi (1972) pointed out that the separation that occurs between a young rhesus monkey and its mother is produced through a mixture of maternal punishment and infant curiosity. And Sroufe (1979) concluded that infant behavior is a vectorial resultant of opposing forces such as wariness and curiosity, security in the familiar, and attraction to the unfamiliar. For all the reasons given, emotions in infants (as well as adults) are complex hypothetical states whose existence and properties can be determined only by a series of inferences. Ekman and Oster (1979) made a similar point when they suggested there is no single, infallible way to determine a person's true emotional state and the use of multiple convergent measures is necessary.

FUNCTION OF EMOTIONAL BEHAVIOR IN INFANTS

From an evolutionary point of view, the newborn organism is most vulnerable to the dangers of the environment. This reality is the basic reason behind the various signals, displays, communication patterns, and behaviors that are found in immature organisms and that are present at or shortly after birth. These various behaviors have effects that increase the chances of survival in the newborn. And because the problems of survival exist from the moment of birth, certain mechanisms must exist both in the child and in the mother or caretaker to help ensure survival. If young organisms had to wait until the infant learned how to attract its mother's attention and support, and if the mother had to learn how to provide it, the chances of species survival would be small. Communication patterns have to work the first time they are used. From this viewpoint, emotions may be thought of, in part, as communication signals emitted by the infant that help increase the chances of survival. Emotions are not disruptive, maladaptive states but rather act to stabilize the internal state of the organism. Emotions are autonomic and behavioral patterns that act to maintain homeostasis rather than to disrupt it. They represent transitory adjustment reactions that function to return the organism to a stable, effective relationship with its immediate environment when that relationship is disrupted. Emotions help the individual maintain a steady state in the face of environmental fluctuations. It is important to recognize that emotional reactions do not always work in this way because of circumstances beyond the control of the individuals who are interacting.

Andrew (1974) suggested that the generalized mammalian response to noxious stimulation is characterized by mouth corner withdrawal, lip retraction, and eye closure. Other behaviors that are often found as part of the protective response pattern are tongue protrusion and lateral shaking of head and body. Vocalizations may imply that the organism is uncomfortable, or lost, or wants something, or is likely to flee. These patterns are found in young organisms as well as mature ones and may be thought of as emotions.

The idea that emotional behaviors in infants have functions has also been elaborated by John Bowlby, an English psychiatrist, in 1969. He suggested that there are at least four systems that work together to control the infant's behavior. The first is the *attachment system,* whose function is to maintain proximity, closeness, or contact between the infant and his or her caretaker. The second system is the *fear/wariness system,* whose function is to help the infant escape or avoid potential dangers. The third is the *exploratory system,* which motivates the infant to play or interact with others and with parts of the environment. The fourth is the *affiliation system,* which prompts acquisition of social skills and connections with a person other than the key attachment figure. It is evident that all these systems (patterns of behavior) play a role in gaining support and nourishment and avoiding dangers. They therefore function to increase the chances of survival. Bowlby believed that these four systems interact and function without the infant being cognitively aware of them (in the adult sense). As the child's intellectual capacities develop, the child may become more aware of the operation of these systems and more able to exercise conscious control over them.

To illustrate some of these ideas, let us examine the work of Myron Hofer (1984), a research psychiatrist who has studied bereavement in young organisms. Table 8.3 shows the typical pattern of acute and chronic signs of bereavement or grief reactions in human adults to the loss of a close family attachment. In the acute stage of bereavement, there is often great agitation, crying, aimless activity, or near total passivity and feelings of muscular weakness. In the chronic stage of bereavement, which may last weeks or months, there is often social withdrawal, decreased concentration, restlessness, anxiety, decreased appetite, sleep disturbances, and depressed mood.

What is of considerable interest is that the infant reacts with very much the same pattern to separation from its mother. In infants, the acute stage is called the phase of *protest,* which may last minutes to hours. It is characterized by agitation, vocalization, searching behavior, passivity, and increased heart rate. If the separation continues, the infant enters the chronic or *despair* phase, which may last for hours or days. In this phase the infant shows decreased social interaction, rocking behavior, changed responsiveness to outside stimuli, decreased food intake, and sleep disruptions, among other signs.

These protest and despair phases have been interpreted as strategies that have evolved because they have survival value. The agitation and vocalization of the initial phase increase the chances that the mother will return to the infant and find the infant. The decreased behaviors of the second phase may help the infant hide from predators or strangers who may be a source of danger to the child. The various physiological changes are believed to be adaptations that reduce risk under these stressful circumstances.

TABLE 8.3. Typical Patterns of Acute Signs of Bereavement

Acute Reactions in Adults	Acute Reactions to Separation in Infants
Agitation	Agitation
Crying	Vocalizations
Aimless activity	Searching activities
Preoccupation with image of deceased	Increased heart rate
Tears	Increased cortisol
Sighing	Increased catecholamines
Muscular weakness	Decreased social interaction and play
Social withdrawal	Mouthing
Decreased attention	Rocking
Restlessness	Variable food intake
Anxiety	Variable responses to stimulation
Variable food intake	Facial expression of sadness
Facial expressions of sadness	Decreased body temperature
Depressed mood	Decreased oxygen consumption
Decreased body weight	Decreased cardiac rate
Sleep disturbance	Decreased growth hormone
Muscular weakness	Decreased T-cell activity
Endocrine changes	
Immunologic changes	

Note. From "Relationships as Regulators: A Psychobiologic Perspective on Bereavement," by M. A. Hofer, 1984, *Psychosomatic Medicine, 46*, p. 191. Copyright 1984 by American Psychosomatic Society. Reprinted with permission.

MUTUAL INTERACTION OF PARENTS AND INFANTS

The previous section has introduced the idea that many patterns of behavior in infants have a function and that the function is to avert or decrease dangers and to increase support, protection, and nourishment. These patterns of behavior are what we may call emotions even though we cannot say much about the mental states of the infant. These behavior patterns act as signals that are sent by the infant to its caretaker, and these signals are in essence attempts to change the behavior of the caretaker. The interesting thing about them is that they work, and many studies have been carried out in recent years to demonstrate this point.

For example, Bowlby (1969) proposed that the attachment that a mother develops for her infant depends to a considerable degree on the crying, smiling, clinging, and sucking behavior of the infant. In an effort to test this hypothesis, Moss and Robson (1968) interviewed 54 mothers and also observed the interaction of these mothers with their infants in their homes. The extent to which the mothers showed caregiving behavior and physical contact was rated. It was found that maternal behavior occurred following 77% of the situations in which the baby cried or fussed. At the age of 1 month, crying of the baby tended to produce the following behavior in the mother: attend, hold the infant close, burp the infant; talk to the infant; imitate his or her vocalizations; engage in mutual visual regard with the infant; and rock the infant. At the age of 4 months, fussing and crying of the female infants tended to initiate talking, imitative vocalization, and mutual visual regard in the mothers. Crying of male infants was more likely to initiate close physical contact. These findings may be interpreted as indicating that an infant's expressive behavior affects others by modifying their behavior toward the infant. The functional value of expressive displays is to modify others' behavior in such a way as to increase the infant's probability of survival.

A study that strikingly reveals the impact of the infant on its caretakers was reported by Frodi and her colleagues. In this investigation (Frodi et al., 1978), a group of mothers and fathers of newborn infants looked at videotape presentations of an infant. Some of the parents were shown a crying baby, and others were shown a smiling baby. The parents were asked to rate their moods on seeing the infants, and at the same time the parents' blood pressure and skin conductance were recorded.

The results showed that parents who viewed the crying baby reported feeling more annoyed, irritated, distressed, disturbed, indifferent, and at the same time less attentive and less happy than the parents who viewed the smiling infant. These results were obtained for both mothers and fathers, although the mothers' ratings tended to be more extreme. When viewing the crying infant, the parents' diastolic blood pressures rose significantly, but no blood pressure changes occurred during the observation of the smiling child. Skin conductance increased while the parents were viewing the crying infant, but it was unaffected when they saw a smiling infant.

Frodi et al. concluded that crying and smiling infants elicit different emotional and physiological reactions from parents. They suggested that crying is perceived as aversive and that parents have a strong desire to terminate this aversive signal from an infant. A smiling infant produces pleasant feelings with little or no arousal. However, both crying and smiling tend to elicit feelings from the parents that incline them to move close to the infant, in one case to stop the crying, and in the other to prolong the smiling. This study strongly supports the concept that infants have a powerful effect on the emotional states of their parents.

That parents have strong effects on the emotional behavior of their infants has also been experimentally demonstrated. Campos, Barrett, Lamb, Goldsmith, and Sternberg (1983) received permission from mothers to allow their 10-month-old infants to explore a visual cliff. This is essentially a large piece of glass mounted across two tables with a space between. On one side, there is a checkered pattern just under the surface of the glass. In the space between the tables, there is a similar checkered pattern placed anywhere from a few inches to 4 feet (1.21 m) below the glass. It was found that when the apparent drop off is about 12 inches (0.3 m), about half of the infants will avoid crossing and half will cross to reach their mother on the other side of the table.

In Campos et al.'s study, the infant was placed at the shallow side of the table while the mother was placed at the other end with an attractive toy. In one condition the mother was instructed to smile at her child, whereas in another she was told to show a fearful expression. The results demonstrated that if the child looked at his or her mother's face, almost all crossed the visual cliff if she was smiling. In contrast, if the mother showed a fearful expression, not one infant crossed the visual cliff. It thus indicates that facial expressions of the mother had a powerful effect on the exploratory behavior of their infant.

Brazelton (1983), a child psychiatrist, has provided many descriptions of the subtle interactions that take place between a mother and her infant. He pointed out that many mothers report that when their infant clings tightly to them and presses their face into the crook of their neck, they feel a tightening sensation in their breasts, followed by a "let down" reflex of milk.

When careful observations are made of a few minutes of apparently pleasant mother–infant interaction, Brazelton found that the smiles and vocalizations of the mother tend to produce the same kind of reactions in the infant, and the smiling and vocalizing of the infant increase the same behaviors in the mother. If the mother is asked to sit in front of her seated infant and maintain an expressionless face with no touching or other interaction, the infant shows a strong reaction. The baby shows repeated attempts to elicit a response from the mother, and when unsuccessful, eventually withdraws attention. This reaction was observed in babies as young as 1 to 4 months. Brazelton concluded that normal mother–infant interactions function as a goal-oriented, reciprocal system in which infants play a major, active role, constantly modifying their expressions and actions in response to the feedback provided by their mothers.

In a study by Trainor, Austin, and Desjardins (2000), speech patterns of 23 mothers were assessed while they were speaking to their 7- to 9-month-old infants and the patterns were compared with those directed at other adults. The mothers were asked to say the words: "Hey, honey, come over here" while imagining each of eight different scenarios. In four scenes, the words were to be addressed to their infants, and in four other scenes, they were to be addressed to an adult. The four emotions implicit in the various scenes were love, comfort, surprise, and fear. Pitch, tempo, and rhythmic contour were measured for each recording.

The analyses revealed that speech directed at infants by their mothers had a higher pitch, a larger pitch range, and a slower tempo and was more rhythmical than speech directed by the same mothers to other adults (Trainor et al., 2000). This was true at least for the emotions of love, comfort, fear, and surprise.

FACIAL EXPRESSIONS IN INFANTS

In the previous chapter, I discussed some evidence relating to the evolutionary basis of facial expressions. In this section, I examine some additional research on this issue. Infants are capable of a great variety of facial expressions. Ekman and Friesen (1976) developed a facial action code that defines 24 rather specific facial expressions. Ekman and Oster (1979) claimed that virtually all of the facial action code movements can be seen in both premature and full-term newborns. Extensive video recordings have been made of infants' facial expressions during the first few months of life. Attempts have been made to establish the meaning of different facial expressions on the basis of two types of criteria: (a) evidence of patterning based on the simultaneous occurrence of independent muscle actions and (b) the timing of particular facial movements. Oster and Ekman reported, for example, that the earliest smiles are produced by the action of a single muscle, but smiles become increasingly complex, in terms of muscle action unit involvements, as they become more related to social interactions.

Given the importance of facial expression in infants, many studies have been concerned with this issue. Ekman and Oster (1979) reviewed the evidence on facial expressions in human infants and arrived at the following conclusions:

1. The facial musculature is fully formed and functional at birth.
2. Distinctive facial expressions resembling certain adult expressions are present in early infancy. Expressions of crying, smiling, disgust, and startle are observable in the first days of life.

3. Three- to 4-month-old infants show differential facial responses to exaggerated facial responses of caretakers.

4. Imitation of certain facial expressions of caretakers (mouth opening and tongue protrusion) has been shown by 2- to 3-week-old infants.

5. Preschool children know what the most common facial expressions look like, what they mean, and what kinds of situations typically elicit them.

6. Facial expressions play a role in social communication.

These generalizations illustrate the important point that facial expressions suggestive of emotions are present at birth and continue to appear long before any language exists. It has been found that the human infant begins to show fragments of facial expressions in the last trimester of pregnancy. In the newborn, smiling may occur as part of one of the sleep states (REM sleep), and in the next 2 months may occur to a wide range of stimulus conditions. Smiling may occur in a 3-month-old while the infant is learning a task even when no one is present. After about 6 weeks, smiles appear in response to the sight of the human face and may also be triggered by rocking the baby or by ringing a bell.

The ethologists have paid the most attention to displays or expressive behavior as signals of emotion, generally without reference to hypothetical subjective states. From their point of view, facial expressions are only one kind of display system that includes such varied communications as warning signals, threat signals, food signals, and territory signals, among others. These displays may be vocal, visual, postural, or olfactory (e.g., production of odors through scent glands or urine). In lower vertebrates, expressive emotional behavior tends to be whole body displays. At higher phylogenetic levels, displays are more discrete, and at the same time, the parts of the display are less highly correlated with each other. Also found at higher levels is less all-or-none behavior and more gradation of signals. Such gradations allows greater flexibility in the expression of meanings.

There is no doubt that facial expressions play a role in social communication. This is true for all infant emotional expressions. Infants do not simply emit signals that have emotional meaning. The signals are part of an interaction between the infant and its caretaker. Parents help shape and organize the expressions of infants by influencing their timing, intensity, and threshold. According to Trevarthen (1977), infants show various movements of their head, trunk, or limbs that are closely synchronized to facial expressions or vocalizations of the mother. There is thus a rudimentary grammar of the sequence of interactions (Plutchik, 1983).

Some of the above points may be illustrated with more detailed information concerning the development of the smile. Data on the development of smiling showed that during the first few weeks infants would occasionally turn their lips into a smile without any identifiable stimulus being present. Such smiles, without eliciting external stimuli, are called *endogenous smiles*. It was discovered that such smiles occurred during REM states, which are normal concomitants of both sleep and drowsiness in infants. The frequency of such endogenous smiles was about one smile for every 2 minutes of REM time in infants about 8 months post conception. At 9 months post conception (i.e., at birth for a normal-term baby), the rate of endogenous smiles is about one for each 8 minutes of REM time. For the next few weeks after birth, the rate of endogenous smiles is about one for each 13 minutes of REM time. Endogenous smiling rapidly decreases by the 3rd of 4th month of life and is rarely seen after the 6th month.

In contrast to the endogenous smile is the *exogenous smile*, which is a smile in response to external stimulation. It is not present at birth but begins to appear around the 1st or the 2nd month as a reaction to various stimuli. Mild nonspecific stimulation, such as ringing a bell or rocking the infant, may trigger a smile. Sometimes the infant shows repetitive smiling to the stimulus, as often as one or two per minute for as long as 10 minutes.

From the age of 6 or 8 weeks on, smiling is best elicited by the sight of a human face, and after 3 or 4 months the mother's face is the most potent elicitor of smiling. Thus, the endogenous smile and exogenous smile are inversely related; as the former disappears, the latter becomes more firmly established.

The onset of the social smile is dependent to some degree on the nature of the caretaking to which the infant is exposed. For example, Gewirtz (1965) studied the development of the smile in four different settings in Israel. He found that infants raised in families and in the stimulating environment of the kibbutz showed social smiling earlier and more persistently than did infants raised in institutional and day nursery settings.

That the initiation of the exogenous smile is under genetic and maturational control is indicated by the work of Fraiberg (1971) on children who are blind from birth. These infants showed the same pattern of smiling in response to multiple stimuli, and the development of smiling had essentially the same time course. The major difference is that social (exogenous) smiling became increasingly responsive to the mother's voice and touch instead of her face.

Because social smiling appears with greater frequency after the age of 3 or 4 months, it can be increasingly influenced by the mother's behavior. Studies have shown that social smiling can be influenced by operant conditioning procedures (i.e., by giving the child rewards for smiling) after this period. Although these studies clearly demonstrate that mothers can reinforce babies, there have been few studies of the reinforcing effects of the baby's smile on the mother. General observations reveal that an infant's smiles increase a mother's attachment to the infant and also tend to increase (attract) new kinds of social stimulation.

In recent years, a distinction has been suggested between *Duchenne smiling*, which involves high cheek raising, and non-Duchenne smiling, which involves a smile without the high cheek raising. The Duchenne smile is said to be a felt smile, whereas the non-Duchenne smile is considered to be an unfelt smile (Surakka & Hietanen, 1998). In a study comparing these two types of smiles in early infancy, a group of 13 infants ranging in age from 1 to 6 months of age were videotaped weekly in face-to-face interactions with their mothers. The presence of the two types of smiles were recorded.

It was found that Duchenne smiles were visually preceded by non-Duchenne smiles. Surakka and Hietanen (1998) concluded that these two "frequently contrasted smiles occur in similar situations, and are often different temporal phases of a continuous emotional process" (p. 31). It is possible that the distinctions previously made may be an artifact of the tendency to categorize (or dichotomize) what are in fact variable, dynamic processes.

ATTACHMENT THEORY

The theory of attachment behavior is based largely on the work of one man, John Bowlby, although many investigators have contributed to it. Bowlby was a British psychiatrist whose experiences during World War II led him to an interest in studying prolonged mother–child separations and deprivation of maternal care. His observations suggested that the deprived infant or young child went through a stage of *distressed protest* followed by stages of *despair* and *detachment* if the separation continued for more than a week.

Bowlby found parallels to these patterns of reaction in the ethological literature. Many birds and mammals show comparable kinds of reactions under similar conditions of separation from mothers. Bowlby concluded that attachment behavior was biologically rooted and the possible basis for long-term affectional bonds. He believed that attachment behavior, that is, the maintenance of close contact with a mother or caretaker, had evolved through natural selection because it increased the chances of survival of an infant through protection by its mother. This idea has been emphasized by all contemporary researchers dealing with attachment behavior (Weinfield, Sroufe, Egeland, & Carlson, 1999). However, the accumulation of knowledge has made contemporary attachment theory a blend of evolutionary biology, ethology, control system theory, and cognitive psychology (Simpson, 1999).

Attachment theory assumes that the infant is equipped at birth with a set of species-characteristic behaviors that increase the likelihood of proximity to its mother. Examples of such behaviors are crying, smiling, and grasping, which act as signals, plus such things as large head, large eyes, soft skin, and other characteristics that appear to attract adults. One of Bowlby's collaborators, Mary Ainsworth, described 13 behaviors that she considered to be examples of attachment-inducing behaviors: crying, smiling, vocalizing, visual–motor orientation, crying when the attachment figure leaves, following, scrambling, burying face in lap, exploring from a secure base, clinging, lifting arms in greeting, clapping hands in greeting, and moving toward the mother (Lamb, Thompson, Gardner, & Charnov, 1985). These behaviors act to attach the infant to its mother, which in turn leads to protection and increased chances of survival.

Separation of the infant from his or her mother is a dangerous situation for the child, and such separation activates all the mechanisms and behaviors the child has available, the most obvious of which is crying. Subsequent studies found that parents who responded promptly and consistently to infant crying had infants who by the end of the first year cried relatively little. It appears that prompt and close bodily contact does not spoil babies or make them fussy (Ainsworth & Bowlby, 1991).

Attachment Patterns in Different Cultures

The study of attachment led to the idea that there are at least three different attachment patterns: *avoidant, secure,* and *ambivalent* or *resistant.* These different patterns may lead to different emotional reactions in children. A series of studies carried out in Western countries (Europe and the United States) led to the conclusion that the majority of infants are *securely* attached but that many are *insecurely* attached (van Ijzendoorn & Sagi, 1999). Research data supported the hypothesis that secure attachment is associated with better control of aggression and better relations to teachers and peers (Meins, 1997). A review of 21 studies of infant–mother attachment in Africa, China, Israel, Japan, Europe, and the United States led to the conclusion that about 21% of infants show an avoidant pattern, 67% show a secure pattern, and 12% show a resistant pattern. There is, however, considerable variability around these means (van Ijzendoorn & Sagi, 1999).

These findings are interesting and suggest some degree of generality in the patterning of attachment behaviors in different cultures. This is not surprising in view of the fact that, from an evolutionary perspective, attachment behaviors evolved for the goal of sustaining reproductive fitness.

Some questions have been raised, however, about the generality of all the basic concepts of attachment theory. The basic hypotheses of attachment theory are that highly responsive caretaking leads to secure attachment, that secure attachment leads to social competence in later years, and that the presence of a secure base allows children to explore and still feel protected.

In a critique of these ideas, Rothbaum, Weisz, Pott, Miyake, and Morelli (2000) compared the American with the Japanese culture. They pointed out that the concept of social competence has a different meaning in Japanese society than it does in American society and, as a result, the connection between secure attachment and social competence is different. They also noted that exploration by Japanese babies is less than that by American babies, implying a different relation between attachment and independence. One implication of these findings is that parent education programs and therapeutic strategies may need to be different in different cultures.

Harlow's Extension of Bowlby's Ideas

Harry Harlow was a psychologist who carried on research in his University of Wisconsin laboratory for many years. He studied the effects on infant monkeys of separating them from their mothers for varying periods of time. Generally, the effects were devastating. Despite adequate food, cleanliness, and environment, the monkeys became severely dysfunctional, rocking back and forth in a corner, sucking or biting their fingers or skin, screeching or crying, walking on their hind legs while clasping their own body, or curling into a ball. When they were allowed to join other monkeys, their behavior was one of panic, and they were unable to engage in normal social interactions.

In one of his early studies, 4 infant rhesus monkeys raised in a group were compared with 6 raised in pairs and 20 raised with real mothers. When the group-raised infant monkeys were tested with peers early in life, they showed less play and less aggression and also showed a great deal of clinging, attachment behavior (Chamove, Rosenblum, & Harlow, 1973). This is seen in Figure 8.3.

In studying such animals, Harlow and his associates began to learn a great deal about the antidote to such disturbed behavior, what he called *contact comfort, or love*. He discovered that young monkeys raised without their mothers showed strong attachments to cloth pads used to cover the cage's floor. When these young monkeys were given the choice of going to a crude wooden model of a mother that supplied milk versus a model that had a terry cloth covering, all the monkeys chose the latter. It appeared that contact comfort was more important than food in these young animals.

These findings were inconsistent with the old idea that hunger, thirst, and sex are the primary drives whereas love and affection are secondary drives learned by association or conditioning. From the old point of view, the mother is loved because she is a secondary reinforcing agent who provides food. This did not seem to be the case in Harlow's study. In addition, the presence of the terry cloth mother (but not the wire mother) provided a secure base from which the infant could explore any strange or novel situation.

Harlow also demonstrated that there are other kinds of attachments besides those between mother and child. His experiments showed that social attachments between female pairs of rhesus monkeys, housed in pairs during their 2nd year of life, outlasted 2 years of separation. When the animals were reunited, no female showed aggression against her previous cage-mate, although she did show aggressive behavior toward unfamiliar females. The reunited pairs generally showed high levels of embracing, grooming, and proximity behavior (Harlow & Mears, 1983). Other bonds that have been identified are the sexual pair bond, the sibling/kinship bond, the parent's complementary caregiving bond, and the friendship bond (George & Solomon, 1999).

FIGURE 8.3. Clinging behavior seen in infant rhesus monkeys raised as a group. From "Monkeys (*Macaca mulatta*) Raised Only With Peers: A Pilot Study," by A. S. Chamove, L. A. Rosenblum, and H. F. Harlow, 1973, *Animal Behaviour, 21,* p. 321. Copyright 1973 by Animal Behavior Society. Reprinted with permission.

One of Harlow's special concerns was with the identification of factors that reduce or ameliorate fear or aggression in animals (and presumably in humans as well). His research demonstrated, consistent with the observations of Bowlby, that complete or partial isolation of infants creates serious disturbances in their solitary behavior as well as in their social interactions. Harlow and his associates then tried to create various procedures that might undo the damage created by isolation. They tried placing them with peers, but the isolates did not know how to play. They tried surrogate mothers—unheated, heated, and rocking—and they achieved acceptance of contact but nothing more.

They achieved success only when they were able to take fear out of the picture by using junior "therapists" (other monkeys). The 3-month-old therapists were just one-half the age of the isolates, young enough to seek gentle contact with other monkeys. The therapists were so gentle that they did not present any threat to the fearful 6-month isolates. At age 3 months, the little rhesus monkeys were just learning to play, and they established playful contact with the isolates, little by little. It took approximately 5 months for complete reversal of the behavioral deficits to occur and a year of this therapy to develop normal play and social interaction. Eventually, maturation produced normal sexual behavior (Harlow & Mears, 1983).

Harlow believed that social play is a key element in undoing the damaging effects of isolation. Play has survival value and prepares the individual for entry into the adult world of social roles and rules.

WHEN DO CHILDREN LEARN EMOTION CONCEPTS?

Much of the previous discussion has dealt with the development and recognition of various emotional expressions in infants and young children. There is, however, another side to the coin. When and how do young children learn to *correctly* use the emotion language appropriate to their culture? There must be some reasonable congruity in children's use of emotion words or communications with peers and parents would be confused and confusing. In recent years, a number of investigations have examined this issue.

Research on children's use of emotion words depends obviously on the child being old enough to use words. Thus, most such research has been done with children from about age 2 or 3 years to adolescence. In some of these studies, the investigator simply asked mothers for their recollections of when their children first used such emotion words as *happy, sad, mad,* and *scared.* In a variant of this kind of study, mothers were asked to keep a diary and to record instances of their child's use of emotion words as well as the contexts. Another approach presented young children with pictures of facial expressions and asked them to identify the emotion seen. Still another method for investigation of this problem is based on filmed interactions of children fighting, crying, kicking, and receiving gifts. The participants were interviewed and asked how the various children in the films feel.

Generally, these studies revealed that the child's ability to make some "correct" inferences about emotions in pictures or in others begins at about the age of 2 or 2½ years. At that time, about half of the children can identify *happy* faces from photographs, and some can identify *sad* or *mad* faces. By age 4 years, *happy* is understood by all children. By 5 years, most children can identify *surprised* and *scared* faces from pictures, and *sad* pictures by age 7. If children are presented with short descriptions of events that might lead a child to feel a particular emotion, 4-year-olds could usually identify *happiness, sadness, anger, disgust,* and *surprise* (Camras & Allison, 1985). When children ages 2 to 5 years were required to make forced-choice judgments between various pairs of facial expressions on photographs, they often confused *mad* with *scared.* When the facial expressions were color movies of actors creating each expression over a 5-second period, most 4-year-olds discriminated all five faces (*happy, sad, mad, surprised,* and *scared;* Smiley & Huttenlocher, 1989).

Also of interest is the fact that children in the sixth and seventh grade who were identified as depressed were aware not only of the sadness they felt but also of their

FIGURE 8.4. A 10-year-old child's drawings of five basic emotions. Courtesy of R. Plutchik.

simultaneous feelings of anger. Eight of 10 depressed children said that depression was a combination of sadness and anger. They were thus aware of the fact that emotions (such as sadness and anger) may blend and interact to produce special qualities that have labels of their own (such as depression). These findings indicated that young children can recognize a number of basic emotions in others by ages 3 or 4 years and that the complex vocabulary of emotion is gradually added much later. By age 10, children recognize that emotions can be mixed, and most children can draw pictures expressive of the basic emotions. This is illustrated in Figure 8.4.

In a study concerned with this problem, 67 children from Grades 2, 4, and 7 were asked to draw emotional expressions of fear, anger, surprise, disgust, happiness, and sadness. Later, a group of adults as well as the children themselves were asked to recognize what emotions were intended by the drawings. It was found that the children were better than the adults at recognizing the expressions and were most accurate for the emotions of happiness and sadness (Missaghi-Laksman & Whissell, 1991).

Although little information is available on the ability of young children to identify verbal expressions of emotion, a study by Baltaxe (1991) dealt with this issue. Audio recordings were made to express the tone patterns associated with anger, happiness, sadness, and neutral. Three and 4-year-old children were asked to match each auditory stimulus with an appropriate emotion–face representation. It was found that correct matching occurred at better than chance levels for each of the audio-presented emotions and that the older children made more correct matches than did the younger ones.

DO CHILDREN UNDERSTAND THE CAUSES
OF EMOTIONS?

A number of studies have been carried out with adults in an effort to determine how consistent they are in judging the causes of different emotions. For example, loss experiences are generally believed to be the origin of feelings of sadness, whereas frustrations of various kinds are generally believed to trigger feelings of anger.

The question to be considered here is how children think about the causes of their emotions. In a study of this question, Harter and Whitesell (1989) obtained open-ended descriptions from children ages 4 through 11 years on the causes of four of the basic emotions: happy, sad, mad, and scared. They compared the responses of the children with those of adults asked the same questions in a study by Shaver, Schwartz, Kirson, and O'Connor (1987).

For happiness or joy, Shaver et al. identified four major categories of causes in adults: (a) getting what you want; (b) being accepted, belonging, receiving affection or love; (c) experiencing highly pleasurable sensations; and (d) achieving a task. In the study of children, 70% indicated that the cause of happiness was getting something they wanted, whereas the other three causes were mentioned infrequently. No age trends were noticed for most of these categories, although happiness resulting from task achievement increased from 2% among young children to 18% among the 9- to 11-year-olds.

With regard to anger, adults described several major causes: physical or psychological pain; loss of power, status, or respect; insult; and things not working out as expected. In children, 62% of the responses corresponded to physical or psychological pain (e.g., being hit, yelled at, or having feelings hurt), whereas most of the rest corresponded to things not working out as expected. These causes were described even in young children and did not change very much with age.

In adults, the emotion of sadness was triggered by five classes of events: (a) loss of a valued relationship, (b an undesirable outcome, (c) feeling rejected or disapproved by others, (d) feeling helpless, and (e) feeling empathy with the sadness of others. The first four of these categories could be identified in the responses of children, but sadness resulting from empathy with the distress of others could not. Some of the categories showed a marked change with increasing age. Sadness resulting from feelings of rejection decreased from 62% in the youngest children to 17% in the oldest. Loss of a valued relationship was a cause of sadness in 14% of the younger children and in 47% of the older ones.

The emotion of fear was described by adults as having three major causes: (a) threat of harm or death, (b) being in an unfamiliar situation, and (c) threat of social rejection. In children, most fears were caused by a threat of harm or being in an unfamiliar situation. Developmental trends were noticed. Threat of harm as a cause of fear decreased from 73% of the 3- to 5-year-old children to 40% of the 9- to 11-year-old children. Fear of unfamiliar situations increased from 25% in the young children to 49% in the older ones.

All of these observations imply that the causes of four basic emotions (joy, anger, sadness, and fear) described by children, when considered in terms of major categories, are pretty much the same as the causes of these same emotions reported by adults. What changes with age are the specific, age-appropriate stimuli (e.g., being gobbled up by monsters vs. being in an automobile accident) that cause or trigger emotional reactions. Somehow, young children by the ages of 3 or 4 years have a fairly accurate sense of the social situations that generate at least a few basic emotions.

This research dealt only with four emotions and therefore had nothing to say about whether the same conclusions hold true for many other emotions such as surprise, disgust, jealousy, pride, and curiosity. On the basis of the research reported in an earlier chapter on the understanding of emotion words, it is likely that the comprehension of these emotion concepts develops relatively late (adolescence or later), and even then only to a limited degree. If we consider most emotions to be mixtures or blends of a small number of basic ones, it is easier to understand why the comprehension of their causes develops late and remains somewhat obscure. The blending of emotions depends on the simultaneous occurrence of many and varied experiences, and the subjective components become fuzzier and more difficult to specify. Despite these problems, it is hoped that future research will help tackle these difficult problems.

It should be noted that there are a number of issues that need to be addressed by research in addition to the ones discussed above. Based on Denham (1998), these issues may be listed as the following:

1. How do children learn to label emotional expressions in other people?
2. What situations elicit emotional reactions of different types?
3. On what basis do children infer the causes of emotions?
4. How do children learn to describe their own emotional experiences?
5. When do children learn that other people's emotional experiences can differ from their own?
6. How do children become aware of emotion regulation strategies?
7. How do children develop a knowledge of emotion display rules?
8. How do children learn to recognize that more than one emotion can be felt simultaneously?

Recent work by Flavell and Miller (1998) has shown that children gradually learn that people can deceive others by showing one emotion even when they feel another, that one's mood can influence how one reacts emotionally to a situation, and that more than one emotion can be experienced at the same time.

SUMMARY

The study of emotions in infants creates a difficult conceptual problem if emotions are defined as inner feelings. This raises the problem of what kind of evidence we should use to infer the existence of emotional states in nonverbal babies. These same issues exist with regard to the judgment of emotions in animals.

The kinds of evidence psychologists use in inferring emotions in infants relate to the similarity between infants and adults on a number of characteristics, such as similarity of eliciting conditions and similarity of effects. Other criteria are that they are generalized reactions affecting many aspects of behavior and physiology simultaneously; that they are usually elicited by important (survival-related) events in the child's life; that they appear to have a sense of urgency; that they have a momentum that makes rapid stops difficult; that they are often associated with approach or avoidance behavior; and that they are usually directed toward other individuals in the environment. These criteria can be used to infer emotions in animals as well.

Studies of human infants and infant animals have led to the conclusion that emotional expressions, including both behavior and sounds, are forms of communication that function to influence other individuals; for example, emotional signals indicate the need for nourishment or protection, and they signal distress of any sort. Such signals increase the probability of social contact with a mother. Because both situations and individuals are complex systems, most emotional signals tend to be mixed signals reflecting two or more emotional systems such as fear and anger. Emotional signals are thus in the service of motives and needs or, put more generally, in the service of survival.

The concept of infant attachment as an expression of emotions has attracted the attention of many researchers, and some of the important ideas related to this domain were presented. When infants are separated from their mothers, patterns of reaction called *protest* and *despair* occur. These strategies have evolved presumably because they have survival value. They tend to stimulate nurturant behavior in the mother or aversive behavior of crying. When mother–infant separation continues for a long time (as in some studies of monkeys), the effects on the infant are extremely disturbing and interfere with later social and sexual behavior.

Because it is evident that children learn to use the language of emotions as they grow, studies have been directed toward assessing the sequence of changes that typically occur. Very young children use only a few emotion words, such as *happy, sad,* and *scared.* As they mature, their emotion vocabulary increases, and their understanding of the elicitors of emotion increases: It is possible to identify prototype elicitors for particular emotions as well as typical types of reactions. Problems of specification arise, however, because older children and especially adults have to learn to recognize and describe the mixed emotions or blends that characterize emotional development.

9 Emotions and Evolution

> Ethology...emphasizes the essential unity of living things and the similarity, in much that is fundamental, between animals and men.
>
> *William H. Thorpe*

PREVIEW

Previous chapters have provided evidence that emotions function to provide information from one individual to another. Such information may influence the behavior of the interacting individuals so that the well-being or survival of the individual expressing the emotion may be enhanced. A simple way of expressing this idea is that emotions are adaptive.

The concept of adaptation is a central notion in evolutionary thinking. The concept relates both to the behavior of individuals attempting to deal with the daily problems of the animate and inanimate worlds and also to the idea of species changes over generations in response to changing environments. This chapter provides a brief introduction to some ideas related to evolution and suggests how they may be connected to ideas about emotions.

From a broad evolutionary point of view, the concept of emotions should apply to most or all living organisms. The idea of continuity of physical structures and biological functioning is central to evolutionary thinking; this implies, as Darwin and many ethologists believe, that emotions can be recognized in all animals. Such a belief implies the need to conceptualize emotions in such a way as to enable us to recognize emotions at all phylogenetic levels. This chapter reviews evolutionary concepts and relates them to emotions.

CHARLES DARWIN was the first to recognize that the concept of evolution should apply not only to the development of physical structures but also to the evolution of mind and emotions. In his book *The Expression of the Emotions in Man and Animals*, which was published in 1872, he gave many illustrations of parallel ways emotions are expressed in different animals. He felt that such observations would provide a basis for generalizations about the origins of various types of expressive behavior, because the expressions of animals, in contrast to those of humans, are not likely to be based on social conventions.

The expansion of research has confirmed Darwin's conception of the basic unity of living systems. There seems to be little question that basic processes exist in common at all levels of biologic development. To fully understand emotions, it is necessary to recognize their evolutionary origins as well as their origins in individual development.

Figure 9.1 illustrates the similarities in the body proportions of the adult male orangutan, chimpanzee, gorilla, and human, all reduced to the same scale. Hair has been omitted and the lower limbs are shown unnaturally straightened to facilitate comparisons

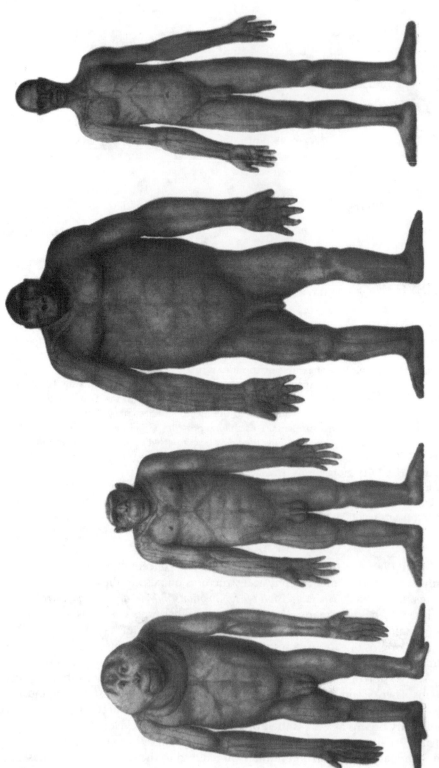

FIGURE 9.1. Body proportions of (from left) adult male orangutan, chimpanzee, gorilla, and human drawn to the same scale. Hair has been omitted and the lower limbs have been straightened to facilitate comparisons. From *The Life of Primates*, by A. H. Schultz, 1969, cover. Copyright 1969 by the Orion Publishing Group. Reprinted with permission.

(Wrangham & Peterson, 1996). This is one way to emphasize the similarities among the higher primates. It is also well known that humans and chimpanzees share over 99% of their genetic makeup.

NATURE OF EVOLUTION

Evolution has often been described as the most general and important idea in biology. Darwin's concept of natural selection implies that many features of each existing species have survival value, and this is as true of an animal's behavior, including its emotional behavior, as it is true of its bodily structures. Behavior, like all of the features of an animal, is a product of evolution. Figure 9.2 shows the timing involved in the evolution of different parts of the human body that humans share with other primates. The time scale is in terms of millions of years ago (Fleagle, 1999).

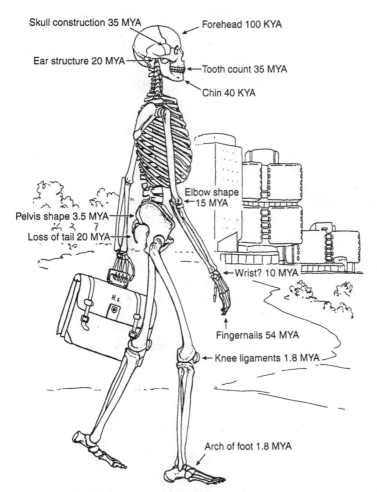

Skull construction 35 MYA

Forehead 100 KYA

Ear structure 20 MYA

Tooth count 35 MYA

Chin 40 KYA

Elbow shape 15 MYA

Pelvis shape 3.5 MYA

Loss of tail 20 MYA

Wrist? 10 MYA

Fingernails 54 MYA

Knee ligaments 1.8 MYA

Arch of foot 1.8 MYA

FIGURE 9.2. The timing of the appearance of distinctive anatomical features of the human skeletons that humans share with other primates. KYA = thousands of years ago; MYA = millions of years ago. From *Primate Adaptation and Evolution*, by J. G. Fleagle, 1999, p. 563. Copyright 1999 by Academic Press. Reprinted with permission.

A cornerstone of the theory of evolution is the concept of *natural selection*. Darwin recognized that the capacity of any given plant or animal population to reproduce was far greater than was needed to keep a constant population size. Many more animals are born than achieve sexual maturity. This meant that, in the long run, the animals that did survive were better equipped, in some way, to live in their environment than those that did not survive. A further implication was that the surviving members of the population would leave offspring that were likely also to be better adapted to their environment. If this process of differential fertility continued over a sufficient number of generations, then major changes could take place in the characteristics of the surviving population.

A simple but interesting example of this process is seen in the development of a black moth in certain areas of England. A gray moth was found over wide areas of the countryside. A black version of this moth appeared in the 19th century as industrialization increased, particularly in certain factory areas. In these locales, there was so much soot in the air that many chimneys and rooftops, and even trees, became blackened by it. Gray moths stood out as easy targets in these areas and were preyed on by birds. Over the course of generations, those moths that showed a darker gray color as examples of naturally occurring variability in color were less likely to be eaten by the predators. The light gray moths produced fewer and fewer offspring, whereas the dark gray moths produced relatively more offspring. In time, there were only black moths and no gray ones. In this case, predation was the cause of differential fertility of one part of the population in relation to another. As a result of pollution control, this moth has since become lighter in most parts of England.

This illustration of natural selection highlights several ideas. Although natural selection affects individuals, it is the population that changes over a period of time. In other words, selective fertility changes the relative distributions of various kinds of genes (or genotypes) in the population. Such changes usually affect the phenotype or overt appearance of a trait. Evolution refers to changes in gene frequencies that occur over the course of generations within interbreeding populations.

A second important idea is the notion of *adaptation*. The changes that took place in the color of the moth population had the effect of decreasing predation. It made the moths less likely to be killed off and thus increased their "fitness" to the environment. The concept of adaptation thus refers to the fitness of a trait or characteristic of a population for a particular environment. If the environment changes, the trait may no longer be adaptive (Gould, 1996). Other examples of adaptations are the color and stereoscopic vision developed by primates for forest living, the keen olfactory sensitivities of certain animals, and the constant (warm-blooded) body temperatures of mammals that allow them to be relatively independent of environmental changes of temperature.

Variables That Affect Genotypes

In the example of the British moth, the frequency of the genes that determine color was affected by predation from other animals. Thus *selective predation* is one kind of variable affecting gene frequencies in a population. Another kind of variable affecting the genotype is *sexual selection*.

In many species there are a number of factors that influence mating success, which in turn affects gene frequencies. Competition between males is one such factor, and it is usually found that more dominant animals have relatively greater reproductive success. However, female mate choice is not always based on dominance. In many species certain male characteristics, such as large antlers in deer, huge colored wings in peacocks, and bright colors in birds, apparently function to attract the female.

In a study of female mate choice in Japanese macaques, the investigators ranked all the males in a troop by *dominance* (determined by the results of dyadic aggressive encounters) and ranked these same males by *attractiveness* based on female mate choice behavior directed toward them (Soltis et al., 1997). It was found that the female macaques often showed mate choice toward lower ranking males, resulting in a near zero correlation between male attractiveness and male dominance. Other variables than dominance apparently affect female mate choice.

A third source of variation in gene frequencies is *mutation*. For reasons that are not fully understood, "spontaneous" changes occasionally occur in the genes. Such mutations are random, and their effects are usually lethal because no complex structure benefits from random interference. Those mutations that do enhance survival often change the gene frequency for a certain characteristic. An example of such an effect is the change in eye color of the common fruit fly due to mutations produced by X-rays.

A fourth source of changes in gene frequencies is called *genetic drift*. This is simply the result of groups of individuals being isolated for long periods from the larger population of which they are a part. Any small differences in gene frequencies between the isolated group and its parent population will tend to become magnified over generations as a result of continued inbreeding and will eventually lead to different genotypes. The fact that human groups were small throughout most of human history, coupled with the fact that social rules differ from group to group, has acted to widen the genetic gaps between populations. Recent reports from geneticists suggest that all the American Indians from the Eskimos in the north to the Algonquians of the east to the Incas and other groups of South America were all descended from a small band of pioneers who crossed the Bering Sea from Asia to Alaska about 12,000 to 15,000 years ago.

Another illustration of the impact of genetic drift may be seen in the differences that have appeared between two isolated groups of squirrel monkeys (genus *Saimiri*). The group "Gothic" lives in the Pacific lowlands of Costa Rica; the group "Roman" lives mainly in Peru and Bolivia. Both groups are part of the same species and differ only slightly in appearance. Both groups live in large troops, eat the same type of fruit and insects, and collect their foods in the same way. In view of these ecological similarities, the differences in social behavior between the two groups are remarkable.

Table 9.1 shows some of the social differences between these groups. For example, the Costa Rican monkeys show little female aggression, and males are dominant to females.

TABLE 9.1. A Comparison of Two Isolated Squirrel Monkey Populations

Costa Rican (Gothic)	Peruvian (Roman) *S. sciureus*
Little female aggression	Frequent female aggression
Males dominant to females	Females dominant to males
Rare food competition	Frequent food competition
No female hierarchy detected	Female dominance hierarchies
Little male–male aggression	Much male–male aggression
Males spatially integrated into group	Females harass males into peripheral positions
Low measures of cortisol in both females and males	Higher measures of cortisol in both females and males

Note. From "Geographic Variation in Behavior of a Primate Taxon: Stress Responses as a Proximate Mechanism in the Evolution of Social Behavior," by S. Boinski. In S. A. Foster and J. A. Endler (Eds.), *Geographic Variations in Behavior: Perspectives on Evolutionary Mechanisms*, 1999, p. 103. Copyright 1999 by Oxford University Press. Reprinted with permission.

No female hierarchy has been detected. The opposite is true for the Peruvian monkeys. The author of the comparative review concluded that

> A primate within its natural habitat must cope with a number of disparate sources of stress-inducing situations in its everyday existence. Some stressors might be mild...while others are severe, such as a successful predatory attempt on another troop member. A reasonable working hypothesis is that geographic variation in stress-response profiles and temperament reflect, at least in part, differential weighting of these factors in the selective regimes in which the taxa evolved. (Boinski, 1999, p. 113)

The four types of factors affecting natural selection, as illustrated by predation, sexual selection, mutation, and genetic drift, all influence gene frequencies in a population. These changes in genotypes over the course of generations are what constitutes evolution. Although evolution implies adaptation or increased fitness, the degree of fitness is related specifically to a given environment. As the environment changes, the degree of fitness changes. These concepts apply to humans as well as to lower animals.

Evolutionary Record and Biological Continuities

Living creatures appeared in the oceans about 3 billion years ago in the form of tiny bacteria. Large bacteria appeared about 1 billion years ago, and small multicellular organisms appeared about 600 million years ago. Fishes appeared in the oceans about 350 million years ago, and reptiles evolved on land about 300 million years ago. The mammals began as tiny nocturnal creatures about 180 million years ago and evolved into the many species we see today. Evidence for humanlike primates is about 2 million years old.

One of the major reasons life was confined to the seas for the first 3 billion years of this planet is that cells could escape the lethal effects of ultraviolet radiation by staying under water. Only very gradually did oxygen develop in the atmosphere, permitting the gradual development of an ozone layer. Protection against lethal radiation developed in a variety of ways, for example, by encasing the embryo in a shell, by internal development of embryos, or by plants sending their germinative roots underground. In addition to local or periodic changes in environmental conditions, the major environmental event was the gradual change on the earth from an atmosphere without oxygen to one with it. This led to a large increase in the size of cells (eukaryotes) and to a change in their system of metabolism. According to Loomis (1988),

> As oxidative metabolism came on line, there was sufficient chemical energy available for bacteria to explore the possibilities of directed cell movement. A set of genes evolved to generate flagella and twirl them such that they moved the whole cell toward attractive compounds and away from repellents. In this way metabolism became coupled to adaptive behavior. (p. 136)

Because no limited environment is optimum for growth indefinitely, there is a strong selective advantage to moving around. The large eukaryotes became predators that engulfed the smaller bacteria. They evolved nuclei, internal membranes to encase their chromosomes, and special intracellular proteins, all adaptations that are found in many living cells. In fact, "all eukaryotic organisms, from algae to trees to elephants, appear to have descended from a single protoeukaryotic cell" (Loomis, 1988, p. 161).

A related idea is the fact that various systems developed millions of years ago that worked so well they have never been improved on. For example, mammalian sperm now use the same flagellum for locomotion that evolved 600 million years ago to keep algae cells near the surface of water. Similarly, the amino acid sequences for both X and B tubulin (the bases of the microtubules that form flagella) are more than 70% similar in yeast, algae, sea urchins, chickens, rats, pigs, and humans. Certain peptide hormones such as insulin and ACTH (adrenocorticotropic hormone) are virtually identical in yeast cells and in human beings. The gene order on the sex chromosome of mice (the X chromosome) is almost identical with that on the human X chromosome. The development of sexual dimorphism (specialization of males for sperm production and females for egg production) is also extremely widespread. The advantage of this system is that variability of genetic potentials increases the chances of individuals successfully dealing with changing or catastrophic environments.

Similarities in evolutionary patterns are also found through studies of development. For example, the similarity of developmental patterns in limb bones is evidence that amphibians, reptiles, and mammals are evolved from a common stock of lobe-fin fish. More than 100 years ago, it had been noted that there are remarkable similarities in the structures that appeared in the early stages of embryogenesis in mammals, amphibians, birds, reptiles, and fish. A small number of developmental genes can radically change the behavior of cells and change an amoeba into a multicelled organism. Loomis (1988) estimated that fewer than 1,400 developmental genes may have been sufficient for the evolution of simple cells into fish, and fewer than 2,500 developmental genes may be sufficient for the embryogenesis of humans: "The important evolutionary differences between a guppy and a primate probably lie in only a few hundred genes" (p. 216).

These various observations, from evolutionary and molecular biology, are presented to emphasize the points that Darwin first made; namely, that evolutionary continuities of structure, function, and development imply continuities of behavioral adaptations and emotional life. Emotions also serve to enhance the possibilities of survival and reproduction. According to Pinker (1999),

> The ultimate function of the mind is survival and reproduction in the environment in which the mind evolved—that is, (in the case of humans) the environment of hunting and gathering tribes in which we have spent more than 99 percent of our evolutionary history, before the recent invention of agriculture and civilizations only 10,000 years ago. (p. 67)

GENERAL EVOLUTIONARY ADAPTATIONS

The process of achieving fitness of a population to a given environment has also led to certain types of adaptations that are quite general and have the effect of making the organism less vulnerable to changes in the environment. For example, the development of genetic mechanisms that produce a constant body temperature (homeothermy) enabled animals to adapt to a wider range of environments. The evolution of lungs made the land environment available to vertebrates.

However, there are even more general adaptations than these. Certain complex chemical molecules evolved to form amino acids. These in turn formed long, chainlike molecules of deoxyribonucleic acid, or DNA, which are the bases of the genes, the reproductive units of all living things. Although evolution has produced many new groups of plants and animals, it has not changed the basic reproductive mechanism of amino acids, DNA, and genes. In other words, evolution does not change whatever works well. Evolution is basically "ultraconservative" (Wilson, 1975).

This idea also applies to the behavior of organisms. All organisms, to survive and maintain their populations, must find food, avoid injury, and reproduce their kind. This is as true of lower animals as it is of higher ones. The nature of the environment creates certain functional requirements for all organisms if they are to survive. Any organism must take in nourishment and eliminate waste products. It must distinguish between prey and predator and between a potential mate and a potential enemy. It must explore its environment and orient its sense organs appropriately as it takes in information about the beneficial and harmful aspects of its immediate world. And in organisms that are relatively helpless at birth and for a while thereafter, there must be ways to indicate the need for care and nurturance. The specific behaviors by which these functions are carried out vary widely throughout the animal kingdom, but the basic prototype functions remain invariant.

A key problem faced by all organism is dealing with danger and threats to survival, but there are only a limited number of modes of reacting that are available. With respect to stimuli arising from within the organism, survival is favored by expulsion or by isolation. With respect to stimuli referring to a source of danger arising from the outer environment, survival is favored by flight, submission, attack, and vocalization, in the order of apparent phylogenetic development. These various modes of reacting to threats to survival are the fundamental bases for emotions.

Scott (1958) elaborated this theme. He suggested that there are only a few general classes of adaptive behavior found in most species and phylogenetic levels. He described them in the following terms: ingestive behavior, shelter-seeking behavior, agonistic (fight-or-flight) behavior, sexual behavior, caregiving behavior, care-soliciting behavior, eliminative behavior, allelomimetic (imitative) behavior, and investigative behavior. These general classes of adaptive behavior clearly apply to the higher animals, but some of the categories are not relevant to the lower ones. For example, fish typically lay eggs and show no parental behavior toward the newborn organisms.

Other examples of behavioral adaptations that have similar functions at various phylogenetic levels are given by Wilson (1975), a leading sociobiologist:

> As my own studies have advanced, I have been increasingly impressed with the functional similarities between invertebrate and vertebrate societies and less so with the structural differences that seem, at first glance, to constitute such an immense gulf between them. Consider for a moment termites and monkeys. Both are formed into cooperative groups that occupy territories. The group members communicate hunger, alarm, hostility, caste status or rank and reproductive status among themselves by means of something on the order of 10 to 100 nonsyntactical signals. Individuals are intensely aware of the distinction between groupmates and nonmembers. Kinship plays an important role in group structure and probably served as a chief generative force of sociability in the first place. In both kinds of society there is a well-marked division of labor, although in the insect society there is a much stronger reproductive component. The details of organization have been evolved by an evolutionary process of unknown precision, during which some measure of added fitness was given to individuals with cooperative tendencies—at least toward relatives. The fruits of cooperativeness depend upon the particular conditions of the environment and are available to only a minority of animal species during the course of their evolution. (p. 4)

Consistent with the views of Scott and Wilson are the studies reported by Roff (1996) concerning the evolution of animal forms. He noted that although millions of animal species have existed over billions of years, the diversity of animal life is limited to approximately 35 basic body plans.

Genetics and Learning

These observations by biologists of similar classes of adaptive behavior identifiable at various phylogenetic levels suggest the following conclusions. During the course of evolution, two general types of adaptation have appeared and can be seen in the most primitive organisms as well as in the most advanced. These types of adaptation are what might be called *innate responses* and *learning*. Even simple protozoa and metazoa show innate (genetically programmed) reactions to certain types of stimulation. The types of stimulation include food objects, gradients of chemical substances in solution, toxic substances, electromagnetic radiation (light), and vibrations at certain frequencies. The reactions to these stimuli are primarily movements toward or away from the stimulus.

The capacity to learn from experience has also evolved. This capacity to benefit from experience is as much a product of evolution as any other species characteristic. Genetic programming determines the limits and nature of the modifications that each individual can undergo as a result of life experiences. For example, ducks will learn to follow any moving object they see shortly after hatching from the egg. This process is called *imprinting*, and although it normally occurs in relation to the mother, the response may become attached to humans or other animals if the mother is absent. However, the timing of the response is under the strict control of the genetic structure of the duck. If young ducks are isolated for a few days and are then presented with an appropriate stimulus (even their own mother), they will not learn to follow. In other words, the amount an animal can learn, the complexity of the stimuli that can be discriminated, and the complexity of the responses that can be made are largely limited by genetic restraints; only the context is determined by experience.

There is another way in which learning relates to evolution. This has been discussed in detail by Breland and Breland (1966), who have used operant techniques with thousand of animals representing over 60 species. In their book, the Brelands pointed out that the vast majority of the species of the earth use only very limited kinds of learning in their interactions with the environment. Most organisms enter the world prepared to cope with it through the use of certain fixed sequences of behavior that are activated by particular species-specific stimuli, or *releasers*. Moths find mates by responding to certain types of odors, most birds have fixed styles of nest building, and fighting behavior is often triggered by particular colors or movements of an animal.

Not all behaviors are equally learnable. For example, although it may take a pigeon days or weeks to learn to pull a string, a chicken can learn this task in a matter of minutes. This is probably due to the fact that the chicken normally eats by pulling worms from the ground, whereas pigeons normally peck at food. It is virtually impossible to get a chicken to vocalize for food reinforcement, whereas other birds can easily be trained to do this (Breland & Breland, 1966). Similarly, efforts to train chimpanzees to use a vocal language have all failed (Kellogg & Kellogg, 1967). The Brelands suggested that the degree to which behavior patterns are rigid and relatively unchangeable depends on the phylogenetic level to which an animal belongs. It also depends on the size of the environmental niche of the animal. Animals that occupy only a small segment of the environment, such as rabbits do, show relatively more fixed behavior sequences than those animals, such as the raccoon, that occupy a broader environmental niche. As one illustration of a factor that influences the size of an environmental niche, it may be noted that animals that eat both meat and plant foods tend to have a wider niche than those that eat plant foods alone.

Concept of Inclusive Fitness

From an evolutionary point of view, the fitness of an individual to an environment is reflected by the individual's reproductive output. From this perspective, fitness is measured by the extent to which one's genes are represented in future generations. This way of conceptualizing fitness has led to the idea that not only individuals but also genes act in "selfish" ways.

A problem that has arisen, however, concerns the existence of altruistic behavior, that is, helping individuals who are not part of one's gene pool. Such behavior has been reported to occur in humans and many other animals.

Evolutionary theory has attempted to deal with this issue by developing a broader concept of inclusive fitness. Total inclusive fitness depends on an individual's reproductive output plus the reproductive output of kin, that is, those who share a portion of the individual's genes. In addition, it is recognized that reproductive effort has at least two parts. One part concerns the complex events surrounding the location of potential mates, courting of potential mates, copulating with a mate, and retention of a mate. The second part concerns the birth and raising of viable offspring who in turn are able to achieve sexual maturity and sire offspring on their own (Simpson, 1999).

Many implications stemmed from this theory of inclusive fitness. Some of these are represented in Figure 9.3. One implication is that males and females usually have different strategies of courtship and mating because of their differential parental investments in

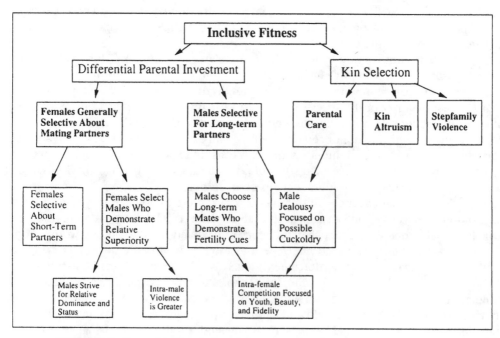

FIGURE 9.3. Some implications of the concept of inclusive fitness in evolutionary psychology. Theories of differential male and female parental investment and kin selection are derived from the general concept. From "Evolutionary Psychology, Cognitive Science, and Dynamical Systems: Building an Integrative Paradigm," by D. T. Kenrick, 2001, *Current Directions in Psychological Science, 10,* p. 14. Copyright 2001 by the American Psychological Society. Reprinted with permission.

the conceiving, development, and growth of offspring. Female selectivity about mates increases competition among males. Kin-selection theory assumes that individuals will favor their own offspring and their genetic relatives and have unfavorable feelings about stepchildren, expressed in the form of greater punishments directed toward stepchildren (Kenrick, 2001).

In a review of the literature on human parental investments from the perspective of evolutionary theory, Geary (2000) described some of the implications of an evolutionary approach to parental investments. Exhibit 9.1 lists some of the implications. Overall, it appears that in most mammalian species males do not provide much direct investment in the well-being of their offspring. Humans are a notable exception, for reasons that are not yet fully understood.

EXHIBIT 9.1. FACTORS ASSOCIATED WITH THE EVOLUTION OF PATERNAL INVESTMENT IN SPECIES WITH INTERNAL FERTILIZATION

1. If paternal investment is necessary for offspring survival, selection favors males who invest in offspring.
2. If paternal investment has little or no effect on survival rate or quality (e.g., size), then selection favors male abandonment, if additional mates can be found.
3. If paternal investment results in a relative, but not an absolute, improvement in offspring survival rate or quality, then selection favors males who show a mixed reproductive strategy. Here, within-species variation is expected, with individual males varying their degree of emphasis on mating effort and parental effort, contingent on social (e.g., male status, availability of mates) and ecological (e.g., food availability, predator risks) conditions.
4. Social and ecological factors that reduce the mating opportunities of males, such as dispersed females or concealed (or synchronized) ovulation, reduce the cost of paternal investment. Under these conditions, selection favors paternal investment if this investment improves offspring survival rate or quality or does not otherwise induce heavy costs on the male.
5. If the certainty of paternity is low, then selection favors male abandonment. Given that any level of parental investment is likely to be costly (e.g., in terms of reduced foraging time), indiscriminate paternal investment is not likely to evolve.
6. If the certainty of paternity is high, then selection favors paternal investment if
   a. such investment improves offspring survival or quality, and
   b. the costs of investment (i.e., reduced mating opportunities) are lower than the benefits associated with investment.
7. If the certainty of paternity is high and the costs, in terms of lost mating opportunities, are high, then selection favors males with a mixed reproductive strategy, that is, expression of paternal investment contingent on social and ecological conditions.

Note. From "Evolution and Proximate Expression of Human Paternal Investment," by D. C. Geary, 2000, *Psychological Bulletin, 126,* p. 60. Copyright 2000 by the American Psychological Association. Reprinted with permission.

Geary (2000) also reviewed the literature on sex differences from an evolutionary point of view. He noted that in almost all cultures men compete with one another for resources (e.g., status or money) and for mates, often by means of physical contests. In contrast, women compete with one another for mates by a nonviolent form of aggression, namely, gossip, criticism, and shunning. Women more than men seek mates who show evidence of cultural success, whereas men tend to focus on physical attractiveness as indicators of fertility. For example, women who have clear skin and wide hips are often considered by men to be more desirable partners.

One further illustration of the value of evolutionary theorizing may be seen in an analysis of the relations between hunger and eating (Pinel, Assanand, & Lehman, 2000). Pinel et al. pointed out that the probable environment in which early humans evolved was characterized by scarcity and unpredictability of food. In such circumstances, humans evolved to eat as much as they could when food was available, so that energy was available at times of future food shortages. In the present-day environment, food is readily available at all times, but the impulse to overeat still exist. This may be an explanation for the widespread obesity seen in many countries.

Proximate and Ultimate Causation

There are several ways one might explain the phenomenon of changes in apparent size that many animals show when dealing with an aggressive encounter. The manes of lions erect, fish expand their fins, birds extend their wings and fluff their feathers, and lizards and some frogs have inflatable pouches.

One explanation for such behavior is based on the identification of the hormonal and neurophysiological changes that are associated with it. This is called *proximate* explanation. Another explanation uses evolutionary concepts such as *resource holding power*. Because size is a cue used by an animal to assess the ability of another animal to successfully defend a territory, the selection of mechanisms that increase apparent size has occurred during the course of evolution in widely dispersed species. The capacity to use size cues to defend resources is thus related to inclusive fitness (Parker, 1974). Although there is a difference of focus when considering individual survival versus genetic survival, it is obvious that they are interrelated and not mutually exclusive. Evolutionary causes of present behavior are referred to as *ultimate* causation.

It is important to emphasize that evolution does not pit genetics against environment as determinants of behavior. All behaviors are based on genetic programs that interact with environmental events. Strictly speaking, it is wrong to say that a behavior is learned or that it is innate, because every behavior must develop in an environment and its development must inevitably be influenced by genetic factors.

Biologists distinguish between proximate and ultimate causation of phenomena. For example, to explain attachment and depressive behaviors, one may try to identify the genetic survival functions such behavior entails. It is known that maternally directed proximity-seeking behavior in young organisms and stressful reactions to maternal separation occur in most mammals studied. If it can be shown that remaining close to the mother has survival value, this would provide an evolutionary or ultimate explanation of a current behavior pattern. To provide a proximate explanation, it is necessary to identify the specific mechanisms that regulate the interactions between a mother and her offspring. Polan and Hofer (1999) showed, through a series of experiments, that the attachment and depressive reactions of young animals involve autonomic, endocrine, thermal, and digestive systems. These are proximate variables and involve norepinephrine-mediated activation, opioid-mediated suckling reward, and benzodiazepine-receptor-mediated separation responses.

Stable and Labile Traits

Hinde (1966) introduced the idea that some characteristics (anatomical, physiological, or behavioral) are *environmentally stable* and others are *environmentally labile*. Examples of stable characteristics are the color of eyes, the body temperature of warm-blooded animals, and the nest-building behavior of most birds. Labile characteristics are illustrated by flute-playing skills in humans and the dancing behavior of circus bears. These terms represent extremes on a theoretical continuum; however, even very stable characteristics can be influenced by marked environmental changes that are outside the range that is usual for a given species. In humans, the learning of a specific language is clearly the result of particular experiences and can vary greatly from one individual to another. However, the age at which humans begin to learn language is similar and quite environmentally stable in all human groups. Thus, the capacity to learn language is under strong genetic control, although the specific words of a language are not.

An interesting analysis of how certain aspects of language are influenced by genetic factors is given by Bornstein (1973). He reviewed the cross-cultural literature on color vision and color naming. Of 98 societies whose languages were examined for color names, it was found that 100% of them had names for black and white (or dark and light), 91% had a name for red, 74% had a name for yellow and/or green, and 55% had a name for blue (Berlin & Kay, 1969). In many societies, no distinction is made between green and blue or between blue and black.

As one examines color-naming systems around the world, the degree of confusion between these primary colors appears to be ordered with increasing skin pigmentation according to the degree of proximity to the equator. The hypothesis Bornstein (1973) proposed is that increased exposure to ultraviolet radiation has led to an increased density of yellow pigmentation at the cornea, the lens, and the pigment epithelium. This results in a decrease in spectral sensitivity to short wavelengths and in a confusion between short wavelength stimuli (blue and green or blue and black) in color naming. The conclusion reached is that dense ocular pigmentation (which has been shown to be subject to genetic inheritance) has a direct effect on the color vocabulary of a given culture.

Another example of a genetic effect on behavior can be found in the studies of bipolar illness in the Amish, a relatively genetically isolated farming community found mostly in Pennsylvania. In this community, extensive family records have been maintained for over 200 years. Through a review of such records, certain family lines were found to be associated with a high risk of depressive illness. Examination of tissues from living individuals descended from these families who were currently experiencing a manic–depressive illness has appeared to demonstrate a gene abnormality (Egeland et al., 1987), although subsequent research with other groups has not confirmed this.

Examples of Environmentally Stable Traits

In lower animals, it is easy to recognize very stable, species-typical behavior patterns. These include such things as migratory behavior, communication and defense behaviors, and parenting and weaning behaviors, to name just a few. In higher animals, variability of behavior is more marked and more subject to influences by environmental sources of stimulation.

The trainability of animals and the importance of learning in shaping their repertoires have led some social scientists to denigrate the role of genetic programs in higher animals, particularly in humans. But all animals, including humans, have a characteristic, genetically influenced ethogram, that is, a set of behaviors that are typical of humans as a species and that distinguish them from all chimpanzees, dogs, and lions. An example of the human ethogram as seen in infants has been reported by Young and Decarie (1977, cited in chapter 8), who found that 8- to 12-month-old human infant shows certain characteristic facial and verbal expressions that include closed-mouth smile, grimace, yawn, blink, sigh, babble, coo, squeal, laugh, wail, and pout. Similarly, the ethogram of chimpanzees include such sounds as pant-hoot, grunt, scream, bark, cough, wraaa, lip smack, roar, growl, and whine (Marler & Tenaza, 1977). The human infant ethogram has over 100 different behaviors or expressions (Plutchik, 1983).

Even personality traits, which are believed by many social scientists to be highly malleable (environmentally labile), have been shown to be under varying degrees of genetic control. Breed differences in dogs have been shown to be associated with characteristic temperamental differences as well as sex differences, and to be quite stable over time (Plutchik, 1971). Such temperamental differences are directly related to the types of functions, such as hunting, tracking, working, or fighting, that dogs were bred for. McGuire and Fairbanks (1977) pointed out that

> Breeding studies, particularly with dogs, have shown that virtually any personality type is under enough genetic control to respond to selection within a few generations. Genetic differences are manifested in increased learning ability, increased plasticity, greater tolerance to stress, as well as the reverse of these tendencies. (p. 29)

A large-scale study of 850 pairs of human same-sex twins has also demonstrated that monozygotic (identical) twins are consistently more alike than dizygotic (fraternal) twins on every personality domain that has been measured. This is especially convincing in view of the fact that parents report similar treatment of cotwins regardless of whether they are identical or fraternal (Loehlin & Nichols, 1976).

Concept of Fitness

In the biological context, there are two different meanings of the word *fitness*. One of these meanings, inclusive fitness, has already been discussed in relation to the idea of fitness to the environment and its consequences for survival of genes in succeeding generations. Such fitness is a species characteristic. The second meaning refers to the ability of individuals to adjust body systems to internal or external changes of the environment. Under conditions of stress, there are changes in heart rate, blood pressure, glucose secretion, hormonal secretions, sweating, and a variety of other activities, all of which prepare the body for action during emergency conditions.

It is important, however, to emphasize that the process of adaptation to stress or emergency conditions does not end with internal changes in biological systems. Those changes function to prepare the individual to act, and it is the action of the entire organism that completes the process of adaptation. Cannon was right when he said that internal changes in the body prepare the organism for flight or fight behavior. Although Darwin had relatively little to say about internal biological processes, he correctly focused his attention on adaptive behaviors of individual animals in response to particular environmental events. Although Freud did not consider internal physiological events or animal behavior, he correctly looked for the adaptational meaning of all human behaviors.

The point being made is that there are certain classes of adaptive behaviors that all organisms show in response to certain special events that occur in their environment (external or internal). These adaptive behaviors are clearly evident in simple form in the lowest animals on the phylogenetic scale. They are also evident in more complex or derivative form in higher animals and in humans. It is reasonable to consider these general classes of adaptive behaviors as the precursors or prototypes of what are called emotions in higher animals.

FUNCTIONS OF EMOTION

A number of writers have discussed the function of emotion. Emotions have been described as a sign of the state of the individual and a way to elicit a response from the receivers of the signal. Expressive emotional behaviors are signals of intentions (Johnston & Scherer, 2000). For example, the alarm calls of vervet monkeys identify a specific type of predator, indicate a state of fear, and signal other monkeys to escape.

Bowlby (1969) proposed that behavior patterns associated with feeding, reproduction, caregiving, attachment, exploration, sociability, and fear-wariness have been selected through evolution because they increase the chances of survival and reproduction. These ideas have been accepted as part of attachment theory (as discussed in chapter 8).

Rolls (1990) suggested that there are at least seven functions of emotional behavior and expressions:

1. To elicit autonomic responses as preparations for crises
2. To adapt reactions to specific local conditions
3. To motivate actions designed to accomplish goals
4. To communicate an intention to others
5. To increase social bonding
6. To influence memory and the evaluation of events
7. To increase the storage of certain memories.

All of these characteristics of emotion help an organism cope with a complex changing environment. Rolls pointed out that even one-celled organisms may attempt to maximize chemical (food) intake of proteins by following concentration gradients that are beneficial and avoiding those that are harmful.

These examples of emotional functions clearly are not limited to human adults and are not limited to individuals who can use language to describe inner feelings. They also apply to children, infants, and animals. There may be some disagreement over the lowest phylogenetic level to which these ideas apply, but a case can be made for the idea that most of these functions apply to all living organisms. This behavior is typical of the species when threatened. The next four chapters discuss the functions of emotion in greater detail.

Adaptive Behavior in Unicellular Organisms

Nicola Ricci, a microbiologist, has pointed out that every single-celled organism from the blue-green algae to the eukaryotic cell is a complete, self-sufficient organism. These cells are exposed to daily risks in their environments. Such cells take in food, excrete waste products, avoid predators, attack prey, reproduce by exchange of genes in many cases, seek safe environments, and explore their microbiological world (Ricci, 1990). These single-celled organisms adapt to the same types of problems faced by higher multicellular organisms.

Single-celled organisms have evolved such specialized features as sensory bristles, flagella, mouth parts, musclelike contractile bundles, and stinging darts. Such cells have existed on earth for over a billion years and still exist today. Figure 9.4 shows a single-celled parasite, *Giardia lamblia*, with two sets of nuclei (that look like eyes) and flagella (tails) that propel the organism through watery environments.

Environments are more frequently dangerous for the individual than benign. For life to continue, organisms must develop adaptations and defenses. Because all organisms depend on other living things for sustenance, a continuous "arms race" exists between prey and predator.

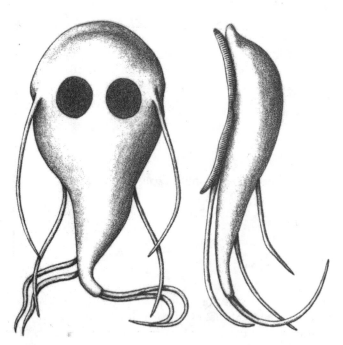

FIGURE 9.4. Drawing of *Giardia camblia*, a single-celled intestinal parasite. The structures that resemble large eyes are nuclei that house the genetic maternal DNA. The side view shows the disk used by the parasite to attach to other cells. The tail-like structures are flagella used to propel itself through its fluid environment. From "Giardia: A Missing Link Between Prokaryotes and Eukaryotes," by K. S. Kabnick and D. A. Peattie, 1991, *American Scientist, 79*, p. 35. Copyright 1991 by The Scientific Research Society. Reprinted with permission.

It is interesting to note the terminology used by scientists to describe the processes involved in infectious disease. Bacteria launch an attack and the immune system puts up a defense. Many pathogens use deception to overcome the defenses. The various deceptions have been placed into three categories by a cell biologist: camouflage, distraction, and mimicry (Goodenough, 1991). Although these terms sound anthropomorphic, they describe the functions very well.

Even in single-celled organisms, genes had to develop the necessary tools needed to interact with other organisms as aggressor, prey, or mate. All organisms have sensors that detect special chemicals as well as gradients of intensity. All organisms have start and stop mechanisms that determine the beginning and end of actions (Chalmers, 1987). Genes that perform essential functions are often found in the same or similar form in organisms as disparate as bacteria and mammals. For example, of the 289 genes known to cause human disease in mutated form, 177 have direct counterparts in the fruit fly. Figure 9.5 shows a phagocyte extending pseudopods toward rod-shaped bacteria to contact and then engulf them.

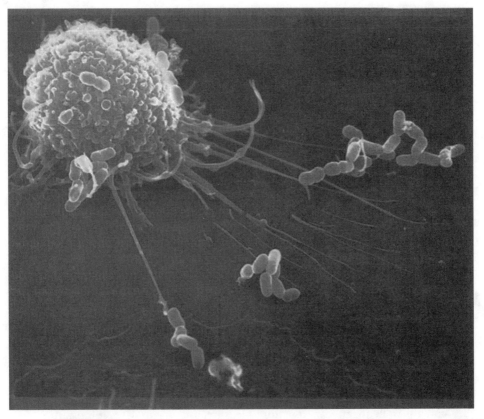

FIGURE 9.5. A single cell extends its pseudopods in response to signals emitted from the rod-shaped bacteria. From "How Cells Crawl," by T. P. Stossel, 1990, *American Scientist, 78,* p. 418. Copyright 1990 by The Scientific Research Society. Reprinted with permission.

Given the fact that emotions are forms of adaptation made to environmental events, is there any reason to limit the application of the term to humans? The observations cited above suggest that emotions may be a general phenomenon found at all phylogenetic levels.

An Evolutionary Definition of Emotions

From an evolutionary point of view, emotions can be conceptualized as certain types of adaptive reactions that can be identified in lower animals as well as in humans. These adaptive patterns have evolved to deal with basic survival issues in all organisms, such as dealing with prey and predator, potential mate and stranger, nourishing objects and toxins. Such patterns involve approach or avoidance reactions, fight and flight reactions, attachment and loss reactions, and riddance or ejection reactions. The evolutionary perspective suggests that these patterns are the prototypes of emotions in higher animals and in humans. These interactional patterns of adaptation may be thought of as the prototypes of fear and anger: acceptance and disgust, and joy and sadness. The subjective feelings that we usually identify as emotions are a relatively late evolutionary development and should not be used as the only or major criteria of the presence of an emotional state.

Emotions are complex, interactional adaptations and must therefore have a variety of expressive forms, each of which can be used to infer properties of the underlying state. Even though the details of the adaptive processes vary among different animals, species, and phyla, depending on the nature of the environment and genetics, the *function* of each pattern of adaptation has remained unchanged throughout all phylogenetic levels. From an evolutionary point of view, emotions are patterns of adaptation that increase the chances of individual and genetic survival.

STUDYING EMOTIONS IN ANIMALS

The observations made so far in this chapter indicate the need to identify systematic ways to infer emotions in animals. The problem in some ways is similar to that involved in inferring the existence of any subjective feeling state in animals. In science, there are many concepts that are not directly observed but are inferences made from various sources of evidence. This is true, for example, of the subatomic particles of physics, the structure of genes and molecules, and concepts related to memory, perception, and learning (e.g., cognitive maps, retroactive inhibition, and neural nets). Emotions, too, are inferences we make based on the actions of other people and on the behavior of lower animals.

The belief in animal feelings is widespread. The Society for the Prevention of Cruelty to Animals is based on the idea that animals can feel pain and can suffer. The contemporary flourishing of animal rights groups is a reflection of the same widespread belief. However, if animals can feel pain and suffering, there is no reason to assume they cannot feel other states as well: anger, fear, affection, pleasure, and disgust. It is important to emphasize that the argument that animals can feel some emotional states does not mean that they can feel all states, nor does it mean that their feelings are exactly like the feelings of humans. If one can justify the probable experience of pain in an animal, one can also justify the probable experience of fear as well. Let us now consider several different proposals about how one can infer emotions in animals.

Donald Hebb on Emotions in Chimpanzees

In a paper written in 1946, Donald Hebb discussed the problem of inferring emotions in chimpanzees. The paper appeared after Hebb had worked for several years at the Yerkes Laboratory for primate studies in Florida, and it described some of his conclusions concerning the problem of how to recognize emotions in animals and in humans.

At the time Hebb worked at the Yerkes Laboratory, it contained 30 adolescent and adult chimpanzees, almost all of whom had been under daily observation for periods of 6 to 19 years. Detailed diary records were kept for each animal by staff members, particularly at times when emotional states were ascribed to the animals. There was thus detailed and intimate knowledge of each animal over most of its lifespan.

With all this information available, Hebb and his colleagues had no reluctance at all in inferring the existence of emotions in these animals. He wrote in 1972,

> The dog is definitely capable of jealousy and occasionally, in some dogs, there are signs of sulking. In the chimpanzee, however, we have the full picture of human anger in its three main forms: anger, sulking and the temper tantrum. The peculiar feature of sulking is refusing to accept what one tried to get in the first place. The peculiar feature of the temper tantrum is the inclusion of apparent attempts at self-injury: the child holding its breath, pulling his hair, banging himself against the wall—and watching meanwhile to see what effect this is having on the adult who is denying him what he wants. There is a purposive element that is also clear in the year-old chimpanzee infant who takes surreptitious looks at his mother in between his attacks of choking to death or pounding his head on the floor. (p. 240)

Hebb went on to point out that not only are such basic emotions as anger, fear, and curiosity seen quite clearly in chimpanzees, but so too is altruistic behavior. Although many philosophers have argued that humans and animals are basically selfish and are governed only by pleasure and pain, there is increasing evidence that altruistic behavior is widely found in the animal kingdom. *Altruism* may be defined as purposive behavior that functions to help another person or animal even at the risk of one's own danger or death. A number of cases have been documented to show that a dolphin, a mammal with a brain that is larger than a human's, will help other dolphins in trouble (e.g., when caught in a net). Two cases are known in which a dolphin helped a human swimmer to reach safety. Adult baboons will deliberately place themselves between their harem, consisting of adult females and younger animals, and a predator such as a lion. Chimpanzees and gorillas observed in the wild have been seen to give help to youngsters in trouble even though it meant going into the dangerous area of the human observer (Hebb, 1972). Hebb concluded that these many instances of altruistic behavior reflect an inferred emotional state and that the capacity for this state is largely a product of evolution rather than learning.

Many important ideas were developed by Hebb as a result of his experiences with the chimpanzees at the Yerkes Laboratory. For example, he emphasized that the names given to emotional behavior are seldom based on the immediate behavior alone; they are based on a knowledge of the animal over an extended period of time. The same behavior might be labeled *fear, nervousness,* or *shyness* depending on a number of factors. In each case the immediate behavior is some form of avoidance, but in the case of fear it is strong, clearly related to an identifiable stimulus and not a common occurrence in that particular animal. Nervousness refers to a long-term characteristic of the animal and is usually recognized by a low startle threshold. Shyness implies that the animal tends generally to avoid strangers. Without knowing something about the stimulus, the details of the behavior, and the animal's typical past behavior, an accurate inference is difficult. In addition, it is evident that the same emotion word, such as *shyness*, can refer both to a temporary state and to a long-term condition akin to a personality trait.

Although a knowledge of the stimulus is very helpful when making an inference about an emotional state in someone else, it is not always, or even often, known. Sometimes, the stimulus is so slight or minimal ("She gets mad over nothing at all") that the observer cannot identify it. More importantly, it implies that there are few, if any, invariable connections between a stimulus and a response. The emotional response is primarily a function of the *meaning* or interpretation one gives to a situation or some aspect of it.

If an inference is made of an emotional state in an animal, is there any way of verifying the judgment? Hebb stated that the validity of the label is seen in its practical ability to predict the animal's behavior. In other words, if an animal is called *shy,* caretakers know what to expect of it in the future. If an animal is called *angry* or *hostile,* the caretakers will know enough to be cautious in its presence. The same point has been made by Masson and McCarthy (1995).

Useful as these labels can be, staff members more often than not refused to utilize them in situations in which the cues were ambiguous. This implies that observers use some kind of implicit weighting of cues to arrive at a probability estimate of the presence of an emotional state.

Another important idea presented by Hebb concerns the significance of subliminal or minimal levels of excitation as factors in the development of emotions. He illustrated this with the following examples (Hebb, 1946):

> In an experiment on avoidance a mounted snake was carried in the experimenter's hands up to the part of the enclosure where Shorty (a chimpanzee) sat. He moved calmly away to another part of the enclosure with no hint of excitement; but when the snake was again brought near him in his new position, he sprang up with hair erect and screaming, and hurled a large piece of timber at the experimenter with excellent aim. The same kind of summation effect is often seen in discrimination training, where a single failure may have no apparent effect but repeated failures lead to sulking, temper tantrums or destructive attacks on the apparatus. In such instances existence of a subliminal excitation is purely a matter of inference...
>
> Individual signs of the development of frustration responses are quite varied. They include the animal's scratching himself, ducking his head, . . . restlessness, moaning, whimpering, and erection of hair . . . knowledge of the species has considerable importance in the interpretation of the associated behavior of emotional excitation. (p. 94)

One implication of this concept of summation of subliminal excitation is the idea that low levels of emotional arousal are inherently vague and relatively undifferentiated. This means that even a human observer may have difficulty labeling his or her own emotional state when it is aroused only to low degree. This idea is probably the basis for some of the variability found in studies of self-attribution of emotions under mild conditions of stress in college students (Schachter & Singer, 1962). It may also help account for the fact that false autonomic feedback can often induce students to label their states as emotions even when objective indices of arousal show minimal levels (Valins, 1966).

Identifying Mental States in Animals

Arnold (1960) pointed out that ascribing emotion to animals is no different in essence than ascribing memory or imagination to animals. She argued that the presence of a similar sensory apparatus in both humans and animals implies that animals have sensory experiences. Similarly, the fact that animals, like humans, can learn implies that they remember earlier situations and have expectations about the future.

It is possible to show parallel sensory experiences in humans and animals in the following way:

1. Animal or human subjects can be tested behaviorally using forced-choice or matching tasks with certain stimulus patterns. No verbal responses are needed for such testing.

2. The effect of these stimulus patterns on the brain can be measured by recording the standard EEG (electroencephalograph) and using computer averaging of visually evoked cortical potentials.

3. Humans with clinical conditions such as cataracts or astigmatism can be compared with animals to which experimental visual deprivations have been produced.

On the basis of these ideas, Millodot and Riggs (1970) used the cortical-evoked potential to measure visual acuity. They found that the strength of the electric potentials obtained from the scalp decreased as vision was decreased through the use of artificial distorting lenses. At the same time, the participant received lower and lower scores on a standard chart test for visual acuity. The authors concluded that they had developed a procedure that could be used to fit corrective lenses to the eyes of nonverbal subjects such as babies and animals. Similar methods have been used to determine the relative sensitivity to color of pigeons and to determine the absolute sensitivity to colors of a 2-month-old baby (Riggs, 1976). It is thus possible to measure inner, private events without recourse to formal language. There are several additional ways that this can be done.

Judging Emotions on the Basis of Choice Behavior

For many years, P. T. Young had been concerned with the concept of choice behavior and its implications for a theory of hedonic states. The word *hedonic* simply refers to the pleasure–displeasure continuum; what Young had tried to do is to reintroduce the concept of pleasure as a meaningful subjective state definable by overt experimental operations.

To carry out this aim, Young (1961) distinguished between the intensity of stimulation and the quality of stimulation. For example, in studies of taste, rats chose to drink from salt solutions of low concentration and tended to avoid salt solutions as the concentration of salt became greater. When sucrose (sweet) solutions were mixed with quinine (bitter) solutions, the rate of ingestion was found to be an algebraic sum of the positive (sweet) and negative (bitter) values of the solution. Similarly, humans rate low-intensity tones as pleasing more frequently than loud tones. Sounds of low pitch are also rated as pleasant more frequently than sounds of high pitch.

These observations and many more examples cited by Young (1961) all imply that a simple one-dimensional activation concept is inadequate. Behavior is not just strong or weak, present or absent. Behavior has a directional aspect, implying a movement toward or away from certain objects or conditions. This idea of bidirectionality of behavior, of both positive and negative forms of activation, is what Young meant by the concept of *affective arousal*. Affective arousal recognizes the reality of attraction and repulsion. For example, foul odors, bitter tastes, or painful burns are not simply at low levels of attractiveness on a unipolar scale of attraction; they are repulsive. Pleasantness is not simply a decrease in pain, but it has a distinctive quality of its own.

Pleasure and pain represent internal states in both humans and animals. Choices tell us that positive or negative feelings are involved, but they do not tell us directly which of any possible positive or negative emotional states are present. For example, the emotional states of affection and curiosity may both lead to approach reactions rather than withdrawals, but these two emotions are quite different from each other. Thus, although choice behavior is a method of communication of inner states, it does not have high precision and must be supplemented with additional types of evidence in order to tell us exactly which emotions are involved.

Judging Emotions on the Basis of Peer Group Behavior

Another important way to identify emotional reactions in an animal (as well as a human) is by observing the behavior of other individuals toward the identified one. There are a number of illustrations of this idea. In his book *The Year of the Gorilla* (1965), ethologist George Schaller described a female gorilla who usually sounded an alarm call when she saw him. However, instead of producing appropriate and typical protective responses from other gorillas in the band, the other animals ignored her. Schaller concluded that what appeared to him as a typical alarm call was interpreted differently by the other gorillas. They apparently recognized that the female was either not afraid, despite the call, or not in danger.

Delgado (1966) gave several illustrations of this same idea. He pointed out that the behavior of one monkey in a colony will produce emotional reactions from other animals. If submissiveness or retaliation is provoked from the other monkeys, it indicates that threat has occurred. Which of these two reactions occurs depends on the relative positions of the animals within the dominance hierarchy; higher dominance animals will retaliate, whereas lower dominance animals will usually become submissive. One can thus identify the nature of the initial emotional stimulus by carefully observing the ensuing behavior of the other animals in the troop.

Another example of this point is given by Delgado in relation to the effects of electrical stimulation of the brain to monkeys and cats. An electrode was placed in the rhinal fissure at the tip of the temporal lobe in a rhesus monkey. Electrical stimulation of this point produced opening of the mouth, rotation of the head, and scratching of the face, a pattern that to a human observer looked aggressive. However, this evoked behavior had no effect on the social behavior of the other members of the monkey colony. In contrast, electrical stimulation of the central gray area of the brain produced behavior that caused the other animals to withdraw, grimace, and show submissive behaviors (Delgado, 1966). We can thus reasonably infer that stimulation of the central gray area produced aggressive behavior whereas stimulation of the rhinal fissure did not, even though there were some superficial similarities in the two patterns of behavior.

Similarly, stimulation of the lateral hypothalamus in the cat produces well-organized attack behavior against other cats. If they retaliate, a full-fledged fight breaks out. Stimulating the anterior hypothalamus produces an aggressive display, which may induce another cat to attack in return. Despite its apparently aggressive display, however, the stimulated cat lowers its head, flattens its ears, withdraws, and does not retaliate. This implies that the apparent aggressive display does not truly reflect a state of aggression. It is evident that the reactive behavior of other animals of the same species provides a basis for judging the existence and type of emotion present in a given, identified animal. This, therefore, represents still another kind of evidence to be used, when available, to infer the presence of emotions in an animal.

These illustrations imply that the study of aggressive and submissive displays is a way of studying emotion regardless of how certain we may or may not be of whether the animal feels *anger* or *fear*. Because emotions are complex phenomena, different aspects may be studied, assessed, and interpreted without necessarily assuming that there is only one gold standard for defining emotion.

The British ethologist Patrick Bateson (1991) described the kind of evidence people use to judge that other people as well as lower animals have subjective experiences, including emotions:

1. They possess receptors (eyes, nose, ears) that are sensitive to the same kinds of stimuli.

2. They possess brain structures that are similar.

3. They use the same types of neurotransmitters in the brain and possess the same types of receptors for opioid substances.

4. Analgesics (pain killers) reduce responses to noxious stimuli and are chosen by animals when they are given a choice.

5. They both try to avoid noxious stimuli.

6. They both learn how to associate neural events with noxious stimuli through conditioning.

Judging Emotions on the Basis of Displacement Behavior

One last illustration is given of a possible method for identifying emotions in lower animals. *Displacement* behavior has been commonly observed in many animals. Such actions have been defined as behavior patterns characterized by their apparent irrelevance to the situation in which they appear. Examples seen in nonhuman primates include scratching, yawning, self-grooming, and body shaking.

It has been reported that such activities tend to occur in situations of conflict between individuals and in situations of social stress (Maestripiere, Schino, Aureli, & Troisi, 1992). They frequently occur during or immediately after agonistic interactions. Scratching often occurs during territorial conflicts in monkeys. When two unfamiliar female macaques are paired in a small cage, there is often a marked increase in the frequency of scratching, self-grooming, and yawning. In general, it appears that monkeys who are uncertain of their relative social status show high levels of displacement activities.

This inference is supported by the fact that the administration of anxiety-increasing drugs (as determined by humans) has the effect of increasing the type and amount of displacement activities as well as the efforts by young animals to seek contact with their mothers. Conversely, administration of anxiety-reducing drugs (as determined by humans) has the effect of decreasing the amount of displacement behaviors.

Psychiatrists have defined anxiety as a state of wariness associated with the anticipation of danger. Displacement activities are commonly observed when an individual is confronting a potential source of danger. For this reason and all the others cited above,

Maestripiere et al. (1992) considered it reasonable to infer the existence of "anxiety" in primates showing displacement activities. These authors also suggested that displacement behaviors serve an adaptive function. They appear to reduce distress. They may possibly also serve a role in communication. They may reveal an animal's mood or motivational state in contest situations in which assessment of another's intentions is important. For example, in captive chimpanzees, self-scratching by a dominant male is frequently followed by appeasement displays by other individuals (Goodall, 1987).

PROBLEMS OF SELF-AWARENESS OF EMOTIONAL STATES

Let us assume that the preceding arguments make plausible the idea that emotions occur in lower animals as well as in humans despite the lack of a verbal repertoire in animals. This now suggests the questions, What about self-awareness in animals? Do animals know that they have emotions?

First, we need to make a distinction between having an experience and being aware of that experience, just as we may distinguish between behaving and being aware of the behavior. Human beings show many behaviors that they are usually not aware of, for example, frowning, breathing, swallowing, and personal mannerisms such as scratching their heads. They may also show various automatic reactions, such as eye blinks, knee jerks, or pupillary contractions, of which they are unaware. Certain types of conditioning can occur without awareness, for example, using plural words because they have been reinforced.

But what about emotions? Do animals know they are having an emotion when they show emotional behavior? Books by Griffin (1976, 1992), a zoologist, takes up the issue of animal awareness. His argument is that research on social communication in bees, orientation and navigation in animals, and language acquisition in chimpanzees suggests the possibility that "conversations" take place between members of a given species and that animals have mental experiences and communicate to satisfy certain goals.

Griffin (1992) pointed out that Behaviorism argued that the study of subjective mental experiences should not be considered as part of the scientific enterprise. However, with the development of cognitive psychology and the recognition that complex mental processes occur in the brain that determine memory, learning, problem solving, and emotions, subjective experience became a valid subject of study. There is still controversy over whether animals are *conscious* beings. Griffin (1992) noted,

> Many scientists who study animal behavior . . . deny the existence or the significance of animal consciousness. Because it is so difficult to prove rigorously whether any given animal is conscious, no matter how ingenious its behavior, scientists have tended to cling to the conservative assumption that all animal behavior is unconscious. (p. 1)

Griffin believed that the evidence of communication in animals, tool use, language acquisition, and emotional reactions (elephants that weep, wolves that mourn, chimpanzees that show compassionate behavior) implies the presence of consciousness.

One set of investigations, however, does provide some information about the issue of self-consciousness. Gallup (1977) presented chimpanzees with a full-length mirror so that they could see their own reflection, under the assumption that self-awareness is based on self-recognition. Within a few days, the behavior changed from the kind that would normally be directed toward another animal to the kind that was clearly self-directed (e.g., grooming parts of the body that could not be seen, picking food from the teeth, or making faces at the mirror). When red paint was placed on the faces of the chimpanzees while they were anesthetized, they showed greatly increased attention to the area after looking in a mirror. This was not true for control animals who had had no previous exposure to the mirror.

This phenomenon of self-recognition (and by implication, self-awareness) has been replicated in orangutans as well as chimpanzees, but every attempt to replicate the phenomenon in other primates—spider monkeys, capuchins, mandrill, and hamadryas baboons—has failed. It is also important to note that not all studies of chimpanzees have replicated these findings and that a British psychologist has criticized both the methodology and the conclusions of these early studies (Heyes, 1994).

An interesting recent study examined the issue of self-awareness in a different way using cowbirds (*Molothrus ater*) as subjects. Cowbirds lay their eggs in other birds' nests such as those of sparrows so that the host birds feed their young. After 6 weeks or so, the juveniles seek out their own species. The problem is: How do they recognize their own species?

In one set of experiments, Hauber, Sherman, and Paprika (2000) dyed the underside of the wings of a group of young cowbirds with black ink. These birds had been removed from the nest of sparrows shortly after hatching and reared separately in visual isolation from all birds. At about 2 months of age, the experimental birds were introduced to two adult female cowbirds, one with wings painted black and one of normal coloring. These encounters were the young cowbird's first visual exposure to other birds.

Over time, it was observed that the young birds spent more and more time with the birds that looked like they did. This was interpreted to mean that the young birds had the ability to inspect themselves, memorize certain physical characteristics, and seek out individuals as social companions that had these characteristics. In more general terms, these findings were interpreted to mean that self-referent matching of a physical characteristic is possible in birds.

Some ambiguity exists in these and other studies as to exactly what is meant by the term *self-awareness*. Partly as a result of such ambiguities, many investigators of animal cognition have focused their attention on the functions that can easily be identified in all animals that reflect the operation of the mind. Such studies are concerned primarily with the processes in the brain that enable individuals to store, represent, and manipulate information. Rather than ask "Is an animal self-conscious," they preferred to study the cognitive processes that enabled these functional activities to occur (Roitblat, 1996).

In the book *Why Elephants Weep*, Masson and McCarthy (1995) discussed a number of these issues. He presented many anecdotes about emotional behavior in animals (e.g., mother love in elephants, sadness and depression) and noted that many animals are able to recognize other animals as individuals and distinguish between them and strangers. Masson reminded us of the great genetic similarity between humans and all other animals, but in particular the other primates. He suggested that it is very easy for most people to attribute personal qualities to animals and to think of some of them as heroes or villains. He wondered why we consider that knowing about an animal's feelings is different from the judgments we make about other people's feelings. He also suggested that we have been led astray by a preoccupation with language as the only sign of a subjective state. These authors wrote, "some cultures lack a word for romantic love, but people in such cultures still have clandestine affairs, refuse arranged marriages, elope, or commit suicide over love" (p. 83).

Emotions Without Awareness

A number of studies have revealed that human adults may show discrepancies between subjective reports of emotions and overt behavior. Here are some illustrations.

In D. Watson's (2000) study of moods involving hundreds of participants, he found that although most people reported that they feel better on sunny days than on rainy days, their rated moods were not correlated with the weather. Similarly, many women said they believed that their menstrual cycle greatly affected their moods, but their daily ratings of mood showed little relation to the phases of the menstrual cycle.

In many psychiatric studies, comparisons have been made between the patients' self-ratings of emotions and ratings made by observers (doctors or nurses). Sometimes the self-ratings match the observer ratings well and sometimes there are great discrepancies. For example, anxiety ratings often show great disagreements between patients and observers, whereas ratings of depression are often in good agreement (Baumann, Eckmann, & Stieglitz, 1985; Lindenmayer, Kay, & Plutchik, 1992; van Praag & Plutchik, 1984).

In a study of the relations between facial expressions of affect and subjective experiences of affect, a group of medication-free patients with schizophrenia were exposed to a series of 4-minute video films designed to arouse feelings of happiness, sadness, fear, and disgust. Their moods were measured by means of a mood scale, and their facial expressions were coded by means of an objective coding system. Results were compared with those of a normal control group (Kring, Kerr, Smith, & Neale, 1993).

The data showed that patients with schizophrenia were less facially expressive than normal participants, but they reported feeling emotions just as intensely as did the normal participants. A discrepancy thus existed in the schizophrenic patients between emotional states and overt behavior.

Psychoanalytic theory and common experiences indicate the extent to which emotional memories of childhood can be forgotten, distorted, or exaggerated. A recent study attempted to determine the extent to which a false memory of an emotional childhood incident could be generated in the participant (Porter, Birt, Yuille, & Lehman, 2000). In this investigation, the parents of those people who had agreed to participate were sent a questionnaire that requested information concerning six emotional events of the participants' childhood. The events concerned such things as accidents, getting lost, being attacked by an animal or another child, or having a serious medical procedure.

Interviewers then used this information to try to create a false memory in the participants by means of guided imagery, repetition, and mild social pressure. In a second and third interview, the participants were asked about the false incident. Responses were placed into three categories: complete, partial, or no false memory. It was found that 26% of the participants created a complete false memory of the emotional event, 30% produced a partial false memory, and 44% produced no false memory. One implication of these findings is that "recovered" emotional memories may sometimes be the result of social pressure rather than a reflection of a real event. Another is that subjective reports of emotional states are not necessarily correct.

An approach to the problem of subjective awareness of emotions involves the use of the *backward masking technique*. In one study using this method, participants were exposed to a picture of a happy, angry, or neutral face for 30 milliseconds. After this brief time, the picture was turned off, and the participants was immediately exposed to a new picture of a neutral face for 5 seconds. This second picture is called the masking stimulus, and it prevents the participant from consciously perceiving the initial target picture (Dimberg, Thunberg, & Elmehed, 2000).

In this study, muscle tension potentials from two facial muscles were measured during the conditioning procedure. The muscles were *zygomatic major*, which elevates the lips to form a smile, and the *corrugator supercilii*, which creates a frown. The results indicated that frowning or smiling facial responses can be evoked without the participant being consciously aware of the eliciting emotional stimuli. These findings further support the idea that emotional reactions can occur without subjective awareness, a phenomenon that is commonly seen in clinical practice.

The problem of studying the development of the language of emotional states can be examined in children. In one such investigation, the development of the language of internal states was determined in a group of normal children and a group of children with Down syndrome. Four groups of children were evaluated: (a) children with Down syndrome who were ages 3 to 4 years, (b) normal children matched on mental age with the Down children, (c) children with Down syndrome ages 6 to 7 years, and (d) normal children matched on mental age with the older Down syndrome children (Beeghly & Cicchetti, 1994).

Mother–child verbal interactions were recorded in various situations, and all examples of internal state words or phrases were noted. These included words related to sensory perception (e.g., smell, taste, touch), physiological states (e.g., fatigue, thirst), positive affect (e.g., pleasure, sympathy), negative affect (e.g., anger, sadness), affective behavior (e.g., kiss, hug, cry), and other internal states.

For all children, there was an increase in internal state language with age. However, the children with Down syndrome produced fewer internal state words overall. It appears that children with Down syndrome who have difficulty with abstract thinking do not learn to use the subjective language of emotion as readily as do cognitively normal children. This does not necessarily mean that their ability to experience and express emotions is impaired.

Measuring Subjective States in Animals

One last example is given to illustrate a way to study subjective states in animals. Lubinski and Thompson (1987) trained pigeons to peck at a key for food or water reinforcement and to make a light go on. The pigeons were then injected with one or another of three agents: a depressant (pentobarbital), a stimulant (cocaine), or saline solution. Pecks to the correct key that matched the pigeons' current internal state were then reinforced. After a 7-month training period, the accuracy of pecking at the correct label for the pigeons' internal state was about 90%.

A new communication task was then set up between pairs of birds. One bird was trained to peck at a key labeled "How do you feel?" This caused all three keys to light up in the cage of the paired bird. If the second bird then correctly pressed the key that indicated its present internal state (i.e., depressed, stimulated, or no drug), the second bird was rewarded, and the first bird was trained to respond with a "Thank you" key press. It took about 40 days of training to obtain a high degree of accuracy of over 90%.

This study was then extended to two new drugs: d-amphetamine (a stimulant) and chlordiazepoxide (a depressant). The communicating bird pressed the key of the drug that was most similar to the newly introduced drugs. The pigeons pressed the cocaine key when injected with amphetamine and the pentobarbital key when injected with chlordiazepoxide, which thus provided an indirect measure of the degree of similarity in the internal states due to these different drugs.

The results of this ingenious study indicated that subjective, private, internal events (produced by drug injections in this case) can be communicated from birds to humans and from one bird to another. This provides strong support for the idea that subjective, internal states of emotion in animals exist and can be communicated.

Given the evidence that has been cited in this chapter, why is the idea of emotional states in animals sometimes treated with skepticism? This issue is considered in the next chapter.

SUMMARY

This chapter examined the evolutionary perspective on the nature of emotions. Such a perspective implies that emotions are complex adaptive patterns of reaction that have effects on the individuals or conditions that elicited the reaction in the first place. The function of these reactions is to increase the chances of survival of the interacting organisms.

To understand this idea more fully, a brief overview of evolutionary theory was presented. One key idea is that all organisms have certain common survival problems to deal with; for example, finding prey and avoiding predators, mating, and rejecting toxic substances. The evolutionary perspective suggests that these basic issues require certain types of adaptive reactions that are common to almost all organisms. Such adaptive patterns are assumed to be the prototypes of emotions as seen in human beings. They are complex states involving adaptive changes in behavior, physiology, and subjective states.

If one accepts these premises, then the problem arises of how to make meaningful inferences about subjective states in animals. This problem is no different in principle than the issue of how to make inferences about subjective states in humans. Previous chapters have revealed how variable and invalid verbal reports of subjective states can sometimes be. General methods need to be developed for assessing the complex, adaptive processes called emotions in both animals and humans.

The chapter reviewed several types of approaches that have been suggested. These include gaining knowledge of an animal's typical behavior, observation of the pattern of reaction to stimuli, and responses of conspecifics to the behavior. Other types of evidence include forced-choice testing procedures and the use of evoked cortical potentials. Such evidence may be interpreted to mean that the subjective aspects of emotions may be a relatively late evolutionary development and therefore only one indicator among many of an emotional state.

10 Emotion and Communication

> The remarkable development of the facial and vocal apparatus for the expression of emotion serves an obvious purpose: Each evolutionary step forward improves the ability of members of the species to communicate with each other.
>
> *Detlev Ploog*

> We respond to gestures with an extreme alertness and, one might almost say, in accordance with an elaborate and secret code that is written nowhere, known by none, and understood by all.
>
> *Edward Sapir*

PREVIEW

From an evolutionary point of view, emotions serve survival functions partly through their role as forms of communication. This chapter examines some of the issues involved in understanding the nature of communication in humans and in animals. Animal communications such as courtship, submissive displays, and warning displays are considered to be aspects of emotional communication. Of particular interest are the sound and speech signals made by animals and humans. Examples are given of bird, tiger, elephant, and primate communications through sound, odor, color, movement, and posture. Emotional displays can also be in conflict and can sometimes act as deceptions. The chapter concludes with a discussion of the question of whether animals have, or can have, a humanlike language. The history of attempts to teach apes to talk, either vocally or by means of sign language, is reviewed. Evidence exists of the use of sign language by bonobo apes to express emotional states.

ALL ANIMALS produce signals of various kinds that have an influence on other animals of the same or different species. Such signals include postural changes, color changes, odor secretions, sounds, light production, electrical fields, and facial expressions. These signals or displays reveal status, internal states, territories, intentions, and emotions (Ploog, 2000).

Social signals, however, must not only be sent but also be received. Over eons of time, there must have been a coevolution of the transmitting and receiving systems for social signals. A baby may cry in distress, but unless the mother somehow recognizes or "knows" what the cry probably indicates, no communication will take place. Studies with monkeys have shown that neuronal cells in the amygdala of the brain respond to pictures of monkey faces, different expressions, direction of gaze, and facial orientations (Hasselmo, Rolls, & Baylis, 1989). This has been interpreted to mean that eye contact creates a circular loop between the sender of a signal and the receiver. The direction of gaze determines the individual on whom focus is directed, whereas the facial expression may indicate the intentions of the sender of the signal. It has been shown that patients with Huntington's disease (a chronic degenerative disease of the brain characterized by irregular, involuntary movements of the limbs and facial muscles) who have impairment in perception of the direction of gaze could not distinguish anger from fear expressions and could not recognize disgust expressions on the face (Sprengelmayer et al., 1996).

COMMUNICATION AND SOCIAL BEHAVIOR

From an evolutionary point of view, social behavior has many advantages. It increases the chances of finding desirable mates. It creates the interactions necessary to raise offspring so they can become reproducing members of another generation. It creates mutually supportive bonds between mates, companions, parents, and children. And it provides the basis for interactions between members of a group that are related to attack, defense, threat, avoidance, and coalitions.

For these functions of social behavior to be effectively carried out, animals, including humans, need to be able to communicate with one another. The following is an example of a green iguana in a social group with a definite dominance hierarchy:

> The top animal is a male easily recognizable by its whitish head, which is distinctively brighter than the head of the other group members. If a top male loses a fight and thereby the top rank, it loses its bright color; within minutes head and body assumed a brownish-green color. With the loss of dominance the animal's social behavior is subject to drastic changes. The color of its head is an indicator of its internal state and the involvement of the autonomic nervous system and hormones. (Ploog, 1992, p. 6)

According to ethologists, the various displays of animals may be labeled in terms of the emotional or motivational state that is most clearly evident. From this point of view, the following list describes many of the specific types of interactions associated with each display:

1. Greeting or recognition displays
2. Courtship displays
3. Mating displays
4. Dominance displays
5. Submissive displays
6. Warning displays
7. Alarm displays
8. Defense displays
9. Challenge displays
10. Distress displays
11. Defeat displays
12. Victory displays
13. Feeding displays
14. Food-begging displays

As a first approximation, it may be said that displays function to communicate emotional information from one animal to another. This may be illustrated in many ways. Chimpanzees make many kinds of sounds. On the basis of an electronic analysis of chimpanzees' sounds, Marler and Tenaza (1977) concluded that about 13 fairly distinct sounds could be identified under natural field conditions, although some degree of gradation was also found. *Pant-hoots* were most frequently heard and were uttered most often by male chimpanzees. These sounds occurred spontaneously while the chimpanzees fed, met with other chimpanzees, ate mammalian prey, and when a group divided into smaller foraging parties. Chimpanzees seemed to listen to distant pant-hoots and then answered them (Tuttle, 1986).

Young chimpanzees often throw noisy tantrums when weaned by their mothers. Adults, particularly dominant males who have been deposed, have also been seen to exhibit tantrums. During grooming, both sexes show quiet panting. Youngsters who have been tickled produce sounds that are suggestive of human laughter.

The sound called a *pant-grunt* has been used to assess the relative status of individuals because subordinate chimpanzees pant-grunt as they move closer to dominant animals. Both males and females emit *wraaa* calls in response to human intruders and predators. In a group of chimpanzees studied by Jane Goodall on the Gombe preserve in Tanzania, wraaa calls were frequently heard following the death of an adult male who fell from a tree. Such calls have been interpreted as indicating fear states.

Studies of sound patterns in gorillas were carried out by Fossey (1983). She described 16 vocalizations and many of the situations associated with them. The older dominant males, generally referred to as silverbacks, sometimes uttered low growls when approached by an animal, with the result that the latter usually retreated. Mildly alarmed adults emitted staccato barks, noted most frequently when a human observer moves suddenly into view. When an adult gorilla was startled by close contact with a dangerous animal such as a buffalo, the gorilla often emitted a loud alarm bark that has been described as a wraaa sound, pitched somewhere between a roar and a scream. Following these wraaa sounds, groups usually moved away from the source of the disturbance. A sound that tended to induce group members to cluster together was the *hoot-bark*. When gorillas heard this sound, many would climb a tree and look around. These various sound patterns reflect both motivational and emotional states.

Alarm Calls in Vervet Monkeys

Ethologists have published many studies that have identified rather specific communication functions of most signals or displays. For example, Seyforth, Cheney, and Marler (1980a) showed that vervet monkey alarm calls function to designate different classes of external danger related to specific types of predators: Animals on the ground respond to leopard alarms by running into trees, to eagle alarms by looking up, and to snake alarms by looking down.

Table 10.1 describes the typical stimuli that tend to produce various types of alarm calls in vervet monkeys (Marler, 1977). Not only does the appearance of various predators produce specific alarm signals but also characteristic and different reactions by the members of the troop.

In a series of field trials, recorded alarm calls were played back to vervet monkeys of different ages. It was found that infants were able to distinguish between general classes of predators, for example, between a terrestrial mammal and a flying bird, but that adults

TABLE 10.1. Vervet Monkey Alarm Calls

Typical Stimulus	Typical Response	Typical Call	Adult Males	Adult and Young Females
Minor mammal predator near	Become alert, look to predator	Uh!	Yes	Yes
Sudden involvement of minor predator	Look to predator, sometimes flee	Nyow!	Yes	Yes
Man or venomous snake—but the chutter is structurally different for man and snake	Approach snake and escort at safe distance	Chutter	Yes (rare)	Yes
Initial sighting of an eagle	Flee from treetops and open area into thickets	Rraup	No	Yes
Initially and after sighting major predator (leopard, lion, eagle)	Attention and then flight to appropriate cover	Threat alarm-bark	Yes	No
After initial sighting of major predator (leopard, lion, eagle)	Flee from thickets and open areas to branches and canopy	Chirp	No	Yes

Note. From "Primate Vocalization: Affective or Symbolic?" by P. Marler. In *Progress in Ape Research*, 1977, p. 137. Copyright 1977 by Academic Press. Reprinted with permission.

could distinguish among predators and other mammals, or eagles and other birds (Seyforth, Cheney, & Marler, 1980a). These observations provide strong support for the idea that the ability to react appropriately to such calls is a genetically determined characteristic. Although the degree of specificity may be influenced by experience, the initial appearance of such abilities does not appear to depend on learning.

After investigating vocalizations of the Japanese monkey (*Maccacca fuscata*), Green (1975) concluded that there are many parallels between human vocalizations and the vocalizations of this monkey: both use shrieks, screams, screeches, and other sounds and they occur in comparable situations.

Sound production in animals has a long evolutionary history. Sounds can be recorded from fish, amphibians, reptiles, birds, mammals, and primates. They occur in different settings and have various effects on the relations between the interacting in-dividuals. In the squirrel monkey, a peep is emitted if the animal is separated from the group. Two types of alarm calls have been identified: one for predators such as eagles and the other for ground-living predators. Other calls are associated with aggressive attacks ("arr" sounds) or with high excitement (shrieks; see Maurus, Streit, Barclay, Wiesner, & Kuehlmorgan, 1988).

Squirrel monkey infants raised by mute mothers in acoustic isolation began to vocalize immediately after birth and expressed all types of adult calls in a few days. This appears to be strong evidence for the genetic basis of call behavior in this species. Further support for this idea comes from the fact that natural calls (cackling, growling, chirping, and shrieking) could be elicited by electrical stimulation of many subcortical areas (e.g., amygdala, hippocampus, medial thalamus, and mamillary body). Destruction of some of these areas produces mutism. This is also true for humans as well as lower animals.

Ploog (1992) described some clinical evidence that reveals a disconnection between expressions of emotion and feelings of emotion. Patients with Parkinson's disease are able to voluntarily control facial muscles but gradually lose spontaneous emotional facial expressions. Their speech also begins to sound flat and unemotional. However, the subjective emotional feelings of such patients are unimpaired. Some neurological conditions produce involuntary laughing and crying, but the patients generally report no emotional experiences during such episodes.

One implication of these observations is that communicative behavior supports the existence of social groups by such functions as the sharing of resources, mutual help, group defense, and child care. Emotions appear to have a major role in effective social behavior. Communication is fundamental to all these actions.

IDENTIFYING THE COMMUNICATION FUNCTIONS OF EMOTIONAL DISPLAYS IN ANIMALS

Most observations of display behaviors of animals are made in more or less natural settings. The conditions cannot generally be manipulated, nor is it possible to know in advance whether a predator is about to appear, whether an infant is about to be weaned, or whether two adults are about to engage in a contest or battle. Therefore, considerable patience and long hours of observations are required. However, many experimental paradigms have also been tried. These include the use of models, recorded calls, and restricted environments. From all of these studies, much insight has been obtained into patterns of animal behaviors, the conditions that tend to trigger such behaviors, and the usual consequences of the behaviors. Some examples are given below of how these kinds of studies are done to reveal connections between emotional states and overt behavior in animals.

Communications in Birds

The literature of ethology is filled with studies on the survival implications of particular patterns of behavior as well as on the communication content of expressions. For example, the function of song in a Florida population of Scott's seaside sparrows was studied by temporarily muting male birds in the field. This procedure left the birds songless for about 2 weeks before recovery. During this time, the songless birds did not acquire mates or lost previously acquired mates. Their territories either shrank or were lost, although new territories were established after voice recovery. The muted birds also experienced more close-range aggressive behavior than controls (McDonald, 1989). It thus appears that bird song in this species influences both reproductive behavior and aggressive interactions.

In a study concerned with sexual competition among female lapwings, a ground-nesting shorebird, the investigators placed a taxidermically mounted model of a female on the ground of a resident female's territory to mimic the presence of an intruder. A mounted male dummy was also used as a comparison. The models were placed on the ground 10 meters from the nest of the resident female (Liker & Szekely, 1997).

The resident females typically made a dash toward the dummy with a retracted neck, fluffed breast feathers, and erected crest. As they got to within 1 meter of the dummy, they performed various displays such as rocking, high-upright posture, and scraping. This was followed by the female pecking at the dummy, hitting it with her wing, or kicking it. Sometimes females dived at the dummy from the air and occasionally hit it with their wings. More aggressive behavior was directed to the female model than to the male model. The investigators interpreted these results as an aspect of female–female competition over male parental care for the young.

Another example of communication in birds may be seen in the studies of food sharing in ravens. A common observation is that the carcass of a deer or moose in a forest may be seen by a raven. It circles above the carcass and then flies off to return later with the group of 40 or more ravens that all join in the feast.

Ravens are known to have a large repertoire of sounds, which include recruitment calls, territorial calls, and attraction calls. When food is seen, a "yell" recruits other ravens to join in the eating. The yell is similar to ones made by young birds when their parents come near or those made by a female when she begs her mate for food. In young adults, the yell attracts other wandering ravens.

In a study of this phenomenon, the experimenters placed carcasses in various remote places in New England and watched and recorded the behavior of ravens, many of which had been previously caught and marked. It was discovered that there were two groups of ravens that came to feed: adult residents of the area and mostly subadult wanderers. The juveniles were allowed little access to the carcasses unless they came in large enough numbers to inhibit the adults' aggressive behaviors. Juvenile calls attracted the other juveniles so that all members of the group could feed. Figure 10.1 illustrates how the sharing of food by ravens depends largely on communication (Heinrich & Marzluff, 1995).

As a final illustration of communication in birds, we may consider a study of male bantam chickens. The subjects were randomly exposed to video pictures of either a raccoon or a hawk, both of which are predators of chickens. In all cases the video images of the aerial and terrestrial predators produced antipredatory responses. To pictures of the hawk, the male chickens crouched down, sleeked their feathers, rolled their heads to fixate upward, and produced aerial alarm calls. In response to the raccoon image, the male chickens moved rapidly to the other end of the cage and produced ground alarm calls while turning round and round (Evans, Evans, & Marler, 1993). It thus appears that many types of birds are able to express alarm calls indicating emotional states that designate to other animals the general nature of the type of predator that has appeared.

How Tigers Communicate by Scent

Thirty-three free-ranging tigers were studied over a 4-year period in the Royal Chitwan National Park in Nepal. Each animal wore a radio collar and could also be identified visually. Because tigers live within fairly clear-cut boundaries within which they hunt and mate, a group of investigators were interested in identifying both the methods of marking boundaries and the functions of the boundaries (Smith, McDougal, & Miquelle, 1989).

To learn the answers to these questions, the investigators recorded five types of marking behavior: (a) spraying of urine on trees; (b) scraping feces, urine, and anal gland secretions on rocks and sand; (c) flattening of vegetation; (d) clawing on trees; and (e) rubbing sprayed trees with their cheeks. It was found that urine spraying of trees was the most frequent territory marker, and the scent was detectable by humans for as long as 3 weeks after spraying. Male tigers generally marked their boundaries more frequently during the

FIGURE 10.1. Sharing by ravens depends largely on communication. (a) Although resident adults try to defend a carcass, (b) a lone juvenile (identified by a white wing tab) will eventually discover it. (c) That juvenile relays the location of the carcass to a roost of other ravens, and (d) the group flies to the carcass and overthrows the resident adults. That cooperation helps young ravens eat consistently, even when food is scarce. From "Why Ravens Share," by B. Heinrich and J. Marzluff, 1995, *American Scientist, 83*, p. 348. Copyright 1995 by The Scientific Research Society. Reprinted with permission.

periods when female tigers were in estrus (i.e., in heat). Consistent with this observation is the fact that most aggressive encounters between male tigers occurred when they were in the vicinity of a female tiger in estrus. Although tigers marked along a network of trails used for travel through their territories, marking was generally more intense at potential contact points between adjoining territories. It thus appears that these various forms of marking behavior are communications between one tiger and another that establish and maintain territorial boundaries as well as express claims on females in reproductive status.

Communicating Aggressive Intent in Elephants

Male African elephants over the age of 25 years show periods of sexual activity and other periods of inactivity. During the sexually active period, there are shorter times during which the male is in a heightened state of aggression, a period called *musth*. During the periods of musth, males are more successful in obtaining mates.

In a study carried out in Amboseli National Park in Kenya, Poole (1989) made observations of a population of 670 elephants, which were all known individually. The aim of her research was to determine the extent to which elephants are able to estimate aggressive intent in each other.

A series of aggressive (agonistic) encounters were observed between pairs of male elephants. Each encounter began with a threat (such as ear waving, chasing, or tusking) by the dominant animal and was concluded when the subordinate animal began to retreat. It was found that generally, when neither of the elephants was in musth, the larger of the two animals was dominant. However, when one elephant of the interacting pair was in musth and the other was not, in most cases the animal in musth was dominant regardless of size. In the relatively few cases in which two musth males challenged each other, serious fights resulted with several deaths and serious injuries. All fights ended with the dominant animal chasing the subordinate one.

What do these findings mean? The ability of small musth males to dominate larger nonmusth males indicates that the musth males are signaling their aggressive intent and that their aggressive fighting abilities are somehow recognized by the other animals. Because the fighting ability of males in the herd changes frequently owing to the presence or absence of musth, all elephants must be able to continually reassess their relative abilities in each contest or encounter. Thus communication of aggressive intent and potential must occur during everyday encounters among elephants.

GENITAL DISPLAY AS COMMUNICATION

Genital display is another form of emotion communication used by animals and humans. Genital displays are often seen in squirrel monkeys. Such displays consist of penile erection, separation of the legs, and specific vocalizations. The displays may be seen in young infants directed at a cagemate; sometimes a squirrel monkey will display to its own image in a mirror. Dominant animals often display to all males but rarely to females (Ploog, 1992). Genital displays appear to be emotional signals that indicate dominance status.

It has also been shown that penile erections can be elicited by mild electrical stimulation of certain parts of the brain; for example, by electrical stimulation of anterior and midline thalamus, the mamillary bodies, cingulate gyrus, and certain hippocampal projections to the septum. In fact, the system from which penile erection can be elicited is widely distributed in the brain. Ploog (1992) interpreted this to indicate that these sexual functions are intimately involved with social behavior, and, in fact, play a regulatory role in maintaining group cohesion.

It is also well known that genital displays in men are widely recognized as signals of power and strength. In many parts of the world, figures with large phalluses were placed in front of homes as guardians. In New Guinea, penis sheaths are still worn (see Figure 10.2). In Japan and India, there are phallus shrines where people go to pray for fertility and strength.

FIGURE 10.2. Some examples of genital displays in man: (*left*) two Papuans of New Guinea; (*next to them*) a Greek God from the National Museum in Athens; (*right*) a house guardian from one of the groups of the South Pacific. From "Ethological Foundations of Biological Psychiatry," by D. Ploog. In H. M. Emrich and W. Wiegland (Eds.), *Integrative Biological Psychiatry*, 1992, p. 13. Copyright 1992 by Springer. Reprinted with permission.

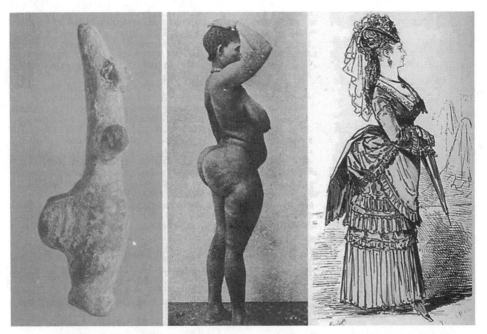

FIGURE 10.3. Examples of sexual signals based on the female form: (*left*) a prehistoric mother goddess figure; (*middle*) a Hottentot woman; (*right*) an illustration of a woman wearing a Victorian bustle. From *Manwatching: A Field Guide to Human Behavior*, by D. Morris, 1977, p. 234. Copyright 1977 by Harry N. Abrams. Reprinted with permission.

Genital displays are only one kind of gender signal. Almost any sexually distinctive characteristic of the male or female can become a sexual signal. With regard to females, their buttocks tend to be more rounded than those of the males and to protrude more. This is also true of the rounded shape of the breasts. This female gender signal can be seen in extreme form in prehistoric mother goddess figures, in Hottentot women, and in women who wore the Victorian bustles (see Figure 10.3).

CAN MONKEYS READ EMOTIONS ON THE FACE?

A study by Miller, Caul, and Mirsky (1967) examined monkeys' ability to read facial expressions. Three rhesus monkeys were trained to press a key to avoid an electric shock each time a certain light went on. When this conditioned avoidance response was well established, the following procedure was introduced. One monkey was arbitrarily selected as the "sender" and another was the "receiver." The receiver monkey could see only the face of the sender monkey on closed-circuit television but could not see the signal light indicating that a shock was coming. The sender monkey was exposed to the signal light indicating that an electric shock was coming. The receiver monkey could avoid getting a shock if he pressed a key within 6 seconds after the stimulus came on. To do this, the receiver monkey would have to be able to recognize a change in the facial expression of the sender monkey (presumably an indication of fear) when the signal light appeared.

During the initial testing of individual monkeys, each one made a correct response (pressed the key within 6 seconds after the signal light came on) in approximately 95% of the trials. When the new procedure was introduced, the percentage of correct avoidance responses of the receiver monkey watching the sender was 77%. This figure was based on all possible pairs, because each monkey had a turn being the sender as well as the receiver. This result clearly indicated that these rhesus monkeys were able to use the expressions on the faces of other monkeys as appropriate cues to influence their own behavior. This finding supports the view proposed by Darwin that facial expressions are communication signals between social animals.

Further important findings resulted from this experiment. Three additional monkeys were tested who had been separated from their mothers at birth and who were then maintained in totally isolated closed cages for the first year of their lives. When tested by themselves, these animals learned to avoid the shock by pressing on the key just as well as did the normal monkeys. When they were placed in receiver roles, their behavior was markedly inferior to those of the normal monkeys.

In other words, when an "isolate" monkey was the sender of facial cues and a normal monkey was the receiver, the percentage of correct avoidance responses was 62%, or slightly less than with two normal monkeys. This indicated that the isolate monkey was sending more or less familiar facial expression cues to the normal receiver monkey. However, when either an isolate monkey or a normal monkey was the sender and an isolate monkey was the receiver, the percentage of avoidance responses was only around 8%. These results imply that monkeys who were socially isolated during the first year of their life tend to show fairly normal facial expressions but are greatly deficient in recognizing the facial expressions of other monkeys. This emphasizes the point that the expression of emotions and the recognition of emotions are two different processes and are affected by different variables. This study thus identifies some of the factors that influence both the expression and recognition of emotions.

CHEMICAL COMMUNICATIONS

Odors are also extensively used as forms of signals. In some animals, the organs of smell are so sensitive that both species and individual identification are possible. Odors that produce emotional reactions are called *pheromones,* and they are widely used by most species, including insects. They have been found to produce alarm reactions, sexual attraction, grooming, exchanging of food, and identification of members of ones own family, caste, or species.

Pheromones in Animals

Although a good deal of research on communications has been concerned with facial expressions and sound signals, for most organisms the ability to sense chemicals in the environment around them is important for survival. Even bacteria respond to certain chemicals, moving toward food and away from toxic substances.

Pheromones are the chemical messages sent and received within the members of a single species. Thus, the spray produced by a skunk to protect itself from a predatory animal is not a pheromone. Agosta (1992), an organic chemist, reviewed much of the research on chemical communications; the material reported here is based on his account.

When an injured minnow is introduced into a tank of water in which other minnows are present, the other fish show a "fright" (or alarm) reaction; they swim away and hide, leap at the surface, or sink to the bottom and become very still. It was eventually discovered that even mild mechanical damage to the skin will cause certain cells of the skin of the fish to discharge the chemical into the water, which in turn produces the alarm reaction. This chemical pheromone is only one of thousands of such chemicals that influence the behavior of the other members of a given species.

Agosta (1992) described the various effects of the chemical messages in human terms. The alarm substance signals "Danger—get out of here!" and bombykol (a pheromone) is the female moth's message "come to me." Other pheromones bear messages such as "The queen is in the hive and all is well," "produce more sex hormones," "we are under attack," and "I am pregnant" (p. 4).

Pheromones have been discovered on algae, mold, and bacteria. They generally function to attract free-swimming male gametes to the females. Studies of invertebrates (such as the sea anemone, nematodes, earthworms, and arthropods like shrimps and lobsters), have revealed alarm pheromones and also sexual attraction, aggregation, trail, and aggression-provoking pheromones.

Of the nearly 1 million insects that have been described, all are believed to secrete pheromones, but only several hundred have actually been identified thus far. Pheromone mimicry has also been discovered. Spiders may mimic a moth's sex attractant to attract moths to their webs. Orchids that depend on insects for their fertilization secrete pheromones that attract insects that attempt to mate with the flower. A bee colony contains a large variety of pheromones. Some influence reproduction, others influence cell construction, and some repel worker bees. Others are alarm signals that mark the site of an attack by an intruder and attract other bees to attack the intruder. Similar sets of pheromones have been discovered in fish, snakes, and some birds.

There are over 4,000 species of mammals; most are nocturnal and have a highly developed sense of smell. The chemical signals of mammals are mainly expressed through urine, feces, and glands in the sex organs and skin.

Are There Pheromones in Humans?

There is less evidence for the existence of pheromones in humans, but some research is consistent with this idea. In one study, investigators blindfolded new mothers immediately after delivery. Each mother was then presented with her own child and two other newborn babies. The mothers were able to identify their own child 61% of the time (vs. 33% expected by chance). Breast-feeding infants, in turn, also became familiarized to their mother's odor even as they transferred their odors to her (see Figure 10.4). When fathers were exposed to the same procedure, their judgments were what would be expected by chance (Agosta, 1992).

Other evidence of the operation of hormones in humans is the phenomenon of *menstrual synchrony*. In one study, a group of "donor" women collected pads of sweat from their underarms and kept careful records of their menstrual cycles. These pads were then used to prepare alcohol solutions of the chemical present in the sweat. A small amount of this solution was applied to the upper lip of each woman in a new group of recipient women three times a week for 13 weeks. A control group of women received only applications of alcohol as a stimulus. After this period of time, the recipients exposed to the sweat solutions had menstrual cycles that had shifted toward the timing represented by the test stimuli. No changes took place in the cycles of the control women. This suggests that the pheromones in humans may have some effect on social bonding and attachment behavior.

In a similar study using alcohol solutions obtained from male underarm sweat, the extracts were applied to women who had unusually long or short menstrual cycles (less than 26 or more than 32 days). After about 14 weeks of exposure to the male extract, the cycles of these women approached the normal cycle length of 29.5 days. No such effect was found in the controls (Agosta, 1992). These studies suggest the possible role of

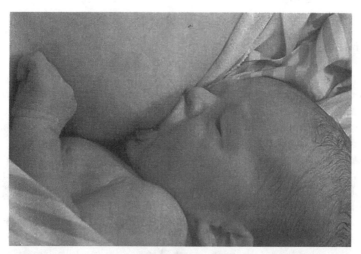

FIGURE 10.4. A breast-feeding infant becomes familiar with its mother's odor and also transfers its own odor to her. From *Chemical Communication: The Language of Pheromones*, by W. C. Agosta, 1992, p. 152. Copyright 1992 by Scientific American Library. Reprinted with permission.

pheromones in synchronizing and regularizing the menstrual cycle of women, which may in turn affect mood states.

In humans, perfumes have been highly desired and used for thousands of years mainly in connection with attempts to create sexual attraction. The basis of many perfumes is either musk obtained from musk deer or a strong odorant obtained from anal glands of the African civet (a member of the cat family). These odors are believed to be types of steroids, but the evidence is not yet in.

CONFLICTS AMONG EMOTIONAL DISPLAYS

Body Posture as a Signal of Conflict

Variations in body postures are also widely used as signals. Figure 10.5 shows the following four distinctive postures in the zebra finch (*Peophila guttata*). Posture (a) is an *aggressive* posture associated both with threat and with pecking behavior; (b) shows a *fearful* vertical posture, the more vertical the posture, the greater the probability of flight. Posture (c) is seen both in a bird *at rest* and in a *frightened* bird that cannot escape; and (d) is a *courtship* posture that is seen just prior to mounting (Morris, 1954). An important point that should be made about these postures, and one that is returned to later, is that intermediate postures are possible. Such intermediate postures reflect the existence of conflicts between impulses—for example, conflict between the impulse to attack and to flee or conflict between the impulse to mount and to withdraw.

This idea of postures reflecting conflicts is more clearly seen in Figure 10.6. Observations of cats in a variety of situations led Leyhausen (1956) to conclude that postural changes of cats expressed the interaction of both fear and aggression. When fear was low, aggressiveness was expressed in one way; however, when fear was high, aggressiveness was expressed by the highly arched back and uplifted tail.

This same idea has been reported in regard to dogs (Lorenz, 1966). Figure 10.7 shows expressions reflecting variations in the intensity of threat shown by a dog. There is also a graded series of changes reflecting increasing likelihood of submissive behavior. These tendencies may simultaneously exist to varying degrees, so that any given facial expression is a transitory resultant of the interaction or conflict of two opposing tendencies.

In black-headed gulls, the conflict between courting and fighting involves the interaction of impulses to attack and impulses to withdraw. In the *oblique* and *aggressive upright* displays shown in Figure 10.8, impulses to attack predominate, but the intensity of motivation is higher with the oblique display. In the *forward* and *anxiety upright* displays, the predominant impulse favors withdrawal. When the impulse to attack is balanced by an equally strong impulse to withdraw, the gull shows the so-called *choking* display. These observations further support the idea that each expression, or display, shown by an animal is most likely a result of the interaction of two or more conflicting impulses.

Displays as Deceptions

Actual fights between animals tend to be relatively rare. Fights are too dangerous for both parties; even the victor may be injured and thus have a lessened chance of survival. Therefore, the most successful way for male animals to achieve dominant status and access to females is through intimidations and threats.

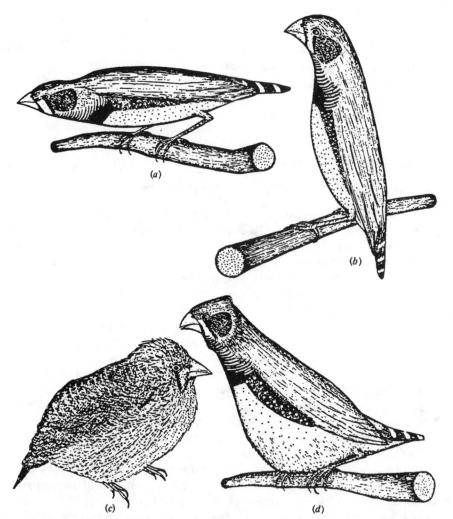

FIGURE 10.5. Distinctive displays in the zebra finch that communicate different affective states: (a) the *aggressive* horizontal posture associated with threats and pecking behavior; (b) the *frightened* sleeked vertical posture; (c) the *submissive* fluffed display; (d) the *courtship* display. From "The Reproductive Behavior of the Zebra Finch (*Peophila guttata*) With Special Reference to Pseudofemale Behavior and Displacement," by D. J. Morris, 1954, *Behaviour, 6,* p. 293. Copyright 1954 by Animal Behaviour Society. Reprinted with permission.

Observations of animals in natural settings indicate that certain features of an animal tend to exaggerate an animal's capabilities or camouflage an animal's weaknesses. For example, male animals with the largest antlers, fangs, or tusks tend to be victors in encounters with males of the same species. To exaggerate apparent size, many animals have evolved face ruffs or beards (or manes). This is illustrated in Figure 10.9.

It is interesting that beards or ruffs only appear on adult males. This is apparently because the most serious conflicts over rank occur among sexually mature males, and the beards represent an aspect of a more general threat display.

FIGURE 10.6. "Aggressive" (threat) and "fear" expressions in the cat. Aggressive postures increase in degree from left to right, and fear postures increase in degree from top down. Almost any observed expression is a combination of both aggression and fear in varying degrees. From *Animal Behavior: A Synthesis of Ethology and Comparative Psychology*, by R. A. Hinde, 1966, p. 262. Copyright 1966 by McGraw-Hill. Reprinted with permission.

EVOLUTION AND COMMUNICATION

The various illustrations of animal communication that have been reviewed indicate that some forms of communication between individuals occur at almost all phylogenetic levels. From an evolutionary point of view, what is the most useful way to interpret these observations?

This question has been extensively examined by Owings and Morton (1998), and the discussion in this section is based on their book. From an evolutionary point of view, why have communication signals appeared in so many species of animals? Owings and Morton suggested that animals need to constantly assess their environments, and signals are used to manage their circumstances. Signaling is favored by natural selection because it substitutes for behavior that is potentially more risky, such as fighting.

Rather than think of communication as a transfer of information from one animal to another, we may consider communication as a two-way process. The actions of each

FIGURE 10.7. "Aggressive" and "fear" expressions in the dog. Aggressive expressions increase from left to right, and fear expressions, indicating readiness to flee, increase from the top down. Different facial expressions in the dog result from the combination of different intensities of fighting and flight impulses. From *Love and Hate,* by I. Eibl-Eibesfeldt, 1971, p. 45. Copyright 1971 by Holt, Rinehart, & Winston. Reprinted with permission.

individual are both cause and effect of the other's behavior. Natural selection favors those individuals who are able to use signals (or displays) to manage the behavior of others in pursuit of their own interest in maintaining their own fitness. According to Owings and Morton (1998), "Animals are negative-feedback systems that work to manage conditions in their own interests" (p. 55). In most situations, the goals of the signaler and the receiver (or perceiver) are different. This implies that animals must assess the information they are offered with skepticism. This is why communication is often a continuing two-way process rather than a single instance of a receiver getting a signal.

In the studies described earlier on vervet monkey calls, it was demonstrated that the monkeys make a typical sound (a *bark*) when they see a leopard, and that audio playback of barks elicited behavior similar to that evoked by the sight of a leopard. A follow-up study by Cheney and Seyforth (1988) examined the effects of repeatedly playing back the barks in the absence of leopards. Although the vervet monkeys still responded to the same signal given by other animals, they began to ignore the playbacks, implying that context was as important as signal.

Owings and Morton (1998) proposed that *assessment* is the basis for all communication systems: "Assessment may be based on anything that another individual does,

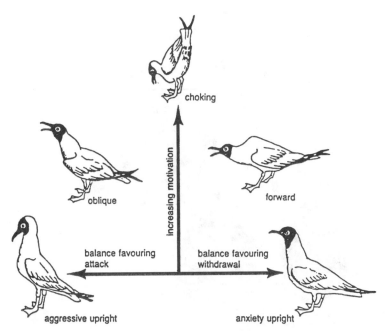

FIGURE 10.8. The displays of the black-headed gull used in courtship and fighting are believed to express different degrees of attack and withdrawal. In the "oblique" or "aggressive upright" displays, aggression predominates. The "forward" and "anxiety upright" positions imply withdrawal impulses. The "choking" display seems to represent a balance of strong attack and withdrawal impulses. From *The Psychology of Fear and Stress*, by J. A. Gray, 1988, p. 241. Copyright 1988 by Cambridge University Press. Reprinted with permission.

e.g., eating, breeding, excreting, fleeing, flying, fighting, sleeping, grooming, walking, etc. If it is used regularly for assessment, it becomes a potential communicative activity such as a signal" (p. 50).

Some examples may help clarify these points. California ground squirrels stimulate a rattlesnake to rattle by kicking earth at it. This is done because squirrels use the sound of rattling to assess the snake's body size and body temperature, two factors that determine how dangerous the snake is to the squirrel's pups.

Female lions roar to maintain contact with other members of their pride. This sound, however, may attract the attention of males who will often kill lion cubs fathered by other males. To prevent this from happening, the females roar together, which acts to intimidate the males.

With regard to vocal displays, because larger individuals usually win in aggressive contests, natural selection increases the likelihood that vocalizations will reflect size. Because larger animals can produce lower frequency sounds than smaller animals (e.g., bass drum vs. snare drum), low, harsh sounds (growls) are often found in nature as signals of potential aggression. Table 10.2 illustrates this observation. Generally, birds and mammals in aggressive emotional states use sounds that are low in frequency, whereas animals in fearful or appeasing states use higher frequency sounds, a point that has been discussed in chapter 8. When both fear and aggression are in conflict, the animal's calls are both harsh and increasing in frequency. Distress screaming is often used by animals to try

FIGURE 10.9. To exaggerate apparent size, many animals have evolved face ruffs or beards (or manes). These are seen only on adult males and are aspects of a general threat display. From "The Evolution of Menace," by R. D. Guthrie, 1973, *Saturday Review of the Sciences, 1,* p. 25. Copyright 1973 by Beeghly. Reprinted with permission.

TABLE 10.2. Animal Sounds Used in Hostile or Friendly Appeasing Contexts

Species	Hostile	Friendly or appeasing
Mallard	Loud harsh *gaeck*	Soft whimpers
Sparrow hawk	Harsh chitter	Whine
Solitary sandpiper	Harsh, metallic sound	Rising shrill whistle
Burrowing owl	*Rasp*	*Eep*
Barn swallow	Deep, harsh stutter	Whine call
Dwarf jay	Harsh rasp	*Shreeup*
Common crow	Growl	Soft and plaintive
Guinea pig	Grunt, snort	Squeak, wheet
Spiny rat	Growl	Twitter, whimper
Pocket mouse	Low, scratchy growl	Whining squeal
Uinta ground squirrel	Growl	Squeal
Maned wolf	Growl	Whine
African elephant	Roaring, rumbling sounds	High frequency sounds
Indian rhinoceros	Roaring, rumbling	Whistling
Pig	Growl	Squeal
Spider monkey	Growl, roar, cough	Chirps, twitter, squeak
Rhesus monkey	Roar, growl	Scratch, squeak

Note. From *Animal Vocal Communication: A New Approach,* by D. H. Owings & E. S. Morton, 1998, p. 243. Copyright 1998 by Cambridge University Press. Reprinted with permission.

to influence a predator that is attacking them. Distress calls are adaptive for several reasons: (a) They may startle a predator into letting go; (b) they may attract the attention of other conspecifics to mob (or attack) the predator; or (c) they may attract a larger predator to compete and possibly allow escape. The adaptive function of a given signal is not always easy to determine; therefore, creative research methods are generally needed. Owings and Morton (1998) concluded that the assessment/management approach

> views communication in terms of the pursuit of self-interest by all participants, the outcomes of their individual regulatory efforts, the mutual exploitation between assessment and management (often identified as a conflict between assessor and manager), and their equal roles in adaptation. (p. 234)

LANGUAGE IN ANIMALS

During the past three decades, several attempts have been made to teach humanlike communication to the great apes. When attempts to teach spoken words were unsuccessful, various researchers beginning with Bernice and Allen Gardner (1978, 1984) tried to teach chimpanzees American Sign Language. Their first chimpanzee trainee was called Washoe, and she acquired her signs in two ways: first by imitating her tutors, and second, by having her hands shaped by her trainers.

On the basis of their experiences with Washoe, the Gardners began a new project with two young chimpanzees, Maja and Pili, who were exposed to a sign language environment from birth. These chimpanzees began to show signing behavior in the 3rd month, and one of them began using two-sign combinations by the age of 6 months.

In an interesting contrast, deaf children of deaf parents have been reported to begin to sign at about 6 months and to use combined signs at about 14 months. Both apes and deaf children occasionally invent signs, and both apes and human children engage in babbling (i.e., make apparently meaningless noises; Miles, 1978).

Do any of the words signed by Washoe refer to emotions? Exhibit 10.1 is a selection of 23 words taken from a longer list of 85 words used by Washoe. Some of these signs appear to refer to emotions, and most imply an internal motivational state. Examples are *good, please, sorry, sweet, dirty, help, hurt,* and *kiss.*

Koko was another primate, a gorilla, who was exposed to a sign language environment from the age of 1 year. Koko was reported to have a vocabulary of about 100 signs after 30 months of training at age 3½ years. A deaf child studied in a similar way had acquired about 132 signs by age 3. At the age of 4½ years, Koko had acquired a signing vocabulary of 225 signs (Patterson, 1978). Exhibit 10.2 lists a set of terms in Koko's vocabulary after 50 months of training. The signs listed in Exhibit 10.1 were also in Koko's vocabulary. The following are examples of signs reflecting inner states and emotions: *kiss, skin pinch, bad, hot, mad, no, frown, like, smile,* and *happy.*

On the basis of her research on Koko, Patterson (1978) concluded that language is a poorly defined communication process that may take many forms. The fact that apes cannot be taught a vocal language does not necessarily mean that they have no language. Anatomical limitations in the apes should not lead to the assumption that apes do not have the neurological and cognitive capacities for language. Animal communication is often quite complex and depends on sound, posture, movement, facial expression, smell, and context. Kingdon (1993) pointed out that dominance and submission relations are quickly recognized through eye contact and eye movements in both apes and humans.

EXHIBIT 10.1. SIGNS IN WASHOE'S VOCABULARY THAT SUGGEST AFFECTIVE STATES

Clean	Please	Kiss
Come-gimme	Sorry	Smell
Drink	Tickle	Yours
Eat-food	Sweet	Good
You	Hurry	Dirty
Listen	Funny	Look
Help	Me	Hug
Out	Hurt	

Note. This list was selected from 85 words used by Washoe that met strict criteria of linguistic use after 36 months of training. From "Linguistic Capabilities of a Lowland Gorilla," by F. Patterson. In F. C. C. Peng (Ed.), *Sign Language and Language Acquisition in Man and Ape*, 1978, p. 168. Copyright 1978 by AAAS Selected Symposium. Reprinted with permission.

The most thorough analysis of language in apes may be found in the book by Savage-Rumbaugh, Shanker, and Taylor (1998). A good deal of their research was carried out with a bonobo named Kanzi. It was only about 25 years ago that primatologists recognized that bonobos were different from chimpanzees although their appearance was quite similar.

EXHIBIT 10.2. SIGNS IN KOKO'S VOCABULARY THAT SUGGEST AFFECTIVE STATES

Me	Good	Come-gimme
You	Hot	Frown
Myself	Mad	Help
Hurt	Sad	Help myself
Kiss	Sorry	Hug-love
Injection	Sweet	Like
Skin-pinch	Stink	Play
Taste	Thirsty	Please
Bad	Can't	Smile
Dirty	No	Happy
Scratch		

Note. This list was selected from 243 words used by Koko after 50 months of training that were used spontaneously and appropriately half the number of days or more in a given month. From "Linguistic Capabilities of a Lowland Gorilla," by F. Patterson. In F. C. C. Peng (Ed.), *Sign Language and Language Acquisition in Man and Ape*, 1978, p. 177. Copyright 1978 by AAAS Selected Symposium. Reprinted with permission.

Chimpanzees tend to be domineering and aggressive, travel in relatively small groups, and show sexual bonding only during the few days a month when females are sexually receptive. Chimpanzees have war parties that have killed chimpanzees of nearby groups as well as infants. In contrast, bonobos live in large groups of nearly equal numbers of males and females. They show few signs of overt aggression toward either males or females and show very high levels of sexual behavior on an almost ongoing basis.

Savage-Rumbaugh, who worked with Kanzi for many years, had no hesitation in describing him as having a short temper, intense emotions, an impulsive personality, and empathy. Because of the vertical posture of humans, the position of the tongue and larynx permits the production of lower pitched, more discriminable vowel sounds. The nasal cavity can be completely closed off from the oral cavity (velar closure). This allows the production of nasal sounds (e.g., "m" and "n") and consonants (e.g., "k" and "g"). These functions are not available in apes. When attempts to teach apes a vocal language failed, it occurred to some investigators to use the sign language or a computer language based on touching of symbols. Figure 10.10 shows Sue Savage-Rumbaugh with Kanzi and the various symbols that were used placed on a computer keyboard. With this method, the subject could simply touch a word symbol (called a *lexigrama*) as a substitute for speaking a word.

FIGURE 10.10. Sue Savage-Rumbaugh showing Kanzi, a bonobo, the computer board containing the lexigrams. Kanzi has shown evidence of comprehension of a large vocabulary of human words as well as an ability to communicate many messages describing his own mental states. From *Apes, Language and the Human Mind,* by S. Savage-Rumbaugh, S. G. Shanker, and T. J. Taylor, 1998 (cover page). Copyright 1998 by Oxford University Press. Reprinted with permission.

Four chimpanzees in addition to Kanzi who were studied by this method—Lana, Sherman, Austin, and Ai—were able to develop vocabularies of between 50 and 150 symbols. By pressing the symbols in the proper order, they could turn on music, watch slides, open a window, cause food and drinks to be offered, and invite people to play. Lana was able to create the sentence, "Please person move M & M into room."

Kanzi, the bonobo, had a vocabulary longer than the 250 signs that were on the computer keyboard. He used vocalizations as well as gestures. For example, he made twisting motions with his hand to ask that someone open a bottle for him. He also rapidly learned to use the lexigrams for *good* and *bad*. He would, for example, "announce his intent to be bad before biting a hole in his ball, tearing up the telephone or taking an object away from someone" (Savage-Rumbaugh et al., 1998, p. 52). On one occasion, Kelly, one of Kanzi's handlers, cut her knee on a can thrown by Kanzi. She cried in pain. Kanzi looked at where he thought the wound was and indicated that another person should pour water on the wound. He then tried to clean the cut. This apparent sign of empathy suggests that Kanzi can recognize that different people have feelings of their own. He can also indicate his feelings. For example, he was able to get the message across that he had a sore throat.

Kanzi also had some simple grammatical rules. When he combined several lexigrams, he placed the goal or object first and his action (chase, carry) last. When he combined a symbol with a gesture, he tended to place the gesture after the symbol.

As observations on Kanzi continued, it became evident that he was able to understand and respond appropriately to complex grammatical sentences. Some requests were so unusual that he could not have responded appropriately without understanding what was said. Some examples follow:

> Put a toothbrush in the lemonade.
> Put the raisins in the shoe.
> Go scare Matata with the toy snake.
> Make the snake bite Linda.
> Put on the monster mask and scare Linda.
> Use the toothbrush and brush Liz's teeth.
> Pour the Coke in the lemonade.
> Hide the toy gorilla.

Kanzi carried out 72% of the requests correctly. Savage-Rumbaugh concluded that Kanzi's ability to understand language is much greater than his ability to produce it (with lexigrams). This is not surprising in view of the fact that for Kanzi to communicate he must point to a rather limited number of symbols. Talking is therefore more difficult than understanding. Bear in mind that even in humans, language is primarily learned by listening rather than speaking. Children's comprehension skills far exceed their production skills.

Kanzi's language behavior had been quite similar to that of a young child to whom we are generally willing to attribute states of mind and emotions. The findings obtained from the study of Kanzi have been confirmed by research on at least three other bonobos.

SUMMARY

The various examples that have been given concerning emotional display behaviors, calls, and signals shown by animals suggest some important conclusions. First, displays generally are related to important events in the life of each animal, events such as threats, attacks, alarms, courtship, mating, social contact, isolation or separation, greetings, appeasement, dominance, submission, and play. Of particular importance is the relation of the display to sex and social rank. Second, it is evident that these displays communicate information from one animal to another, and although the amount of information may be limited, the displays have some impact on the survival prospects of the animals involved. Third, most displays appear to be species characteristics that generally appear even in young animals without much opportunity for learning. Most animals immediately seem to recognize these species-typical displays and react appropriately. These observations suggest that there is a genetic basis for many of the signals. Fourth, the various communication signals often occur in combination with one another. Impulses to attack can be expressed at the same time as impulses to withdraw; impulses to mate can be expressed at the same time as impulses to dominate. These conflicting impulses produce expressions that reflect the conflicts. Fifth, display behaviors express impulses of various kinds. However, one must use indirect evidence to decipher the meaning of the expressions that are observed; it is not always easy to interpret the survival implications of a particular display or to know exactly what impulses are involved. Much of this is also relevant to humans.

Last and most important in the present context, these illustrations and the conclusions drawn from them reveal some important things about emotions. Display behaviors tell us something about emotions, but they are not emotions. Displays are outward behavioral expressions of the complex states we call emotions. Emotions are the states we infer from impulses to actions, internal states, and triggering stimuli. Emotions are about the important events in an animal's life related to issues of survival. They generally occur in special circumstances, are fairly transient, often involve brief but intense arousal, and act to help the animal return to a more *normal* unaroused state, that is, the state that existed before the triggering stimulus occurred. From this point of view, the whole complex pattern of inner and outer activity acts to deal with emergencies and tries to restore the homeostatic balance within an organism. Emotions are not just feelings but may be conceptualized as homeostatic devices (patterns of inner and outer action) that are designed to maintain a relatively (normal) steady state of the individual in the face of environmental emergencies. Emotions represent transitory adjustment reactions that function to return the organism to a stable, effective relationship with its immediate environment when that relationship is disrupted.

11

Emotions and the Brain

All plants and the most primitive animals get along well enough without nervous systems, for the distinctive nervous functions, that is, irritability, conductivity, and integration, are essential properties of all protoplasm.

C. Judson Herrick

PREVIEW

An extensive literature has developed over the years that is concerned with the brain and the role that it plays in emotion. To understand this literature, one needs to have some familiarity with the structure and function of the nervous system in general and with the biochemical systems that act as neurotransmitters. In addition, because much of this research is carried out on lower organisms, we need a sense of the extent to which the nervous systems of lower and higher animals are related. We need also to approach this research literature with a critical mind, particularly in view of the problem of how we are to define the concept of emotion in a lower animal.

This chapter deals with these and other issues. It traces the development of the nervous system as we ascend the evolutionary scale. This is followed by a description of basic brain structures and systems that are believed to be involved in emotions. The chapter also presents an account of the major theories of how the brain is involved in emotions.

ANIMALS WITHOUT NERVOUS SYSTEMS: IS THE CONCEPT OF EMOTION RELEVANT?

In earlier chapters, we looked at some of the similarities in expressions of emotions in humans and lower animals. We have seen how animals express alarm, aggression, courtship, threats, affiliation, and play. We have seen how the biologist John Paul Scott (1980) has recognized a few major classes of adaptive behavior that are found in almost all species. He called these adaptations *ingestive behavior* (eating), *shelter-seeking behavior, agonistic* (fight-or-flight) *behavior, sexual behavior, care-soliciting behavior* (from a young animal toward its mother), *caregiving behavior* (from adults toward young organisms), *eliminative behavior* (getting rid of waste products or inner toxins), *allelomimetic* (imitative) *behavior,* and *exploratory* (including play) *behavior.* His point is that most organisms engage in these types of activities even though they do them in different ways. A cat cares for its kittens in a different way than a bird cares for its young, but the function of caring is the same in both. Similarly, an attack by a shark is different from an attack by a pit bull, yet both can be recognized as engaging in agonistic behavior.

These ideas may be summarized in the following way: To survive and maintain their populations, all organisms must find food, avoid injury, and reproduce their kind. This is as true of lower animals as it is of higher ones. The nature of the environment creates certain functional requirements for all organisms if they are to survive. Any organism must take in nourishment and eliminate waste products. It must distinguish between prey and predator and between a potential mate and a potential enemy. It must explore its environment and orient its sense organs appropriately as it takes in information about the beneficial and harmful aspects of its immediate world. And in organisms that are relatively helpless at birth and for a while thereafter, there must be ways of indicating the need for care and nurturance. The specific behaviors by which these functions are carried out vary widely throughout the animal kingdom, but the basic prototype functions remain the same (Plutchik, 1980). But the logic of these parallels should not stop at monkeys, cats, or ants. Several studies by molecular biologists have implied that we should expand our view of adaptive processes to encompass even single-celled organisms.

An Italian biologist, Nicola Ricci (1990), pointed out that every protozoan is a functional unit, and that single-celled organisms carry out a whole series of important activities, that is, feeding, reproduction, sexually related behavior, avoidance of danger, search for safety, colonization of new habitats, and predatory behavior. Ricci (1990) concluded: "Protozoon behavior . . . is the complex and variable adaptive response of protozoa to the problem of reconciling their necessities and activities with varied and constantly changing external conditions, by means of which response the organism equilibrates its relationship with the environment" (p. 1048).

A molecular biologist, Ursula Goodenough, has been studying the immune system for many years. She pointed out that a common metaphor used to describe infectious disease is warfare; bacteria or viruses launch an attack, and the immune system puts up a defense. But many pathogens do not take on the human body directly; they use deceptive techniques to get at their targets and survive. For example, some bacteria camouflage themselves so that the immune system does not recognize them as foreign (this is true for the HIV virus, which is one of the reasons it is so difficult to deal with). Another strategy of pathogens is a process by which it resembles a known substance and thus gets past the defenses (as in rabies). Goodenough (1991) added,

> The key discrimination made by the detection apparatus of the immune system is between self and nonself. The body continually asks, in effect, "Does this molecule belong to me, or is it part of an invading organism?" . . . If a molecule is recognized as self, it is spared; if it is perceived as nonself, destructive mechanisms are set in motion to kill the cell with which it is associated. (p. 347)

These ideas have been presented to suggest that organisms without nervous systems can still engage in relatively complex behaviors that are *functionally* similar to the complex behaviors seen in animals with nervous systems. If we think of aggression and defense as being related to emotions, then even very simple organisms can be said to show aggression and defense. If emotions are believed to apply to all living things, then they can be considered to be functional adaptations for dealing with life problems and emergencies. This view places less emphasis on subjective reports or feelings that are only available from normal human adults and that may not always be accurate. The extent to which such feelings are available to lower organisms is one that may never have a satisfactory answer. However, this functional way of thinking about emotions allows us to examine the possible relations between brain mechanisms at any phylogenetic level and emotions (broadly defined in terms of adaptations).

Following the same line of thinking, the neurophysiologist Paul MacLean (1986) pointed out that any organism of a complex, highly evolved type mimics what have been fundamental processes of individual cells over evolutionary times. These processes refer to internal signals of need for food to maintain metabolism, the presence of catabolites (waste products of metabolism) that need to be expelled, and the presence of stimuli outside the organism that need to be avoided or approached.

Finally, on this issue, we should consider the ideas of John Bonner (1962), a biologist writing about some of the fundamental ideas in biology. He pointed out that the cells of all animals and plants (with the exception of bacteria), from the smallest amoeba to the largest whale, are constructed roughly the same way. They all have a nucleus containing the chromosomes that hold the genes that are the basis of inheritance. This is surrounded by cytoplasm containing various particles. There are at least three functions: (a) The cell takes in fuel (food) and converts the energy of the fuel to cell movement; (b) the cell reproduces or duplicates parts of itself; and (c) the cell is responsive to environmental stimuli, including other cells. This third function is also called the *property of irritability,* which is a property of all cells even without an elaborated nervous system.

Bacteria are smaller than cells and have a simpler internal structure. Despite this, bacteria have evolved many different ways to obtain energy. Besides using carbohydrates, fats, and proteins, like most cells, some species of bacteria derive energy from photosynthesis, and some from the oxidation of sulfur, iron, or methane gas. Bacteria have two kinds of sexual mechanisms, one of which involves the union of "male" and "female" cells and the mixing of their genetic material.

Why did single-celled organisms become multicellular? The probable answer is that larger organisms can develop new methods for taking in food and new methods of movement, and they may enter new environments not easily available to smaller ones. But an increase in size creates problems as well, for example, how to establish support to facilitate movement. One experiment in size expansion led to the development of plants, the other to the development of animals, both invertebrates and vertebrates. This process took over a billion years to occur. Plants solved these problems by becoming immobile, sun-catching energy converters, whereas animals became mobile and obtained energy through preying on other animals or by converting the energy of plants.

As the increase in size occurred in animals, the need for a mobile animal to obtain information about its near and far environments increased. This led to the development of both sensory and motor systems with a corresponding need to integrate and coordinate their activities. Such integration was provided by an elementary nervous system that provided a specialization of the inherent property of irritability that all cells possess, along with an increase in the speed and complexity of signaling.

THE EVOLUTION OF THE BRAIN

Studies of evolution indicate that the single-celled protozoa gave rise to three lines: the sponges, the jellyfish, and the flatworms. From these simple combinations of cells eventually arose worms, arthropods (insects, spiders), and mollusks (snails, clams, squid), and then echinoderms (starfish), and finally the chordates (bilaterally symmetrical animals with spinal cords). Primitive examples of chordates are the jawless fish (hagfish and lamprey eels). Vertebrates that evolved later are sharks, amphibia (frogs and salamanders), reptiles, birds, and mammals.

In bilaterally symmetrical animals, several important changes took place in the nervous system in the course of evolution. At the head end of the animal where the mouth is and where a visual system began to develop, there was an increase in the relative number of neurons. This process is called *cephalization*, and it presumably increased the capacity of the organism to make coordinated movements in response to sensory inputs.

In vertebrates, the nervous system is made up of the spinal cord and brain, as well as peripheral nerves that extend from the central nervous axis to all parts of the body. A vertebrate animal is basically a series of segments (fundamentally like an earthworm), though this plan is not externally obvious. However, the spinal column remains segmented, and each segment has a pair of spinal nerves connecting sense organs and muscles. Simple coordinations are possible by this means. For example, in humans this would be illustrated by the knee-jerk reflex or by pupillary contraction in response to light. Visceral organs are partly regulated by such reflexes. Sweating, evacuation of bladder and bowel, and local vasoconstriction and vasodilatation in response to cutaneous cold and warmth are examples.

This form of integration is not adequate for the organism as a whole, and as a result several other neural structures were formed at the head end of the animal. One was

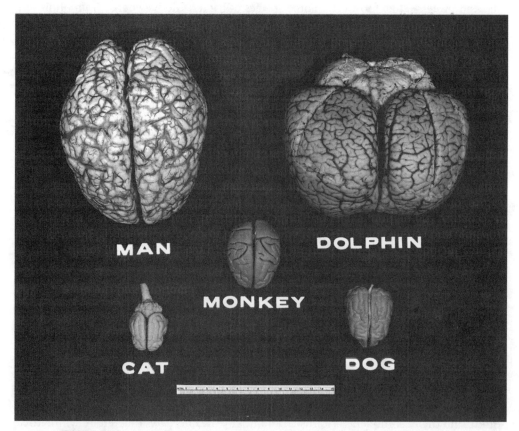

FIGURE 11.1. A comparison of brain size and fissuring in man, dolphin, monkey, cat, and dog.

TABLE 11.1. Comparison of Some Mammalian Brains

	Man	Chimpanzee	Macaque	Indian elephant	Cat	Rat	Mouse
Weight of entire brain (mean grams)	1400	435	80	4717	25	25	.02
Ratio of brain weight to body weight	0.02	0.007	0.05	0.0015	0.008	0.005	0.015

an expansion of the spinal cord to integrate breathing reflexes. Another was the development of the *reticular formation*, which exerts facilitating and inhibiting effects on nerve impulses received from all levels. Anatomically, reticular substance appears unspecialized and consists of a maze of interconnected nerve fibers, with cell bodies evenly distributed within it. However, modern neuroscience research has begun to identify a good deal of neurochemical and functional specialization, so that it is more accurate to consider the reticular formation as made up of multiple systems.

When mudfishes emerged from the water to become amphibians, fins were transformed into legs, and quadrupedal locomotion required more complicated coordination than swimming. This change from water to land began about 300 million years ago and led to the development of a basic brain pattern that has remained similar from reptiles to humans.

The key bilateral structures of the brain are the medulla, the midbrain, the thalamus, and the cerebral cortex. These structures have a hollow center or core called *ventricles* through which flows cerebrospinal fluid. The spaces inside the two cerebral hemispheres are called *lateral ventricles,* the space in the thalamus and hypothalamus is called the *third ventricle,* and the space inside the medulla is called the *fourth ventricle,* which in turn is continuous with the spinal canal. In higher vertebrates, the relative sizes and positions of these structures vary greatly, but the underlying plan remains the same.

Figure 11.1 shows photographs of the brains of five animals: the cat, dog, monkey, human, and dolphin. It is evident that the brain gets larger, and the outermost layer, the cortex, becomes increasingly fissured or convoluted. The brain of a human being weighs about 1,400 grams. In contrast, the brain of a kangaroo, which is of equal body weight to a man, weighs only 60 grams. Similarly, the cortex or outer layer of brain tissue of a man is about four times the area of that of a chimpanzee. The brain of a dolphin is larger than that of a human, but it should not be assumed that large brains necessarily mean very high cognitive capacities. Table 11.1 compares several animals on brain weight and on the ratio of brain weight to body weight. Figure 11.2 shows a comparison of brain size of four primates: a tarsier, lemur, chimpanzee, and human.

AN OVERVIEW OF THE MAJOR BRAIN STRUCTURES

As animals evolved and increased in size, some method of coordination of the animal's multiple activities and functions became necessary if it was to survive. Humans belong to the *phylum chordata*, animals with backbones. The nervous system of animals began as a tubelike structure (a neural tube) that had three enlargements: a *forebrain* (prosencephalon) associated with olfaction, a *midbrain* (mesencephalon) associated with

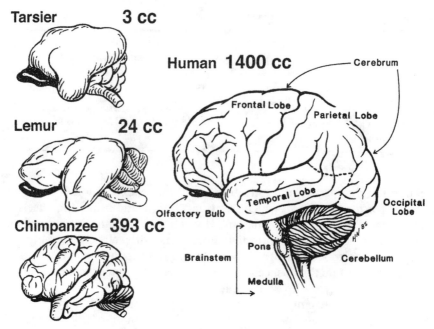

FIGURE 11.2. Lateral view of the brains of a tarsier, a lemur, a chimpanzee, and a human, showing differences in size of parts of the brain. From *Primate Adaptation and Evolution* (2nd ed.), by J. G. Fleagle, 1999, p. 307. Copyright 1999 by Academic Press. Reprinted with permission.

vision, and a *hindbrain* (rhombencephalon) associated with equilibrium and vibration. The complex brains of higher vertebrates have developed by superimposition of new structures (neural cells and fiber bundles) on this primordial brain. The brains of all existing vertebrates are built around a central tube (ventricles) through which cerebrospinal fluid constantly flows.

A *neocortex* first appears at the level of the reptiles. It receives neural impulses from all sensory modalities. The neocortex increases in size during the course of evolution and compresses the old (or paleo) cortex, which become identified as the *hippocampus* and the *pyriform* lobe. Further expansion of the neocortex occurs through the development of an intricate series of fissures and folds that greatly increases the surface area of the neocortex.

The brain and the spinal cord are connected by a series of ascending and descending nerve tracts. The cell bodies of these tracts are mostly located in the *medulla*, an enlargement at the rostral or head end of the spinal cord. Injury to these nuclei will affect respiration, heart rate, eye and facial movement, balance, and tongue movement.

The *pons* is a further continuation of the brain stem and contains ascending and descending fibers as well as nerve nuclei for cranial nerves concerned with chewing movement and salivation. The pons also contains generators for producing rapid eye movements during sleep.

The *midbrain* is the most anterior (frontal) extension of the brain stem that still shows the tubelike structure of the spinal cord. The dorsal (tectum or roof) part of the midbrain contains major relay nuclei for the auditory and visual systems in humans. Some information processing takes place there as well. The relay nuclei are called *inferior*

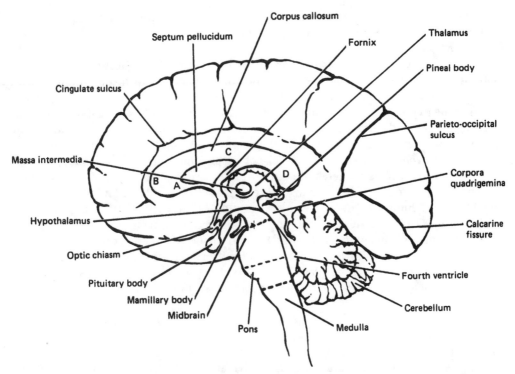

Corpus callosum

Septum pellucidum

Fornix

Thalamus

Pineal body

Cingulate sulcus

Parieto-occipital sulcus

Massa intermedia

C

B A

D

Corpora quadrigemina

Hypothalamus

Calcarine fissure

Optic chiasm

Pituitary body

Mamillary body

Midbrain

Pons

Medulla

Fourth ventricle

Cerebellum

FIGURE 11.3. Medial view of the left hemisphere showing major areas of the human brain. From *The Human Brain: A Photographic Guide,* by N. Gluhbegovic and T. H. Williams, 1980, p. 194. Copyright 1980 by Harper & Row. Reprinted with permission.

(meaning below) and *superior* (meaning above) *colliculi.* Other nuclei found in the midbrain control eye movement. The relative size of these various nuclei are generally related to the behavioral importance of the sensory or motor modality involved. Thus, bats that rely heavily on auditory information have enlarged inferior colliculi.

What is important to emphasize about these brain stem structures is that they are surprisingly uniform from fish to man, and they manage quite well to coordinate a lower animal's behavior. For example, if all brain tissue above the midbrain is removed in a cat, it can still walk to some degree, purr, eat if food is placed in the mouth, sleep, and show signs of emotional behavior. The midbrain also has important connections to the limbic system (described later). Some of the major brain structures in humans are shown in Figure 11.3 and are described below.

The *cerebellum* is a relatively large structure that is highly convoluted and lies over the pons. It is very well developed in birds. It receives connections from the auditory and visual systems, the vestibular (balance) system, some visceral organs, and the cerebral cortex or neocortex. It sends fibers to the thalamus. If removed, for example, in a cat, the animal shows uncoordinated movements.

The *thalamus* is an extremely complex structure with many nuclei, some of which receive inputs from sense organs and some from the neocortex, whereas others relay information to other centers of the brain. Information from the eye is relayed from the thalamus to the visual cortex, and information from the ear is relayed from the thalamus to auditory cortex. Some nuclei project to the reticular formation and some to the limbic system (described below). Neural information from the olfactory system does not pass through the thalamus. This structure has been called the "gateway to the neocortex" (Gellhorn & Loofbourrow, 1963).

The *hypothalamus* refers to a group of nuclei that lie adjacent to the ventral (bottom) part of the third ventricle. It has neural connections with the pituitary gland and has an important role in regulating the secretion of certain hormones in the body. Nuclei in the hypothalamus have influences on eating, drinking, sexual behavior, temperature regulation, and certain emotional expressions. It has connections with parts of the old cortex (such as the amygdala and hippocampus) and with the olfactory system.

The *cerebral cortex* is a layer of cells about 2–3 millimeters thick that surrounds the cerebrum. Fish have no cerebral cortex, amphibians have only a rudimentary one, and birds have a small one. In humans, it is estimated that 9 of the 12 billion neurons in the brain are found in the neocortex. Nerve impulses from each of the senses project to specific parts of the neocortex. In addition to sensory receiving areas, there are motor areas that control movements of the body muscles, and "association" cortex that is believed to have something to do with the elaboration of sensory information in so-called higher intellectual functions. There are several other brain structures and systems that play a major role in emotions. These are the amygdala and the limbic system.

The Amygdala

The *amygdala* is a part of the old cortex and consists of several nuclei that lie buried deep within the temporal lobe. In the rat, at least 34 nuclei have been identified (Alheid, de Olmos, & Beltramino, 1995). The amygdala has neural connections with many other parts of the brain, including the right somatosensory cortex, the hypothalamus, the septal area (an area near the hypothalamus in the midline or medial plane), the thalamus, the hippocampus, the olfactory system, and the reticular formation. Different inputs from most of the sensory systems of the cortex arrive at the amygdala. Some of these are shown in Figure 11.4.

Injury to the amygdala in humans through trauma or disease has been known to produce psychomotor epilepsy. Such epileptic seizures are brief periods of confusion with no subsequent memory for the period of the seizure. Electrical stimulation of the amygdala produces an array of autonomic reactions, including respiratory, cardiovascular, gastrointestinal, uterine, and pupillary changes.

More than 50 years ago, a study was done in which physiologists removed both temporal lobes in monkeys (including the amygdala) and discovered a wide variety of effects. Wild animals became emotionally unresponsive to visual, auditory, tactile, and taste stimuli and would eat feces and meat. Although they were not blind, the animals did not seem to recognize objects and placed all kinds of food and nonfood objects in their mouth. There was a decrease in their social activity and an increase in their sexual activity. They even attempted copulation with members of other species. The amygdalectomized animals decreased their social rank and became increasingly withdrawn. This pattern of changes has come to be known as the Kluver–Bucy syndrome, after the physiologists who first identified it. In an analysis of this phenomenon, Aggleton and Mishkin (1986) interpreted amygdalectomy as a way to disconnect cortical sensory systems from diencephalic nuclei that regulate emotional reactions.

The Kluver–Bucy syndrome has occasionally been reported in humans. A 19-year-old man with epilepsy underwent bilateral removal of the anterior temporal lobes. After the operation, this patient was unable to recognize close relatives, and he showed increased

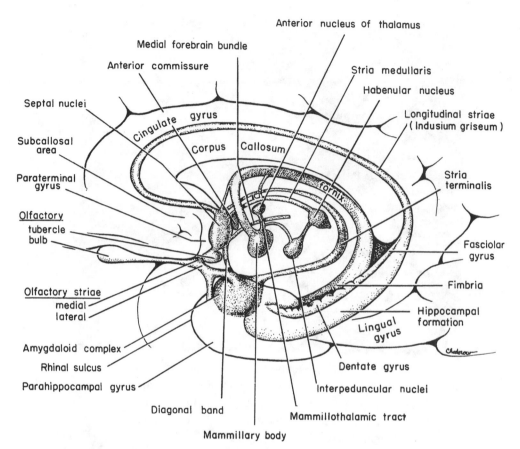

FIGURE 11.4. Semischematic drawing showing the anatomic relationship of amygdala, hippocampus, other components of the limbic system, and part of the olfactory pathway. From *Human Neuroanatomy*, by M. B. Carpenter and J. Sutin, 1985, p. 329. Copyright 1985 by Williams & Wilkins. Reprinted with permission.

sexual activity and appetite. At the same time, he revealed a severe memory deficit as well as a lack of emotional responsiveness (Clarke & Brown, 1990). In this patient both cortical areas and parts of the amygdala were removed.

There are few observations of removal or injury to the amygdala alone in humans. One of the few exceptions has been reported by Adolphs, Damasio, Travel, Cooper, and Damasio (2000). They studied a human patient (S.M.) who had selective bilateral damage to the amygdala. Figure 11.5 shows magnetic resonance images of the brain of this woman indicating that almost all of the damage is confined to the right and left amygdalas.

This patient did not show most of the signs of the Kluver–Bucy syndrome, but she did mislabel facial expressions of fear, surprise, and anger and was unable to adequately judge the similarity between different facial expressions. She was also unable to acquire a conditioned skin conductance response to an aversive loud noise. These observations did not mean that she experienced no fear or did not know verbally what fear is. Further research has indicated that lesions in the right parietal cortex reduced the ability of humans to recognize emotions from facial expressions (Adolphs, Damasio, Travel, Cooper,

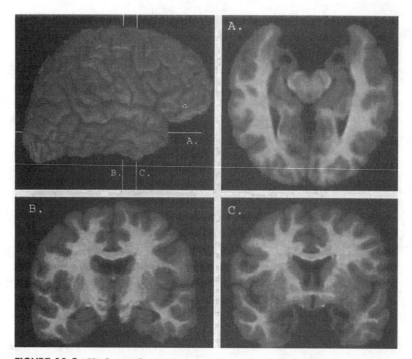

FIGURE 11.5. High-resolution magnetic resonance images of patient S.M., who has selective bilateral amygdala damage. *Top left:* Three-dimensional reconstruction of S.M.'s brain, showing planes of sections. A: Horizontal section at level of amygdala. B: Coronal section at level of hippocampus. C: Coronal section at level of amygdala. From "The Human Amygdala and Emotion," by R. Adolphs, 1999, *The Neuroscientist,* 5, p. 128. Copyright 1999 by Sage Science. Reprinted with permission.

& Damasio, 1996). Ventral frontal cortex has also been found to be involved in the recognition of emotions (Hornak, Rolls, & Wade, 1996).

Research by other investigators has revealed a variety of possible roles for the amygdala. For example, electrical stimulation of the anterior and medial nuclei of the amygdala induces ragelike behavior, whereas stimulation of the central and lateral nuclei suppressed it (Shaikh & Siegel, 1994). Electrical stimulation of the amygdala can induce fear with associated autonomic changes (Gloor, 1990). Lesions of the medial nucleus have been reported to reduce sexual receptivity in female rats.

Lesions in the rat amygdala central nucleus reduced the heart rate orienting response to acoustic startle stimuli. The medial amygdaloid nucleus has receptors for both estrogen and testosterone. Social play is reduced in male rats after lesions of the amygdala. Sex differences in reactions have also been reported (Rasia-Filho, Londero, & Archavol, 2000). It appears that there is a great variety of behavior associated with either electrical stimulation or lesioning of the amygdaloid complex.

Another investigation is relevant to this conclusion. In this study by Isenberg, Silbersweig, et al. (1999), healthy volunteers were instructed to name the color of words of either threat or neutrality, presented in different colored inks. Threat words included *destroy, death, evil, gun, rape, poison, loathe, kill, punish,* and *blame.* While volunteers were naming the colors, brain activity was measured by using a PET (positron emission tomography) scan. Electrical activation of both amygdalas was significantly greater during the color naming of threat words than during the color naming of neutral words. Activation was also found in several other areas during this procedure—the posterior hippocampal gyrus and left premotor area. The authors concluded that the results indicated that the amygdala plays a role in the perception and response to verbally threatening stimuli and is not related to selective attention. It is not reported whether the procedure aroused subjective feelings of fear or anger in the participants.

The Limbic System

In 1937 the neurologist, J. W. Papez, proposed the existence of certain brain pathways that mediate emotional experience. He pointed out that the word *emotion* refers to both a way of acting (emotional expression) and a way of feeling (subjective experience) and that different parts of the brain were involved in these two aspects of emotion.

Walter Cannon had assumed that the hypothalamus was the integrating center for the emotions but that it was intimately connected to many other brain structures. Neural impulses from the hypothalamus to the cortex of the brain were assumed to be the origin of emotional experience. Neural impulses from the hypothalamus to various motor centers were assumed to be the basis for emotional expression. Papez's proposal attempted to identity some of the other brain structures involved in emotions.

He pointed out that nerve impulses that come from the receptor organs of the body, the eyes, ears, skin, and muscles, all go first to various parts of the thalamus. At this point, the impulses break up into three major pathways. One pathway goes to various structures (such as the corpus striatum) and coordinates *movement patterns*. A second pathway goes to lateral parts of the cerebral cortex and handles the *stream of thought*. The third pathway goes through the hypothalamus to the mammillary body to the medial wall of the cerebral hemispheres and handles the *stream of feeling*. These ideas were partly based on fact and partly speculative. He then went on to describe other brain structures that are probably tied into the circuits for the stream of feeling.

Of particular interest to Papez was the hippocampus. This structure is located deep inside the temporal lobes of the brain and was believed to be an integrating center for olfactory (smell) impressions. He pointed out, however, that lesions of the hippocampus are often known to be associated with rabies, a disease that produces intense rage and convulsive symptoms. He therefore hypothesized that the hippocampus is involved both in emotional expressions and in experience.

In addition to the hippocampus, Papez cited evidence to suggest that several other brain structures are involved in the various phases of emotional behavior and consciousness. These other structures include the hypothalamus, the anterior thalamic nuclei, the hippocampus, and their interconnections. These structures have usually been considered to serve olfactory functions alone, but the evidence for this belief is weak. Although the evidence for Papez's proposal was not overwhelming, the proposal itself stimulated a good deal of interest by neurologists on the problem of how brain structures are related to emotions. During the next several decades, several investigators experimentally examined the hypotheses proposed by Papez and greatly expanded our knowledge of brain anatomy as related to emotions.

PAUL MACLEAN AND THE VISCERAL BRAIN

One prominent investigator who has devoted a good deal of research to understanding the role of the limbic system is Paul MacLean, a neurophysiologist. He has spent much of his career at the National Institute of Mental Health studying the neurology and behavior of the squirrel monkey. He pointed out that the course of evolution has, in a sense, overlapped three different types of brains, and despite differences in structure, they must function together. The oldest type of brain is found in reptiles; the second is inherited from lower mammals; and the third is a late development in terms of evolution, found most highly developed in the primates. The earlier types of brains are basically olfactory brains. In lower animals, many brain structures are connected with the activity of smell which, from an adaptive point of view, plays an important role in food gathering, courtship, mating, and warning of predators. Brain centers for correlating smell, taste, oral, and visceral sensations have a relatively large development in primitive animals, but in the course of evolution a new cortex, or neocortex, develops that exerts more and more control over adaptive behavior. MacLean suggested that the olfactory brain structures continue to exercise a large degree of control over visceral activity such as sweating, heart rate, and blood pressure, even in higher primates, and should be called a *visceral brain*.

Structures that MacLean called the visceral brain include the hippocampal gyrus (a part of the temporal lobe), the mammillary body (a small structure found at the back of the hypothalamus), the anterior thalamic nucleus, and the cingulate gyrus (found on the medial surface of the cerebrum). The fornix is a large bundle of fibers connecting the hippocampus to the mammillary body. Additional structures that are considered by MacLean to be part of the visceral brain are the amygdala and the septum (found near a juncture of the thalamus and the frontal lobes).

Although these structures are prominent in animals that rely greatly on a sense of smell, some of these structures, such as the hippocampus and the cingulate gyrus, reach a high level of development in humans (and an even higher level in whales and dolphins), for whom the sense of smell is limited. It therefore seems likely that the olfactory brain (or rhinencephalon) has functions in addition to olfaction. MacLean proposed that it is largely involved in the control of visceral and emotional activities.

In a later paper, MacLean (1963) pointed out that what he called a visceral brain in 1949 is now more often called the *limbic brain*. A series of investigations have tried to systematically determine the functional characteristics of limbic structures. For example, several studies have shown that bilateral injuries or lesions of the temporal lobes (which eliminate the normal functions of the amygdala and the hippocampus, among other structures) tend to make wild and dangerous animals passive, tractable, and hypersexed (the Kluver–Bucy syndrome).

Other studies carried out by MacLean have been concerned with the effects of electrical stimulation of small areas of the brain. Such experiments have found, for example, that stimulation of the amygdala produces patterns of behavior related to eating or swallowing and behaviors related to searching or fighting. Electrical stimulation of the hippocampus, or of the septum to which it is connected, frequently produced penile erection and grooming reactions. It thus appears evident that these limbic system structures are involved in the integration of oral behaviors, sexual behaviors, and agonistic (fight-or-flight) behaviors; in other words, *emotional behaviors*.

MacLean pointed out that his researches have repeatedly shown that very small changes in the location of the stimulating electrode tip often produced very marked changes in emotional behaviors. For example, at one point in the brain, stimulation may produce penile erection. One millimeter away, stimulation may produce ragelike reactions or vocalizations suggestive of fear. The proximity of brain structures associated with such diverse emotional behaviors may be a possible explanation, he suggested, of the frequently noted connection in humans between scary experiences and aggressive encounters.

FIGURE 11.6. In the communal situation, the male squirrel monkey may display penile erection in the act of courtship, or as illustrated, it may display to another male as a means of exerting and establishing dominance. In each case, the display is performed with the thighs spread and the erect penis thrust almost into the face of the other animal. From "Display of Penile Erection in Squirrel Monkey (*Saimiri sciureus*)," by D. W. Ploog and P. D. MacLean, 1963, *Animal Behavior Monographs, 11,* p. 35. Copyright 1963 by Animal Behavior Society. Reprinted with permission.

He speculated that the spread of neural impulses to adjacent structures may account for some of the mixed emotions people report.

One of the most interesting aspects of MacLean's discussion of the brain and emotions is his attempt to relate his concepts about the visceral brain to the behavior of animals in natural environments. For example, in squirrel monkeys, penile erection is used as a form of display; that is, as a social signal to other monkeys. As illustrated in Figure 11.6, the male squirrel monkey displays his penis both in courtship and in dominance situations. The thighs are spread and the erect penis is thrust almost up into the face of the other animal. If a male receiving a display does not remain submissive during this time, the other male may attack him. Observations have shown that who displays to whom is directly correlated with dominance rank in the group. This suggests a close connection between courtship and dominance (sex and aggression).

In his elaboration of these ideas, MacLean suggested that the reptilian part of the brain is quite capable of carrying out complex forms of social and emotional behavior, including the following: (a) establishing a territory, (b) ritualistic displays in defense of territory, (c) intraspecies fighting, (d) hunting, (e) formation of social groups, (f) courtship displays, (g) and mating. It is important to emphasize that in naturalistic situations with animals, the establishment of a territory is an essential prelude to mating and breeding. Thus it is understandable that territory, defense, fighting, courtship, and mating are closely interrelated. It is also worth noting that most display behaviors in animals are innate; for example, a squirrel monkey raised in isolation will display to other monkeys when first placed in proximity to them.

Studies carried out in MacLean's laboratory on squirrel monkeys have revealed some of the major limbic pathways. For example, electrical stimulation of the amygdala and parts of the hippocampus elicits biting, mouthing, and eating activities. Electrical stimulation of the septum and cingulate gyrus elicits penile erection. And in areas in and around parts of the hypothalamus, it elicited oral, genital, or aggressive behavior. He interpreted this as indicating that the same neural mechanisms may be involved in combat, whether as a prelude to eating or mating. A third limbic pathway does not involve the olfactory system but sends nerve fibers from the hypothalamus to the cingulate gyrus, and then to the neocortex. Stimulation along this pathway elicits penile erection. The concern of the limbic system, overall, thus seems to be the regulation of feeding, fornication, fighting, and fleeing.

Further research on limbic structures used the method of *evoked potentials*. Tiny microelectrodes may be placed into small groups of neurons and any electrical signal recorded. MacLean found that stimulation of all sensory systems—olfaction, vision, hearing, touch, pressure, and taste—elicited electrical signals in individual cells of different parts of the limbic system. For example, visual stimulation elicited evoked responses in the hippocampus.

MacLean (1984) also suggested that there are three main forms of behavior that characterize the evolutionary transition from reptiles to mammals: (a) nursing in conjunction with maternal care, (b) vocal communication for maintaining maternal–offspring contact, and (c) play. The separation call (or isolation call) of young mammals (e.g., dogs, monkeys, babies) probably functions to maintain contact with the mother and with other members of a social group.

It is also of interest that the cingulate cortex has a high concentration of opiate receptors and that morphine intake (which blocks receptor action at certain dose levels) eliminates the separation call. It has also been found that naloxone, a substance that acts as an antagonist of morphine, reinstates the separation call. Lesions of the cingulate area tend to reduce opiate craving in humans.

Emotions and Psychomotor Epilepsy

MacLean (1986) described one other set of data that throws light on the functioning of certain limbic structures in humans. Psychomotor epilepsy (also called temporal lobe epilepsy and complex, partial seizures) in humans is known to result from abnormal electrical discharges in certain limbic structures that are usually triggered by head injury or diseases. For unknown reasons, many such abnormal foci arise in the hippocampus and spread to other parts of the limbic system. Depending on the particular areas that are activated, a person with epilepsy will experience several strange sensations (the *aura*) at the beginning of an epileptic attack. Examples of these sensations include feelings of nausea, choking, hunger, thirst, a need to urinate, distorted sounds, hallucinations, disturbances in one's sense of reality, and disturbances of emotion. Patients with epilepsy may report feelings of elation, anger, or sadness.

To evaluate this kind of information, MacLean reviewed the many reports in the world literature that describe the subjective feelings associated with psychomotor epilepsy. He was interested in trying to identify the kinds of subjective emotional feelings patients reported. His review led him to conclude that about six emotions were reported by patients during their auras. One was fear. For example, a 23-year-old medical student stated that he invariably had an aura consisting of a peculiar sensation in the upper part of his abdomen and an intense feeling of fear. A 42-year-old newspaper editor described his aura as "a feeling of impending disaster. It's a horrible sensation." Several neurosurgeons have reported that electrical stimulation of parts of the hippocampus or amygdala in conscious patients during brain surgery for removal of part of the temporal lobe elicited feelings of fear.

Anger, too, has been reported as part of the epileptic aura in as many as 17% of the cases. One patient seen by MacLean was so guilt-ridden by his unpredictable attacks on other people that he attempted to commit suicide. Another reported that during his aura "I just get an electrical feeling, and it goes all the way through me; it starts in my head and then it makes me do things I don't want to do—I get mad." Feelings of disgust and depression have also been reported.

Not all feelings connected with the aura are unpleasant. There are many reports of pleasurable, pleasant, joyful, or even ecstatic feelings. One epileptic women said, "My fingertips began to vibrate thrillingly, and then the sensation passed to my head, giving me the most ecstatic physical pleasure."

These various reports concerning patients with psychomotor epilepsy strongly suggest that some parts of the limbic system are involved in the generation of emotional states. In these studies, evidence exists of abnormal electrical activity in various limbic structures, based on EEG recordings, CAT scans, or surgical records. As these electrical changes spontaneously recur from time to time, the various emotional feelings associated with the epileptic aura also occur. The fact that fear and rage experiences are more common than other types of emotional experiences may be related to the fact that medial temporal structures (involving the amygdala and hippocampus) are more susceptible to injury and disease than those in other lobes.

These reports by MacLean of a connection between psychomotor epilepsy and emotional feelings have been largely confirmed by Ervin and Martin (1986). They reviewed the work of neurosurgeons and neurologists concerned with electrical stimulation of various brain points in conscious patients following brain surgery for relief of epilepsy. These observations revealed that stimulation of the cortex of the brain never elicits emotional responses, whereas stimulation of limbic structures often does. For example, one patient who was stimulated at a ventral amygdaloid site cursed, struck out, and smashed a heavy panel with her fist. A few seconds later she apologized for her act and could not imagine what had motivated her to do it.

Examination of the records of 2,000 cases of epilepsy corroborated the fact that individuals commonly feel various emotions associated with the aura preceding the epileptic attack. These included feelings of anger, fear, pleasure, sadness, disgust, acceptance, anticipation, and surprise. An illustration of one of these reactions may be seen in a 28-year-old woman who had a friendly personality, with no evidence of maladjustment. The epileptic attack would begin with a shivering feeling in the abdomen, a general feeling of weakness, and a feeling of sadness, accompanied by some fearfulness. No associated motor or sensory changes occurred, and there were no hallucinations. The attacks lasted for about 3 minutes. Electroencephalograph evidence indicated some electrical abnormality in the posterior parts of both temporal lobes. All these observations support the idea that limbic structures have an important role in the processing of information and the expression of emotions. Most of the remainder of this chapter reviews the theories of several neuroscientists who have contributed important ideas about the relations of brain function to emotions.

ROBERT HEATH AND THE NEURAL SUBSTRATE FOR EMOTION

Since the mid-1940s, Robert Heath has carried out detailed studies, in his laboratory at Tulane Medical School, of brain physiology and biochemistry in human patients and in animals. This research has led to an expanded view of the neural bases of emotion.

The evidence that Heath (1992) used to justify his ideas is of diverse types. Electrical stimulation at neocortical locations in patients has little or no effect on emotions. Lobotomies generally did not change the emotional behavior of patients with schizophrenia. In contrast, ablation of subcortical sites often produced profound disturbances of memory as well as of emotional behavior. Electrical stimulation of subcortical centers in patients who were able to report their thoughts and feelings demonstrated that scientists could elicit pleasurable feelings by stimulating septal areas and unpleasant feelings by stimulating parts of the hippocampus. Using evoked potentials to map the interrelated anatomic network led Heath to identify the following areas as involved in emotional expressions:

1. Septal region, hippocampus, and amygdala.
2. Subcortical sensory relay nuclei for audition (medial geniculates), vision (lateral geniculates), somatic sensation (posterior ventral lateral thalamus), and vestibular proprioception (fastigial nucleus of the cerebellum).
3. Sites involved in facial expression and eye movement (superior colliculus, third nerve nuclei, inferior olive in the pons).
4. Midbrain nuclei that have been found to contain large amounts of the major neurotransmitters of the brain. Dopamine is found in the substantia nigra, norepinephrine in the locus coereleus, and serotonin in the raphe nuclei.

These and other observations led Heath to conclude that the conventional limbic system was only a small part of the system involved in emotional behavior. All major parts of the brain—hindbrain, midbrain, and forebrain—participate in emotional states. This condition makes sense in view of the fact that emotions generally involve widespread bodily changes of the skeletal muscles (such as postural changes or facial expression) as well as the autonomic system, and changes also in perception and appraisal. Of special interest is the fact that Heath discovered pleasure-inducing sites that act functionally to inhibit activity at aversive sites.

The Pleasure System

To learn about the functions of subcortical systems in humans, in the early 1950s, Heath studied 106 intractably ill patients who allowed the implantation of tiny electrodes into deep parts of their brain. In some cases the electrodes were left for a few days, and in others for as long as 8 years. In some cases, Heath also implanted very fine tubes or cannulas used to introduce chemicals into the brain.

Heath found that when patients reported pleasurable feelings, neural changes consistently occurred in recordings from the septal region, deep cerebellum, and dorsal lateral amygdala. When he administered addictive-type drugs such as marijuana and cocaine through the cannulas, patients most often reported pleasurable feelings when the septal area was stimulated.

After Olds and Milner (1954) demonstrated that rats would repetitively self-stimulate certain areas of their brains with small electric currents, Heath tried this technique with some of his patients. He found that patients would repeatedly stimulate sites in the pleasure system, but particularly the rostral septal area. Introduction of acetylcholine, a neurotransmitter, into septal areas also produced pleasant feelings and in one patient, it induced orgasms. At the same time, activity in the hippocampus, an aversive system, was inhibited. This reciprocal relation worked for physical pain as well as unpleasant feelings. The result was that Heath was able greatly to reduce the pain of metastatic cancer by electrically stimulating the pleasure system. He could similarly reduce epileptic seizure activity by septal stimulation.

The Aversive System

Heath interviewed patients while using the deep electrodes to record electrical changes in various brain structures. When the patients reported unpleasant feelings or memories, he noted electrical changes from such nuclei as the hippocampus, the medial amygdala, and the cingulate gyrus. When he administered electrical stimulation to these sites, the most common responses were feelings of fear, anger, and sometimes violent behavior. Three patients, who periodically became violent and psychotic, showed abnormal electrical activity in the hippocampus and at sites in the amygdala. Electrical stimulation of the hippocampus and the dorsal lateral amygdala tended to induce seizures in experimental animals and patients. Electrical and chemical stimulation (acetylcholine) of the septal region consistently reduced the incidence of seizures in patients with epilepsy and also reduced abnormal electrical activity in the hippocampus. Heath concluded that there is an inverse relationship between the pleasure system (represented primarily by the septal region) and the aversive system (represented primarily by the hippocampus).

Heath further concluded that the earlier concept of a limbic system as the basis for emotions is too limited. Almost all parts of the brain play a role in determining the expression of emotions, in behavior, and in verbalizations reflecting inner feelings. Most important is the concept of pleasure and aversion systems interacting in reciprocal ways. However, not all neurophysiologists have placed equal importance on these observations, and several researchers have proposed other theories about the neural mechanisms underlying emotion.

JOSE M. R. DELGADO: EMOTIONS AND THE FRAGMENTAL ORGANIZATION OF BEHAVIOR

Jose Delgado is a neurophysiologist who, through a long series of investigations mainly at the Yale Medical School, has contributed to our understanding of brain mechanisms in emotion. He has demonstrated, for example, that there are three types of brain structures in relation to emotions. In the first type, electrical brain stimulation produces no observable effects that can be considered emotional. Examples of such structures are the motor cortex, the pulvinar (a part of the thalamus), and the substantia nigra. When

TABLE 11.2. Offensive–Defensive Manifestations in the Cat

Vocal signs	Expressive sounds	Autonomic signs	Functional behaviors
Growling	Alerting	Pupil dilation	Circling
Hissing	Retracting ears	Salivation	Prowling
Spitting	Unsheathing claws	Piloerection	Stalking
Snorting	Arching back	Sweating	Pouncing
High-pitched	Lashing tail	Urination	Striking with paws
screaming	Showing teeth	Defecation	Biting
	Opening mouth	Respiratory increase	Chasing
	Snarling		Fighting
	Pawing floor		Cringing
			Hiding
			Escaping

Note. From *Emotions*, by J. M. R. Delgado, 1966, p. 114. Copyright 1966 by Brown. Reprinted with permission.

electrically stimulated, the second type of structure will produce behavioral manifestations of emotion but will not produce subjective experiences of emotion. An example of such a structure is the anterior part of the hypothalamus. The third type of structure will produce both emotional behavior and emotional experience when electrically stimulated, as researchers have demonstrated in the central gray area of the midbrain, in the posteroventral nucleus of the thalamus, the tectal area of the thalamus, and in certain parts of the hippocampus (Delgado, 1966).

However, Delgado has done far more than provide us with a kind of emotion atlas of the brain. He has pointed out that whatever an emotion is, it is not simply a subjective feeling. He emphasized that one may express emotional states in so many different ways that no one single aspect (such as reported feelings) is the final or ultimate criterion of its existence. This idea implies that we can recognize emotions in lower animals as well as in humans. Illustrations of the kinds of evidence he used include the following: how animals behave with purposeful effects, such as the killing of another animal; the way other animals of the same type react (e.g., submissive behavior of monkeys toward an aggressive male); and the willingness of an animal to work to induce an emotion in itself, as we see in electrical self-stimulation studies. In addition to these kinds of indices, many expressive behaviors reflect emotions. Table 11.2 provides a list of cat behaviors that are related to offensive or defensive actions.

The variety of such behaviors led Delgado to his theory of the *fragmental organization of behavior*. Each item of behavior listed in the table is involved not only in emotional expressions but also in other types of activities. For example, licking may be part of eating, exploring, playing, and mothering. It is unlikely that the motor pattern of licking has a separate representation in the brain for each type of activity. A more plausible hypothesis is that one neural center organizes licking behavior, but nerve impulses from other parts of the brain activate this center, depending on the initiating stimulus (e.g., food, a novel object, a baby, and so forth). The result is that simple fragments of behavior (such as licking, hissing, or biting) may become part of different sequences of action and thus take on different functional meanings.

This idea implies that there is no single brain circuit for anger or pleasure but that there must be a group of structures that play a role in integrating the various behaviors that define each emotion. Consistent with this theory is the fact that electrical stimulation of different brain locations can produce the same emotion. For example, electrical stimulation of the lateral hypothalamus and midbrain central gray areas has produced aggressive attacks, but stimulation of the frontal lobes or occipital cortex never has.

JAAK PANKSEPP: NEURAL CONTROL SYSTEMS FOR EMOTIONS

Jaak Panksepp, a physiological psychologist, believes that emotions are complex psychophysiological–behavioral reactions of organisms to various kinds of stimuli. His investigations over several years have concerned the identification and study of emotional command circuits in the brain. He stated that research has identified at least seven such emotive circuits, although the possibility exists of finding additional circuits in the future (Panksepp, 2000; Panksepp & Miller, 1996).

Panksepp believed that certain types of stimuli or environmental events tend to produce emotional reactions. For example, restraint is one kind of event that triggers *rage* reactions; pain triggers *fear*; social losses trigger *panic*; and positive incentives such as social contact trigger *expectancy.* Panksepp cautioned us not to misinterpret the use of these particular terms, because a variety of other related words could be used just as well, such as hate and anger instead of rage, alarm and anxiety instead of fear, loneliness and grief instead of panic, and hope and curiosity instead of expectancy. He further assumed that certain general attributes define emotive command circuits, including the following:

1. The underlying circuits are genetically prewired and respond to major life-challenging circumstances (e.g., threat, pain, and loss).

2. The circuits organize behavior by activating or inhibiting movement patterns and autonomic and hormonal changes that have been adaptive during the evolutionary history of the species (e.g., biting, flight, distress cries, and sniffing).

3. Emotive circuits can come under the control of neutral stimuli through conditioning.

4. Emotive circuits interact with brain mechanisms that influence appraisal, decision making, and consciousness. (Panksepp, 1986, p. 96)

Panksepp believed that it is a mistake to view emotion primarily as a state of aroused autonomic reactivity. The evidence now available demonstrates that emotion is fundamentally associated with several well-organized behavioral patterns related to survival such as attack, flight, and exploration, which autonomic changes support or reinforce.

Panksepp defined *emotive command circuits* as two-way avenues of communication that simultaneously recruit several brain structures and functions in response to life-challenging situations. They transmit information from sense organs, association cortex, and memory stores to limbic structures as well as to other parts of the nervous system. The final result of this complex interplay is the individual's integrated and appropriately adaptive behavior. A brief description of each of the basic emotional systems follows.

1. *The seeking/expectancy system:* This neural system controls certain aspects of individuals' engagement with the environment; individuals explore, investigate, and try to anticipate the rewards to be found in the environment. Administration of addictive drugs such as amphetamines can greatly increase the sensitivity of this system. Animals will self-stimulate the areas of the brain involved with this system (the dopamine neurotransmitter system).

2. *The rage system:* Animals can be made more sensitive to anger-arousing stimuli by administration of gonadal steroids. There is a decline in aggressive responses with aging. The medial nuclei of the amygdala and the medial nuclei of the hypothalamus are believed to be involved in rage responses. Panksepp also believed that many of these neural circuits are activated at the same time by life events but to varying degrees. Such interactions are what produce the more complex (or blended) emotions and social bonding in general.

3. *The fear system:* Key structures involved in the fear system are the amygdala, the medial hypothalamus, and the central gray areas of the midbrain. Increases in response to fear-precipitating stimuli can be produced by electrical stimulation of the amygdala.

4. *The lust system:* Erotic impulses may partly overlap with the joy experiences related to play. A decline in sexual drive with age occurs in all species, but the rate of decline is related to an animal's sexual experiences and also to the degree of neocortical development of each species. Sex hormones influence the changes in sexual impulses over the life span and differs somewhat in males and females.

5. *The care/nurturance acceptance system:* In all mammals acceptance and nurturance are mediated by specific brain circuits. Females of most species show stronger tendencies to respond with nurturance (accepting) behavior than do males. Accepting behavior is seen first in terms of responses to the young of a species but may be continued into adult life.

6. *The separation distress/panic system:* This neural system generates separation calls or distress vocalizations in mammals. They appear very early as survival-related mechanisms in young organisms, as ways of obtaining care and nurturance from mothers. In all species the distress vocalizations decline as the organism matures.

7. *Play and dominance systems:* These neural systems control the appearance and decline of the rough-and-tumble activities of childhood. Panksepp assumed that the activation of play circuits is a major source of joy that organisms experience through social interactions. Early play may also be a basis for social dominance. For example, in rat societies, animals that have exhibited the highest levels of juvenile play tend to become dominant. Sports activities may be an expression of the playful dominance impulses.

Although research data are far from unanimous on the exact nature of the emotive command circuits, data from animal and human studies suggest certain key structures for each. In addition, various neuromodulators, peptides, and neurotransmitters are also involved. Table 11.3 summarizes Panksepp's views.

In this table, the major brain structures believed to be involved in each emotive command system represent only a partial list. It is obvious that cranial nerves must be involved in these circuits as well as spinal and autonomic reflexes of various kinds. For

TABLE 11.3. Key Neuroanatomical and Neurochemical Factors Related to Basic Emotion Systems in the Mammalian Brain

Basic emotional systems	Key brain areas	Key neuromodulators
Seeking or expectancy	Nucleus accumbens—VTA; mesolimbic mesocortical outputs; lateral hypothalamus—PAG	DA (+); glutamate (+); many neuropeptides; opioids (+); neurotensin (+)
Rage or anger	Medial amygdala to BNST; medial and perifornical hypothalamus to dorsal PAG	Acetylcholine (+); glutamate (+)
Fear or anxiety	Central and lateral amygdala to medial hypothalamus and dorsal PAG	Glutamate (+) many neuropeptides; DBI; CRF; CCK; alpha-MSH; NPY
Lust or sexuality	Corticomedial amygdala; BNST; preoptic and ventromedial hypothalamus; lateral and ventral PAG	Steroids (+); vasopressin and oxytocin; LH-RH; CCK
Care or nurturance	Anterior cingulate; BNST; preoptic area; VTA; PAG	Oxytocin (+); prolactin (+); DA (+); opioids (+/−)
Panic or separation	Anterior cingulate; BNST and preoptic area; dorsomedial thalamus; dorsal PAG	Opioids (−); oxytocin (−); prolactin (−); CRF (+); glutamate (+)
Play or joy	Dorsomedial diencephalon; parafascicular area; ventral PAG	Opioids (+/−); glutamate (+); ACh (+)

Note. The monoamines serotonin and norepinephrine are not indicated because they participate in nonspecific ways in all emotions. The higher cortical zones devoted to emotion, mostly in frontal and temporal areas, are not indicated. ACh = Acetylcholine; BNST = bed nucleus of stria terminalis; CCK = cholecystokinin; CRF = corticotropin-releasing factor; DA = dopamine; DBI = diazepam-binding inhibitor; LH-RH = lutenizing hormone-releasing hormone; MSH = melanocyte-stumulating hormone; NPY = neuropeptide Y; PAG = periaqueductal gray; VTA = ventral tegmental area. The minus sign (−) indicates the inhibition of a prototype while the plus sign (+) indicates activation of a prototype. From "Emotions as Natural Kinds Within the Mammalian Brain," by J. Panksepp. In M. Lewis and J. M. Haviland-Jones (Eds.), *Handbook of Emotions* (2nd ed.), 2000, p. 151. Copyright 2000 by Guilford Press. Reprinted with permission.

example, the trigeminal facial nerve is involved in the control of biting (rage), the occulomotor cranial nerves are involved in eye movements and foraging, and several cranial nerves are involved in the vocalizations of separation distress. Because emotions tend to be associated with characteristic sounds, each circuit may influence respiratory and vocal controls to generate the whines, screeches, screams, and coos identified with different emotions. Similarly, the circuits influence autonomic and skeletal muscle reactions that produce the changes in skin color, skin temperature, sweating, shivering, erection of hair, and cardiovascular responses characteristic of emotions. These ideas that Panksepp developed represent an important approach to understanding the relations between emotions and the brain.

DETLEV PLOOG: NEUROETHOLOGY AND THE VOCAL EXPRESSION OF EMOTIONS

Detlev Ploog is a neurophysiologist and ethologist who has carried out his research at the Max Planck Institute in Germany. He has been involved in a long-term program concerned with identifying the neural mechanisms that underlie species-typical behavior. This approach is common in medicine, in which researchers attempt to find similarities and differences between lower animals and humans in such things as the organs of the body, the immune system, and the brain.

One example of Ploog's research deals with the neuroethology of social signaling, particularly vocal signaling. The following review is based on his analyses of this issue (Ploog, 1986, 1992, 2000).

From an evolutionary point of view, the ability to produce sounds has a long history. We see the rudimentary beginnings of a pharynx capable of sound production in lungfish. Further development occurs in amphibia (e.g., frogs) and in mammals in the differentiation in the laryngeal (vocal cord) musculature. In humans, movements of the tongue, lips, and soft palate produce verbal language with only minor involvement of the vocal cords. In contrast, both humans and animals produce nonverbal sounds almost exclusively with the vocal cords.

The neuroethological approach compares the vocal behavior of lower and higher animals and attempts to relate the differences to both lifestyle and brain systems. As a limited example, male frogs have about five calls: One is a mating call that attracts females, and another is a call that threatens other males. Both are species specific. In contrast, the squirrel monkey has many calls with variants of each that serve as communication signals.

How can one learn about the role of the different vocal signals? One approach is to see how often one type of call follows another. This pattern gives some idea of the similarity of motivations associated with each call. Another approach is to implant tiny electrodes in the brain of the monkey and find sites from which different calls may be elicited. Researchers then give the animal an opportunity to turn the electrical current on or off by itself, thus providing an index of how aversive (unpleasant) or pleasant the inner state is for each call. Investigators assume that the lower the self-stimulation rate for a particular call, the greater the aversiveness of the inner state connected with that call.

Using these procedures, Ploog and his colleagues identified the properties of 15 types of calls in the squirrel monkey. They are grouped into five classes as follows:

1. Warning signals include sounds described as *clucking, yapping*, and *alarm peeps*.

2. Protest signals include sounds described as *groaning, cawing*, and *shrieking*. They vary from signs of slight uneasiness to intense threat.

3. Challenging signals include sounds described as *purring, growling*, and *spitting*.

4. Desire for social contact signals include sounds described as *chirping, isolation peeps*, and *squealing*. They act to draw another group members' attention to the caller.

5. Companionship signals include sounds described as *twittering, chattering*, and *cackling*. They seem to confirm social bonds or attachment.

A comparison of all the calls shows one feature in common: The more intense the expression of aggression, the greater the frequency range of the call. The fact that these species-typical calls relate to such emergency and survival-related events as warning, protest, challenge, aggression, social contact, and companionship implies that they are one kind of expression of emotion.

The Innateness of Calls

Several investigators directed studies toward the question of whether these squirrel monkey calls were innate or learned by social experience. In one study, infant monkeys were raised by mothers who were unable to make any sounds at all. Although deprived of vocal experience, the infants began to vocalize immediately after birth, and they produced all types of adult calls. In another study, infant monkeys who were deafened on the 4th day of life produced vocal calls typical of the species. In a third study, researchers exposed infant monkeys raised without experience of species-typical vocalizations to tape recordings of alarm calls by adult monkeys. One call was an *alarm peep* for bird predators and the other was *yapping,* the alarm call for predators on the ground. The infant monkeys showed an immediate flight response to the mother in both cases. It thus appears that both the production of species-typical calls and the perception of such calls are innate.

The Cerebral Organization of Vocal Behavior

Electrical stimulation studies of the brain of the squirrel monkey have revealed a good deal about the brain mechanisms underlying species-specific vocal signals. Stimulation of the neocortex never elicits vocalizations in the squirrel monkey. When researchers stimulate various subcortical structures, they elicit species-typical expressions such as growls, shrieks, groans, and chirps. Investigators found locations in the hypothalamus, the thalamus, and the midbrain that produced vocalizations on stimulation. A section of the central gray area of the dorsal midbrain will yield vocalizations when stimulated in amphibians, reptiles, cats, dogs, and monkeys.

Ploog's research suggests a hierarchical system of organization for vocal expression in the brain. One level concerns the cranial nerves that determine movements of the larynx musculature and associated respiratory movements. The second level is represented by the central gray area of the midbrain, from which electrical stimulation can elicit many normal calls. Destruction of this area causes mutism. The third level includes four different areas that mediate different motivational states such as threats, warnings, fear, and aggression, connected with vocalizations. These structures include the amygdala, the lateral hypothalamus, the dorsomedial hypothalamus, and the mediodorsal thalamus. The fourth level is represented by part of the cingulate gyrus, which is believed to exert a facilitating or inhibiting effect on activation of lower levels.

A comparison of monkeys and humans in vocal expression reveals that brain injury of certain neocortical areas in monkeys has little or no effect on their vocal behavior, although it may have marked effects on humans. Destruction of the anterior cingulate cortex in humans causes temporary mutism and a long-term speech defect but has no effect on monkeys' spontaneous vocalizations in a social situation. Injury to the mouth area of the motor cortex may paralyze the vocal cords in humans but have no effect on a monkey's vocalizations. It appears that the voluntary control over vocal expression is a late evolutionary development. Only humans have gained direct cortical control over the voice.

Implications

Vocal behavior is clearly related to important survival issues in the life of an animal. It is used to express such things as warnings, threats, fear, aggression, social needs, and comfort, states that are clearly emotional. Thus, the study of vocal behavior is an aspect of the study of emotion.

From an evolutionary point of view, it is advantageous for an individual to communicate its likelihood of future action and for the receiver of the communication to understand it. For this to happen, there appears to be a gradual modification of a behavior pattern connected with a certain motivational state to make it more conspicuous. The ethologists call this change of behavior into a conspicuous signal *ritualization,* and the form of the ritualized behavior a *fixed-action pattern.* Examples of fixed-action patterns are head-nodding in lizards in competitive situations and species-typical songs in birds, which act as territory markers and mate attractors. Although fixed-action patterns are genetically programmed and relatively constant in their expression, which pattern is carried out at a given time depends on the motivational state of the animal as well as on stimulus conditions. Ploog (1986) concluded, "Since social signals are expressions of emotions, we must concede that vertebrates—whether at a high or low evolutionary level—express emotions when they communicate via signals" (p. 189).

DESCARTES' ERROR: MIND AND BODY ARE SEPARATE

A neuroscientist, Antonio Damasio, who is both a researcher and a clinician, has described his ideas about the nature of mind and brain in a book called *Descartes' Error* (1994). His views are based on extensive clinical experience with patients experiencing the effects of brain lesions, disease, or injuries as well as research with humans and animals.

He pointed out that the most fully studied neurotransmitters—that is, dopamine, norepinephrine, acetylcholine, and serotonin—originate from neurons in the brain stem or basal forebrain, and that their axons terminate in many parts of the brain: neocortex, limbic system, basal ganglia, and thalamus. In primates, increases in serotonin act to inhibit aggressive behavior, and the blocking of serotonin tends to be associated with impulsive and aggressive behavior. Structures in evolutionarily older parts of the brain, such as the brain stem, hypothalamus, amygdala, and cingulate region, act to regulate homeostasis in body systems without which there would be no survival. Survival depends on respiration, oxygen, nutrients, appropriate fight-or-flight behavior, sexual behavior, care of offspring, and suitable amounts of light and temperature.

According to Damasio (1994), an example of homeostatic regulations involving an interaction between brain and body is the fact that

> sadness and anxiety can alter the regulation of sexual hormones, causing not only changes in sexual drive but also variations in the menstrual cycle. Bereavement, again a state depending on brainwide processing, leads to a depression of the immune system such that individuals are more prone to infection and, whether as a direct result or not, more likely to develop certain types of cancer. (p. 120)

An important idea Damasio proposed is that humans and lower animals have nervous systems that are "prewired" to respond to certain significant features of the environment, significant in the sense that they are related to threats to survival. Such features include size, relative motion (as in flying predators), certain sounds such as growling, and certain colors. To elicit an emotional reaction, an individual does not need to recognize the python, eagle, or panther as such. All that is necessary is that the key features of a source of danger be received by the amygdala. This will often produce a rapid initial response, to be followed later by a "rational" reaction. Conscious emotional feelings, at least in primates with large neocortices, are considered by Damasio to be a cortical response to a subcortical reaction. From this point of view, feelings are just as cognitive as any other image or idea, and just as dependent on cortical functioning.

Despite his concern with brain function in both internal and behavioral homeostasis, Damasio pointed out that reductionism can go too far. For example, reducing depression to a statement about levels of serotonin is not a satisfactory explanation: "Discovering the chemicals involved in emotions and moods is not enough to explain how we feel" (Damasio, 1994, p. 160). Emotional functioning is a multicausal phenomenon whose complete understanding requires knowledge of environmental events, cognitive assessments, brain mechanisms, and response possibilities, at the very least.

JOSEPH E. LE DOUX: EMOTIONAL EVALUATION AND BRAIN SYSTEMS

Joseph Le Doux is a physiological psychologist who has been interested in identifying the neural pathways that underlie emotions. However, he pointed out an ambiguity in the meaning of the word *emotion* as we customarily use it. Some researchers have studied emotion as reflected in *expressions*, some have been concerned with the *subjective experience* of emotions, and still others have been interested in the *evaluation* of sensory inputs to determine their significance to the individual. For each meaning of the word there may be a different underlying neurophysiology.

In a chapter in the *Handbook of Physiology,* Le Doux (1987) reviewed many of the studies concerned with the neurophysiology and neuroanatomy of emotions. His ideas were updated in the book *The Emotional Brain* (1998) and in a new chapter (Le Doux & Phelps, 2000). Although his views apply to emotions in general, his research has been focused on the emotion of *fear* as studied in lower animals.

Much of his research involved fear conditioning in the rat. In these studies, a tone is sounded, followed by a brief, mild electric shock to the rat's feet. After a few such pairings, the rat stops all activity when the tone is sounded and shows a typical *freezing posture*; it crouches down and remains motionless, the fur stands up, blood pressure and heart rate rise, and stress hormones are released into the blood.

Fear conditioning has been studied in humans, baboons, monkeys, dogs, cats, rabbit, rats, pigeons, lizards, fish, snails, and fruit flies, and the neural basis of such conditioning is believed to be similar in all the vertebrates. Le Doux decided to examine all parts of the auditory system to determine which were necessary for the development of fear conditioning using a tone as the conditioned stimulus. He found that damage to the auditory cortex had no effect on conditioning but that when the auditory thalamus or the auditory midbrain was damaged, no conditioning occurred.

Further work showed that electrical stimulation of the rat amygdala (particularly the central nucleus) elicited freezing behavior. Lesions of the central nucleus were found to interfere with or limit various measures of conditioned fear, such as freezing behavior, autonomic responses, suppression of pain, and stress hormones release. Le Doux also found that the lateral nucleus of the amygdala received the conditioned stimulus inputs during fear conditioning and transmitted them to the central nucleus, which in turn transmitted them to other areas of the nervous system such as the lateral hypothalamus or the auditory cortex.

The theory that Le Doux suggested is based on these studies plus the fact that auditory signals take about 12 milliseconds to reach the amygdala and almost twice as long to reach the neocortex. The thalamic pathways thus can provide a fast signal to warn an individual that something dangerous may be present, but a detailed knowledge of what the danger is must wait until the neocortex receives and integrates several messages from different sense organs as well as from memory.

For a long time, investigators accepted the idea that the limbic system is the structural basis for emotions, but recent research has raised questions about exactly what structures constitute the limbic system as well as what role they serve. After reviewing the literature, Le Doux suggested that the most acceptable way to describe the limbic system is in terms of certain forebrain areas: the hippocampus, the cingulate gyrus, the rhinal cortex (olfactory projection areas), the amygdala, and the orbitofrontal cortex. These areas and some of their connections are shown schematically in Figure 11.7.

Connections Between Sensory Cortex and Limbic Forebrain

Sensory inputs are relayed through thalamus to primary receiving areas (koniocortices). Koniocortices project locally to unimodal association areas, which in turn project to areas in which sensory input converges (polymodal association zones) and to limbic forebrain. Polymodal cortex projects to complex (supramodal) association cortex and to limbic areas. Limbic areas also receive inputs from supramodal cortex and some limbic areas (rhinal cortices and hippocampus) qualify as supramodal cortex.

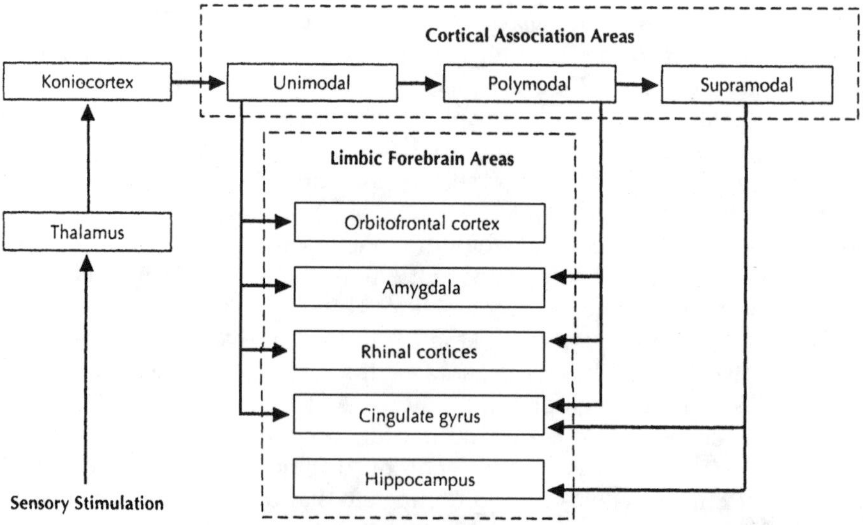

FIGURE 11.7. Schematic diagram showing connections between sensory cortex and limbic structures. From "Emotion," by J. E. Le Doux. In F. Plum (Ed.), *Handbook of Physiology: The Nervous System: Vol. 5. Higher Functions of the Brain*, 1987, p. 210. Copyright 1987 by the American Physiological Society. Reprinted with permission.

Inputs from most senses go to relays in the thalamus and from there to primary receiving areas of the neocortex. The primary sensory receiving areas have projections to association areas of the neocortex, which in turn have relays to several limbic structures. This schema applies to most of the senses; the olfactory system, however, does not have a thalamic relay but goes directly to areas in the neocortex as well as the amygdala. The amygdala receives afferent nerve impulses not only from the neocortex and thalamus but also from visceral pathways.

One of the complex issues about which little is known is the problem of how the emotional systems of the brain produce the movements of face, posture, and attack or retreat in an ongoing interaction between two individuals. Such adaptations clearly require intimate relations between sensory and motor systems mediated by evaluations of the nature of the interaction. For adaptive emotional behavior to occur, there must be some way in which stimulus inputs may be compared with stored information in the brain. This process of appraisal must be widespread throughout the animal kingdom, for without such a capacity, an organism could not survive (Le Doux, 1984).

Partly because of research on the Kluver–Bucy syndrome, it seems likely that appraisal processes are somewhat tied to the functioning of the amygdala as well as parts of the temporal lobe. Studies of monkeys with split-brains and a destroyed amygdala on one side has demonstrated normal behavior when they view the world through the hemisphere with the intact amygdala. In contrast, the monkeys were tame and fearless to threatening stimuli when the only eye that was open was connected to the hemisphere with the destroyed amygdala. The amygdala contains receptors for hormones such as steroids, which also influence emotional states.

One of Le Doux's major contributions was his demonstration that classical conditioning of fear, using auditory cues and shock, requires no cortical participation (at least in rats). It appeared that a thalamic–amygdala linkage is sufficient. This phenomenon does not mean that emotions can occur without cognitions, only that we need to have a broader conception of cognition, because even without cortical participation, the brain needs to distinguish between an emotional event and a nonemotional event.

After reviewing these many anatomic and physiological studies, Le Doux came to the following conclusions.

1. Emotion is not a unitary phenomenon. It consists of appraisal, expressive, and feeling aspects.

2. A preliminary evaluation of the emotional significance of sensory inputs occurs without conscious awareness probably in neurons located in the amygdala.

3. Mechanisms that evaluate stimulus significance are phylogenetically old and are distributed widely throughout the animal kingdom.

4. The neural mechanisms underlying emotional *experience* are phylogenetically recent. They are connected to the development of language and related cognitive processes. Le Doux also concluded that much adaptive processing will remain inaccessible to the conscious, feeling person.

5. Consciousness will only be understood by studying the unconscious processes that make it possible.

6. All functions are the properties of integrated systems rather than of isolated brain areas.

7. The only way to understand how emotions result from brain function is to study emotions one at a time.

8. "Each animal has to detect the particular things that are dangerous to it, but there is an evolutionary economy to using universal response strategies—withdrawal, immobility (freezing), (defensive) aggression, submission (appeasement), and universal physiological adjustments" (Le Doux, 1998, p. 133).

9. Subjective emotional experience, like the feeling of being afraid, results when we become consciously aware that an emotion system of the brain, like the defense system, is active.

10. Contrary to cognitive appraisal theories, the core of an emotion, at least in rats, is not an introspectively accessible conscious representation.

THE INFLUENCE OF DRUGS ON EMOTIONS

Thus far, we have considered the issue of brain and emotion in terms of studies of electrical and chemical stimulation of selected sites in the brain, in terms of self-stimulation studies, and in terms of the effects of lesions (either experimentally created in animals or as resulting from epilepsy or illness). Another line of research throws light on the role of the brain in emotion: the treatment with medications of individuals with emotional disorders.

In the early 1950s, for the first time, physicians used new medications called *neuroleptics* for the treatment of schizophrenia. The treatments were remarkably effective for many patients, and even those who had lived on the back wards of large state hospitals for many years would often show rapid improvement. These findings started the major drug companies on intensive searches for other kinds of medications that would be helpful in treating various psychiatric disorders.

From a clinical point of view, there are several major emotional disorders (with many interactions and variants): depressive disorders, anxiety disorders, aggressive disorders, cognitive disorders, and pleasure disorders. The depressive disorders are characterized by symptoms such as feelings of sadness; loss of interest in usual activities; difficulties in sustaining attention; sleeping and eating too much or too little; and suicidal thoughts, gestures, or acts. Multiple fears, palpitations, shortness of breath, hot flashes or chills, and feelings of depersonalization (i.e., feelings of unreality or detachment) characterize the anxiety disorders. Such symptoms as loss of control of aggressive impulses, assaultive acts, destruction of property, cruelty, fighting, and impulsivity characterize the aggressive disorders. Cognitive disorders such as dementia are related to loss of cognitive functioning. Symptoms such as anhedonia (loss of feelings of pleasure) or its opposite, mania, characterize the pleasure disorders. Such symptoms as inflated self-esteem, racing thoughts, increased sexual activity, decreased need for sleep, and distractibility define mania.

Over the years, clinicians have found many drugs that are reasonably effective in dealing with each of these emotional disorders. The following section is a brief, oversimplified view of neurotransmitters and how they may be related to emotions.

NEUROTRANSMITTERS AND EMOTIONS

Nerve messages in the central nervous system are passed from neuron to neuron across junctions called *synapses*. As the electrical nerve impulse is transmitted along a nerve axon, various chemicals are simultaneously transmitted along the axon in very tiny tubes called *microtubules*. At the synapse, neurotransmitter chemicals are produced and stored in a presynaptic area before being released into the space between cells. The adjoining cells have postsynaptic receptors that the neurotransmitters activate to elicit an electrical signal sent down the dendrites to the cell body.

For a long time, researchers believed that only a few chemicals acted as neurotransmitters, but in recent years, they have identified many new ones, although they do not yet clearly understand their role in normal brain functioning. The neurotransmitters that have been most studied are dopamine, serotonin, norepinephrine, and acetylcholine. Neurons that use dopamine for neurotransmission are widely scattered throughout the central nervous system, usually as major projections from the medial forebrain bundle. Many studies have shown that brain sites from which high levels of self-stimulation may be obtained are typically areas of high concentration of dopamine cells. A deficiency of dopamine tends to produce tremors and muscular rigidity; an excess of dopamine may produce some of the symptoms of schizophrenia. Serotonin neurons have their cell bodies in the upper pons and midbrain. They project to the limbic system, the basal ganglia, and the cerebral cortex. Low levels of serotonin in these structures are believed to have some relations to depression, anxiety, violence, and schizophrenia.

Norepinephrine as a central nervous system neurotransmitter is found mainly in the locus ceruleus in the pons. The axons of these neurons have connections with the limbic system, the thalamus, and the cerebral cortex, and researchers believe them to have some regulatory effect on attention and emotion. A deficiency of norepinephrine may be associated with depression.

Acetylcholine is found in the reticular system, and its neurons project to the cortex, limbic system, and thalamus. Clinicians use acetylcholine drugs to treat the Parkinsonian (movement disorder) side effects of antipsychotic medication. Some researchers report excessive levels of acetylcholine production to possibly be related to depression.

Although researchers know a great deal about the biochemistry of these various neurotransmitters, their role in the genesis of emotional disorders is not well established. Pharmaceutical companies continue to develop new medications that influence neurotransmission (mainly through one or more of these four systems) to treat emotional disorders. Their efforts have been somewhat successful, because we now know various classes of medications that can reduce the extreme emotional changes we see in psychiatric patients. Table 11.4 summarizes the major classes of drugs used to reduce extreme manifestation of emotions. These observations are consistent with the conclusions a variety of other research methods have yielded: that there exist sites, pathways, and systems in the brain that regulate and control the expression and experience of emotions.

TABLE 11.4. Classes of Medications That Reduce the Experience of Certain Emotions

Emotion	Type of medication
Depression	Tricyclics, Monoamine Oxidase Inhibitors (MAOIs), Selective Serotonin Reuptake Inhibitors (SSRIs)
Anxiety	Benzodiazepams
Aggression	Serenics* (Selective Serotonin Reuptake Inhibitors)
Mania	Lithium, Neuroleptics

*Serenics is the name given to a new class of medications that influences certain serotonergic receptors.

SOME IMPLICATIONS OF KNOWLEDGE
OF BRAIN FUNCTIONING

It is important to emphasize that an understanding of how the brain works and the development of theories about the brain are not academic exercises. Some important practical and clinical implications result from this knowledge. To illustrate this point, we may consider the implications of neurobiology for the understanding and treatment of addictions.

It has long been known that mild electrical stimulation of certain limited parts of the brain can be rewarding. Animals given control over the administration of the electrical stimuli will often self-stimulate themselves to exhaustion. Studies have shown that positive reinforcing effects are usually associated with stimulation of the medial forebrain bundle, a complex pathway connecting the forebrain and the midbrain. Further studies have revealed that reinforcing effects are related to increases in synaptic dopamine levels in the brain. Blocking of dopamine receptors will reduce or eliminate the reinforcing effects of cocaine and amphetamine.

Opiates such as heroin and morphine work by a similar mechanism. They activate all dopamine-containing cells of the ventral tegmental area and the substantia nigra, and most drug effects can be blocked by dopamine antagonists. Opiates are known to have multiple effects. They can relieve the distress associated with pain, withdrawal symptoms (from any source), and isolation or loss of social attachments. Evidence shows that the mechanism of opiate physical dependence is different from the system of positive reinforcement associated with the medial forebrain bundle. In this case, morphine stimulation of the periventricular gray areas (either systemically or directly into the brain) will produce physical dependence that injections of opiate antagonists such as naloxone or naltrexone can block (Wise, 1988).

One implication of these findings is that many drugs of abuse probably activate the same neural systems. This inference is consistent with the belief shared by many rehabilitation programs that total abstinence from all drugs is a condition of treatment. The possibility also exists that nicotine, alcohol, and caffeine may stimulate the same systems so that such "recreational" drugs also should not be part of the addict's intake of substances.

A second implication of these studies of the brain is that drug treatment of addictions will be inadequate as long as it deals only with the withdrawal symptoms associated with avoidance of drugs of abuse. This is because a great deal of the craving for opiates and stimulants is associated with activation of the positive reward system of the medial forebrain bundle. Successful drug abuse treatment therefore requires approaches that have a twofold effect: reduction of withdrawal symptoms and reduction of craving.

SUMMARY

This chapter has provided a brief overview of brain evolution from single-celled organisms to humans. All living organisms need to deal with certain basic adaptive challenges that relate to prey and predator, exploring and mating. One may argue that these fundamental patterns of behavioral adaptations are the functional prototypes of emotions as usually observed in humans.

A review is given of the development of the nervous system from amphibia to humans. The major brain structures are briefly defined and their interrelations described. Particular attention is given to the amygdala and the limbic system, which have been considered by many neuroscientists to be important parts of the organizing systems for emotions and emotional expressions.

Several theories are reviewed that imply that the neural circuits underlying emotions are genetically prewired and primed to respond to important life-challenging circumstances. They use autonomic and hormonal changes to increase the organism's adaptive responses to emergency situations. Because emotional reactions such as fear can be conditioned to previously neutral stimuli, it is evident that emotion circuits must interact with those neural systems related to sensation, assessment, memory, decision making, and consciousness. Knowledge of brain systems in emotion has many practical therapeutic implications, some of which are briefly described.

12 Love and Sadness in Everyday Life

> Nature has placed mankind under the governance of two sovereign masters, *pain* and *pleasure* .... They govern us in all we do, in all we say, in all we think.
>
> *Jeremy Bentham*

PREVIEW

Two emotions that are a frequent part of everyday life and about which a great deal has been written are love and sadness. Not only are both a part of every person's life, but they also represent opposites in that one is based on receiving, gaining, and attachment, whereas the other is based on loss of a valued attachment or on deprivation.

This chapter begins with a review of ideas about love as reflected in Western culture from the time of the Bible to the present day. It reveals the many meanings of the word love as it has evolved over the centuries. In recent years, some degree of consensus exists on the idea that love is a complex mixed state with many elements and even on what those elements may be. Love is also examined in the context of attachment theory.

The second part of the chapter concerns the nature of sadness and its offshoot, depression. Evidence indicates that depression is very common and that women report experiencing it more frequently than men. Theories of depression are described, as well as several approaches to the treatment of depression. The final chapter focuses on the important topic of what happens when emotional functioning "goes wrong" and people develop emotional disorders particularly anxiety and aggression.

LOVE

Love has been a focus of human attention perhaps more than any other emotion. It is a favorite topic for novelists and poets, philosophers and clerics, and everyone else as well. We are all an eager audience in the desire to know and empathize with love.

Early Western Views

The concept of heterosexual love was already part of Western thought more than 4,000 years ago, and it is often mentioned in the Old and New Testaments of the Bible. Of great interest is the fact that the word for *love* is used in a variety of contexts, so that it is evident that several meanings were attached to it.

In the Old Testament, love is used to note passionate feelings between men and women, family affection as parent for child, and theological concerns as an expression of

God's feelings for humans. It also includes the feelings of people for God and the feelings of people for other people (as in *love your neighbor*). In most passages in which the word occurs in the Bible, the word *accept* or *adopt* could probably be substituted for it. Other connotations of love are compassion, delight in, attachment, preference, and loyalty. In the *Song of Songs,* love designates sexual desire for a woman or man. In other places in the Bible, it means affection and esteem. Almost 4,000 years ago, the word *love* was used to describe the loyalty and friendship between independent and equal rulers and between king and subjects.

With the onset of Christianity, concepts of love began to change. Possibly because of the Roman emphasis on sensuality, the early Christians developed a strong counter-reaction characterized by a preoccupation with asceticism and celibacy. The concept of virginity became honored and marriage with multiple wives was abolished (Murstein, 1974). A practice called *syneisaktism* appeared, in which men and women could live in the same household but with strict continence as *spiritual lovers*. The attempt to repress sex led to a strong preoccupation with it, and more was written about sex than about love.

By the 12th century, a new phenomenon called *courtly love* appeared in Europe. Although there is controversy among historians about its origins, the forms it took are well known. Poets and musicians of that period described love as a burning passion that must be spontaneous; therefore, love within the confines of a contractual marriage was considered impossible and must be sought elsewhere.

A book written in the 12th century listed rules to describe the qualities of courtly love. Here are some of them:

- A true lover does not desire to embrace in love anyone except his beloved.
- The easy attainment of love makes it of little value; difficulty of attainment makes it of great worth.
- When a lover catches sight of his beloved, his heart palpitates.
- A person who is truly in love eats and sleeps very little.
- A true lover is constantly possessed by the thought of his beloved.

These ideas, emphasized by the troubadours of southern France, were quickly eliminated by the Albigensian Crusade at the beginning of the 13th century. In their place, new ideas extolled the difference between *pure* and *sensual* love. To love women as sexual objects was wrong; to love the manifestation of God in women was considered to be desirable.

The Puritans' Ideas

The Puritans in the colonial period in America considered love as sexual passion to be a threat to one's commitment to God. Love was not a prerequisite to marriage; marriage was based on the shared values of thrift, piety, and industriousness. The wife was expected to be submissive. The poor of that period carried out courtship by *bundling,* which meant that unmarried couples could sleep in the same bed without undressing to get to know one another prior to marriage. Several methods prevented physical contact, including placing a wooden board in the middle of the bed or restricting the young girls' clothing in various ways. After marriage, adultery was a severely punished sin, and adulterers were fined, whipped, and branded. Divorce was rare.

Later American Ideas

As American economic life changed, more and more people moved from farms to cities. Women received the right to vote, and other entitlements and social relations between men and women also changed. Both men and women became relatively emancipated from their parents and experienced the sense of free choice in love and marriage partners. With free choice came an increased emphasis on finding the right partner based on ideas of romantic love.

Many people associated certain stereotyped ideas with romantic love, such as the idea that love occurs at first sight, that for each person there is only one true love, that romantic love is irrational and immature, and that women are more romantic than men. In a series of other surveys in America, a majority of women reported their belief that men lose romantic interest in their wives after marriage and become more interested in sports and business than do women. At the same time, more than half of the women saw their own role as primarily *mother* rather than *wife*. In studies of lower-class marriages, women perceived their husbands as domineering, controlling, jealous, impulsive, and given to too much drinking, whereas men described their wives as temperamental, emotional, demanding, irritating, and irrational (Murstein, 1974).

The Impact of Freud

Early in the 20th century, the writings of Freud and other psychoanalysts introduced many complexities into our ways of thinking about love. Psychoanalysts believe that unconscious drives based on infant and childhood experiences strongly influence humans. Sexuality is believed to begin at birth in the striving for pleasure and then passes through various stages—oral, anal, and phallic—before reaching the final adult stage of sexuality. Humans can express the drive for pleasure in many ways, but it always requires an object toward which it is directed. When the object is another person, the experience is called *dependent* or *anaclitic love,* but when the person himself or herself is taken as the object of the pleasure, the experience is called *narcissism.*

If a person has strong narcissistic drives, he or she tends to fall in love with someone who resembles him or her psychologically or in terms of past history. If a man is the dependent type, he may seek a love relationship with a woman who will take care of him in a motherly way, whereas a dependent woman may seek a protective, fatherlike person. From the Freudian viewpoint, a happy love relation is one that has many infantile elements of which the individual in love is often not aware (A. Freud, 1946).

Research Studies of Love

For many years, academic psychologists largely ignored the subject of love, but beginning in the 1970s, a gradually increasing literature has attempted to conceptualize the nature of love. An early study concerned the difference between *loving* and *liking* (Rubin, 1973). On the basis of a review of novelists' and scientists' descriptions of friendship and love, Rubin concluded that *love* implied idealization of another person, willingness to do things for that person, the desire for sharing, and sexual attraction, among other things. *Liking* of another person implied respect of the other, as well as a sharing of common interests. Rubin constructed a Romantic Love Scale that included such items as "I will do almost anything for___" and "If I could never be with___ I would feel miserable." An example of a liking item is "I have great confidence in___'s good judgment."

Using a somewhat similar methodology, Pam, Plutchik, and Conte (1975) identified five major components of a love relationship: respect, congeniality, physical
attraction, attachment, and altruism. A self-report questionnaire, the *Love Scale*, was
developed to measure each of these components. Examples of items for each scale
follows:

- *Respect scale:* "You feel privileged to know him (her)."
- *Attachment scale:* "You feel more secure when you are with him (her)."
- *Attraction scale:* "You spontaneously want to express affection toward him (her)."
- *Congeniality scale:* "You and he (she) can work it out when you disagree."
- *Altruism scale:* "You go out of your way to do things he (she) will enjoy."

Several groups of people completed the Love Scale about someone they believed
they were in love with, or someone they were dating, and also in relation to a friend. Scores
on the scales clearly differentiated the love relation from the other types of relations on
four of the five scales, as well as on total score. Based on the findings, the most important
aspects of a love relationship appear to be physical attraction and attachment. The two
most important aspects of a dating relationship seem to be congeniality and physical
attraction, and the two most important aspects of a friendship appear to be congeniality
and respect. The results, however, indicate that there is no sharp line of demarcation
between a love relationship and a dating relationship, and it is likely that they blend into
one another.

Sternberg (1986) proposed another way of conceptualizing love relationships. He
suggested that love always involves the components of intimacy, passion, and commitment in various combinations. A triangular model that helps us understand the differences
among various types of love describes this idea. For example, according to Sternberg's
model, romantic love primarily involves intimacy and passion, whereas companionate
love primarily involves intimacy and commitment. Sternberg also believed that each of
these three components tends to follow a certain time course as a love relationship continues. Passion rises rapidly to a maximum and then gradually decreases. Both commitment
and intimacy increase more slowly and then tend to remain stable. If these patterns change
appreciably, the relationship is likely to be disrupted.

Shaver and Hazan (1988) proposed an approach to understanding love based on
evolutionary biology. They pointed out that fundamentally love is an emotion whose
characteristics are a result of the interaction of three behavioral systems: attachment, caregiving, and sexual mating. Using the work of Bowlby (1960, 1969, 1979) as a basis, they
suggested that falling in love is the establishment of an attachment bond and that maintaining an attachment bond is a source of security. The establishment of a bond leads both
to care soliciting and caregiving, and, in adults, under the influence of hormonal and other
elicitors, to sexual behavior as well. The complex of feelings associated with these states is
believed to be what most adults experience as love.

It is also obvious that these three behavior systems may exist in isolation or interact
in a variety of ways. The love of a parent for a child is a form of attachment and caregiving
behavior without sex. This characteristic is also true of the relationships between friends.
In professional settings, experts may provide medical or mental health caregiving services
without either of the other two systems. In rape, the offender activates the sexual system
without attachment or caregiving.

Shaver and Hazan (1988) pointed out the similarities between infant caregiver attachment and adult romantic love. Close proximity and contact define attachment behaviors in children. In adult lovers, there is usually a preoccupation with touching, caressing, and kissing. In children, separation from the attachment figure causes intense distress, which also happens when adult lovers are unavoidably separated. Children wish to share discoveries and reactions with their attachment figures, and lovers typically have a strong need to give gifts to each other. Childhood attachments lead to baby talk and a special quality of mothering talk. Adult lovers also sometimes use baby talk and engage in childlike playfulness. Shaver and Hazan concluded that this approach to understanding love within a broad evolutionary context offers a developmental perspective on the evolution of this complex state.

The Function of Love: Attachment Theory

Attachment theory, as part of an evolutionary approach to emotions, has played an interesting role in contemporary theories of romantic relationships in general and love in particular. To update Shaver and Hazan's (1988) study, Fraley and Shaver (2000) elaborated the basic tenets of their model and some of the implications. Their central propositions are as follows:

1. The emotional dynamics of infant–caregiver relationships and adult romantic relationships are determined by the same biological system. A key element of such dynamics is physical or psychological proximity to a caregiver or romantic partner, which in turn produces a feeling of safety and security.
2. Individual differences in adult attachment behavior reflect an individual's attachment history. Children are believed to develop an *internal working model* that represents a kind of description of expectations and interactions of events related to attachment experiences. If parents were warm and available, children grow up to become adults who are more likely to initiate friendly interactions with others. In contrast, if parents were rejecting or unpredictable, this might lead to similar behaviors when their children become adults.
3. Romantic love involves the interaction of attachment, caregiving, and sex. This implies that different biological systems are involved in the experience and expression of romantic love.

From an evolutionary point of view, there are at least four questions that need to be answered to provide a complete explanation of a behavior:

1. What factors influence the appearance of this behavior?
2. How did this behavior develop over time?
3. What is the function of this behavior?
4. What are the evolutionary origins of this behavior?

Fraley and Shaver (2000) suggested that evolution (natural selection) has borrowed the attachment system to increase bonds between adult mates, which may also increase the chances of survival of offspring. The fact that human children are dependent for such a long time (twice as long as chimpanzees) implies that the genetic success of a father cannot be measured solely by how many children he has. His genetic fitness depends on how many of his children reach sexual maturity and are able to have children of their own. These ideas deal only with some of the basic questions about romantic love, and more research is needed.

Human Mating and Attachment

Love is often related to mating, but the nature of the relation is not entirely obvious. Proponents of evolutionary theory have in recent years elaborated a theory of sexual strategies as the basis for mating. Because males can reproduce their genes with minimal involvement in contrast to the personal and energy costs to females, it has been argued that males desire to copulate with as many females as possible, whereas females are more cautious and seek mates who can provide support for a developing child (Buss & Schmidt, 1993). In partial support of these ideas, a study of thousands of college students in 37 cultures found that male students report preferring young and physically attractive women for potential mates, whereas female students prefer men with high social status and earning power (Buss, 1989). Such findings, however, are reports of preferences and not a description of real-life mate choices. Many people are unaware of the reasons for their actual mating choices. In support of these ideas, a twin study has shown that the mate choices of identical twins are no more alike than the mate choices of randomly selected pairs (Lykken & Tellegen, 1993).

Despite the high rate of divorce in some societies, most humans tend to stay with their mates for a fairly long period of time (H. E. Fisher, 1992). Why is this so? Hazan and Diamond (2000) suggested that the attachment system keeps mated adults together at least long enough for their offspring to reach reproductive age, which in turn increases the likelihood of the parents' genes being passed to future generations. They suggested that sex serves not only a reproductive function but also an attachment function, and it is attachment that prolongs the pair-bond.

Another finding apparently inconsistent with sexual strategies theory is the fact that both men and women prefer partners who are kind, understanding, and intelligent. When several women were asked to indicate their future mate choices in terms of high status versus agreeableness, most preferred the agreeable mate (Graziano, Jensen-Campbell, Todd, & Finch, 1997). When men and women were asked to indicate what facial features were most appealing, both groups largely agreed on size of smile (as a cue to warmth), large eyes (as a sign of childlike features that elicit a caregiving reaction), and prominent cheekbones (as a sign of sexiness; Cunningham, Druen, & Barbee, 1997).

These and other observations were interpreted by Hazan and Diamond (2000) as implying that both men and women seek similar qualities in a mate. Pair selection is based on the combination of attachment, caregiving, and sexual systems, and it functions to hold reproductive partners together at least long enough for offspring to reach reproductive age. Hazan and Diamond suggested that there are three factors that largely determine mate choices: physical proximity to a potential partner (*propinquity*), frequent contact with a potential partner (*familiarity*), and romantic infatuation (*reciprocal interest*). Future research will be examining these hypotheses.

SADNESS AND DEPRESSION

In the 17th century, British clergyman and scholar Robert Burton wrote a book called *The Anatomy of Melancholy*. It consisted of a large compendium of ideas and examples of the symptoms of emotional illness as it was understood at the time. It was assumed that depression or melancholy is produced by an excess of black bile in the body. It included many examples of melancholy in scholars and in nuns, and Burton buttressed his arguments with extensive quotations from Latin sources. The book has been reprinted many times and is easily available today (e.g., Burton, 2000). A copy of the cover in the 1628 edition is shown in Figure 12.1.

The layperson often thinks of sadness and depression as more or less synonymous. Clinicians, however, recognize that the depressed person is not only sad; there are mixed feelings of pessimism and hopelessness and possibly anger as well. Depression is thus a complex, mixed emotion. In 1969, Davitz asked college students to describe the ways they feel when they are depressed. The many descriptions of depression that Davitz gathered led to the conclusion that depression is a complex internal state having many elements. There are physical symptoms (*tired, sleepy*), negative feelings about oneself (*feel vulnerable*), impulses to action (*want to withdraw*), and physiological changes (*no appetite*). Any one class of descriptions is only a partial image of the complex state of depression. Not every student had all these feelings, but any one person might report several of these elements.

If people describe depression in these terms, it is evident that such feelings can happen to anyone. However, if we consider depression from the point of view of psychiatrists, depression is a mental illness and must take certain characteristic forms to justify treatment with medication, psychotherapy, or hospitalization. In the *Diagnostic and Statistical Manual of Mental Disorders,* the American Psychiatric Association (1994) defined a *major depression* in terms of such symptoms as feeling sad, losing interest or pleasure in usual activities, gaining or losing weight, having trouble sleeping or sleeping too much, having trouble concentrating or making decisions, and suicidal thoughts.

Psychiatrists add some qualifications to these criteria of major depression. For one thing, these feelings cannot be the result of an organic or medical condition about which the individual has just learned, nor should they be part of the normal reaction to the death of a loved one. The following is an illustration:

> At age 16, Claire had become anorexic–bulimic. She went through periods of eating very little and losing weight, followed by binge eating associated with vomiting. Even though Claire did not report being depressed, the family pediatrician prescribed an antidepressant that seemed to help. Gradually, the anorexic–bulimic eating pattern disappeared, and Claire went to college. In her 4th year there, she began to feel increasingly depressed. She felt sad, hopeless, tired, had impaired appetite, and was unable to concentrate on her work. She consulted a psychiatrist, who could not identify a specific precipitating incident for the current depression. Claire was given an antidepressant, which was somewhat helpful in reducing the depression but which had some unacceptable cardiovascular side effects. Another antidepressant greatly reduced the depression. At the same time, psychotherapy was also included as part of the treatment.

Other kinds of depression are recognized apart from major depression. The two other most important mood disorders are called *dysthymia* and *bipolar disorder* (the latter is also called *manic–depressive illness*). The essential feature of dysthymia is a feeling of sadness along with certain associated symptoms, such as those listed for major depression, that last for at least 2 years. One may think of it as a chronic state of depression.

For some patients, a totally opposite mood called a *manic state* either precedes or follows the *depressed state*. Manic states sometimes confuse the inexperienced observer because they do not seem at first to interfere with a person's ability to function. For example, a manic person may feel very good about herself or himself and feel able to handle

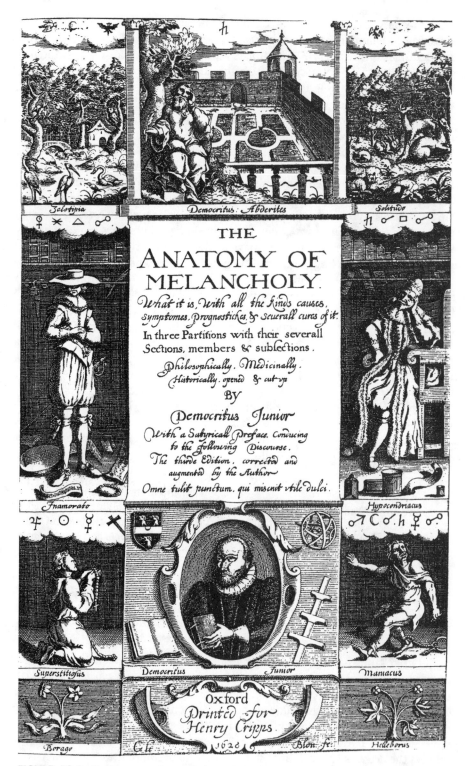

FIGURE 12.1. Front page from Robert Burton's *The Anatomy of Melancholy*, first printed in 1628. The book describes the symptoms, causes, prognostications, and cures for melancholy with many case histories.

any challenge. This person will often report feeling rested after only 3 hours of sleep. The manic person talks a lot, has racing thoughts, and is easily distracted. While in this state, the person is particularly concerned with doing pleasurable things such as buying wildly or engaging in indiscriminate sexual activity. Quite often, such manic individuals do not consider anything wrong with their behaviors, but their spouses, parents, and other relatives are deeply troubled by them.

Reactive vs. Endogenous Depression

Clinicians usually recognize a spectrum of depression-related conditions. This spectrum ranges from feelings of sadness (feeling blue), to normal reactions of grief, to reactive depressions, and to endogenous depressions. Sadness reactions and normal grief reactions tend to be brief and are associated with sad thoughts and feelings. Endogenous depressions are generally prolonged, often lasting for many months or more, and they decrease an individual's ability to function normally. In addition to sad feelings and thoughts, people with depression have difficulty with sleep, appetite, and general activity; the risk of suicide is greatly increased as well. The major difference between reactive and endogenous depressions is that a specific event such as the death of a family member, loss of a job, failure in school, or rejection by a lover usually triggers the former. In contrast, endogenous depressions occur out of the blue and usually have no association with a clear-cut triggering event.

Over the years, an extensive literature has developed for dealing with reactions to loss and factors related to recovery from loss. Early psychoanalytic writings proposed that the period of mourning was a time that gradually enabled a bereaved individual to disconnect his or her attachment from the lost object. However, Bowlby (1980) pointed out that many people who experienced loss retained a strong feeling of the continued presence of the lost person. Apparently, the ability to stay connected to the lost person, through memory and through rituals, is an effective way to cope with the loss (Klas, Silverman, & Nickman, 1996).

When deaths are sudden, as in accidents, suicides, or homicides, the bereaved person may sometimes develop trauma symptoms. These have been called *posttraumatic stress disorder (PTSD)* in servicemen who have experienced battle but the term has been applied to other stressful situations as well. In one study, individuals whose spouses had died from violent death showed more PTSD symptoms over a 2-year period than did a comparison group in which spouses had died of other causes (Bonanno & Kaltman, 1999).

In an attempt to summarize the literature, these authors suggested that an understanding of bereavement must involve the identification of the major factors that influence the grieving process. These include the age of the lost individual, his or her reproductive value, the age and sex of the grieving person, the unexpectedness of the loss, the presence of social supports, and the nature of one's cultural attitude toward the loss. These authors also pointed out that the presence of attachment bonds toward the lost person provides comfort, supports one's identity, and rewards efforts at coping. In a broad sense, these efforts made by the bereaved person are attempts at emotion regulation.

The Epidemiology of Depression

Epidemiology refers to large-scale studies of population groups done to determine what factors seem to be associated with particular illnesses or mental conditions.

Researchers attempt to identify risk factors, conditions that increase the likelihood of a person developing a particular disorder. For example, we know that risk factors for heart disease include such things as high blood pressure, high cholesterol levels, smoking, and a sedentary lifestyle.

With regard to depression, several risk factors have also been identified.

- *Age:* The onset of unipolar depressions usually occurs in young adults, but the highest prevalence of depression occurs in the mid-40s. Bipolar disorders tend to occur at a younger age, with a peak onset in the mid-20s; a third of all cases have an onset in adolescence. These disorders first appear at a younger age in women than in men. The average number of unipolar major depressions in a lifetime is 4, although some individuals may have as many as 15 to 20. In the general population, bipolar episodes occur about 10% to 20% as frequently as unipolar depressions. However, for patients in whom bipolar episodes occur, their frequency is higher, with a median lifetime frequency of about 10 (Goodwin, 1985).

- *Sex:* A great deal of research reveals that women are more likely than men to show unipolar depression. Studies reported during the past 30 years in various parts of the United States generally show that women have about twice the likelihood of unipolar depression compared with men. Similar studies in England, Scotland, and Israel report comparable findings (Nolen-Hoeksema, 1987). Efforts to explain these differences as artifacts due to variations in income, reporting biases, and types of symptoms reported fail to account for them. Biological explanations have focused on changes in women's hormonal levels and to sex-linked chromosomal effects. Studies in these areas have been inconsistent.

- *Other demographic factors:* Various studies show that separated and divorced people have higher rates of depression than those people who are married and those who have never married. Depressive symptoms occur more frequently in lower socioeconomic classes than in those of higher classes. However, researchers report bipolar symptoms more frequently in people with higher social and educational achievements. Rates of depression in African Americans and White Americans do not differ, nor are there differences in depression among religious groups (Lobel & Hirschfeld, 1984).

A large-scale mail study of 38,000 people in Great Britain tried to identify variables that correlated with depression (J. Harrison, Barrow, Gask, & Creed, 1999). It was found that such variables as absence of a confidante, long-term physical illness, unemployment, being female, single parenthood, and living alone were predictors of depression, particularly in young adults (ages 18–34 years).

Nolen-Hoeksema's (1993) review suggested that women have greater exposure to stress or traumas of various kinds because of their relative lack of social power compared with that of men. For example, women are much more likely to be the victims of sexual assaults. In addition, some studies, but not all, suggest that girls tend to be more dependent than boys and that these gender differences may increase in adolescence. Nolen-Hoeksema also pointed out that boys are more likely to take action of some kind to relieve their distress, whereas girls tend to focus on inner feelings. She concluded that biological, social, and psychological systems interact to influence one's level of vulnerability to depression.

Causes of Depression

The most obvious causes of depression are unpleasant and disruptive life events. These events include such things as death of a parent, spouse, or other member of one's family; loss of a job or promotion or another sign of devaluation; failure to accomplish important goals; and other personal losses such as separation or divorce. Studies show that patients with depression have had significantly more such loss experiences than other types of psychiatric patients and that suicidal patients have significantly more loss experiences than other psychiatric patients as well as greater degrees of depression (Plutchik, 2000b).

Despite these findings, it is also obvious that not everyone who experiences a major loss develops a major depression. Most people are able to cope with such losses in a variety of ways, such as through finding social supports, redirecting one's energy, and improving shortcomings if they exist. The individuals who react to *bad* life events with depression are likely to be people who are *vulnerable;* such vulnerability may be related to experiences that occurred long before the bad event. Examples of vulnerability factors that seem to increase the impact of an unpleasant life event are unemployment, lack of a close relationship with a friend or partner, and childhood loss of a parent (Brown & Harris, 1978). Other vulnerability factors include a previous history of depression, suicide attempts, and poor performance at school. In addition, people who see themselves as defective, inadequate, worthless, and failures, and who see the future as bad, are more likely to react with overt depression to unpleasant life events than others. People who are quick to blame themselves when things do not go well and who tend to evaluate events in extreme terms as good or bad also have the cognitive style of thinking that predisposes to depression (Beck, 1983).

Another possible vulnerability factor has been examined by Feingold and Mazzella (1998). They carried out a meta-analysis of 222 studies published over the past 50 years that were concerned with sex differences in attractiveness and body image. A meta-analysis is a statistical way of combining the results of many studies that may have used different populations and methods. In most studies, physical attractiveness was rated by two or more judges not acquainted with the participants. Body image was usually measured by self-ratings of degree of satisfaction with each part of one's body or by global ratings of satisfaction with one's appearance.

On average, it was found that male participants rated themselves as more physically attractive than did female participants, although female participants were more variable in their judgments about themselves. These results are probably not due to actual differences in physical attractiveness, because the judges generally rated the women as better looking than the men. The differences between men and women was greatest in adolescence and gradually decreased so that there was less of an average difference among adults.

In terms of changes over the 50-year period, it was found that an increasing number of women were dissatisfied with their body image and self-judgments of physical attractiveness. These findings may possibly be related to social pressures on women to be thin and to the increases in the number of women having eating disorders.

It has gradually become evident that depression occurs in situations other than resulting from unpleasant life events. This discovery was made by accident. Many years ago, researchers discovered that patients with hypertension could be treated effectively with the drug reserpine. In most patients, it worked quite well in reducing blood pressure levels, but in about 15% of the patients a serious side effect occurred; they became severely depressed. This observation, along with others, led to an increasing volume of research on the biochemical mechanisms that underlie depression.

One hypothesis that has guided much of this research is that depression results from decreases in the availability of neurotransmitters in the brain, particularly serotonin and norepinephrine. Autopsy data have revealed low concentrations of serotonin and its metabolites in the brains of suicidal or depressed patients. These metabolites tend also to be present in lower-than-normal amounts in the cerebrospinal fluid of depressed patients. When a neurotransmitter has served its purpose, it is destroyed or rendered inactive in a variety of ways. One way is by conversion to an inactive substance called a neurotransmitter metabolite, which then appears in various fluids of the body: cerebrospinal fluid, blood, and urine, for example. Further support for the role of neurotransmitters in depression is the fact that most antidepressant drugs act by making serotonin or norepinephrine more available for neural transmission in the brain.

Depression and Physical Illness

Physicians have noticed that many illnesses are known to cause depression. For example, hypothyroidism, a disorder of low thyroid production, is frequently associated with clinical depression. Cushing's disease, a dysfunction of the adrenal glands, tends also to be associated with depression. This type of connection is also sometimes seen in individuals who have syphilis, multiple sclerosis, mononucleosis, pancreatic cancer, and ulcerative colitis. It is not always evident whether the disease causes the depression or whether knowledge of the illness causes the depression, but sometimes these patterns are found even when the patient is unaware that he or she has any physical illness.

Physicians have also found that several medications tend to induce depressions in particularly sensitive individuals. As stated earlier, antihypertensive agents such as reserpine induce depression in 15% of patients. This tendency is also true of anti-Parkinson agents such as L-dopa and various hormones such as cortisol, estrogen, and progesterone. It thus appears that not only can unpleasant life events induce depression, but imbalances of neurotransmitters in the brain and changes in various hormones in the body can as well. One result of this latter fact is that depressions sometimes occur without a known or identifiable cause.

THE TREATMENT OF DEPRESSION

Given the heterogeneity of depressive syndromes, it is not surprising that clinicians have developed a large variety of methods for the treatment of depression. Table 12.1 summarizes some of the therapeutic approaches that are being used. Because it provides a brief definition for each treatment modality, only two of the more frequently used methods are described here in more detail.

Cognitive–Behavioral Therapy

This approach to treatment assumes that our emotions are a consequence of the ways that we think about ourselves and about the world. If for any reason we think of ourselves as insecure, dependent, helpless, and apathetic, and if we anticipate that the future will only bring unpleasant events, it is difficult not to be depressed. If, however, we feel competent, interested in things, and expectant of pleasant experiences in the future, it is hard to become depressed. Cognitive–behavioral therapy attempts to get the

TABLE 12.1. Overview of Treatment Approaches to Depression

Modality	Definition
Behavioral therapy	A form of psychotherapy that focuses on modifying faulty behavior rather than basic changes in the personality. Instead of probing the unconscious or exploring the patient's thoughts and feelings, behavior therapists seek to eliminate symptoms and to modify ineffective or maladaptive patterns by applying basic learning techniques and other methods. Brief treatment.
Relaxation training	Teaches techniques to help clients learn to relax, including biofeedback and guided imagery. Brief treatment.
Self-control therapy	Encourages depressed clients to attend to positive events, to set realistic self-expectations, to increase self-reinforcement and decrease self-punishment. Brief treatment.
Social skills training	Teaches clients communication and social interaction skills. Brief treatment.
Cognitive therapy	A psychotherapeutic approach based on the concept that emotional problems are the result of faulty ways of thinking and distorted attitudes toward oneself and others. The therapist takes the role of an active guide who helps the patient correct and revise perceptions and attitudes by citing evidence to the contrary or eliciting it from the patient himself or herself. The therapist uses cognitive and behavioral techniques to correct distortions of thinking associated with depression, that is, pessimism about oneself, the world, and the future. Brief treatment.
Interpersonal psychotherapy	A form of psychotherapy in which the therapist seeks to help the patient to identify and better understand interpersonal problems and conflicts and to develop more effective ways of relating to others. The therapist focuses on client's current interpersonal relationships. Helps clients learn more effective ways of relating to others and coping with conflicts in relationships. Brief, focused treatment.
Psychodynamic psychotherapy	Any form or technique of psychotherapy that focuses on the underlying, often unconscious drive and experiences that determine behavior and adjustment. Usually long treatment.
Feminist therapy	A form of psychotherapy that views symptoms as reactions to cultural oppression rather than simply as intrapsychic phenomenon. It focuses on empowerment of the clients. Clients are helped to understand that depression stems, in part, from the cultural role of women in society. Typically open ended.
Marital and family therapy	Treatment of marital partners or parents and children. Wide range of treatment strategies, including insight-oriented and systems-oriented therapy, communication skills training, and reinforcement strategies. May be time limited or open ended.

continued

TABLE 12.1. (*continued*)

Modality	Definition
Group therapy	Psychotherapy in a group setting. Typically led by a trained therapist. May be interpersonally oriented, behaviorally oriented, or insight oriented. Provides cohesiveness and support, sharing of feelings and experiences, feedback about interpersonal skills, and problem solving.
Support	Peer self-help and consciousness-raising groups, People provide support for each other in a setting that encourages sharing feelings and innovative problem solving, may be leader-led or leaderless. Typically open ended.
Pharmacotherapy	The use of pharmacological agents in the treatment of mental disorders in conjunction with psychotherapy.
Electroconvulsive treatment	The patient is prepared by administration of barbiturate anesthesia and injection of a chemical relaxant. An electric current is then applied for a fraction of a second through electrodes placed on the temples, which immediately produces a two stage seizure (tonic and clonic). The usual treatment is bilateral, but unilateral stimulation of a nondominant hemisphere has been introduced in order to shorten the period of memory loss that follows the treatment.

Note. From *Women and Depression: Risk Factors and Treatment Issues,* by E. McGrath, C. P. Keita, B. R. Strickland, and N. F. Russo (Eds.), 1990, p. 29. Copyright 1990 by the American Psychological Association. Reprinted with permission.

depressed person to change his or her thinking styles, to avoid unpleasant situations, to plan one's time more effectively, and to be more assertive about one's wishes. Therapists attempt to help patients decrease negative thoughts about themselves and their futures. They encourage responsibility, assertiveness, and an active lifestyle, and they use homework assignments to help get patients involved in difficult tasks. Sometimes they teach social skills and new coping styles. Several studies have revealed that these methods often produce beneficial changes in depressed patients.

Psychodynamic Therapy

This treatment modality is based on Freudian psychoanalytic concepts and is widely used in private practice to treat depression as well as other conditions. This approach is based on the idea that a patient's current depression is influenced not only by a current loss but also by certain types of early life experiences. These early life experiences may be related to a real or fantasized loss of a parent, they may be related to fears associated with the strong attachments children develop to one or another of their parents, and there may be constitutional or temperamental factors involved as well. Treatment requires uncovering these early fantasies and relating them to current issues in the patient's life, including his or her relationship to the therapist. This process usually takes a long time and is quite unstructured compared with the other methods. It should be emphasized that therapists often use medications in conjunction with these various psychological treatments.

In a review of all 17 controlled studies of combined psychotherapy and pharmacology published between 1974 and 1984, Conte, Plutchik, Wild, and Karasu (1986) found that combined treatment produced a significantly better reduction in depression for outpatients with unipolar depression than did the placebo conditions. However, they also discovered that the combined treatment was only marginally superior to either psychotherapy alone or pharmacotherapy alone. These effects varied depending on whether the patients had reactive or endogenous types of depression.

How Antidepressants Work

Over the years, a great deal of research has shown that increasing the amount of serotonin involved in neurotransmission is the most effective pharmacologic treatment for depression. But how does serotonin work?

For many years, it was believed that new neurons are not created in the adult brain. Recent work, however, has demonstrated the birth of new neurons from existing neurons (called *neurogenesis*) in the hippocampus of adult rats, monkeys, and humans. Neurons also continue to be created throughout life in the *olfactory bulb*. In the dentate gyrus of the hippocampus of rats and mice, about 1,000 to 3,000 new neurons per day are formed (Jacobs, van Praag, & Gage, 2000).

When the body is exposed to certain stressors, hormones called *glucocorticoids* are released into the bloodstream and dispersed throughout the body. These hormones have been found to suppress the formation of new neurons in the hippocampus. For example, a rat exposed to the odor of a fox, one of its natural predators, will show a suppression of neural cell proliferation in the dentate gyrus, a part of the hippocampus.

In humans, through use of magnetic resonance brain imaging, it was found that a group of women with recurrent major depression had smaller hippocampal volumes than an age-matched control group, thus implying that neurogenesis was not occurring in the depressed women. It is also well known that patients with temporal lobe epilepsy show a large loss of cells in and around the hippocampus. Such patients are generally at high risk for depression.

When a drug that releases serotonin into the central nervous system is injected into adult rats, there is a two to threefold increase in cell division in the dentate gyrus and an increase in new neurons. A nearly similar result was found through the use of Prozac (which increases the availability of serotonin at synapses), as well as through the use of chronic electroconvulsive shock.

These findings help account for a well-known, but puzzling phenomenon; that is, that it typically takes 3 to 6 weeks for an antidepressant to become effective. In the light of the new findings on neurogenesis, this may be due to the time it takes for newly created hippocampal neurons to mature and integrate into existing brain circuitry. These results also help explain the fact that clinically depressed patients have a variety of memory defects; this may be because the hippocampus is involved in memory.

THE FUNCTION OF SADNESS AND DEPRESSION

From the point of view of several theories reviewed in previous chapters, emotions serve a function for the individual. What functions do sadness and depression have?

To infer the function of a particular emotion, one needs to identify the events that generally trigger the emotion and the events that generally follow the appearance of the emotion. In the case of sadness, the most common precipitating event is the loss of something important to the individual. This loss often results in characteristic facial expressions and vocalizations (such as crying or distress signals). Such distress signals typically produce a sympathetic response in adults who are exposed to them, a feeling often followed by some attempt at helpful actions. This sequence is probable and need not work exactly this way in every case. However, a helping response should occur often enough to have some long-term beneficial effects on individuals who exhibit this kind of distress signal. Under these conditions, evolutionary forces will operate on the pattern of distress response to loss because it is a survival-related pattern. To summarize this point, the function of sadness signals seems to be to elicit helpful behaviors from other people. Depression may be considered to be an extreme and persistent distress signal that continually seeks to solicit help from others.

Most writers on emotion describe sadness as a *negative* emotion, presumably because of the circumstances that bring it about. However, if sadness creates a helping response in times of great distress, then perhaps it may be considered to be a *positive* emotion. This issue was examined by Barr-Zisowitz (2000), a psychiatrist, and she presented some interesting observations:

> Lester Little (1998) found sadness and patience appraised as virtues in response to injustice in medieval monasticism. My own work on sadness in premodern England and North America discovered a highly valued sadness. Seventeen-century English diaries revealed subjects faced with difficulty who regarded patience and wisdom as solutions and were proud of their sadness. To be doleful was sometimes seen as the opposite of being sinful. . . . Melancholia as a subject of admiration fascinated many intellectuals in this period. How totally negative could such virtuous emotions feel? (p. 610)

Barr-Zisowitz (2000) also pointed out that sadness is highly valued in many Asian societies as a part of the path to salvation. In France, in the 18th century, tears were considered enjoyable and were considered a sign of compassion. It has been reported that in Tahiti, a person who has experienced grief is encouraged to try to minimize it because it is associated with fatigue and lack of drive. The Inuit Eskimos try not to get sad about issues for which they have no solution. In some societies, sadness is transformed (consciously or unconsciously) into anger. Barr-Zisowitz concluded that the willingness of individuals to use the word *sadness* with a positive or a negative connotation is related to views about anger, individualism, passivity, and where one is in a social hierarchy.

SUMMARY

Two very different emotions that are quite common in everyday life are love and sadness. Both are the core of many works of literature, and both have certain interesting relationships to one another. Love is frequently described in Western civilization and is a frequent theme in the Bible. Only in recent years has love been studied as an object of scientific investigation.

Current research has revealed that love can be considered as a complex state having a variety of components such as respect, attraction, and attachment. Other descriptions of love claim that it can be playful or a form of possessiveness. Attachment theory has attempted to understand love from an evolutionary point of view and has suggested that love results from an interaction of three biobehavioral systems: the attachment system, the caregiving system, and the mating system.

In contrast to love, which is associated with the experience of attachment, caregiving, and care receiving, sadness is associated with the loss of an important attachment or bond. Sadness, or its more chronic state, depression, is also a complex condition with multiple elements and expressions. Clinicians recognize a spectrum of sadness-related conditions that vary from feeling blue, to transient grief reactions to the loss of a family member, to endogenous depressions that seem to appear from nowhere and may last months or even years.

We know now that depression is more likely to occur in women than men, although no generally accepted explanation has yet been found for this difference. Evidence also exists for biochemical variables as well as genetic factors that may affect the likelihood of depression. Although psychiatrists often treat depression with the use of medications, psychological treatments include the use of cognitive–behavioral methods and psychoanalytic methods, and both approaches have been found to be effective. Finally, it is evident that sadness and depression usually serve a function for the affected individual. These emotions tend to elicit helping behavior from other people.

13 Understanding Emotional Disorders

Life is filled with pain and suffering.
Buddhist principle

PREVIEW

A book on emotions could not be considered complete without some discussion of what happens when our emotions do not function adequately: in other words, when an emotional disorder exists. This chapter examines what clinicians mean when they write about emotional illness or emotional problems. In part, this means that some emotions are too extreme or persistent or that some emotions are absent or too limited.

To illustrate these ideas, this chapter provides detailed descriptions of emotions frequently seen as problems in clinical practice; namely fear/anxiety and anger/aggression, and their derivatives, suicide and violence. Included are descriptions of the epidemiology of anxiety disorders, the psychological and biological theories used to interpret and treat them, and a discussion of the adaptive functions of fear and anxiety.

A parallel description is given of the subjective experience of anger and its correlates in the form of violence directed toward oneself or toward other people. Many variables influencing suicide risk are described as well as many of the overlapping variables influencing violence toward others. The chapter concludes with a discussion of the function of anger and aggression and of methods for the control of anger and violence.

WHAT IS AN EMOTIONAL DISORDER?

The ancient Greeks were among the first to describe emotional tendencies and their exacerbations in humans. Hippocrates suggested that all human beings have emotional dispositions based on bodily fluids consisting of one of four types or their combinations. The *melancholic type* was described as depressed and anxious. The *choleric type* was irritable and impulsive. The *phlegmatic type* was peaceful, passive, and controlled. And the *sanguine type* was optimistic and sociable. This classification in slightly modified form has remained popular for 2,000 years. In the 20th century, attempts have been made to relate these ideas to concepts of introversion and extroversion and to the many factor-analytic studies of personality.

Most clinicians agree that it is useful to classify mental or emotional illnesses. Such classifications can assist clinicians when making treatment decisions and can make sure that different investigators doing research are dealing with the same conditions. Despite the evident usefulness of diagnostic categories, psychiatrists have had great difficulty deciding just how many emotional disorders there are. For example, in 1917, the classification system used by the American Psychiatric Association included 59 mental disorders. In 1952, when they made the first major revision of the diagnostic system, there were 111 disorders. The 1987 revision of the *Diagnostic and Statistical Manual of Mental Disorders (DSM)* lists 261 possible diagnoses. The fourth revision of *DSM*, published in 1994, listed 397 disorders. Are people becoming more mentally ill, or are psychiatrists making finer and finer distinctions (Salzinger, 1999)?

Psychologists have not been entirely satisfied with this *DSM* system. They believe that such disorders as "luteal phase dysphoric disorder" (i.e., premenstrual tension), "nicotine dependency" (i.e., smoking too much), and "hypoactive sexual desire disorder" (not wanting sex often enough) as well as other examples are not mental disorders but rather problems in living (Follette & Houts, 1996; Maddox, 1993). Maddox suggested that the distinction between normal and abnormal is an extremely difficult decision to make and that the question of what behaviors should be changed are primarily questions of value, not of science. He also questioned the tendency to turn problems of living into pathological diagnoses.

In contrast to this view, Wakefield (1999) proposed an evolutionary account of disorders. His argument is that disorders are failures of evolutionarily designed mechanisms to perform their "natural" functions. For example, mood disorders may be considered to be "failures of naturally selected emotional systems that regulate fear, anxiety, sadness, and joy, and thought disorders [are] failures of brain mechanisms naturally selected to enable us to think rationally" (p. 383). He further pointed out that

> The fight-or-flight response has been argued to be maladaptive in today's society of constant stressful interaction and has been suggested as a factor in the growth of heart disease, but still it is not considered a disorder because it is how humans are designed. (p. 385)

From Wakefield's (1999) point of view, some inappropriate emotional responses are considered to be disorders and some are not. Uncomplicated grief over the loss of a loved one is not a disorder, nor is fear of snakes or heights, or other typical fears. However, when a mechanism (such as fear) responds when there is, in fact, no danger (as in cases of panic disorder or generalized anxiety disorder), then it may be inferred that some evolutionarily designed mechanism is unable to perform its natural function (Wakefield, 1996). A detailed analysis of these and related issues may be found in Widiger and Clark (2000). One important point they emphasized is that because of the extensive concurrence of symptoms from different diagnoses in the same individual, future *DSMs* may not be composed of individual diagnoses but will consist of symptom cluster dimensions for the rating or evaluation of psychopathology.

Despite what we intuitively know about emotions and their obvious importance in life, we might have some difficulty finding exactly the right words if we are asked to describe or define them. We might be uncertain of the best ways to describe what we think we are feeling. Thinking about feeling is not the same as feeling, and the language we use to reconstruct inner experiences is not always up to the task. Sometimes poets and novelists, with their subtle evocations of language and metaphor, catch the nuances of feeling better than we ourselves can.

Patients with posttraumatic stress disorder have been described as often using metaphors to describe their inner states. Some of their comments include "I feel like I am in a cave and can't get out" and "I feel like a pressure cooker" (see Meichenbaum, 1994). As patients improve, their metaphors often change.

From a clinical point of view, patients or clients seek psychological counseling or psychotherapy for one or more of four reasons (Plutchik, 2000b):

1. Patients may experience certain emotions such as depression, anxiety, or anger, too often or too strongly.

2. Patients may experience certain emotions too weakly or infrequently. They complain of being unable to show affection, trust, anger, or assertiveness.

3. Patients complain of difficulty in getting along with people. For example, parents make them feel guilty, bosses make them feel resentful, children disappoint them, and lovers create anxiety.

4. Patients may complain of severe conflict between two or more emotions: fear and anger, resentment and wishes for attachment, independence and dependence.

To support the idea that emotions are intimately involved in almost all clinical encounters, Plutchik (2000b) examined the symptoms and diagnostic categories described in the *DSM–IV* (American Psychiatric Association, 1994). He showed that almost all diagnoses include some dysfunction or problem with emotions. This is obvious in such conditions as *depression*, *dysthymia*, the various *anxiety disorders*, *manic episode*, and *obsessive–compulsive* disorders. It is also true for *schizophrenia* (e.g., "flat or inappropriate affect"; American Psychiatric Association, 1994, p. 288) and all the personality disorders as well. For example, the *dependent personality disorder* is described as "has difficulty expressing disagreement with others because of fear of loss of support or approval" (p. 668). The *histrionic personality disorder* is described as "shows self-dramatization, theatricality, and exaggerated expressions of emotion" (p. 568). The *paranoid personality disorder* is described as "perceives attacks on his or her character or reputation that are not apparent to others, and is quick to react angrily or to counterattack" (p. 638). These examples suggest that for most diagnoses there is at least one or more symptoms that explicitly refer to emotional states.

Of great importance is the fact that psychotherapists often see symptoms in a different way than patients do. Symptoms are seen as symbols or expressions of "something else," and that something else is determined largely by theory. Psychoanalysts see the meaning of symptoms in underlying conflicts (usually unconscious). Other clinicians see symptoms in terms of an individual's inadequate coping with life's crises. Some see symptoms as resulting from missing capabilities in individuals, which limit their ability to cope with frustrations or interpersonal conflicts. Other clinicians claim that the presence of symptoms points to inadequate underlying affect *scripts* that determine how individuals react emotionally to a wide variety of life situations. Symptoms can also be interpreted to reflect struggles for power in the hierarchical relations characteristic of all relationships. Clinicians also may interpret symptoms as reflecting the failure of the environment to meet the developing individual's basic, innate needs or propensities.

There is one additional way in which emotions enter into our ideas about psychopathology. Almost everyone agrees that the concept of emotion applies not only to subjective feelings that human adults can describe in words. Because emotions are complex states with multiple elements, sometimes a disconnection occurs between different parts of this complex emotional chain of events. Thus, for example, it is possible to have a free-floating anxiety without an awareness of the source of the anxiety (i.e., without an appropriate cognitive appraisal). It is possible to be depressed without knowing why one is depressed, or angry without an awareness of the source of anger. It is even possible to have the physical signs of a panic attack without any subjective feeling of fear or anxiety

(Kushner & Beitman, 1990). Psychiatrists also report masked anxiety or masked depression, in which signs of anxiety or depression exist without the individual being aware of them. And psychosomatic equivalents are often reported in which a physical illness appears, presumably in place of, or in reaction to, strong emotions. The following is an example:

> A patient was admitted to the hospital with complications of diabetes, chest pain, shortness of breath, and rapid breathing. The medical evaluation was negative, with no evidence of a heart or lung condition. The patient was referred to a psychiatrist who concluded that the patient was apparently experiencing repeated panic attacks that involved typical symptoms of panic, such as chest pains, palpitations, dizziness, cold flushes, sweating, and trembling. The patient, however, denied feeling either anxiety or depression, and insisted on a medical interpretation of his problem, namely, low blood sugar.

To provide a more precise understanding of emotional disorders, the following sections deal with two groups of emotions frequently seen in clinical practice. These are fear and anxiety, and anger and aggression. Included are descriptions of anxiety states, panic disorders, theories of anxiety, and their treatment. The sections on anger and aggression include the functions of aggression, the interactions of suicide and violence, and the control of anger.

FEAR AND ANXIETY

[handwritten: × emotions elicit Physiological Response]

Everyone knows what fear is. Anyone who has been in an accident or has been threatened by someone bigger or more powerful has probably felt fear. The subjective experience is usually described as unpleasant, and the accompanying physiological signs such as sweating, rapid heart beat, and trembling are disturbing in themselves. Our language probably has more synonyms for the word *fear* than for any other emotion term. It also contains several expressions that seem to be related to fear, for example:

> "I feel butterflies in my stomach."
> "I was scared stiff."
> "My hair stood on end."

Fortunately, in the ordinary course of events, most dangerous situations that induce fear are transient, and the fear experience is brief. However, some unusual aspects of fear seem puzzling. Many people have intense fears of things—moths, insects, caterpillars, and birds, for example—that could not possibly hurt them. In the lives of most people, contacts with such creatures are rare events; yet people fear them more than such dangerous objects as electrical outlets, cars, and guns. These fears are so common that psychologists have given them special names and have compiled long lists of such phobias. Table 13.1 briefly defines 22 phobias, and the possibilities are endless.

Another puzzling thing about fear is the fact that some people experience uncontrollable panic attacks, usually without a clearly provoking incident. These panic attacks are often so severe that medication and psychiatric intervention may be necessary.

[handwritten margin note: anxiety] Clinicians are particularly interested in fear because they consider it to be the central ingredient of anxiety, a state that is believed by many psychoanalytically oriented clinicians to be the basis of neurosis and many psychiatric conditions. Depression rarely occurs without associated fear or anxiety, and anger and aggressive reactions in people are often a result of fear.

TABLE 13.1. Some Common Phobias

Phobia	Fear of
Acrophobia	High places
Agoraphobia	Open places
Algophobia	Pain
Astraphobia	Thunder and lightning
Claustrophobia	Confined places
Coprophobia	Excreta
Hematophobia	Sight of blood
Hydrophobia	Water
Lalophobia	Speaking
Mysophobia	Dirt or contamination
Necrophobia	Dead bodies
Nyctophobia	Darkness, night
Pathobia	Disease, suffering
Peccatophobia	Sinning
Phonophobia	Speaking aloud
Photophobia	Bright lights
Sitophobia	Eating
Taphophobia	Being buried alive
Thanatophobia	Death
Toxophobia	Being poisoned
Xenophobia	Strangers
Zoophobia	Animals

Note. From *The Psychology and Biology of Emotion,* by R. Plutchik, 1994, p. 338. Copyright 1994 by HarperCollins. Reprinted with permission.

*disorders

Part of the problem in defining anxiety is that it has acquired several different connotations in ordinary usage. For example, one might say "I am anxious about my job interview tomorrow," meaning that the individual is worried about the outcome of this particular encounter. Someone might also say, "I am anxious to go on a safari to Africa," meaning in this case that the individual is eager to go. Psychiatrists use the term *anxiety* as a theoretical term referring to an underlying basis of neurosis. Many psychologists use the term as a description of "a sense of uncontrollability focused largely on possible future threats, danger, or other upcoming potentially negative events, in contrast to *fear,* where the danger is present and imminent" (Barlow, 2000, p. 1249). Fear thus seems to be considered an imminent reaction to a dangerous situation, whereas anxiety is an anticipatory fear.

The following case is from the American Psychiatric Association's (1987) *DSM–III–R Case Book* and is designed to illustrate the clinical manifestation of anxiety:

A 27-year-old married electrician complained of dizziness, sweating palms, heart palpitations, and ringing of the ears. He had also experienced dry mouth and throat, periods of uncontrollable shaking, and a constant "edgy" and watchful feeling that had often interfered with his ability to concentrate. These feelings have been present most of the time over the previous two years; they have not been limited to discrete periods.

Because of these symptoms the patient had seen a family practitioner, a neurologist, a neurosurgeon, a chiropractor, and an ear, nose and throat specialist. He had been placed on a hypoglycemic diet, received physiotherapy for a pinched nerve, and told he might have "an inner ear problem."

He also had many worries. He constantly worried about the health of his parents. His father, in fact, had had a myocardial infarction two years previously, but was now feeling well. [The patient] also worried about whether he was "a good father," whether his wife would ever leave him (there was no indication that she was dissatisfied with the marriage), and whether he was liked by coworkers on the job.

For the past two years the patient had few social contacts because of his nervous symptoms. Although he sometimes had to leave work when the symptoms became intolerable, he continued to work for the same company he joined for his apprenticeship following high school graduation. He tried to hide his symptoms from his wife and children, to whom he wanted to appear "perfect," and reported few problems with them as a result of his nervousness. (p. 262)

Clinical Descriptions of Anxiety Disorders

Because of the theoretical and practical importance of anxiety, clinicians have attempted to identify the many faces of anxiety disorders with the hope that such distinctions may be of value in deciding on appropriate treatments. For example, in the *DSM–IV* (American Psychiatric Association, 1994), psychiatrists identified the following major types of anxiety disorders: panic disorders, social phobia, specific phobia, obsessive–compulsive disorder, posttraumatic stress disorder, and generalized anxiety disorder.

Consider two anxiety disorders, social phobia and panic disorder. A person with social phobia has an unusually strong fear of other people's scrutiny or evaluation. The fear of embarrassment or humiliation is overwhelming and leads the individual greatly to restrict his or her interactions with others. Sometimes the fear is limited to such things as being unable to speak in a group, or to urinate in a public lavatory, or to write in front of people without trembling. In other cases, the fear may be general and involve many of the above signs in the same person.

When the phobic person is faced with the need to enter into the feared situation, strong anticipatory anxiety occurs. If the individual forces himself or herself to enter the phobic situation, he or she usually experiences intense anxiety. Typically, most such individuals go to great lengths to avoid the situation that creates such unpleasant feelings.

Social phobias usually begin in late childhood or early adolescence. The disorder is often chronic and appears more frequently in males than females. Because the phobic person recognizes that his or her fear is unreasonable and sometimes tries to cope with the problem by means of alcohol or drugs, the danger of substance abuse is great.

According to Sheehan (1983), a psychiatrist, clinically significant anxiety usually starts with a group of symptoms that occur suddenly, without warning, and for no apparent reason. Initially these symptoms may occur without a subjective feeling of anxiety.

In an early stage of clinical anxiety, the individual may feel lightheaded, dizzy, and unbalanced; he or she may have difficulty breathing, palpitations, chest pain, choking feelings, tingling or numbness in some part of the body, hot flashes, nausea, diarrhea, headaches, or a feeling of being outside of or detached from one's own body. At some point, the individual enters a second stage, which consists of subjective feelings of panic and terror that occur, apparently at random, "out of the blue." Because of the great variety of symptoms that occur, diagnosis is sometimes difficult, and the patient often develops hypochondriacal attitudes about his or her own body. If the panic attacks persist, most patients develop one or more phobias depending on where the person happens to be when the panic attacks occur. (This does not imply that all phobias in the general population develop this way.)

As the phobias become extreme, they may take the form of agoraphobia (for example), a fear of public places, crowds, cars, tunnels, and highways. Anticipatory anxiety develops as the individual begins to feel frightened in anticipation of a panic attack. Finally, as the individual finds it difficult to cope with the ordinary events of everyday life, as well as normal family responsibilities, he or she becomes pessimistic and depressed. The depression may include strong feelings of guilt as well as suicidal thoughts.

Panic Disorder

The most dramatic expressions of anxiety disorders are panic attacks. These experiences usually occur spontaneously without an obvious cause, although sometimes the sense of being trapped in an elevator, an airplane, or a tunnel triggers them. The central feature of a panic attack is an overwhelming feeling of terror. In addition, many physical sensations occur such as chest pains and dizziness, as well as certain characteristic thoughts such as fear of dying or going crazy. The following is an illustration:

> Marie had been dating Adam for about six months. She had always felt nervous in restaurants, so when Adam invited her to a good restaurant for her birthday she was upset but, in order not to disappoint him, decided to go. As they entered the restaurant she had the urge to turn and run. She sat down with her back to the window. As she faced the crowded room she felt out of control. Her breathing was too fast. Everything around her was becoming strange and unreal. She ordered a double scotch straight in the hope that the drink would relieve her anxiety. All of a sudden her heart started beating faster. She could feel the pounding in her chest; then a flushing sensation in her face. Her throat tightened, and Marie felt that she was going to choke. Beads of sweat broke out on her forehead; a rushing sensation rose from her stomach up through her chest, then came a sinking sensation in the bottom of her stomach. She felt dizzy, lightheaded, and panicky. As she stood up her hands were shaking and her legs felt like rubber. She staggered to the ladies' room. Gradually the symptoms diminished. (Sheehan, 1934).

Several studies in Europe and the United States have tried to determine the prevalence of various types of anxiety disorders. When researchers compared three cities in the United States with cities in Switzerland, Germany, and Korea, they found that the prevalence of panic disorders over a 6-month period varied over the small range of 0.6% to 1.5%, or approximately 1 person in 100 (see Humble, 1987). The prevalence of agoraphobia in these cities was somewhat higher, with 3 to 6 people in 100 reporting this problem. In all these investigations, women had a higher prevalence of anxiety disorders than did men, ranging from one and one-half to four times higher. In a comparison of two American and three European cities, the likelihood that a person would experience any type of anxiety disorder during a lifetime was between 10% and 20%. Here again, women had about twice the lifetime prevalence as compared with men. Similar sex differences have been reported in several large-scale studies (Gater et al., 1998; Lewisohn, Gotlib, Lewisohn, Seeley, & Allen, 1998).

Family studies have raised the possibility of genetic factors in anxiety. In one such study, researchers compared the first-degree relatives (i.e., father, mother, siblings, and children) of 41 patients with panic disorders with the first-degree relatives of 41 normal control individuals. It was found that the patients' relatives had a lifetime risk of panic disorders of 24.7%, whereas relatives of control individuals had a lifetime risk of 2.3%. Of great interest is the fact that the risk of generalized anxiety disorder was about the same in the relatives of both groups (Crowe, Noyes, Pauls, et al., 1983). This observation suggests that panic disorder may have a different etiology and course compared with other forms of anxiety disorder. It is also noteworthy that alcoholism is twice as common in families of panic patients than in families of the control individuals (Harris, Noyes, Crowe, et al., 1983). This finding is consistent with the belief that alcohol is a common self-prescribed remedy for symptoms of anxiety.

To evaluate further genetic factors in anxiety and depression, researchers in Australia carried out a twin study involving 3,798 pairs of identical and fraternal twins (Kendler, Heath, Martin, & Eaves, 1986). They asked each twin about current symptoms of anxiety and depression, including such things as insomnia, loss of interest, and feelings of panic. Using a mathematical model, Kendler et al. estimated the relative importance of genetic and environmental factors with regard to each symptom. They found that genetic factors accounted for 34% to 46% of the causes of anxiety, with specific life events such as trauma or loss accounting for the rest. These findings were interpreted as implying that genetic factors have a large effect in determining vulnerability to anxiety and that traumatic life events trigger specific anxiety symptoms. Plomin, De Fries, Mchearn, & McGuffin (1997) concluded that several different genes contribute to the potential for developing anxiety disorders.

When one considers the onset and cause of anxiety disorders, the findings are different for the subtypes of anxiety. Social phobias tend to appear first in childhood or adolescence and rarely thereafter. The onset of panic disorders and agoraphobias tends to occur in late adolescence or early adulthood, with an average age of onset of about 26 years (Humble, 1987).

Psychiatrists have pointed out that there seem to be at least two kinds of anxiety. One is a feeling of *panic* that occurs at unpredictable times. The second is called *anticipatory anxiety,* which is a fear that the panic attack will recur. One reason for the distinction is that anticipatory anxiety may be temporarily reduced by sedatives that have little or no effect on panic attacks. At the same time, antidepressant medications seem to be able to block panic attacks but have no effect on anticipatory anxiety.

Klein (1981) proposed that the development of panic disorder and agoraphobia was linked to disturbed separation experiences in children. His studies found that about one third to one half of all adult patients with panic disorder or agoraphobia had histories of intense separation anxiety as children. Many of them exhibited school refusal or developed nausea and stomachaches when expected to go to school. If they could be induced to go to school, they experienced worries that some disaster would occur to their parents or that their home was burning down. Many such children can be successfully treated with the same medications that reduce panic attacks in adults. Barlow (2000) reviewed evidence on the contribution of childhood experiences to the later development of anxiety. Several studies have demonstrated an effect of early parenting experience on later anxiety. Of particular importance in the later development of anxiety are experiences that reduce the child's sense of control.

THEORIES OF ANXIETY

The False-Alarm Hypothesis of Panic Disorder

In recent years there have been several important contributions to our understanding of fear and anxiety. In reviewing theories of anxiety, Windmann (1998) noted that purely psychological theories of panic disorder assume that panic arises from a connection between threat experiences and an individual's perception of his or her own bodily symptoms. This process is called *cognitive misinterpretation* and is assumed to be irrational. A problem with this approach appears to be that there is no unambiguous temporal sequence relating cognitions, feelings, and physiological changes; in other words, what comes first? Many studies have shown that patients with panic disorders or with generalized anxiety disorder demonstrate a tendency to selectively detect, focus on, store, retrieve, and recall anxiety-related information. It is still not clear whether panic attacks are a cause or a consequence of the disorder (McNally, 1994).

Another view of anxiety, proposed by Beck and Clark (1988), states that the brain has an early warning system, which is a rapid, involuntary, unconscious, nonrational, and automatic response to minimal signs of danger. Such fast responding has high evolutionary value and increases an individual's chances of survival. In such situations, false detection of danger may occur. When such false detection is frequent, the possibility exists of an anxiety disorder.

These ideas are consistent with the findings of Le Doux (1998), who showed that the amygdala of the brain receives direct input from the sensory thalamus. This enables the amygdala to detect danger signals even if connections to the neocortex are disconnected. Le Doux (1986) also noted that unconscious, automatic reactions to danger signals by the amygdala are evolutionarily adaptive because false-positive responses to nonthreatening stimuli do little harm, whereas false-negative reactions to real dangers can be fatal.

Windmann (1998) referred to her theory as a "false-alarm hypothesis of panic disorder." She assumed that when the amygdala alarm system detects a danger, it triggers physiological responses and directs attention to the threat. If, however, there is no real danger, the cortex registers bodily fear symptoms such as palpitations, feelings of restlessness, and dizziness and misinterprets the (relatively) harmless bodily symptoms, thus producing a panic state.

The Triple Vulnerability Theory

Barlow (2000) considered anxiety to be a sense of lack of control that an individual feels in relation to possible future dangers. All anxiety is thus anticipatory. Anxiety, however, is not pathological until it becomes chronic. Panic is a primitive fear response, but one in which the individual is unable to specify the antecedent condition.

For chronic anxiety to develop in an individual, the triple vulnerability theory assumes that there are three general classes of events that need to be involved. The first is a *biological* or *genetic vulnerability*. Genetic studies cited by Barlow apparently suggest that 30% to 50% of the variability in chronic anxious behavior can be attributed to genetic factors. At present the genes are not known, but there appears to be good reasons to believe in their existence.

The second vulnerability is what Barlow called *psychological vulnerability*. This idea refers to the fact that some individuals have learned to cope well with uncontrollable, unpredictable dangerous events, whereas others have not. Early parenting styles have been shown to influence the general sense of control in children.

The third vulnerability was called *specific-stimulus vulnerability.* This implies that some children learn that certain specific objects or events are very dangerous, particularly somatic sensations. Such objects or events tend to become the focus of one's fears. For an individual to develop chronic anxiety in any one of its forms, all three types of vulnerability must exist. These ideas have provided the basis for a research program that is ongoing (Barlow, 2000).

The Unconscious Activation of Anxiety Theory

Ohman (2000) has made many contributions to our understanding of anxiety. He pointed out that fear/anxiety can be considered to be both an emotional state and a personality trait, a point I have also emphasized (Plutchik, 1997). A factor analysis of questionnaire data on self-reported fears identified four general categories of fears:

1. *Fears of interpersonal events:* for example, criticism, rejection, conflicts, and aggression from others.
2. *Fears of existential problems:* for example, death, injury, illness, blood, and surgery.
3. *Fears of animals:* for example, animals, insects, and reptiles.
4. *Fears related to spaces:* for example, open spaces, closed spaces, and solitary travel.

It can be seen that these types of fears have significance in the context of evolution and have undoubtedly been shaped by natural selection.

Ohman (2000) stated that it is not the fear/anxiety response that is maladaptive but the fact that it appears in inappropriate settings or is too easily aroused. He also believed that the amygdala is an evaluator of dangerous situations for the individual but only in a limited way, because it responds automatically only to certain features of the danger stimulus. To provide experimental support for these ideas, he used a backward-masking conditioning technique that provides a means of presenting fear stimuli outside of an individual's conscious awareness.

Several such studies revealed that the unconscious exposure to the feared stimulus (such as a picture of a spider or a snake) had a stronger unpleasant effect on the anxiety of phobic participants than of control participants even when they were unaware of the nature of the stimulus. It was also possible for Ohman (2000) to demonstrate unconscious conditioning to masked snakes or spiders but not to masked flowers or mushrooms. Ohman concluded that these results imply that dangerous stimuli may directly activate physiological and emotional responses even in the absence of conscious recognition of the stimuli. These findings help explain the often stated idea that phobias are irrational. Other data cited by Ohman (2000) indicate that patients with anxiety disorders have a strong tendency to attend to danger signals in the environment and to expect dangers to appear.

An interesting observation reported by Ohman (2000) concerned the effects of prior expectations on subjective feelings. Participants were given a lactate infusion, which has often been reported to induce feelings of anxiety. Some participants, however, were told to expect an anxiety reaction from the infusion, whereas others were told to expect positive feelings. Results showed that the people given the anxiety instructions reported unpleasant tensions. Some of those given the positive expectations reported positive feelings to the infusion, whereas others reported negative ones. These results were interpreted as emphasizing the multiplicity of factors that determine a verbal report of an emotional state.

THE TREATMENT OF ANXIETY

Therapists who have a cognitive or behavioral orientation toward psychotherapy generally believe that they can effectively treat ordinary fears and phobias by systematic desensitization. This procedure requires the client to learn to relax the muscles at will and to then confront the feared object or situation in graded steps in imagination. Sometimes the graded exposure to the feared object is carried out in vivo, that is, in an actual series of graded encounters. Researchers have reported this procedure to be more effective than desensitization performed in imagination. Further research has apparently shown that gradual desensitization is not needed. Any therapy seems to work that encourages the client to confront the phobic situation (Klein, Zitrin, Woerner, et al., 1983).

Clinicians with a psychodynamic orientation believe that anxiety occupies a unique position among the emotions in that it is considered to be the cause of repression, other ego defenses, and symptom formation. In psychoanalytic theory, the belief that emotions can be repressed creates the problem of how to identify and change a state that even the patient cannot identify.

Psychoanalysts assume that various transformations occur in the expression of an emotion so that its presence can be judged only on the basis of indirect evidence. Such indirect evidence comes from dreams, free associations, slips of the tongue, postures, facial expressions, and voice quality. It is also assumed that verbal reports of emotion by a patient are not always accurate and that self-deception is a common event. In addition, because emotions seldom occur in a pure state but have many subjective and historical links connected with them, psychoanalysis attempts to determine the elements of the complex state. For a detailed discussion of some of the procedures that may be used by any clinician to uncover emotions, see Plutchik (2000b).

THE FUNCTION OF FEAR AND ANXIETY

In 1967, English ethologist Desmond Morris asked children viewing a zoo program on television which animal they liked most and which they disliked most.

The characteristics of the most liked animals are that they all have hair rather than feathers or scales; most have flat faces, facial expressions, the capacity to manipulate small objects, and a more-or-less vertical posture. Morris (1967) suggested that the popularity of an animal is directly related to the human-like features it has.

The animals the children disliked most shared one important feature: They are dangerous to humans. When one examines the reasons the children gave for disliking snakes and spiders, the two highest ranked responses focus on "slimy and dirty" and "hairy and creepy." Morris (1967) proposed that this response implies either that snakes and spiders have a strong symbolic significance or that humans have a powerful inborn response to avoid these animals. Consistent with this second idea is the fact that both monkeys and chimpanzees appear to have a strong aversion to snakes. This aversion is true even in young animals that have had little opportunity to learn how dangerous snakes can be (Seyforth, Cheney, & Marler, 1980a, 1980b).

From an evolutionary point of view, the development of phobias (avoidance re-actions) to dangerous animals has obvious survival value. The fact that some individuals have a lower threshold of reaction is consistent with the likelihood of a normal distri-bution of sensitivity thresholds to danger. Humble (1987) suggested the possibility that some individuals' unusual sensitivity to anxiety reactions may be of value to a commu-nity threatened by vague or hidden dangers (such as predators lying in wait), despite the distress it may cause these individuals. It is also likely that brain mechanisms evolved to handle dangerous emergency situations as rapidly as possible and that the existence of panic disorders reflects a dysfunction in this brain system.

It is probable that at least two different fear mechanisms have evolved to deal with threats to survival. One mechanism is to organize the body for flight and to focus all attention on this one goal. The second way the primitive brain system protects the individual from danger is to briefly shut off consciousness, inhibit reflex action, and cause fainting. This passive reaction to danger is likely when running away is impossible, but passivity may also decrease the chances of discovery and attack, and thus may have some survival value.

Trower and Gilbert (1989) suggested another way of looking at the function of fear and anxiety. Most mammals and especially primates live in social groups that are organized and stabilized by means of dominance hierarchies. That each individual enacts a role that defines his or her position within the hierarchy maintains cohesiveness of the group. If someone else of higher dominance status threatens another group member, escape from the group is rarely possible if the individual is to survive without the group's support. The result is usually some form of submissive ritual or gesture that allows the threatened individual to remain in the group. Thus, researchers assume that social anxiety evolved as a method for maintaining group cohesion. According to this theory, the socially anxious person has an appraisal and coping style that focuses on threats and loss of status in a hostile and competitive world.

ANGER AND AGGRESSION

Anger is an emotion that almost everyone feels at one time or another. A wide variety of incidents can provoke it, from waiting in a long line, to hearing someone ad-vocating abortion rights (or its opposite), to having your property stolen or your body violated. Anger generates an impulse to retaliate, attack, or injure the source of the provo-cation. People do not always act on such impulses, and when most people try to assess the possible results of retaliation, it may (or may not) inhibit the action. Thus, researchers consider anger to be an inner feeling that people do not necessarily express in overt be-havior.

Although we usually think of a specific event triggering anger, we also recognize that individuals can sometimes appear to be angry or irritable most of the time, regardless of the situations in which they find themselves. In such cases, we think of the individual as exhibiting a personality trait or as having a disposition based on anger. We give a variety of names to such traits—*hostile, irritable, spiteful, quarrelsome, cantankerous,* and *sarcastic*—but all have the common element of implied anger or attack.

The concept of *aggression* is a more complex idea than that of anger and is associ-ated with a long history of theoretical ideas. Aggressive behavior is usually considered to be acts of attack and intentions to do harm to others. In humans, the idea of intention is part of our legal system in that an accidental injury or death is considered a less serious crime than deliberate injury or death.

One problem that arises concerns whether it is possible to describe anger and aggression in lower animals for which subjective reports are not available. For example, a distinction between predatory behavior and aggressive behavior is often made (Jones, 1995). Predatory behavior is simply a way organisms obtain food. Predators are not angry at their prey animals. Their behavior in predatory settings has been described as excited and playful. Such behavior belongs in the confidence/mastery system and not the competitive/territorial system (Jones, 1995). Aggression in the latter sense is connected with angry feelings and actions and is often associated with establishing one's position in a dominance hierarchy. When two animals compete for the same resources, an attack or fight often occurs.

Aggression has also been described as a theoretical construct, an inner state of the brain and body, that may sometimes be expressed in the form of violent behavior, or not, depending on the presence or absence of inhibiting forces. This way of defining aggression has been shown to have considerable heuristic value in studies of suicide (Plutchik, 2000a). The state of anger is simply one monitor or indicator that the aggressive impulse has been activated.

Clinicians have pointed out that humans compete not only for resources but also for pride related to position. People react with rage to infringement on their perceived territory and to symbolic injuries to self-esteem. Rage is also strongly associated with shame. Scheff and Retzinger (1991) made a historical case for the German shame of defeat in World War I being a strong element in the rise of Nazism and the cruelty and rage associated with it.

Blanchard and Blanchard (1984) carried out a survey in Hawaii with several thousand college students, finding that a few situations seem to trigger most angry reactions. Apparently, anger occurs when individuals perceive a challenge to something they regard as symbolically or actually belonging to them or to a group with which they identify. A loss of status, dominance, or authority such as demotion or loss of a job also generates anger. Property damage and injury are also likely to elicit anger, at least to some degree. Blanchard and Blanchard interpreted these findings as indicating that conflicts between individuals over dominance relations and conflict over control of important resources such as food and sex are most likely to initiate anger.

If we consider aggression in a broader sense, for example, in relation to such things as alcoholism and suicide, other insights are available. In a large-scale survey of Americans, it was found that male binge drinkers of alcohol were three times more likely to express violence toward their wives than were nondrinkers (Kaufman, Kantor, & Strauss, 1987). It has also been reported that married men in treatment for alcoholism were four times more likely to be physically aggressive to their wives than were nondrinkers (O'Farrell & Murphy, 1995). On the basis of five clinical studies, Murphy and O'Farrell (1996) reported that more than 50% of the wives of men seeking alcoholism treatment had been physically assaulted in the previous year.

In a series of studies concerned with the relations between suicide and violence, I identified many risk factors as possible correlates of suicidal or violent behavior (Plutchik, 2000a). I identified at least 62 variables that are possible risk factors for suicidal behavior. These include depression, all other types of mental illness, personality disorders, number of life problems, impulsivity, a history of family violence, trait anxiety, rejection by one's father, early loss of mother or father, easy access to weapons, previous psychiatric treatment, alcohol and drug abuse, minimal family support, frequent mobility, sexual conflicts, and poor reality testing.

Risk factors for expressions of violence have also been identified. These include schizophrenia, alcohol and drug abuse, antisocial personality disorder, violence in one's own family, troubled early school experiences, previous suicidal behavior, history of fire setting, number of life problems, loss of mother or father at an early age, easy access to weapons, high testosterone levels, multiple suicide attempts, school failure, crowding, use of cocaine or amphetamines, number of behavioral problems in first-degree relatives, depression, and disturbed reality testing (Plutchik, 2000a).

What is also interesting about this compilation of risk factors is the overlap that has been found between the risk factors for suicide and those for violence directed toward others. On the basis of these and other findings, I proposed a two-factor model of the relations between suicide and violence toward others (Plutchik, 2000a). A fundamental premise of the model is that whether or not an aggressive impulse is expressed in overt behavior depends on many variables, some of which act as amplifiers of the aggressive impulse and some as attenuators of the aggressive impulse. The vectorial interactions of these factors at any given moment determine whether the aggressive impulse exceeds the threshold and is then expressed in overt behavior. A key element of the model is that some variables determine whether the violent behavior will be directed at oneself in a suicidal act, whereas different variables determine whether the violent behavior will be directed toward other people. Several studies have provided results consistent with the model (Plutchik, 1995a; Plutchik, Botsis, & van Praag, 1995). The following is an illustration:

> Marnie is an 18-year-old college freshman at a large university 400 miles from her home. The first month or two was exciting, but then she began to feel increasingly lonely. She was not comfortable with her roommates and felt dominated by them. When each of her roommates found boyfriends, she felt even more depressed. Although she had been a good student in high school, she was not doing well at college. She was ashamed to tell her parents about her sad feelings and her loneliness.
>
> Marnie found that she felt better after drinking a lot of beer, and she began to spend more of her time in the local pubs. One night she met a male student at the bar who offered to drive her home. He stopped at a deserted place and cajoled her into having sex with him. When he did not call or see her again she became increasingly depressed and one night ingested about 20 aspirin tablets. Her roommates discovered her in a groggy condition and got her to the nearest hospital in time to have her stomach pumped.

THE INTERACTION OF SUICIDE AND VIOLENCE

Newspapers periodically remind us of the close connection between violence and suicide. Headlines frequently tell us of people who commit murder and then suicide. The Guyana incident with Jim Jones is one well-known example; another occurred in Oklahoma where a postal worker shot 14 coworkers and then killed himself. At Columbine High School, in Littleton, Colorado, 2 students shot 15 other students and then shot themselves.

A few reports have looked at the statistics of homicide followed by suicide. A study by West (1966) examined data in England and Wales for the period from 1954 to 1961. He reported that the rate of murder followed by the suicide of the murderer was 33%. In contrast, it was 42% in Denmark, 22% in Australia, 4% in Philadelphia, 2% in Los Angeles (Allen, 1983), and 1%–2% in North Carolina (Dalmer & Humphrey, 1980). The Los Angeles study (Allen, 1983) found that in the majority of the homicide–suicide cases, the reason for the murder seemed to be an unbalanced, quarrelsome love relationship between husband and wife or lovers. The following newspaper account is an example:

Man shoots ex-lover, kills her fiancé

Former suitor commits suicide after shooting 3. Monticello groom-to-be was slain early yesterday—his wedding day—and his fiancée and brother were both shot by a spurned lover in the house where the couple were to be married, authorities said. The assailant later shot himself to death, police said. Manuel Saldana, 36, was to marry Emily Rodriguez at Saldana's home in a working-class neighborhood in Monticello, about 75 miles northwest of New York City. But Saldana was shot to death outside his raised-ranch house about 3 a.m. after arguing with Rodriguez's former boyfriend Eusbio Torres. Rodriguez told police that Torres, 34, entered Saldana's yard and triggered an alarm light. Saldana and his 34-year-old brother, Jose, went outside to talk to Torres, who was distraught over the upcoming marriage. Torres shot the brothers with a .22 caliber rifle, killing Manuel Saldana and wounding Jose Saldana in the shoulder and back, police said. Torres then shot Rodriguez twice through a storm door before fleeing into woods behind the house. Torres committed suicide soon after the shootings. Police found Torres' body about 4 a.m. in his apartment off the village's main street. Torres had been arrested in an assault on an ex-wife about three years ago. (1992, p. 2)

Other evidence of a connection between violence and suicide comes from the literature on the effects of crowding in prisons (Cox, Paulus, & McCain, 1984). A review of this literature indicated that population increases in prisons are associated with increased rates of suicide, disciplinary infractions (violence), psychiatric commitment, and death. Conversely, decreases in prison populations were associated with decreases in assaults, suicide attempts, and death rates.

In the early part of the 20th century, "epidemics of insanity" were reported among rubber and rayon workers accidentally poisoned by carbon disulfide. These workers showed symptoms of depression, extreme irritability, uncontrolled anger, and acute mania, and there were many cases of attempted suicide as well as homicide. Suicide may thus be a reaction to extreme states of stress that produce a cognitive disorientation. It often expresses a sense of hopelessness that an individual feels in circumstances beyond his or her control. The strong connection between aggression expressed outwardly and aggression expressed toward oneself is consistent with this view.

Ethologists have pointed out that aggressive behavior serves to increase the probability of access to resources, helps deal with conflict among individuals, and increases the chances of successful courtship and mating. In addition, neurophysiological research over many decades has established the existence of brain structures that organize patterns of aggressive behavior (e.g., lateral hypothalamus, ventral tegmental areas, midbrain central gray area, and the central and anterior portions of the septum). Research has also shown that various neurotransmitter systems are involved in the expression of aggression. Low serotonin levels have been reported to be associated with a risk of violent behavior (Baumgarten & Grozdanovic, 1995; Maes & Coccaro, 1998).

Finally, literature on behavioral genetics has revealed that many, if not most, emotional characteristics are heritable. Studies show that aggressivity is inheritable in mice and dogs (Fuller, 1986), and human studies of personality and temperament also indicate significant genetic components in assertiveness, extraversion, and dominance (Loehlin, Horn, & Willerman, 1981; Loehlin & Nichols, 1976; Wimer & Wimer, 1985).

A review of the literature on predation within species (i.e., cannibalism) has demonstrated that the killing and eating of an individual of one's own species is widespread.

Researchers have observed it in about 1,300 species, including humans (Polis, 1981), and it appears to have a strong genetic component, although the availability of food supplies can affect its frequency. In some species, cannibalism has a major influence on population size. It has been observed in at least 14 species of carnivorous mammals: lion, tiger, leopard, cougar, lynx, spotted hyena, golden jackal, wolf, coyote, dingo, red fox, arctic fox, brown bear, and grasshopper mouse. In most such cases, adults prey on immature animals and cubs. Schankman (1969) also reported cannibalism in 60 human cultures.

This brief overview suggests that aggressive behavior may have fundamental importance for survival and for regulation of populations in humans and lower animals. The evidence clearly indicates that neurological structures and biochemical processes are intimately connected with aggressive behavior and that there are genetic contributions to the individual differences one sees in aggressive traits.

THE FUNCTIONS OF ANGER AND AGGRESSION

It is evident that experiences of anger are commonplace and expressions of aggression widespread. Why is this true? What functions do anger and aggression have in human life?

The literature dealing with aggression is vast. It deals with aggression in both animals and humans and covers the range from reef fish fighting over territories to human societies battling one another over ideologies and plunder. Controversies abound over the question of how best to interpret the diversity of observations concerning aggression.

Psychoanalysts have had much to say about aggression. Freud (1922) suggested that aggression is the oldest impulse of all and can be seen even in primitive organisms. Sullivan (1956) pointed out that the purpose of anger is not to enable us to escape threatening or injurious situations but to destroy them or drive them away. Anger is most likely to occur in connection with situations that contain barriers to desired goals.

Cannon (1929) wrote,

> The rage response (crouching body, frowning brow, firm lips, clenched or grinding teeth, growled threats, tightened fists, etc.) is a complex attitude which we do not have to learn—its occurrence is a part of our native inheritance. It is a constant and uniform type of behavior, having features in common in widely scattered races of men and even in lower animals so that the nature of the attitude is at once understood without the necessity for words. It is a permanent mode of reaction; whether in childhood or old age, it differs only in minor details . . . . Any hampering or checking of activity, or opposition to one or another primary impulse brings it out. . . . These are the properties of a simple reflex, such as sneezing or coughing. (p. 243)

Scott (1980) described aggression as one of nine basic adaptations that almost all organisms make. Despite the fact that aggressive behavior patterns are widely distributed, the intensity of expression of each pattern may vary greatly both within and between species. We readily see this viability through the efforts of countless generations to domesticate wild animals. For example, Siamese fighting fish and Paradise fish belong to the same family, and in the wild both types are known for their aggressiveness. However, unlike the Siamese fighting fish, the Paradise fish have been bred for docility so they can be kept together and sold commercially to fish hobbyists.

Similarly, the brown Norway rat appeared in the United States about the time of the American Revolution and was recognized as a fierce animal with high readiness to attack other animals or humans. As biologists and psychologists became interested in using these animals for research, animal suppliers began to domesticate new strains that would be timid and easy to handle. This inbreeding was successful within 8 to 10 generations. Researchers have shown that 70% of wild rats will attack and kill mice, whereas only about 12% of domesticated rats will do the same (Karl, 1956).

One sees this same process in domestic chickens. Most are bred for passivity and productivity, but a small group of roosters were bred for fighting ability. These specially bred roosters are so aggressive they will fight to the death in cockfights that are still prevalent in parts of the United States and many other countries.

Similarly, just as dogs were bred for herding of animals, for pointing at prey, for work, or for cuteness and cuddliness, others were selected in the past for their ability to fight. This trait is true of all the terriers, which are relatively insensitive to pain, with tough skin on their necks and shoulders and strong jaws and teeth. In the fox hunts of England, beagles would be used in packs to locate a fox until the fox ran into a hollow tree trunk or a hole in the ground, at which point a terrier would be sent in to drag the terrified but still dangerous fox out of the hole.

These examples illustrate the fact that aggressiveness in animals is based on genetic predispositions that selective breeding can modify. However, the fact that the overt, or phenotypic, expression of aggression can be modified does not mean that the capacity for aggression is eliminated. It is necessary to distinguish between the potential capacity to destroy and actual destructive behavior. Selective breeding changes the average threshold for reacting aggressively to a stimulus, but it does not do this uniformly for all members of a group. Some animals will remain aggressive (or passive, as the case may be). In any case, once someone or something has exceeded the threshold for provoking aggression, even in a passive animal, the pattern of evoked aggression will take much the same form as in an animal with a low threshold for aggression. A peaceful pussycat can be provoked into a screeching rage under certain conditions.

These observations about the genetics of aggressive behavior are consistent with other types of evidence. In chapter 11, we considered how neural systems in the brain organize and control the expression of aggressive behavior. Researchers have often demonstrated that electrical stimulation of certain hypothalamic and amygdaloid nuclei in the brain will evoke attack behavior in humans as well as lower animals. Some brain tumors, particularly in the temporal lobe, may be associated with increased levels of irritability and with unprovoked destructive outbursts. In most cases, if the tumor is successfully removed, the aggressive outbursts subside. Diffuse head injuries, rabies, and some kinds of epilepsy may also produce irritable and aggressive behaviors. Increases in hormones such as testosterone will increase aggressiveness in animals and, to some degree, in humans as well (Moyer, 1983). The following example describes a case in which temporal lobe disease influenced the expression of aggression.

> A very capable young engineer gradually became increasingly aggressive toward his wife and other people. On many occasions, and apparently with little provocation, he would exhibit extreme forms of aggressive behavior. He broke down doors in his house, threatened to stab his wife, and threatened to shoot his neighbors. He was referred to a psychotherapist for treatment who came to the conclusion that the patient's impulsive attacks were irrational and out of proportion to the precipitating events and to his neurotic problems. The patient was referred for medical evaluation and was discovered to have temporal lobe disease, which was treated successfully by medication.

All this evidence for the innate character of aggressive reactions raises the question of purpose. From an evolutionary point of view, what is the function of anger and violent behavior? Or, to put this another way, what survival functions does it serve?

Konrad Lorenz (1966), the well-known ethologist, discussed this issue at length. He pointed out that Darwin's expression "the struggle for existence" is sometimes erroneously interpreted as the conflict between different species. The struggle Darwin meant was the competition between members of the same species. Typical prey–predator relations exemplify conflicts between different species (interspecific conflict). In nature, a balance typically develops between the weapons of attack and those of defense. Fights between prey and predator never go so far as to cause extinction of the prey; a state of equilibrium is almost always established between them.

Lorenz also pointed out that fights between predator and prey do not generally involve overt expressions of emotion in the predator (i.e., growling, laying the ears back, erection of hair or fur, and so on). However, many animals will attack ferociously if an enemy surprises them at less than a certain critical distance. This observation suggests a territorial function for aggressive behavior, and that is, to space out a given population of animals to avoid exhausting all sources of nutrition in a given area. This function, basically true for nutritional competitors of the same species, is found in fish, birds, and many mammals including primates. Colors of coral fish function to identify members of each species so that the spatial distribution of competitors is easy to accomplish. The songs of birds play a similar role in acoustically defining territories, and the scent of urine or feces tends to mark the territories of many mammals.

A second function of aggression is to select the strongest male animals for reproduction through rival fights. Zebras, bison, antelopes, and other grazing animals form large herds but do not engage in territorial aggression because there is enough food for all. Nevertheless, males of these species fight each other violently. Winners of the fights play a major role in fathering future generations. The survival value of herd defense results in selective breeding for size and strength in males.

A third function of aggression is to defend offspring, readily seen in many animals and particularly in humans. In this case, aggressiveness is not limited to one sex, and females may be more aggressive than males.

A fourth function of aggression is to establish a dominance or hierarchical structure within a group. Such a social structure acts to stabilize relations among members of a group and thus maintains group cohesion, undoubtedly a property that contributes to the likelihood of survival of members of the group. A dominance hierarchy also has another function. In such systems, tension usually exists between individuals who hold immediately adjoining positions in the rank order. When conflicts occur between two or more low-ranking individuals, high-ranking ones usually intervene to protect the weaker ones. Observers have also seen that members of primate groups tend to pay most attention to older, high-ranking individuals and will imitate and learn from such individuals only (Lorenz, 1966).

In summary, ethologists suggested at least four functions of aggression: (a) It tends to space the members of a group within an environment in accordance with the food resources that are available, (b) it selects strong males for the protection of the group and for the fathering of future generations, (c) it serves to protect offspring under conditions of danger or threat, and (d) it creates a hierarchical system within a social group that provides stability for the group. These are obviously important contributions of aggression, and they help to explain the persistence of aggression in living organisms.

Anger in Humans

Novaco (1976) described another way of looking at the adaptive functions of anger and aggression when he pointed out that anger has several useful functions in humans. First, it increases the energy or intensity with which we act to accomplish our goals. It is interesting to see normally quiet, friendly people marching in front of an abortion center, shouting, threatening, and sometimes fighting with police and picketers on the other side of this controversial issue. Anger arousal induces a sense of power that may facilitate the attainment of personal goals. Second, anger displays serve an expressive function; they quickly reveal how an individual feels and an intention to quarrel or fight. This will often influence the behavior of another individual. Third, individuals often use anger expressions to intimidate others and to give the impression of a strong, threatening presence. The success of such expressions in determining an individual's reputation may increase his or her ability to gain resources and survive in the face of threats. Fourth, Novaco suggested that anger reduces anxious feelings of vulnerability. Anger blunts feelings of personal insecurity and prevents feelings of helplessness from reaching levels of conscious awareness. Last, recognition of signs of anger in others and in oneself may alert the individual to use coping strategies that may be effective in resolving conflicts.

The fact that anger has so many positive values for individuals helps to explain what sometimes seems like a puzzling fact: Many people enjoy getting angry. It is therefore misleading to describe anger as a negative emotion. It is probably more accurate to think of anger and fighting as potentially creating pleasant feelings of arousal and excitement, triumph, and joy if victorious, or sadness and pain if unsuccessful.

The Dark Side of Aggression

Although there are many reasons for thinking of aggression as having some useful functions, many people are concerned about the dark side of aggression; that is, the fact that aggression can be abusive, dangerous, destructive, and homicidal. How can we best understand this aspect of aggression?

Murder rates in the United States have been considerably higher than those in all European countries (measured in terms of the number of homicides per 100,000 population). For example, in 1990, the homicide rate in the United States was 9.4, whereas the British rate was 1.5; the Netherlands, 0.9; Sweden, 1.5; France, 1.1; and Germany, 1.0. However, to obtain some perspective on these figures, they may be compared with estimates made by historians for earlier periods of Europe. In the 14th century in London, the homicide rate was estimated to be almost 50 per 100,000 population. In Amsterdam in the 15th century, the rate was over 47, and in 15th-century Stockholm it was 42. These rates declined so that in the 19th century, the rate for England was 0.9, for Amsterdam it was 1.4, and for Stockholm it was 3.0. Of great interest is the fact that the homicide rate in the United States in 1900 was only 1.0 (Rhodes, 1999).

A social historian named Norbert Elias (1939/1994) has described the civilizing process from the Middle Ages to the present. He reported that fear was endemic in the Middle Ages, and warriors of the feudal groups of that time loved battle. Violence was the usual method for settling personal disputes in all classes of society. Revenge, jealousy, and competition were important sources of violent conflicts.

Private violence settled disputes in a world in which public sources of settlement were quite limited. Gradually, the development of courts of law displaced personal violence as a way of settling disputes, and the power to punish became limited only to the government (or the representatives of the king). Vengeance was gradually transferred from the victims' relatives to the state. To remind people of the possibilities of severe punishment for crimes, executions were made public, and mutilated bodies of criminals were often hung on posts along the road leading into each city. In several places in the modern world, the use of capital punishment for crime deterrence is still practiced.

Sources of Violence

A sociologist named Lonnie Athens (1997) has spent many years studying the most violent offenders incarcerated in the jails of the United States. He has developed a theory of how extreme forms of violence develop in an individual, the kinds of violence that often result in homicides.

Athens (1997) proposed that violent criminals go through four stages of a process he called *violentization*. He called the first stage *brutalization*, which has several aspects. *Violent subjugation* occurs when an authority figure such as a parent or gang leader uses coercion to force the individual to submit to his or her authority. A second aspect is *retaliation* for past disobedience or present disrespect. A third aspect is *personal horrification*, which means that the individual is exposed to the violent subjugation of someone cherished, such as a mother or sibling. A fourth aspect is *violent coaching* by someone whose task is to instruct the individual in violent behavior. Such a violence coach might be a parent, or relative, or gang member.

Coaches use a variety of techniques to inculcate violence. These include *story-telling* (with the violent actor as the hero), *ridicule*, *haranguing* (ranting about hurting other people), *besiegement* (social rewards for engaging in violence and penalties for not engaging), and *celebrity* (development of a sense of notoriety).

By going through all these experiences, an individual moves from being a victim of brutalization to being a ruthless aggressor. The person is then ready to attack people physically with the serious intention of harming or killing them despite little or no provocation. The norm in that individual's life is that physical violence is the most effective means of settling conflicts.

Athens (1997) emphasized that his theory does not necessarily apply to a person who commits a homicide during a robbery or because of jealousy alone. He is referring to people who are chronically violent. These ideas, interesting as they are, need to be subject to extensive research by others before they can be accepted as valid.

THE CONTROL OF ANGER

When anger occurs in extreme form, it is likely that someone will be injured. This fact is the basis for the many forms of social control that are used to limit the overt expression of anger.

The oldest and most common method for reducing anger and violence is the use of punishment. Punishment may be either physical, as in spankings, or psychological, as the following incident illustrates:

> A mother was waiting in a cashier's line in a department store. Her 7-year-old son was restlessly walking along the nearby aisle, touching everything he passed.
> The mother became increasingly agitated and finally began to talk loudly to her son.

She began with the following remark.

"Stop touching everything."

Her son ignored her and continued to touch the merchandise. She then said, "You're stupid. I can't wait for you to go back to school. Boy, am I going to go out and celebrate."

The son said nothing but continued to touch things on the counters. The mother then said, "If you don't stop touching things I'm going to hit you so hard your teeth will rattle."

The boy ignored the mother, made no remarks, and continued to wander along the aisles. After a brief hesitation the mother said, "When we get home, if your room is clean I may let you go out and play."

This threat finally roused the son to respond. He looked at his mother and said, "But my room is clean."

The mother answered, "Well, it didn't look clean to me. When we get back I'll look at it and decide if I want to let you go out and play." (Plutchik & Plutchik, 1990, p. 35)

Many people believe that punishment reduces violent behavior, but evidence suggests that it has undesirable effects as well. The punishing parent may be a role model for the punished child, who learns that violence is a good technique for getting what one wants. This observation is consistent with various studies that have shown that angry parents tend to produce angry children.

Another technique for dealing with anger and its offshoot, violence, is the use of timeout from social reinforcement when certain clearly defined violent behaviors occur. Such behaviors include tantrums, self-injury, attacks on other children or teachers, screaming, biting, and destruction of property. When a child engages in such behavior, he or she is placed in a timeout room for a relatively short period. This procedure, when used consistently, is quite successful in reducing incidents of outbursts of anger.

Rewarding behavior that is incompatible with anger and violence is another approach to reducing anger. Children or patients are given tokens that may be exchanged for desirable rewards at a later time. If the tokens reward behavior that is incompatible with violent behavior, the violence is likely to gradually decrease.

The American Psychological Association (1999) has been concerned with the problem of violence among teenagers and has developed a series of readings and programs that have begun to be widely used. The approach uses forums in schools, community centers, and religious buildings that involve teen youths and their parents in exploring issues of violence. These include such things as the recognition of warning signs of violence, the role of parent–child communication, and the role of peer groups, television, literature, and weapons. In 1999, over 50,000 youths were involved in these forums.

Finally, counseling, psychotherapy, and psychopharmacology are used in many situations to try to reduce or avert violent behaviors in individuals. To provide a theoretical foundation for such efforts, Gross (1999a, 1999b) described the emerging field of emotion regulation. He concluded that people attempt to regulate their emotions in at least five ways:

1. by selecting the situations in which they wish to be
2. by modifying the situations in which they find themselves
3. by changing their focus of attention
4. by reinterpreting the situation they are in or the events that are occurring
5. by modifying their own responses.

These methods of emotion regulation reflect the ideas introduced in recent years that are concerned with the concept of *emotional intelligence.* Goleman (1995) suggested that many individuals achieve success in life because they have emotional intelligence as well as cognitive intelligence. In his book, Goleman described the five broad areas of emotional intelligence that he considered to be central to this concept:

1. *emotional self-awareness:* recognizing one's own emotions, understanding the causes of feelings
2. *managing emotions:* anger management, expressing less aggressive behavior, handling stress, less social anxiety
3. *harnessing emotions productively:* responsibility, self-control
4. *empathy:* sensitivity to others' feelings, good at listening
5. *handling relationships:* able to resolve conflicts, assertive, cooperative and helpful.

These concepts have stimulated many researchers to develop these ideas and to find ways to measure them. For example, Saarni (1999) described the skills of emotional competence. In addition to the ones listed by Goleman (1995), she suggested the following:

1. ability to use the vocabulary of emotions
2. ability to reciprocally share emotions
3. ability to accept one's own emotional experiences, regardless of how unique or eccentric they are.

Although these are useful ideas, Davies, Stankov, and Roberts (1998) raised some relevant questions. Using a large sample, they investigated the relations among measures of emotional intelligence, traditional cognitive abilities, and personality. They found low reliability for most of the emotional intelligence subscales. They also found that many of the emotional intelligence scales correlated highly with personality scale measures, thus suggesting that emotional intelligence may in fact be an aspect of personality. These issues are in the process of fuller exploration. "Empirical research on emotional intelligence is still in its infancy" (Salovey, Bedell, Detweiler, & Mayer, 2000, p. 516).

In 1932, Albert Einstein sent a letter to Sigmund Freud asking him if he had any ideas about how to reduce the risk of war. In his interesting letter of response, Freud presented the following idea:

> If willingness to engage in war is an effect of the destructive instinct, the most obvious plan will be to bring Eros, its antagonist, into play against it. Anything that encourages the growth of emotional ties between men must operate against war. These ties may be of two kinds. In the first place they may be relations resembling those toward a loved object, though without having a sexual aim. There is no need for psychoanalysis to be ashamed to speak of love in this connection, for religion itself uses the same words: "Thou shalt love thy neighbor as thyself." This, however, is more easily said than done. The second kind of emotional tie is by means of identification. Whatever leads men to share important interests produces this community of feeling, these identifications. And the structure of society is to a large extent based on them. (Freud, 1932, p. 283)

SUMMARY

A true understanding of emotions should provide insight into disorders of emotion. It appears that we can recognize emotional disorders in several different ways. For example: (a) when some emotions are extreme or persistent, (b) when some emotions are absent or too limited, and (c) when strong emotions are in conflict.

Two of the most troubling emotions that clinicians see in practice are anxiety and anger. Individuals express anxiety in social phobias and panic disorders as well as in other ways. Epidemiological studies indicate that anxiety disorders are more likely to occur in women and to have a possible genetic component. The treatment of anxiety disorders often uses medication and a variety of psychological procedures such as psychotherapy, systematic desensitization, and confrontation. Various studies suggest that fear and anxiety have certain adaptive functions and in many dangerous circumstances may contribute to the possibility of survival.

Anger is a frequent emotional experience, but in extreme form it may lead to violence toward oneself in the form of suicide attempts or to violence toward others. In fact, there is a persistent belief among clinicians that suicide and violence are two sides of the same issue. Various studies, in fact, show that many of the same variables influence the risk of both suicide and violence. For example, crowding in prisons increases both homicide and suicide rates. There are also many reports of individuals who murder someone and then commit suicide.

Ethological studies of aggression in animal populations suggest that such behavior has a role in regulating conflicts and populations and thus has survival value. Genetic studies and brain stimulation studies (cited in chapter 11) imply that innate factors have an influence on aggression systems in the brain. Despite this tendency, it is possible to control the overt expression of violent behavior by several methods, including punishment, timeout, catharsis, psychodrama, psychotherapy, and medication.

References

Abercrombie, H. C., Schaefer, S. M., Larson, C. L., Oakes, T. R., Lindgren, K. A., Holden, J. E., et al. (1998). Metabolic rate in the right amygdala predicts negative affect in depressed patients. *NeuroReport, 9,* 3301–3307.

Adolphs, R. (1999). The human amygdala and emotion. *The Neuroscientist, 5,* 125–137.

Adolphs, R., Damasio, H., Travel, D., Cooper, G., & Damasio, A. R. (1996). Cortical systems for the recognition of emotion in facial expression. *Journal of Neuroscience, 16,* 7678–7687.

Adolphs, R., Damasio, H., Travel, D., Cooper, G., & Damasio, A. R. (2000). A role for somatosensory cortices in the visual recognition of emotion as revealed by three-dimensional lesion mapping. *Journal of Neuroscience, 20,* 2683–2690.

Aggleton, J. P., & Mishkin, M. (1986). The amygdala: Sensory gateway to the emotions. In R. Plutchik & H. Kellerman (Eds.), *Biological foundations of emotion* (Vol. 3, pp. 281–300). New York: Academic Press.

Agosta, W. C. (1992). *Chemical communication: The language of pheromones.* New York: Scientific American Library.

Ainsworth, M. D. S., & Bowlby, J. (1991). An ethological approach to personality development. *American Psychologist, 46,* 333–341.

Alheid, G. F., de Olmos, J. S., & Beltramino, C. A. (1995). Amygdala and extended amygdala. In G. Paxinos (Ed.), *The rat nervous system* (pp. 495–578). San Diego, CA: Academic Press.

Allen, B., & Potkay, C. R. (1981). On the arbitrary distinction between states and traits. *Journal of Personality and Social Psychology, 4,* 916–928.

Allen, N. H. (1983). Homicide followed by suicide: Los Angeles, 1970–1979. *Suicide and Life-Threatening Behavior, 13,* 155–165.

American Psychiatric Association. (1987). *Diagnostic and statistical manual of mental disorders* (3rd ed., rev.). Washington, DC: Author.

American Psychiatric Association. (1994). *Diagnostic and statistical manual of mental disorders* (4th ed.). Washington, DC: Author.

American Psychological Association. (1999). *Warning signs for parents.* Washington, DC: Author.

Anderson, J. R. (1996). ACT: A simple theory of complex cognition. *American Psychologist, 51,* 355–365.

Andrew, R. J. (1963). The origin and evolution of the calls and facial expressions of the primates. *Behavior, 20,* 1–109.

Andrew, R. J. (1974). Arousal and the causation of behavior. *Behavior, 51*, 135–136.

Arieti, S. (Ed.). (1974). *American handbook of psychiatry.* New York: Basic Books.

Arnold, M. B. (1960). *Emotion and personality* (2 vols.). New York: Columbia University Press.

Arnold, M. B. (1970). Perennial problems in the field of emotion. In M. B. Arnold (Ed.), *Feelings and emotions* (pp. 169–186). New York: Academic Press.

Aronoff, J., Barclay, A. M., & Stevenson, L. A. (1988). The recognition of threatening facial stimuli. *Journal of Personality and Social Psychology, 54*, 647–655.

Athens, L. (1997). *Violent criminal acts and actors revisited.* Urbana: University of Illinois Press.

Attneave, F. (1974). How do you know? *American Psychologist, 29*, 493–500.

Averill, J. R. (1975). A semantic atlas of emotional concepts. *JSAS Catalog of Selected Documents in Psychology, 5*, 330. (Ms. No. 421)

Baltaxe, C. A. (1991). Vocal communication of affect and its perception in three- to four-year-old children. *Perceptual and Motor Skills, 72*, 1187–1202.

Bargh, J. A., & Ferguson. M. J. (2000). Beyond behaviorism: On the automaticity of higher mental processes. *Psychological Bulletin, 126*, 925–945.

Barlow, D. H. (2000). Unraveling the mysteries of anxiety and its disorders from the perspective of emotion theory. *American Psychologist, 55*, 1247–1263.

Barr-Zisowitz, C. (2000). "Sadness"–Is there such a thing? In M. Lewis & J. M. Haviland-Jones (Eds.), *Handbook of emotions* (2nd ed., pp. 607–622). New York: Guilford Press.

Bateson, P. (1991). Assessment of pain in animals. *Animal Behavior, 42*, 827–839.

Baumann, U., Eckmann, F., & Stieglits, R. D. (1985). Self-rating data as a selecting factor in clinical trials of psychotropic drugs. *European Archives of Psychiatry and Neurological Science, 235*, 65–70.

Baumgarten, H. G., & Grozdanovic, Z. (1995). Psychopharmacology of central serotonergic systems. *Pharmacopyschiatry, 28*, 73–79.

Beck, A. T. (1983). Cognitive therapy of depression: New perspectives. In P. J. Clayton & J. E. Barrett (Eds.), *Treatment of depression: Old controversies and new approaches* (pp. 265–284). New York: Raven Press.

Beck, A. T., & Clark, D. A. (1988). Anxiety and depression: An information processing perspective. *Anxiety Research: An International Journal, 1*, 23–36.

Beeghly, M., & Cicchetti, D. (1994). Child maltreatment, attachment, and the self system: Emergence of an internal state lexicon in toddlers at high social risk. *Development and Psychopathology, 6*, 5–30.

Bendig, A. W. (1956). The development of a short form of the Manifest Anxiety Scale. *Journal of Consulting Psychology, 20*, 384–387.

Benesh, M., & Weiner, B. (1982). On emotion and motivation: From the notebooks of Fritz Heider. *American Psychologist, 37*, 887–895.

Benson, P. J., Campbell, R., Harris, T., Frank, M. G., & Tovee, M. J. (1999). Enhancing images of facial expressions. *Perception and Psychophysics, 61*, 259–274.

Benton, D. (1989). Measuring animal aggression. In R. Plutchik & H. Kellerman (Eds), *The measurement of emotions* (Vol. 4, pp. 261–292). New York: Academic Press.

Ben-Ze'ev, A. (2000). *The subtlety of emotions.* Cambridge, MA: MIT Press.

Berlin, B., & Kay, P. (1969). *Basic color terms: Their universality and evolution.* Berkley, CA: University of California Press.

Birch, H. C., Thomas, A., Chess, S., & Hertzig, M. E. (1962). Individuality in the development of children. *Developmental Medicine and Child Neurology, 4*, 370–379.

Blackmore, S. (1999). *The meme machine.* Cambrige, UK: Oxford University Press.

Blanchard, D. C., & Blanchard, R. J. (1984). Affect and aggression: An animal model applied to human behavior. In R. J. Blanchard & D. C. Blanchard (Eds.), *Advances in the study of aggression* (Vol. I, pp. 56–78). New York: Academic Press.

Block, J. (1957). Studies in the phenomenology of emotions. *Journal of Abnormal and Social Psychology, 54*, 358–363.

Boinski, S. (1999). Geographic variation in behavior of a primate taxon: Stress responses as a proximate mechanism in the evolution of social behavior. In S. A. Foster & J. A. Endler (Eds.), *Geographic variations in behavior: Perspectives on evolutionary mechanisms* (pp. 95–113). New York: Oxford University Press.

Bonanno, G. A., & Kaltman, S. (1999). Toward an integrative perspective on bereavement. *Psychological Bulletin, 125*, 760–776.

Bond, M., Gardner, S. T., Christian, J., & Sigal, J. J. (1983). Empirical study of self-rated defense styles. *Archives of General Psychiatry, 40*, 333–338.

Bonner, J. T. (1962). *The ideas of biology.* New York: Harper & Row.

Bornstein, M. H. (1973). Color vision and color naming: A psychological hypothesis of culture difference. *Psychological Bulletin, 80*, 257–285.

Bowlby, J. (1960). Grief and mourning in infancy and early childhood. In R. Eissler (Ed.), *Psychoanalytic study of the child.* (Vol. 15, pp. 9–52). New York: International Universities Press.

Bowlby, J. (1969). *Attachment and loss: Vol. 1. Attachment.* New York: Basic Books.

Bowlby, J. (1979). *The making and breaking of affectional bonds.* London: Tavistock.

Bowlby, J. (1980). *Loss: Sadness and depression* (Attachment and Loss, Vol. 3). New York: Basic Books.

Brain, P. F. (1981). Differentiating types of attack and defense in rodents. In P. F. Brain & D. Benton (Eds.), *Multidisciplinary approaches to aggression research* (pp. 53–78). Amsterdam: Elsevier/North Holland.

Brazelton, T. B. (1976). Early parent–infant reciprocity. In V. C. Vaughan III & T. B. Brazelton (Eds.), *The family: Can it be saved?* (pp. 31–44). New York: YearBook Medical.

Brazelton, T. B. (1983). Precursors for the development of emotions in early infancy. In R. Plutchik & H. Kellerman (Eds.), *Emotions in early development* (Vol. 2, pp. 35–56). New York: Academic Press.

Breland, K., & Breland, M. (1966). *Animal behavior.* New York: Macmillan.

Brenner, C. (1975). Affects and psychic conflict. *Psychoanalytic Quarterly, 44*, 5–28.

Brody, C., Plutchik, R., Reilly, E., & Peterson, M. (1973). Personality and problem behavior of third-grade children in regular classes. *Psychology in the Schools, 10*, 196–199.

Brown, C. W., & Harris, T. O. (1978). *Social origins of depression.* London: Tavistock.

Buck, R. (1984). *The communication of emotion.* New York: Guilford Press.

Buck, R. (1999). The biological affects: A typology. *Psychological Review, 106*, 301–336.

Buechler, S., & Izard, C. E. (1983). On the emergence, functions, and regulation of some emotion expressions in infancy. In R. Plutchik & H. Kellerman (Eds.), *Emotions in early development* (Vol. 2, pp. 293–314). New York: Academic Press.

Buirski, P., Kellerman, H., Plutchik, R., Weininger, R., & Buirski, N. (1973). A field study of emotions dominance, and social behavior in a group of baboons *(Papio anubis)*. *Primates, 14*, 67–78.

Buirski, P., & Plutchik, R. (1991). Measurement of deviant behavior in a Gombe Chimpanzee: Relation to later behavior. *Primates, 32*, 207–211.

Buirski, P., Plutchik, R., & Kellerman, H. (1978). Sex differences, dominance, and personality in the chimpanzee. *Animal Behavior, 26*, 123–129.

Burton, R. (2000). *The anatomy of melancholy*. New York: Review Books Classic.

Buss, D. M. (1989). Sex differences in human mate preferences: Evolutionary hypotheses tested in 37 cultures. *Behavioral and Brain Science, 12*, 1–49.

Buss, D. M., & Schmitt, D. P. (1993). Sexual strategies theory: An evolutionary perspective in human mating. *Psychological Review, 100*, 204–232.

Cacioppo, J. T., Berntson, G. G., Larsen, J. T., Poehlmann, K. M., & Ito, T. A. (2000). The psychophysiology of emotion. In M. Lewis & J. M. Haviland-Jones (Eds.), *Handbook of emotions* (2nd ed., pp. 173–191). New York: Guilford Press.

Campos, J., Barrett, K., Lamb, M., Goldsmith, H., & Sternberg, C. (1983). Socioemotional development. In P. H. Mussen (Ed.), *Handbook of child psychology: Vol. 2. Infancy and developmental psychology* (pp. 783–915). New York: Wiley.

Camras, L. A. (2000). Surprise! Facial expressions can be coordinative motor structures. In M. Lewis & I. Granic (Eds.), *Emotion, development and self-organization* (pp. 370–376). New York: Cambridge University Press.

Camras, L. A., & Allison, K. (1985). Children's understanding of emotional facial expressions and verbal labels. *Journal of Nonverbal Behavior, 9*, 84–94.

Cannon, W. B. (1929). *Bodily changes in pain, hunger, fear and rage*. New York: Appleton.

Carpenter, M. B., & Sutin, J. (1985). *Human neuroanatomy*. Baltimore: Williams & Wilkins.

Cattell, R. B. (1957). *Personality and motivation: Structure and measurement*. New York: Harcourt Brace Jovanovich.

Chalmers, N. R. (1987). Developmental pathways in behavior. *Animal Behavior, 35*, 659–674.

Chamove, A. S., Rosenblum, L.A., & Harlow, H. F. (1973). Monkeys (*Macaca mulatta*) raised only with peers: A pilot study. *Animal Behavior, 21*, 316–325.

Chapman, R. L., Kipfer, B. A., & Wentworth, H. (Eds.). (1977). *Dictionary of American Slang*. New York: HarperInformation.

Cheney, D. L., & Seyforth, R. M. (1988). Assessment of meaning and the detection of unreliable signals by vervet monkeys. *Animal Behaviour, 36*, 477–486.

Chiera, E. (1938). *They wrote on clay*. Chicago: University of Chicago Press.

Clancy, J., & Noyes, R., Jr. (1976). Anxiety neurosis: A disease for the medical model. *Psychosomatics, 17*, 90–93.

Clarke, D. J., & Brown, N. S. (1990). Kluver–Bucy syndrome and psychiatric illness. *British Journal of Psychiatry, 157*, 439–441.

Clore, G. L., Ortony, A., & Foss, M. A. (1987). The psychological foundations of the affective lexicon. *Journal of Personality and Social Psychology, 53*, 751–766.

Conte, H. R., & Plutchik, R. (1981). A circumplex model for interpersonal traits. *Journal of Personality and Social Psychology, 2*, 823–830.

Conte, H. R., Plutchik, R., Wild, C. V., & Karasu, T. B. (1986). Combined psychotherapy and pharmocotherapy for depression: A systematic analysis of the evidence. *Archives of General Psychiatry, 43,* 471–479.

Coren, S. (1994). *The intelligence of dogs: Canine consciousness and capabilities.* New York: Free Press.

Cosmides, L., & Tooby, J. (2000). Evolutionary psychology and the emotions. In M. Lewis & J. M. Haviland-Jones (Eds.), *Handbook of emotions* (pp. 91–115). New York: Guilford Press.

Cox, V. C., Paulus, P., & McCain, G. (1984). Prison crowding research: The relevance for raising prison standards and a general approach regarding crowding phenomena. *American Psychologist, 39,* 1148–1160.

Crowe, R. R., Noyes, R., Pauls, D. L., & Slymen, D. (1983). A family study of panic disorder. *Archives of General Psychiatry, 40,* 1065–1069.

Cunningham, M. R., Druen, P. B., & Barbee, A. P. (1997). Angels, mentors, and friends: Trade-offs among evolutionary, social, and individual variables in physical appearance. In J. A. Silpson & D. T. Kennik (Eds.), *Evolutionary social psychology* (pp. 109–140). Mahwah, NJ: Erlbaum.

Dalmer, S., & Humphrey, J. A. (1980). Offender–victim relationships in criminal homicide followed by offender's suicide: North Carolina 1972–1977. *Suicide and Life-Threatening Behavior, 10,* 106–118.

Damasio, A. R. (1994). *Decartes' error.* New York: G. P. Putnam's Sons.

Darwin, C. (1958). *The autobiography of Charles Darwin and selected letters* (F. Darwin, Ed.). New York: Dover. (Original work published 1892)

Darwin, C. (1965). *The expression of the emotions in man and animals.* Chicago: University of Chicago Press. (Original work published 1872)

Davies, M., Stankov, L., & Roberts, R. D. (1998). Emotional intelligence: In search of an elusive construct. *Journal of Personality and Social Psychology, 75,* 989–1015.

Davis, R. C. (1934). The specificity of facial expressions. *Journal of Genetic Psychology, 10,* 42–58.

Davitz, J. R. (1969). *The language of emotions.* New York: McGraw-Hill.

Davitz, J. R. (1970). A dictionary and grammar of emotion. In M. Arnold (Ed.), *Feelings and emotions: The Loyola Symposium* (pp. 251–258). New York: Academic Press.

Deacon, L. W. (1977). *The symbolic species: The co-evolution of language and the brain.* New York: W. W. Norton.

De Bonis, M., De Boesk, P., Perez-Diaz, F., & Nahas, M. (1999). A two-process theory of facial perception of emotions. *Life Sciences, 322,* 669–675.

Delgado, J. M. R. (1966). *Emotions.* Dubuque, IA: Brown.

Dember, W. N. (1974). Motivation and cognitive revolution. *American Psychologist, 29,* 161–168.

Denham, S. A. (1998). *Emotional development in young children.* New York: Guilford Press.

De Sousa, R. (1987). *The rationality of emotion.* Cambridge: MA: MIT Press.

de Waal, F. (1982). *Chimpanzee politics.* London: Jonathan Cape.

de Waal, F. (1989). *Peacemaking among primates.* Cambridge, MA: Harvard University Press.

Dimberg, U., Thunberg, M., & Elmehed, K. (2000). Unconscious facial reactions to emotional facial expressions. *Psychological Science, 11,* 86–89.

Dore, F. Y., & Kirouac, G. (1985). Identifying the eliciting situations of six fundamental emotions. *Journal of Psychology, 119*, 423–440.

Duchenne de Boulogne, G. B. (1990). *The mechanism of human facial expression.* New York: Cambridge University Press. (Original work published 1862)

Egeland, J. A., Gerhard, D. S., Paula, D. L., Sussex, J. N., Kidd, K. K., Allen, C. R., et al. (1987). Bipolar affective disorders linked to DNA markers in Chromosome 11. *Nature (London), 325*, 783–787.

Eibl-Eibesfeldt, I. (1971). *Love and hate.* New York: Holt, Rinehart, & Winston.

Eibl-Eibesfeldt, I. (1973). *The expressive behavior of the deaf-and-blind-born.* In M. von Cranach & I. Vine (Eds.), *Social communication and movement* (pp. 163–193). New York: Academic Press.

Eibl-Eibesfeldt, I. (1979). *The biology of peace and war.* New York: Viking.

Eibl-Eibesfeldt, I., & Sutterlin, C. (1990). Fear, defense and aggression in animals and man: Some ethological perspectives. In P. F. Brain & S. Parmigiani (Eds.), *Fear and defense* (pp. 310–332). London: Harwood.

Ekman, P. (1976). *Pictures of facial affect.* Palo Alto, CA: Consulting Psychologists Press.

Ekman, P. (1992). An argument for basic emotions. *Cognition and Emotion, 6*, 169–200.

Ekman, P. (1993). Facial expression and emotion. *American Psychologist, 48*, 384–392.

Ekman, P. (1994). Strong evidence for universals in facial expressions: A reply to Russell's mistaken critique. *Psychological Bulletin, 115*, 268–287.

Ekman, P., & Friesen, W. V. (1971). Constants across cultures in the face and emotion. *Journal of Personality and Social Psychology, 17*, 124–129.

Ekman, P., & Friesen, W. V. (1976). Measuring facial movement. *Environmental Psychology and Nonverbal Behavior, 1*, 56–75.

Ekman, P., Friesen, W. V., & Ancoli, S. (1980). Facial signs of emotional experience. *Journal of Personality and Social Psychology, 39*, 1125–1134.

Ekman, P., Friesen, W. V., & Simons, R. C. (1985). Is the startle reaction an emotion? *Journal of Personality and Social Psychology, 49*, 1416–1426.

Ekman, P., & Oster, H. (1979). Facial expressions of emotion. *Annual Review of Psychology, 30*, 527–554.

Elias, N. (1994). *The civilizing process.* Oxford, England: Blackwell. (Original work published 1939)

Ellis, A. (1962). *Reason and emotion in psychotherapy.* New York: Lyle Stuart.

Ervin, F. R., & Martin, L. (1986). Neurophysiological bases of the primary emotions. In R. Plutchik & H. Kellerman (Eds.), *Emotion: Theory, research and experience: Vol. 3. Biological foundations of emotion* (pp. 145–172). New York: Academic Press.

Evans, C. S., Evans, L., & Marler, P. (1993). On the meaning of alarm calls: Functional reference in an avian vocal system. *Animal Behavior, 46*, 23–38.

Feingold, A., & Mazzella, R. (1988). Gender differences in body image are increasing. *Psychological Science, 9*, 190–195.

Feleky, A. M. (1914). The expression of the emotions. *Psychological Review, 20*, 33–41.

Feyereisen, P. (1986). Production and comprehension of emotional facial expressions in brain-damaged subjects. In R. Bruyer (Ed.), *The neuropsychology of face perception and facial expression* (pp. 124–129). Hillsdale, NJ: Erlbaum.

Fisher, G. A. (1997). Theoretical and methodological elaborations of the circumplex model of personality traits and emotions. In R. Plutchik & H. R. Conte (Eds.), *Circumplex models of personality and emotions* (pp. 245–269). Washington, DC: American Psychological Association.

Fisher, H. E. (1992). *Anatomy of love.* New York: W. W. Norton.

Flavell, J. H., & Miller, P. H. (1998). Social cognition. In D. Kuhn & R. S. Siegler (Eds.), *Handbook of child psychology: Vol. 2. Cognition, perception, and language* (pp. 851–898). New York: Wiley.

Fleagle, J. G. (1999). *Primate adaptation and evolution* (2nd ed.). San Diego, CA: Academic Press.

Follette, W. C., & Houts, A. C. (1996). Models of scientific progress and the role of theory in taxonomy development: A case study of the DSM. *Journal of Consulting and Clinical Psychology, 64,* 1120–1132.

Fossey, D. (1983). *Gorillas in the mist.* Boston: Houghton-Miffin.

Fraiberg, S. (1971). Smiling and stranger reactions in blind infants. In J. Helimuth (Ed.), *Exceptional abnormalities* (pp. 112–125). New York: Brunner/Mazel.

Fraley, C., & Shaver, P. R. (2000). Adult romantic attachment: Theoretical developments, emerging controversies, and unanswered questions. *Review of General Psychology, 4,* 132–154.

Freedman, T. G. (1974). *Human infancy: An ethological perspective.* Hilisdale, NJ: Eribaum.

Freud, A. (1946). *The ego and the mechanisms of defense.* New York: International Universities Press. (Original work published 1936)

Freud, S. (1922). *Beyond the pleasure principle.* London: Hogarth Press.

Freud, S. (1932). Why war? In J. Strachey (Ed. & Trans.), *Collected papers* (pp. 273–287). New York: Basic Books.

Freud, S. (1936). *Studies on hysteria* (A. A. Brill, Trans.). New York: Nervous and Mental Disease Publications. (Original work published 1895)

Freud, S. (1959). Inhibitions, symptoms, and anxiety. In J. Strachey (Ed. & Trans.), *The standard edition of the complete psychological works of Sigmund Freud* (Vol. 20, pp. 77–175). London: Hogarth Press. (Original work published 1926)

Freud, S., & Breuer, J. (1936). *Studies on hysteria* (A. A. Brill, Trans.). New York: Nervous and Mental Disease Publication Company. (Original work published 1895)

Fridlund, A. J. (1994). *Human facial expression: An evolutionary view.* San Diego, CA: Academic Press.

Frijda, N. H. (1986). *The emotions.* New York: Cambridge University Press.

Frijda, N. H. (2000). The psychologist's point of view. In M. Lewis & J. M. Haviland-Jones (Eds.), *Handbook of emotions* (pp. 59–74). New York: Guilford Press.

Frodi, A. N., Lamb, M. E., Leavitt, L. A., Donovan, W. L., Neff, C., & Sherry, D. (1978). Fathers' and mothers' responses to the faces and cries of normal and premature infants. *Developmental Psychology, 14,* 190–198.

Fulcher, J. S. (1942). "Voluntary" facial expressions in blind and seeing children. *Archives of Psychology, 38* (Whole No. 272).

Fuiller, J. L. (1986). Genetics and emotions. In R. Plutchik & H. Kellerman (Eds.), *Emotion: Theory, research, and experience: Vol. 3. The biological foundations of emotions* (pp. 199–218). New York: Academic Press.

Galati, D., Miceli, R., & Sini, B. (2000). Judging and coding facial expression of emotions in congenitally blind children. *International Journal of Behavioral Development, 24,* 266–278.

Galati, D., Scherer, K. R., & Ricci-Bitti, P. E. (1997). Voluntary facial expression of emotion: Comparing congenitally blind children with normally sighted encoders. *Journal of Personality and Social Psychology, 73*, 1363–1379.

Galati, D., & Sini, B. (1998a). Echelonnement multidimensionnel de termes du lexique francais des emotions: Une comparison entre trois procedes d'analyse. [Multidimensional structure of French terms for emotions: A comparison between three analytic procedures] *Les Cahiers Internationaux de Psychologie Sociale, 37*, 76–96.

Galati, D., & Sini, B. (1998b). Les mots pour dire les emotions: Recherche sur la structure du lexique emotional italien. [Words to describe emotion: Research on the structure of the Italian emotional lexicon]. *Revue de Semantique et Pragmatique, 4*, 139–161.

Galati, D., Sini, B., Ferrer, S. E., Vilageliu, O. S., & Mateos Garcia, P. M. (1998).

Gallup, G. G., Jr. (1977). Self-recognition in primates: A comparative approach to the bidirectional properties of consciousness. *American Psychologist, 32*, 329–338.

Gardner, H. (1983). *Frames of mind: Theory of multiple intelligences*. New York: Basic Books.

Gardner, R. A., & Gardner, B. T. (1978). Comparative psychology and language acquisition. *Annals of the New York Academy of Sciences, 309*, 37–76.

Gardner, R. A., & Gardner, B. T. (1984). A vocabulary test for chimpanzees (*pan troglodytes*). *Journal of Comparative Psychology, 98*, 381–404.

Gater, R., Tansella, M., Korten, A., Tiements, B. G., Mavreas, V. G., & Olatawura, M. O. (1998). Sex differences in the prevalence and detection of depressive and anxiety disorders in general health care settings: Report from the World Health Organization collaborative study on psychological problems in general health care. *Archives of General Psychiatry, 55*, 405–414.

Gautier-Hion, A., Bourliere, F., Gautier, J. P., & Kingdon, J. (1988). *A primate radiation: Evolutionary biology of the African guenons*. New York: Cambridge University Press.

Geary, D. C. (2000). Evolution and proximate expression of human paternal investment. *Psychological Bulletin, 126*, 55–77.

Gellhorn, E., & Loofbourrow, G. N. (1963). *Emotions and emotional disorders*. New York: Hoeber Durscon.

Gendolla, G. H. E. (2000). On the impact of mood on behavior: An integrative theory and a review. *Review of General Psychology, 4*, 378–408.

George, C., & Solomon, J. (1999). Attachment and caregiving: The caregiving behavioral system. In J. Cassidy & P. R. Shaver (Eds.), *Handbook of attachment* (pp. 649–677). New York: Guilford Press.

Gewirtz, J. L. (1965). The course of infant smiling in four child-rearing communities in Israel. In B. M. Foss (Ed.), *Determinants of infant behavior*. New York: Wiley.

Gloor, P. (1990). Experimental phenomena of temporal lobe epilepsy: Facts and hypotheses. *Brain, 113*, 1673–1694.

Gluhbegovic, N., & Williams, T. H. (1980). *The human brain: A photographic guide*. New York: Harper & Row.

Goleman, D. (1995). *Emotional intelligence: Why it can matter more than IQ*. New York: Bantam.

Goodall, J. (1987). *The chimpanzees of Gombe: Patterns of behavior*. Cambridge, MA: Belknap.

Goodall, J. (1990). *Through a window: My thirty years with the chimpanzees of Gombe*. Boston: Houghton-Mifflin.

Goodenough, F. L. (1932). Expression of the emotions in a blind–deaf child. *Journal of Abnormal and Social Psychology, 27*, 328–333.

Goodenough, U. W. (1991). Deception by pathogens, *American Scientist, 79*, 344–355.

Goodwin, F. K. (1985). Epidemiology and clinical description of depression. In S. H. Snyder (Ed.), *Biopsychiatric insights on depression.* Summit, NJ: Psychiatric Diagnostic Laboratories of America.

Gough, H. G. (1960). The Adjective Checklist as a personality assessment research technique. *Psychological Reports, 6*, 107–122.

Gould, S. J. (1996). The tallest tale. *Natural History, 5*, 18–25.

Graham, C. A., Janseen, E., & Sanders, S. A. (2000). Effects of fragrance on female sexual arousal and mood across the menstrual cycle. *Psychophysiology, 37*, 76–84.

Gray, J. A. (1988). *The psychology of fear and stress* (2nd ed.). New York: Cambridge University Press.

Gray, J. A. (1990). Brain systems that mediate both emotion and cognition. In J. A. Gray (Ed.), *Psychobiological aspects of relationships between emotion and cognition* (pp. 269–288). Hillsdale, NJ: Erlbaum.

Graziano, W. G., Jensen-Campbell, L. A., Todd, M., & Finch, J. F. (1997). Interpersonal attraction from an evolutionary psychology perspective: Women's reactions to dominant and prosocial men. In J. A. Silpson & D. T. Kennik (Eds.), *Evolutionary social psychology* (pp. 141–167). Mahwah, NJ: Erlbaum.

Green, D. P., Goldman, S. L., & Salovey, P. (1993). Measurement error masks bipolarity in affect ratings. *Journal of Personality and Social Psychology, 64*, 1029–1041.

Green, S. (1975). Communication by a graded vocal system in Japanese monkeys. In L. A. Rosenblum (Ed.), *Primate behavior* (Vol. 4, pp. 61–78). New York: Academic Press.

Greenberg, L. S., & Paivio, S. C. (1997). *Working with emotions in psychotherapy.* New York: Guilford Press.

Griffin, D. R. (1976). *The question of animal awareness.* New York: Rockefeller University Press.

Griffin, D. R. (1992). *Animal minds.* Chicago: University of Chicago Press.

Gross, J. J. (1999a). Emotion and emotion regulation. In L. A. Pervin & O. P. John (Eds.), *Handbook of personality: Theory and research* (2nd ed., pp. 525–552). New York: Guilford Press.

Gross, J. J. (1999b). The emerging field of emotion regulation: An integrative review. *Review of General Psychology, 2*, 271–299.

Guilford, T., & Dawkins, M. S. (1991). Receiver psychology and the evolution of animal signals. *Animal Behavior, 42*, 1–14.

Guthrie, R. D. (1973). The evolution of menace. *Saturday Review of the Sciences, 1*, 22–260.

Harlow, H. F., & Mears, C. E. (1983). Emotional sequences and consequences. In R. Plutchik & H. Kellerman (Eds.), *Emotions in early development* (Vol. 2, pp. 171–198). New York: Academic Press.

Harlow, H. F., & Suomi, S. J. (1970). The nature of love simplified. *American Psychologist, 25*, 161–168.

Harris, E. L., Noyes, R., Crowe, R.R., & Chaudry, D. R. (1983). Family studies of agoraphobia: Report of a pilot study. *Archives of General Psychiatry, 40*, 1061–1064.

Harrison, J., Barrow, S., Gask, L., & Creed, F. (1999). Social determinants of GHQ score by postal survey. *Journal of Public Health, 21*, 283–288.

Harrison, R. H. (1986). The grouping of affect terms according to the situations that elicit them: A test of a cognitive theory of emotion. *Journal of Research in Personality, 20*, 252–266.

Harter, S., & Whitesell, N. R. (1989). Developmental changes in children's understanding of single, multiple, and blended emotion concepts. In C. Saarni & P. L. Harris (Eds.), *Children's understanding of emotion* (pp. 310–336). New York: Cambridge University Press.

Harvard, S. R., Steklis, H. D., & Lancaster, J. (Eds.). (1977). Origins and evolution of language and speech. *Annals of the New York Academy of Sciences, 280*, 544–561.

Haskins, R. (1979). A causal analysis of kitten vocalizations: An observational and experimental study. *Animal Behavior, 27*, 726–736.

Hasselmo, M. E., Rolls, E. T., & Baylis, G. C. (1989). The role of expression and identity in the face-selective responses of neurons in the temporal visual cortex of the monkey. *Behavioral and Brain Research, 32*, 203–218.

Hauber, M., Sherman, P., & Paprika, D. (2000). Self-referent phenotype matching in a brook parasite: The armpit effect in brown-headed cowbirds (*Molothrus ater*). *Animal Cognition, 3*, 113–117.

Hauser, M. D. (1996). *The evolution of communication.* Cambridge, MA: Bradford Press.

Hazan, C., & Diamond, L. M. (2000). The place of attachment in human mating. *Review of General Psychology, 4*, 186–204.

Heath, R. G. (1992). Correlation of brain activity with emotion: A basis for developing treatment of violent–aggressive behavior. *Journal of the American Academy of Psychoanalysis, 20*, 335–346.

Hebb, D. O. (1946). Emotion in man and animal: An analysis of the intuitive processes of recognition. *Psychological Review, 53*, 88–106.

Hebb, D. O. (1972). *Textbook of psychology.* Philadelphia: W. B. Saunders.

Heider, F. (1958). *The psychology of interpersonal relations.* New York: Wiley.

Heider, K. G. (1991). *Landscapes of emotion: Mapping three cultures of emotion in Indonesia.* New York: Cambridge University Press.

Heinrich, B., & Marzluff, J. (1995). Why ravens share. *American Scientist, 83*, 342–349.

Heyes, C. M. (1994). Reflections on self-recognition in primates. *Animal Behavior, 47*, 909–919.

Hinde, R. A. (1966). *Animal behavior: A synthesis of ethology and comparative psychology.* New York: McGraw-Hill.

Hjortsjo, C. H. (1970). *Man's face and mimic language.* Malmo, Sweden: Nordens Boktrycheri.

Hoeksma, J. B., Sep, S. M., Vester, F. C., Groot, P. F. C., Sijmons, R., & de Vries, J. (2000). The electronic mood device: Design, construction, and application. *Behavior Research Methods, Instruments, and Computers, 32*, 322–326.

Hofer, M. A. (1984). Relationships as regulators: A psychobiologic perspective on bereavement. *Psychosomatic Medicine, 46*, 183–197.

Hornak, J., Rolls, E. T., & Wade, D. (1996). Face and voice expression identification in patients with emotional and behavioral changes following ventral frontal lobe damage. *Neuropsychologia, 34*, 247–261.

Howard, P. J. (1994). *The owner's manual for the brain.* Austin, TX: Leornian Press.

Hoyt, D. P., & Magom, T. M. (1954). A validation study of the Taylor Manifest Anxiety Scale. *Journal of Clinical Psychology, 10*, 357–361.

Humble, M. (1987). Aetiology and mechanisms of anxiety disorders. *Acta Psychiatrica Scandanavica, 76*(Suppl. 335), 15–30.

Isenberg, N., Silbersweig, D., Engelien, A., Emmerich, S., Malavade, K., Beattie, B., et al. (1999). Linguistic threat activates the human amygdala. *Proceedings of the National Academy of Sciences, 96*, 10456–10459.

Izard, C. E. (1971). *The face of emotion.* New York: Appleton-Century-Crofts.

Izard, C. E. (1972). *Patterns of emotions: A new analysis of anxiety and depression.* New York: Academic Press.

Izard, C. E. (1979). *The maximally discriminative facial movement coding system (Max).* Newark: University of Delaware, Instructional Resource Center.

Izard, C. E. (1990). Facial expressions and the regulation of emotions. Journal of *Personality and Social Psychology, 58*, 487–498.

Izard, C. E. (1991). *The psychology of emotions.* New York: Plenum Press.

Izard, C. E., Fantauzzo, C., Castle, J., Haynes, M., Rayias, M., & Putnam, P. (1995). The ontogeny and significance of infants' facial expressions in the first 9 months of life. *Developmental Psychology, 31*, 997–1015.

Izard, C. E., & Tompkins, S. (1966). Affect and behavior: Anxiety as a negative affect. In C. D. Spielberger (Ed.), *Anxiety and behavior.* New York: Academic Press.

Jacobs, B. L., van Praag, H. M., & Gage, F. H. (2000). Depression and the birth and death of brain cells. *American Scientist, 88*, 340–345.

James, W. (1884). What is emotion? *Mind, 19*, 188–205.

James, W. (1890). *The principles of psychology.* New York: Holt, Rinehart & Winston.

Jerison, H. J. (1973). *Evolution of the brain and intelligence.* New York: Academic Press.

Johnston, T., & Scherer, K. R. (2000). Vocal communications of emotion. In M. Lewis & J. M. Haviland-Jones (Eds.), *Handbook of emotions* (pp. 220–235). New York: Guilford Press.

Jones, J. M. (1995). *Affects as process: An inquiry into the centrality of affect in psychological life.* Hillsdale, NJ: Analytic Press.

Jurgens, U. (1979). Vocalization as an emotional indicator: A neuroethological study in the squirrel monkey. *Behavior, 69*, 88–117.

Karasu, T. B. (1992). *Wisdom in the practice of psychotherapy.* New York: Basic Books.

Karl, P. (1956). The Norway rats killing response to the white mouse: An experimental analysis. *Behaviour, 10*, 81–103.

Karp, E. (1968). *Charles Darwin and the Origin of Species.* New York: American Heritage.

Kaufman, K., Kantor, G., & Strauss, M. A. (1987). The "drunken bum" theory of wife beating. *Social Problems, 34*, 213–230.

Kellogg, W. N., & Kellogg, L. A. (1967). *The ape and the child.* New York: Macmillan. (Original work published 1933)

Kelly, K. L., & Judd, D. B. (1955). *The ISCC–NBS method of designating colors and a dictionary of color names* (National Bureau of Standards Circular 553). Washington, DC: U.S. Government Printing Office.

Keltner, D., Kring, A. M., & Bonanno, G. A. (1999). Fleeting signs of the course of life: Facial expression and personal adjustment. *Current Directions in Psychological Science, 8,* 18–22.

Kemper, T. D. (1987). How many emotions are there? Wedding the social and the autonomic components. *American Journal of Sociology, 93,* 263–271.

Kendler, K. S., Heath, A., Martin, N. G., & Eaves, I. J. (1986). Symptoms of anxiety and depression in a volunteer twin population. *Archives of General Psychiatry, 43,* 213–221.

Kenrick, D. T. (2001). Evolutionary psychology, cognitive science, and dynamical systems: Building an integrative paradigm. *Current Directions in Psychological Science, 10,* 13–17.

Kentridge, R. W., & Appleton, J. P. (1990). Emotion: Sensory representation, reinforcement, and the temporal lobe. In J. A. Gray (Ed.), *Psychobiological aspects of realtionships between emotion and cognition* (pp. 191–208). Hillsdale, NJ: Erlbaum.

Kingdon, J. (1993). *Self-made man and his undoing.* New York: Simon & Schuster.

Kinsey, A. C., Pomeroy, W. B., & Martin, C. E. (1948). *Sexual behavior in the human male.* Philadelphia: W. B. Saunders.

Klas, D., Silverman, P. R., & Nickman, S. L. (Eds.). (1996). *Continuing bonds: New understandings of grief.* Washington, DC: Taylor & Francis.

Klein, D. F. (1981). Anxiety reconceptualized. In D. F. Klein & J. G. Robkin (Eds.), *Anxiety: New research and changing concepts* (pp. 235–263). New York: Raven Press.

Klein, D. F., Zitrin, C. M., Woerner, M. C., & Ross, D. C. (1983). Treatment of phobias: II. Behavior therapy and supportive psychotherapy: Are there any specific ingredients? *Archives of General Psychiatry, 40,* 139–145.

Kleinginna, R. R., & Kleinginna, A. M. (1981). A categorized list of emotion definitions, with suggestions for a consensual definition. *Motivation and Emotion, 5,* 345–379.

Kring, A. M., Kerr, S. L., Smith, D. A., & Neale, J. M. (1993). Flat affect in schizophrenia does not reflecte diminished subjective experience of emotion. *Journal of Abnormal Psychology, 102,* 507–517.

Kushner, M. G., & Beitman, B. D. (1990). Panic attacks without fear: An overview. *Behavior Research and Therapy, 28,* 469–479.

Lamb, M. E., Thompson, R. A., Gardner, W., & Chamov, E. L. (1985). *Infant–mother attachment.* Hillsdale, NJ: Erlbaum.

Landauer, T. K. (1998). Learning and representing verbal meaning: The latent semantic analysis theory. *Current Directions in Psychological Science, 7,* 161–164.

Landis, C. (1924). Studies of emotional reactions: II. General behavior and facial expression. *Journal of Comparative Psychology, 4,* 447–509.

Langs, R. (1990). *Psychotherapy: A basic text.* Northvale, NJ: Jason Aronson.

Lazarus, R. S. (1981). A cognitist's reply to Zajonc on emotion and cognition. *American Scientist, 36,* 222–223.

Lazarus, R. S. (1991). *Emotion and adaptation.* New York: Oxford University Press.

Lazarus, R. S. (2000). Reason and our emotions: A hard sell. *The General Psychologist, 35,* 20–25.

Lazarus, R. S., Averill, J. R., & Opton, E. M., Jr. (1970). Towards a cognitive theory of emotion. In M. Arnold (Ed.), *Feelings and emotions* (pp. 207–232). New York: Academic Press.

Lazarus, R. S., & Folkman, S. (1984). *Stress, appraisal and coping.* New York: Springer.

Lazarus, R. S., & Lazarus, B. N. (1994). *Passion and reason: Making sense of our emotions.* New York: Oxford University Press.

Le Doux, J. E. (1984). Cognition and emotion: Processing functions and brain systems. In M. S. Gazzeniga (Ed.), *Handbook of cognitive neuroscience* (pp. 267–289). New York: Plenum.

Le Doux, J. E. (1986). Sensory systems and emotion: A model of effective processing. *Integrative Psychiatry, 4,* 237–248.

Le Doux, J. E. (1987). Emotion. In F. Plum (Ed.), *Handbook of physiology: Section I. The nervous system: Vol. 5. higher functions of the brain* (pp. 675–687). Bethesda, MD: American Physiological Society.

Le Doux, J. E. (1998). *The emotional brain.* London: Weidenfeld & Nicolson.

Le Doux, J. E., & Phelps, E. A. (2000). Emotional networks in the brain. In M. Lewis & J. M. Haviland-Jones (Eds.), *Handbook of emotions* (pp. 157–172). New York: Guilford Press.

Leff, J. (1977). The cross-cultural study of emotion. *Culture, Medicine, and Psychiatry, 1,* 317–350.

Lemerise, E. A., & Dodge, K. A. (2000). The development of anger and hostile interactions. In M. Lewis & J. M. Haviland (Eds.), *Handbook of emotions.* New York: Guilford Press.

Levenson, R. W., Ekman, P., & Friesin, W. V. (1990). Voluntary facial expression generates emotion-specific nervous system activity. *Psychophysiology, 27,* 363–384.

Lewisohn, P. M., Gotlib, I. H., Lewisohn, M., Seeley, J. R., & Allen, N. B. (1998). Gender differences in anxiety disorders and anxiety symptoms in adolescents. *Journal of Abnormal Psychology, 107,* 109–117.

Leyhausen, P. (1956). Cited in R. A. Hinde (Ed.), *Animal behavior: A synthesis of ethology and comparative psychology* (p. 262). New York: McGraw-Hill.

Lieberman, P. (1975). *On the origins of language.* New York: Macmillan.

Liker, A., & Szekely, T. (1997). Aggression among female lapwings: Vanellus vanellus. *Animal Behaviour, 54,* 797–802.

Lindenmayer, J. P., Kay, S. R., & Plutchik, R. (1992). Multivantaged assessment of depression in schizophrenia. *Psychiatry Research, 42,* 199–207.

Little, L. (1998). Anger in monostic surses. In B. Rosenwein (Ed.), *Anger's past* (pp. 9–35). Ithaca, NY: Cornell University Press.

Lobel, B., & Hirschfeld, R. M. A. (1984). *Depression: What we know* (NIMH No. ADM-85-1318). Rockville, MD: U.S. Government Printing Office.

Loehlin, J. C., Horn, J. M., & Willerman, L. (1981). Personality resemblance in adoptive families. *Behavior Genetics, 11,* 309–330.

Loehlin, J. C., & Nichols, R. C. (1976). *Heredity, environment, and personality: A study of 850 sets of twins.* Austin: University of Texas Press.

Loomis, W. F. (1988). *Four billion years.* Sunderland, MA: Sinauer Associates.

Lorenz, K. (1966). *On aggression.* New York: Harcourt Brace Jovanovich.

Lorr, M., & McNair, D. M. (1984). *Manual: Profile of Mood States: Bipolar form.* San Diego, CA: Educational and Industrial Testing Service.

Lubinski, D., & Thompson, T. (1987). An animal model of the interpersonal communication of interoceptic (private) states. *Journal of Experimental Analysis of Behavior, 48,* 1–15.

Lykken, D. T., & Tellegen, A. (1993). Is human mating adventitiuns or the result of lawful choice? A twin study of mate selection. *Journal of Personality and Social Psychology, 65,* 56–68.

Lyons, M. J., Campbell, R., Plante, A., Coleman, M., Kamachi, M., & Akamatsu, S. (2000). The Noh mask effect: Vertical viewpoint dependence of facial expression perception. *Proceedings of the Royal Soceity of London B, 267,* 2239–2245.

MacLean, P. D. (1963). Phylogenesis. In P. H. Knapp (Ed.), *Expressions of the emotions in man* (pp. 16–35). New York: International Universities Press.

MacLean, P. D. (1984). Evolutionary psychiatry and the triune brain. *Psychological Medicine, 14,* 1–3.

MacLean, P. D. (1986). Ictal symptoms relating to the nature of affects and their cerebral substrate. In R. Plutchik & H. Kellerman (Eds.), *Biological foundations of emotion* (Vol. 3, pp. 61–90). New York: Academic Press.

Maddox, J. E. (1993). The mythology of psychopathology: A social cognitive view of deviance, difference and disorder. *The General Psychologist, 29,* 34–45.

Maes, M., & Coccaro, E. F. (Eds.). (1998). *Neurobiology and clinical views on aggression and impulsivity.* New York: Wiley.

Maestripiere, D., Schino, G., Aureli, F., & Troisi, A. (1992). A modest proposal: Displacement activities as an indicator of emotions in primates. *Animal Behavior, 44,* 967–979.

Mahoney, M. J. (1977). Reflections on the cognitive-learning trend in psychotherapy. *American Psychologist, 32,* 5–12.

Marler, P. (1977). Primate vocalization: Affective or symbolic? In P. Marler (Ed.), *Progress in ape research* (pp. 21–40). New York: Academic Press.

Marler, P., & Tenaza, R. (1977). Signaling behavior of apes with special reference to vocalization. In T. A. Sebeok (Ed.), *How animals communicate* (pp. 43–61). Bloomington: Indiana University Press.

Marsh, P. (1988). *Eye to eye: How people interact.* Topsfield, MA: Salem House.

Marvin, R. S., & Britner, P. A. (1999). Normative development: The ontogeny of attachment. In J. Cassidy & P. R. Shaver (Eds.), *Handbook of attachment: Theory, research, and clinical applications* (pp. 44–66). New York: Guilford Press.

Masson, J. M., & McCarthy, S. (1995). *When elephants weep.* New York: Dell.

Maurus, M., Streit, K.-M., Barclay, D., Wiesner, E., & Kuehlmorgan, B. (1988). A new approach to finding components essential for intraspecific communication. In D. D. Todt, P. Godeking, & D. Symmes (Eds.), *Primate vocal communication* (pp. 69–87). Berlin: Springer.

McDonald, M. V. (1989). Function of song in Scott's seaside sparrow *Ammodramus Mantimus peninsulae. Animal Behavior, 38,* 468–485.

McDougall, W. (1921). *An introduction to social psychology.* Boston: Luce.

McGrath, E., Keita, C. P., Strickland, B. R., & Russo, N. F. (Eds.). (1990). *Women and depression: Risk factors and treatment issues.* Washington, DC: American Psychological Association.

McGuire, M. T., & Fairbanks, L. A. (1977). Ethological psychiatry. In M. T. McGuire & L. A. Fairbanks (Eds.), *Ethological psychiatry* (pp. 1–40). New York: Grune & Stratton.

McNally, R. J. (1994). *Panic disorder: A critical analysis.* New York: Guilford Press.

Meichenbaum, D. (1994). *A clinical handbook/practical therapist manual for assessing and treating adults with post-traumatic stress disorder (PTSD)*. Waterloo, Ontario, Canada: Institute Press.

Miles, L. W. (1978). Language acquisition in apes and children. In F. C. C. Peng (Ed.), *Sign language and language acquisition in man and ape* (AAAS Selected Symposium, pp. 105–116). Washington, DC: American Association for the Advancement of Science.

Miller, R. E., Caul, W. F., & Mirsky, I. R. (1967). Communication of affects between feral and socially isolated monkeys. *Journal of Personality and Social Psychology, 7*, 231–239.

Millodot, M., & Riggs, L. A. (1970). Refraction determined electrophysiologically. *Archives of Opthalmology, 84*, 272–278.

Missaghi-Laksman, M., & Whissell, C. (1991). Children's understanding of facial expression of emotion: II. Drawing of emotion-faces. *Perceptual and Motor Skills, 72*, 1228–1230.

Moody, R. A., Jr. (1979, February). Laughter and humor in medical practice. *Behavioral Medicine*, pp. 25–29.

Moore, T. V. (1948). *The driving forces of human nature*. London: Heinemann.

Morris, D. J. (1954). The reproductive behavior of the zebra finch (*Peophila guttatal*) with special reference to pseudofemale behavior and displacement. *Behaviour, 6*, 271–322.

Morris, D. (1967). *The naked ape*. New York: McGraw-Hill.

Morris, D. (1977). *Manwatching: A field guide to human behavior*. New York: Harry N. Abrams.

Morris, D., Collett, P., Marsh, P., & O'Shaughnessy, M. (1979). *Gestures: Their origins and distribution*. New York: Stein & Day.

Morton, B. E. (1986). Biochemical studies of regional brain activities during emotional behavior. In R. Plutchik & H. Kellerman (Eds.), *Biological foundations of emotion* (pp. 381–394). New York: Academic Press.

Morton, E. S. (1977). On the occurrence and significance of motivation: Structural rules in some bird and mammal sounds. *American Naturalist, 111*, 855–869.

Moss, H. A., & Robson, K. S. (1968, August). *The role of protest behavior in the development of the mother–infant attachment*. Paper presented at the meeting of the American Psychological Association, San Francisco, CA.

Moyer, K. E. (1983). Biological bases of aggressive behavior. In R. Plutchik & H. Kellerman (Eds.), *Biological foundations of emotion* (Vol. 3, pp. 219–236). New York: Academic Press.

Murphy, C. M., & O'Farrell, T. J. (1996). Marital violence among alcoholics. *Current Directions in Psychological Science, 5*, 183–186.

Murstein, B. I. (1974). *Love, sex and marriage through the ages*. New York: Springer.

Myllyniemi, R. (1997). The interpersonal circle and the emotional undercurrents of human sociability. In R. Plutchik & H. R. Conte (Eds.), *Circumplex models of personality and emotions* (pp. 271–298). Washington, DC: American Psychological Association.

Neisser, U. (1963). The imitation of man by machine. *Science, 139*, 193–197.

Nelson, R. (1995, November 22). Scientists at Johns Hopkins discover a genetic basis for aggressive behavior in male mice. *Time*, 5.

Nesse, R. M. (1990). Evolutionary explanations of emotions. *Human Nature, 1*, 261–289.

Nesse, R. M. (1998). Emotional disorders in evolutionary perspective. *British Journal of Medical Psychology, 71*, 397–415.

Nesse, R. M. (2000). Is depression an adaptation? *Archives of General Psychiatry, 57*, 14–20.

(1992, April 19). *New Rochelle Standard Star*, p. X.

Nihara, K., Foster, R., Shellhaas, M., & Leland, H. (1970). *AAMD Behavior Scales*. Washington, DC: American Association on Mental Deficiency.

Nolen-Hoeksema, S. (1987). Sex differences in unipolar depression: Evidence and theory. *Psychological Bulletin, 101*, 259–282.

Nolen-Hoeksema, S. (1993). *Sex differences in depression*. Stanford, CA: Stanford University Press.

Novaco, R. W. (1976). The functions and regulation of the arousal of anger. *American Journal of Psychiatry, 133*, 1124–1128.

Oatley, K., & Jenkins, J. M. (1996). *Understanding emotions*. Malden, MA: Blackwell.

O'Farrell, T. J. & Murphy, C. M. (1995). Marital violence before and after alcoholism treatment. *Journal of Consulting and Clinical Psychology, 63*, 256–262.

Ohman, A. (2000). Fear and anxiety: Evolutionary, cognitive, and clinical perspectives. In M. Lewis & J. M. Haviland-Jones (Eds.), *Handbook of emotions* (pp. 573–593). New York: Guilford Press.

Olds, J., & Milner, P. (1954). Positive reinforcement produced by electrical stimulation of septal area and other regions of rat brain. *Journal of Comparative and Physiological Psychology, 47*, 419–427.

Ortony, A., Clore, G. L., & Collins, A. (1988). *The cognitive structure of emotions*. New York: Cambridge University Press.

Ortony, A., & Turner, T. J. (1990). What's basic about basic emotions? *Psychological Review, 97*, 315–331.

Osgood, C. E., Suci, C. J., & Tannenbaum, P. H. (1957). *The measurement of meaning*. Urbana: University of Illinois Press.

Owings, D. H., & Morton, E. S. (1998). *Animal vocal communication: A new approach*. Cambridge, England: Cambridge University Press.

Pam, A., Plutchik, R., & Conte, H. R. (1975). Love: A psychometric approach. *Psychological Reports, 37*, 83–88.

Panksepp, J. (1982). Toward a general psychobiological theory of emotions. *Behavioral and Brain Sciences, 5*, 407–468.

Panksepp, J. (1986). The anatomy of emotions. In R. Plutchik & H. Kellerman (Eds.), *Biological foundations of emotion* (Vol. 3, pp. 91–124). New York: Academic Press.

Panksepp, J. (1990). Gray zones at the emotion/cognition interface: A commentary. In J. A. Gray (Ed.), *Psychobiological aspects of realtionships between emotion and cognition* (pp. 289–304). Hillsdale, NJ: Erlbaum.

Panksepp, J. (2000). Emotions as natural kinds within the mammalian brain. In M. Lewis & J. M. Haviland-Jones (Eds.), *Handbook of emotions* (pp. 137–156). New York: Guilford Press.

Panksepp, J., & Miller, A. (1996). Emotions and the aging brain: Regrets and remedies. In C. Magai & S. H. McFadden (Eds.), *Handbook of emotion, adult development, and aging* (pp. 2–22). San Diego, CA: Academic Press.

Papez, J. W. (1937). A proposed mechanism of emotion. *Archives of Neurology and Psychiatry, 38*, 725–743.

Parker, G. A. (1974). Assessment strategy and the evolution of fighting behavior. *Journal of Theoretical Biology, 47,* 223–243.

Parrott, A. C., & Lasky, J. (1998). Ecstacy (MDMA) effects upon mood and cognition: Before, during and after a Saturday night dance. *Psychopharmacology, 139,* 261–268.

Patterson, F. (1978). Linguistic capabilities of a lowland gorilla. In F. C. C. Peng (Ed.), *Sign language and language acquisition in man and ape* (AAAS Selected Symposium, pp. 161–202). Washington, DC: American Association for the Advancement of Science.

Picard, R. W. (1997). *Affective computing.* Cambridge, MA: MIT Press.

Pinel, J. P. R., Assanand, S., & Lehman, D. R. (2000). Hunger, eating, and ill health. *American Psychologist, 55,* 1105–1116.

Pinker, S. (1999). How the mind works. *The General Psychologist, 34,* 65–70.

Platman, S. R., Plutchik, R., Fieve, R. R., & Lawlor, W. (1969). Emotion profiles associated with mania and depression. *Archives of General Psychiatry, 20,* 210–214.

Platman, S. R., Plutchik, R., & Weinstein, B. (1971). Psychiatric, physiological, behavioral, and self-report measures in relation to a suicide attempt. *Journal of Psychiatric Research, 8,* 127–137.

Plomin, R., De Fries, J. C., McLearn, G. E., & McGuffin, P. (1997). *Behavioral genetics: A primer* (3rd ed.). New York: Freeman.

Ploog, D. (1986). Biological foundations of the vocal expressions of emotions. In R. Plutchik & H. Kellerman (Eds.), *Biological foundations of emotion* (Vol. 3, pp. 173–198). New York: Academic Press.

Ploog, D. (1992). Ethological foundations of biological psychiatry. In H. M. Emrich & W. Wiegland (Eds.), *Integrative biological psychiaty* (pp. 3–35). New York: Springer.

Ploog, D. (2000). Evolutionary biology of emotion. In F. Henn, N. Sartorus, H. Helmchen, & H. Lauter (Eds.), *Contemporary psychiatry: Vol 1. Foundations of psychiatry* (pp. 309–326). New York: Springer.

Ploog, D. W., & MacLean, P. D. (1963). Display of penile erection in squirrel monkey *(Saimiri sciureus). Animal Behavior Monographs, 11,* 32–39.

Plotkin, H. (1998). *Evolution in mind: An introduction to evolutionary psychology.* Cambridge, MA: Harvard University Press.

Plutchik, R. (1958). Outlines of a new theory of emotion. *Transactions of the New York Academy of Sciences, 20,* 394–403.

Plutchik, R. (1962). *The emotions: Facts, theories, and a new model.* New York: Random House.

Plutchik, R. (1970). Emotions, evolution, and adaptive processes. In M. Arnold (Ed.), *Feelings and emotions: The Loyola Symposium* (pp. 1–14). New York: Academic Press.

Plutchik, R. (1971). Individual and breed differences in approach and withdrawal in dogs. *Behaviour, 40,* 302–311.

Plutchik, R. (1976). The self-inventory: A measure of irrational attitudes and behavior. *Rational Living, 11,* 31–33.

Plutchik, R. (1980). *Emotion: A psychoevolutionary synthesis.* New York: Harper & Row.

Plutchik, R. (1983). Emotions in early development: A psychoevolutionary approach. In R. Plutchik & H. Kellerman (Eds.), *Emotion: Theory, research, and experience: Vol. 2. Emotions in early development* (pp. 221–258). New York: Academic Press.

Plutchik, R. (1989). Measuring emotions and their derivatives. In R. Plutchik & H. Kellerman (Eds.), *The measurement of emotions* (Vol. 4, pp. 1–36). New York: Academic Press.

Plutchik, R. (1990). Emotions and psychotherapy: A psychoevolutionary perspective. In R. Plutchik & H. Kellerman (Eds.), *Emotions, psychopathology, and psychotherapy* (Vol. 5, pp. 3–41). New York: Academic Press.

Plutchik, R. (1994). *The psychology and biology of emotion.* New York: HarperCollins.

Plutchik, R. (1995). A theory of ego defenses. In H. R. Conte & R. Plutchik (Eds.), *Ego defenses: Theory and measurement* (pp. 13–37). New York: Wiley.

Plutchik, R. (1997). The circumplex as a general model of the structure of emotions and personality. In R. Plutchik & H. R. Conte (Eds.), *Circumplex models of personality and emotions* (pp. 17–46). Washington, DC: American Psychological Association.

Plutchik, R. (2000a). Aggression, violence, and suicide. In R. Maris, L. Berman, & M. Silverman (Eds.), *Comprehensive textbook of suicidology and suicide prevention.* New York: Guilford Press.

Plutchik, R. (2000b). *Emotions in the practice of psychotherapy: Clinical implications of affect theories.* Washington, DC: American Psychological Association.

Plutchik, R., Botsis, A. J., & van Praag, H. M. (1995). Self-esteem, sexual, and ego functions as correlates of suicide and violence risk. *Archives of Suicide Research, 1,* 1–12.

Plutchik, R., & Conte, H. R. (Eds.). (1997). *Circumplex models of personality and emotions.* Washington, DC: American Psychological Association.

Plutchik, R., Conte, H. R., Weiner, M. B., & Teresi, J. (1978). Studies of body image: IV. Figure drawings in normal and abnormal geriatric and nongeriatric groups. *Journal of Gerontology, 33,* 68–75.

Plutchik, R., & Kellerman, H. (1974). *Manual of the Emotions Profile Index.* Los Angeles, CA: Western Psychological Services.

Plutchik, R., & Kellerman, H. (Eds.). (1989). *The measurement of emotions.* New York: Academic Press.

Plutchik, R., McFarland, W. L., & Robinson, B. W. (1966). Effects of current intensity on self-stimulation rates and escape latencies and their relationships to behavior evoked by brain stimulation in rhesus monkeys. *Journal of Comparative and Physiological Psychology, 61,* 181–188.

Plutchik, R., & Plutchik, A. (1990). Communication and coping in families. In E. A. Blechman & M. J. McEnroe (Eds.), *Emotions and the family: For better or for worse* (pp. 35–51). New York: Erlbaum.

Polan, H. J., & Hofer, M. A. (1999). Psychological origins of infant attachment and separation responses. In J. Cassidy & P. R. Shaver (Eds.), *Handbook of attachment: Theory, research, and clinical applications* (pp. 162–197). New York: Guilford Press.

Polis, C. A. (1981). The evolution and dynamics of intraspecific predation. *Review of Ecology and Systematics, 12,* 225–252.

Poole, J. H. (1989). Announcing intent: The aggressive state of musth in African elephants. *Animal Behavior, 37,* 140–152.

Pope, H. G., Jr., Kouri, E. M., & Hudson, J. I. (2000). Effects of supraphysiologic doses of testosterone on mood and aggression in normal men. *Archives of General Psychiatry, 57,* 133–140.

Porter, S., Birt, A. R., Yuille, J. C., & Lehman, D. R. (2000). Negotiating false memories:

Interviewer and rememberer characteristics relate to memory distortion. *Psychological Science, 11*, 507–510.

Posner, M. I., & Di Girolamo, G. J. (2000). Cognitive neuroscience: Origins and promise. *Psychological Bulletin, 126*, 873–889.

Rasia-Filho, A. A., Londero, R. G., & Archavol, M. (2000). Functional activities of the amygdala: An overview. *Journal of Psychiatry and Neuroscience, 25*, 14–23.

Redican, W. K. (1982). An evolutionary perspective on human facial displays. In P. Ekman (Ed.), *Emotion in the human face* (2nd ed., pp. 212–282). New York: Cambridge University Press.

Rhodes, R. (1999). *Why they kill: The discoveries of a maverick criminologist.* New York: Alfred A. Knopf.

Ricci, N. (1990). The behavior of ciliated protozoa. *Animal Behavior, 40*, 1048–1069.

Richards, T. W., & Simons, M. P. (1941). The Fels child behavior scales. *Genetic Psychology Monographs, 24*, 259–309.

Riggs, L. A. (1976). Human vision: Some objective explorations. *American Psychologist, 31*, 125–134.

Rilling, M. (2000). John Watson's paradoxical struggle to explain Freud. *American Psychologist, 55*, 301–312.

Rinn, W. E. (1984). The neuropsychology of facial expression: A review of the neurological and psychological mechanisms for producing facial expressions. *Psychological Bulletin, 95*, 52–77.

Ritvo, L. B. (1990). *Darwin's influence on Freud: A tale of two sciences.* New Haven: Yale University Press.

Roff, D. A. (1996). The evolution of genetic correlations: An analysis of patterns. *Evolution 50*, 1392–1403.

Roitblat, H. L. (1996). Animal cognition. In W. Bechtel & G. Graham (Eds.), *A companion to cognitive science* (pp. 14–19). Oxford, England: Blackwell.

Rolls, E. T. (1990). A theory of emotion and its application to understanding the neural basis of emotions. In J. A. Gray (Ed.), *Psychobiological aspects of realtionships between emotion and cognition* (pp. 161–190). Hillsdale, NJ: Erlbaum.

Roseman, I. J., Spindel, M. S., & Jose, P. E. (1990). Appraisals of emotion-eliciting events: Testing a theory of discrete emotions. *Journal of Personality and Social Psychology, 59*, 899–915.

Rothbaum, F., Weisz, J., Pott, M., Miyake, K., & Morelli, G. (2000). Attachment and culture: Security in the United States and Japan. *American Psychologist, 55*, 1093–1104.

Rozin, P., & Fallon A. (1987). A perspective on disgust. *Psychological Review, 94*, 23–41.

Rubin, Z. (1973). *Liking and loving: An invitation to social psychology.* New York: Holt, Rinehart, & Winston.

Russell, J. A. (1983). Two pan-cultural dimensions of emotion words. *Journal of Personality and Social Psychology, 45*, 1281–1288.

Russell, J. A. (1989). Measures of emotion. In R. Plutchik & H. Kellerman (Eds.), *The measurement of emotions* (pp. 83–112). New York: Academic Press.

Russell, J. A. (1994). Is there universal recognition of emotion from facial expression? A review of methods and studies. *Psychological Bulletin, 115*, 102–141.

Rusting, C. L. (1998). Personality, mood, and cognitive processing of emotional information: Three conceptual frameworks. *Psychological Bulletin, 124*, 165–196.

Saarni, C. (1999). *The development of emotional competence.* New York: Guildford Press.

Salovey, P., Bedell, B. T., Detweiler, J. B., & Mayer, J. D. (2000). Current directions in emotional intelligence research. In M. Lewis & J. M. Haviland-Jones (Eds.), *Handbook of emotions* (pp. 504–522). New York: Guilford Press.

Salzinger, K. (1999). Words, words, words: The psychologist's dilemma. *The General Psychologist, 34*, 17–21.

Savage-Rumbaugh, S., Shanker, S. G., & Taylor, T. J. (1998). *Apes, language, and the human mind.* New York: Oxford University Press.

Savitsky, J. C., Izard, C. E., Kotsch, W. E., & Christy, L. (1974). Aggressor s response to the victim's facial expression of emotion. *Journal of Research in Personality, 7*, 346–357.

Scarr, S., & Salapatek, P. (1970). Patterns of fear development during infancy. *Merrill–Palmer Quarterly of Behavior and Development, 16*, 53–90.

Schachter, S., & Singer, J. E. (1962). Cognitive, social, and physiological determinants of emotional state. *Psychological Review, 69*, 379–399.

Schaller, G. (1965). *The year of the gorilla.* Chicago: University of Chicago Press.

Schankman, P. (1969). *Le roti et le bouilli:* Levi-Strauss theory of cannibalism. *American Anthropologist, 71*, 54–69.

Scheff, T. J., & Retzinger, S. M. (1991). *Emotions and violence: Shame and rage in destructive conflicts.* Lexington, MA: Lexington Books.

Scherer, K. R. (1986). Vocal affect expression: A review and a model for future research. *Psychological Bulletin, 99*, 143–165.

Scherer, K. R. (1989). Vocal measurement of emotions. In R. Plutchik & H. Kellerman (Eds.), *The measurement of emotions* (Vol. 4, pp. 233–260). New York: Academic Press.

Schlosberg, H. (1941). A scale for the judgment of facial expressions. *Journal of Experimental Psychology, 29*, 497–510.

Schweder, R. A., & Hoidt, J. (2002). The cultural psychology of the emotions: Ancient and new. In M. Lewis & J. M. Haviland-Jones (Eds.), *Handbook of emotions* (pp. 397–414). New York: Guilford Press.

Scott, J. P. (1958). *Animal behavior.* Chicago: University of Chicago Press.

Scott, J. P. (1980). The function of emotions in behavioral systems: A systems theory analysis. In R. Plutchik & H. Kellerman (Eds.), *Theories of emotion* (Vol. 1, pp. 35–56). New York: Academic Press.

Scoville, R., & Gottlieb, C. (1980). Development of vocal behavior in Peking ducklings. *Animal Behavior, 28*, 1095–1109.

Seyforth, R. M., Cheney, D. L., & Marler, P. (1980a). Monkey responses to three different alarm calls: Evidence of predator classification and semantic communication. *Science, 210*, 801–803.

Seyforth, R. M., Cheney, D. L., & Marler, P. (1980b). Vervet monkey alarm calls: Semantic communication in a free-ranging primate. *Animal Behavior, 28*, 1070–1094.

Shaikh, M. B., & Siegel, A. (1994). Neuroanatomical and neurochemical mechanisms underlying amygdaloid control of defensive rage behavior in the cat. *Brazilian Journal of Medical and Biological Research, 27*, 2759–2779.

Shaver, P. R., & Hazan, C. (1988). A biased overview of the study of love. *Journal of Social and Personal Relationships, 5,* 473–501.

Shaver, P., Schwartz, J., Kirson, D., & O'Connor, C. (1987). Emotion knowledge: further explorations of a prototype approach. *Journal of Personality and Social Psychology, 52,* 1061–1086.

Sheehan, D. V. (1983). *The anxiety disease.* New York: Scribner.

Shields, S. A. (1984). Distinguishing between emotion and nonemotion: Judgments about experience. *Motivation and Emotion, 8,* 355–369.

Simpson, J. A. (1999). Attachment theory in modern evolutionary perspective. In J. Cassidy & P. R. Shaver (Eds.), *Handbook of attachment* (pp. 115–161), New York: Guilford Press.

Skinner, B. F. (1989). The origins of cognitive thought. *American Psychologist, 44,* 13–18.

Smiley, P., & Huttenlocher, J. (1989). Young children's acquisition of emotional concepts. In C. Saarni & P. L. Harris (Eds.), *Children's understanding of emotions* (pp. 112–131). New York: Cambridge University Press.

Smith, J. L., McDougal, C., & Miquelle, D. (1989). Scent marking in free-ranging tiger, *Panthera tigris. Animal Behavior, 37,* 1–10.

Smith, W. J., Chase, J., & Lieblich, A. K. (1974). Tongue showing: a facial display of humans and other primate species. *Semiatrica, 11,* 201–246.

Soltis, J., Mitsunaga, F., Shimizu, K., Nozaki, M., Yanaagihara, Y., Domingo-Roura, X., et al. (1997). Sexual selection in Japanese macaques. II: Female mate choice and male–male competition. *Animal Behavior, 54,* 737–746.

Spelke, E. S. (2000). Core knowledge. *American Psychologist, 55,* 1233–1243.

Spezzano, C. (1993). *Affect in psychoanalysis: A clinical synthesis.* Hillsdale, NJ: Analytic Press.

Spielberger, C. D., Gorsuch, R. L., & Lushene, R. E. (1970). *STAI Manual for the State–Trait Inventory.* Palo Alto, CA: Consulting Psychologist Press.

Spitz, R. (1957). *No and yes: On the genesis of human communication.* New York: International Universities Press.

Sprengelmayer, R., Young, A. W., Calder, A. J., Kormat, A., Lange, H., Homberg, V., et al. (1996). Loss of disgust: Perception of faces and emotions in Huntington's disease. *Brain, 119,* 1647–1665.

Sroufe, L. A. (1979). Socioemotional development. In J. D. Osofsky (Ed.), *Handbook of infant development* (pp. 149–203). New York: Wiley.

Stein, N. L., Trabasso, T., & Liwag, M. D. (2000). A goal appraisal theory of emotional understanding: Implications for development and learning. In M. Lewis & J. M. Haviland-Jones (Eds.), *Handbook of emotions* (pp. 173–191). New York: Guilford Press.

Stenberg, C. R., & Campos, J. J. (1990). The development of anger expressions in infancy. In N. L. Stein, B. Leventhal, & T. Trabasso (Eds.), *Psychological and biological approaches to emotion* (pp. 33–59). Hillsdale, NJ: Erlbaum.

Sternberg, R. J. (1986). A triangular theory of love. *Psychological Review, 93,* 119–135.

Sternberg, R. J., & Grigorenko, E. L. (2001). The (mis)organization of psychology. *American Psychological Society Observer, 14,* 1–20.

Storm, C., & Storm, T. (1987). A taxonomic study of the vocabulary of emotions. *Journal of Personality and Social Psychology, 53,* 805–816.

Storm, C., & Storm, T. (1998, August). *The English lexicon of interpersonal affect*. Paper presented at the meeting of the International Society for Research on Emotion, Wuerzburg, Germany.

Stossel, T. P. (1990). How cells crawl. *American Scientist, 78*, 408–423.

Strongman, K. (1987). *The psychology of emotion*. New York: Wiley.

Strum, S. C. (1988). *Almost human: A journey into the world of baboons*. New York: Random House.

Sullivan, H. S. (1956). *Clinical studies in psychiatry*. New York: W. W. Norton.

Surakka, V., & Hietanen, J. K. (1998). Facial and emotional reactions to Duchenne and non-Duchenne smiles. *International Journal of Psychophysiology, 29*, 23–33.

Taylor, J. A. (1953). A personality test for manifest anxiety. *Journal of Abnormal and Social Psychology, 48*, 285–290.

Thompson, J. (1941). Development of facial expressions of emotion in blind and seeing children. *Archives of Psychology, 37*, 264–299.

Tomkins, S. S. (1962). *Affect imagery consciousness: Vol. I. Positive affects*. New York: Springer.

Tomkins, S. S. (1963). *Affect imagery, consciousness: Vol. II. Negative affects*. New York: Springer.

Tomkins, S. S. (1970). Affect as the primary motivational system. In M. Arnold (Ed.), *Feelings and emotions* (pp. 101–110). New York: Academic Press.

Tomkins, S. S. (1980). Affect as amplification: Some modifications in theory. In R. Plutchik & H. Kellerman (Eds.), *Emotion: Theory, research, and experience: Vol. 1. Theories of emotion* (pp. 141–164). New York: Academic Press.

Tomkins, S. S. (1991). *Affect imagery, and consciousness: Vol. III. Negative affects: Anger and fear*. New York: Springer.

Tomkins, S. S. (1992). *Affect, imagery, and consciousness: Vol. IV. Cognition*. New York: Springer.

Tomkins, S. S., & McCarter, R. (1964). What and where are the primary affects? Some evidence for a theory. *Perceptual and Motor Skills, 18*, 119–158.

Trainor, L. J., Austin, C. M., & Desjardins, R. N. (2000). Is infant-directed speech prosody a result of the vocal expression of emotion? *Psychological Science, 11*, 188–195.

Trevarthen, C. (1977). Descriptive analysis of infant communicative behavior. In H. R. Schaffer (Ed.), *Studies in mother–infant interaction*. New York: Academic Press.

Trower, P., & Gilbert, P. (1989). New theoretical conceptions of social anxiety and social phobia. *Clinical Psychology Review, 9*, 19–35.

Tuttle, R. H. (1986). *Apes of the world*. Park Ridge, NJ: Noyes.

Vaillant, L. M. (1997). *Changing character. Short-term anxiety-regulating psychotherapy for restructuring defenses, affects, and attachments*. New York: Basic Books.

Valins, S. (1966). Cognitive effects of false heart-rate feedback. *Journal of Personality and Social Psychology, 4*, 400–408.

van Hooff, J. A. R. A. M. (1973). A structural analysis of the social behavior of a semi-captive group of chimpanzees. In M. von Cranach & I. Vine (Eds.), *Social communication and movement* (pp. 253–288). New York: Academic Press.

Van Ijzendoorn, M. N., & Sagi, A. (1999). Cross-cultural patterns of attachment: Universal and contextual dimensions. In J. Cassidy & P. R. Shaver (Eds.), *Handbook of attachment* (pp. 713–741). New York: Guilford Press.

Van Lawick-Goodall, J. (1973). The behavior of chimpanzees in their natural habitat. *American Journal of Psychiatry, 130,* 1–12.

van Praag, H. M., & Plutchik, R. (1984). Depression-type and depression-severity in relations to the risk of violent suicide attempts. *Psychiatry Research, 12,* 333–338.

Varley, H. (1980). *Colour.* London: Marshall Editions.

Vaughn, B. E., & Bost, K. K. (1999). Attachment and temperament: Redundant, Independent, or Interacting influences on interpersonal adaptation and personality development? In J. Cassidy & P. R. Shaver (Eds.), *Handbook of attachment* (pp. 198–225). New York: The Guilford Press.

Wakefield, J. C. (1996). DSM–IV: Are we making diagnostic progress? *Contemporary Psychology, 41,* 646–652.

Wakefield, J. C. (1999). Evolutionary versus prototype analyses of the concept of disorder. *Journal of Abnormal Psychology, 108,* 374–399.

Wallbott, H. C., & Scherer, K. R. (1989). Assessing emotion by questionnaire. In R. Plutchik & H. Kellerman (Eds.), *Emotion: Theory, research, and experience: Vol 4. The measurement of emotions* (pp. 55–82). New York: Academic Press.

Warren, S. L., Emde, R. N., & Sroufe, L. A. (2000). Internal representations: Prediciting anxiety from children's play narratives. *Journal of the American Academcy of Child and Adolescent Psychiatry, 39,* 100–107.

Watson, D. (2000). *Mood and temperament.* New York: Guilford Press.

Watson, D., Clark, L. A., & Tellegen, A. (1988). Development and validation of brief measures of positive and negative affect: The PANAS Scales. *Journal of Personality and Social Psychology, 54,* 1063–1070.

Watson, J. B., (1919). *Psychology from the standpoint of a behaviorist.* Philadelphia: Lippincott.

Watson, J. B. (1924). *Psychology from the standpoint of a behaviorist* (2nd ed.). Philadelphia: Lippincott.

Watson, J. B. (1929). *Psychology from the standpoint of a behaviorist* (3rd ed.). Philadelphia: Lippincott.

Watson, J. B., & Rayner, R. (1920). Conditioned emotional reactions. *Journal of Experimental Psychology, 3,* 1–14. (Reprinted in *American Psychologist, 2000 55,* 313–317)

Webster's Third New International Dictionary (1971). Chicago: G. & C. Merriam.

Wehrle, T., Kaiser, S., Schmidt, S., & Scherer, K. R. (2000). Studying the dynamics of emotional expression using synthesized facial muscle movements. *Journal of Personality and Social Psychology, 78,* 105–119.

Weinfield, N. S., Sroufe, L. A., Egeland, B., & Carlson, E. A. (1999). The nature of individual differences in infant–caregiver attachment. In J. Cassidy & P. R. Shaver (Eds.) *Handbook of attachment* (pp. 68–88). New York: Guilford Press.

Weisman, A. D. (1965). *The existential core of psychoanalysis: Reality sense and responsibility.* Boston: Little, Brown.

West, D. J. (1966). *Murder followed by suicide.* London: Heinemann.

White, G. M. (2000). Representing emotional meaning: Category, metaphor, schema, discourse. In M. Lewis & J. M. Haviland-Jones (Eds.), *Handbook of emotions.* New York: Guilford Press.

Widiger, T. A., & Clark, L. A. (2000). Toward DSM–V and the classification of psychopathology. *Psychological Bulletin, 126,* 946–963.

Wilson, E. O. (1975). *Sociobiology: The new synthesis.* Cambridge, MA: Harvard University Press.

Wimer, R. E., & Wimer, C. C. (1985). Animal behavior genetics: A search for the biological foundations of behavior. *Annual Review of Psychology, 36,* 171–218.

Windmann, S. (1998). Panic disorders from a monistic perspective: Integrating neurobiological and psychological approaches. *Journal of Anxiety Disorders, 12,* 485–507.

Wise, R. A. (1988). The neurobiology of craving: Implications for the understanding and treatment of addiction. *Journal of Abnormal Psychology, 97,* 118–132.

Woodworth, R. S. (1938). *Experimental psychology.* New York: Holt, Rinehart and Winston.

Wrangham, P., & Peterson, D. (1996). *Demonic males: Apes and the origins of human violence.* New York: Houghton-Mifflin.

Young, C., & Decarie, T. (1977). An ethology-based catalogue of facial/vocal behavior in infancy. *Animal Behavior, 25,* 95–107.

Young, P. T. (1961). *Motivation and emotion.* New York: John Wiley & Sons.

Zajonc, R. B. (1980). Feeling and thinking: Preferences need no inferences. *American Psychologist, 35,* 151–175.

Zajonc, R. B., Murphy, S. T., & Inglehart, M. (1989). Feeling and facial efference: Implications of the vascular theory of emotion. *Psychological Review, 96,* 395–416.

Author Index

Subject Index

Abreaction, 36
Abuse, family, ix
Acetylcholine, 277, 284, 289
Action readiness, 99, 107
Active emotions, 6
Adaptations, evolutionary. *See* Evolutionary
    adaptations
Adaptive behaviors, 261–262
Adaptive emotions, 6–8
Addiction, 290
Addition (of numbers), 51
Adjective checklists, 95, 117–118, 120–121
Adolescence, 302, 331
Affect families, 93–94
Affect Imagery Consciousness (Sylvan Tomkins),
    92
Affect in Psychoanalysis (Charles Spezzano),
    62, 100
Affective arousal, 229–230
Affective memory, 48
Affects, 36
    characteristics of, 100
    emotions vs., 62–63
Affects as Process (Joseph Jones), 101
Affect system, motivational system vs., 93
Affiliation system, 195
Affinitive system, 132
African Americans, 302
Age factor, 302
Agency appraisal, 53
Aggression, 322–332. *See also* Anger
    in baboons, 178
    in cats, 230–231
    drugs affecting disorders of, 288
    in elephants, 244
    functions of, 326–330
    in mice, 10
    in muted birds, 241

in rats, 134–135
and suicide, 324–326
Aggressive system, 132
Agonistic behavior, 261
Agoraphobia, 317, 318
Ai (chimpanzee), 258
Ainsworth, Mary, 201
Alarm calls, 239–241
Albigensian Crusade, 294
Alcohol, 290
Alcoholism, 318, 323
Allelomimetic behavior, 261
Almost Human (Shirley Strum), 178
Altruism, 227
Altruism scale, 296
American Psychiatric Association, 312
American Sign Language, 255
Amish, 221
Amphetamines, 280, 290
Amygdala, 268–271
    and anxiety, 319, 320
    and aversive system, 277
    and communication, 237
    and emotional evaluation, 287
    and emotional states, 276
    and emotion control, 280
    and epilepsy, 275
    and homeostasis, 284, 285
    and pleasure system, 277
    stimulation of, 274
    and vocal expression, 283
Anaclitic love, 295
The Anatomy of Melancholy (Robert Burton),
    298–300
Anesthesia, 33, 34
Anger, 5. *See also* Aggression
    as adaptive/maladaptive emotion, 6–7
    as basic emotion, 72, 75

367

About the Author

Robert Plutchik, PhD, is professor emeritus of psychiatry and psychology at the Albert Einstein College of Medicine, as well as adjunct professor at the University of South Florida. He has taught at Columbia, Hostra, Yeshiva, and Long Island Universities and lectured widely in the United States and in many countries around the world, including New Zealand, Greece, Austria, China, Japan, Colombia, Germany, Israel, Argentina, and Canada. He spent two years at the National Institute of Mental Health participating in brain research. He has been director of Program Development and Clinical Research at the Bronx Psychiatric Center in New York City and later became associate director of the Psychiatry Department at Jacoby Hospital, an affiliate of the Albert Einstein College of Medicine.

Dr. Plutchik's work is internationally recognized, and he has been invited to contribute articles on emotions to the *World Book Encyclopedia; The Academic American Encyclopedia;* and the *International Encyclopedia of Neurology, Psychiatry, Psychoanalysis, and Psychology.* He has also published several books on the subject of emotions, including *Emotion: A Psychoevolutionary Synthesis; Emotion: Theory, Research, and Experience; The Psychology and Biology of Emotion; Ego Defenses, Theory, and Measurement; Circumplex Models in Personality and Emotions;* and *Emotions in the Practice of Psychotherapy.* Dr. Plutchik has authored or coauthored over 265 articles and 46 chapters.